Bond's Top 100 Franchises

2004 EDITION

Robert E. Bond, Publisher
Stephanie Woo, Editor
Annabelle Louie, Editorial Assistant
Kimberly Tsau, Editorial Assistant

Source Book Publications
Serving the Franchising Industry
1814 Franklin Street, Suite 820
Oakland, CA 94612
510.839.5471

ISBN 1-887137-31-9

DISCLAIMER

BOND'S TOP 100 FRANCHISES is based on data submitted by the franchisors themselves. Every effort has been made to obtain up-to-date and reliable information. As the information returned has not been independently verified, we assume no responsibility for errors or omissions and reserve the right to include or eliminate listings and otherwise edit and present the data based on our discretion and judgment as to what is useful to the readers of this directory. Inclusion in the publication does not imply endorsement by the editors or the publisher. Errors brought to the attention of the publisher and verified to the satisfaction of the publisher will be corrected in future editions. The publisher specifically disclaims all warranties, including the implied warranties of merchantability and fitness for a specific purpose.

This publication is designed to provide its readers with accurate and authoritative information with regard to the subject matter covered. It is sold with the understanding that neither the author nor the publisher is engaged in rendering legal, accounting or other professional services. If legal advice or other expert assistance is required, the services of a competent professional person should be sought.

From a Declaration of Principles jointly adopted by a Committee of the American Bar Association and a Committee of Publishers.

Cover Design by Joyce Coffland, Artistic Concepts, Oakland, CA.

ISBN 1-887137-31-9

Printed in the United States of America.
10 9 8 7 6 5 4 3 2 1

BOND'S TOP 100 FRANCHISES is available at special discounts for bulk purchase. Special editions or book excerpts can also be created to specifications. For details, contact **Source Book Publications**, 1814 Franklin Street, Suite 820, Oakland, CA 94612. Phone: (510) 839-5471; FAX: (510) 839-2104.

Preface

At its best, purchasing a franchise is a time-tested, paint-by-the-numbers method of starting a new business. It avoids many of the myriad pitfalls normally encountered by someone starting anew and vastly improves the odds of success. It represents an exceptional blend of operating independence with a proven system that includes a detailed blueprint for starting and managing the business, as well as the critical on-going support. But purchasing a franchise is clearly not a fool-proof investment that somehow guarantees the investor financial independence.

At its worst, if the evaluation and investment decision is sloppy or haphazard, franchising can be a nightmare. If things don't work out, for whatever reason, you can't simply walk away. You are still responsible for the long-term lease on your retail space, the large bank loan that underwrote your entry into the business and/or the binding, long-term financial obligation to the franchisor. While it is easy to sell a profitable business, an unprofitable business will most likely result in a significant financial loss. If that loss is all equity, that might be an acceptable risk. If, however, you still have obligations to the bank, landlord and others, your hardship is greatly compounded. This says nothing about the inevitable stress on a marriage and one's own self-esteem.

Your ultimate success as a franchisee will be determined by two factors:

1. The homework you do at the front-end to ensure that you are selecting the optimal franchise for your particular needs, experience and financial resources.

2. Your commitment to work hard and play by the rules once you have signed a binding, long-term franchise agreement. For most new franchisees in the retail industry, this involves working 60+ hours per week until you can justify delegating some of the day-to-day responsibilities. It also requires being a team player — not acting as an entrepreneur who does his or her own thing without regard for the system as a whole. A franchise system is only as good as the franchisees make it. This means following the script.

Another harsh reality, unfortunately, is that there is no such thing as the Top 100 franchises. Similarly, there isn't a list of the Top 10 colleges, the Top 5 professional basketball players or the Top 3 sports cars. Like everything else in life, the beauty is in the eye of the beholder. Picking the optimal retail franchise is a good example. What appeals to me, even after exhaustive and, hopefully, well-thought-out research, may not appeal to you or be appropriate for you. Whereas I might be prepared to work 70-hour weeks for the first year my new business is open, you might not. Whereas I might be willing to invest $500,000 in a specific franchise concept, you might feel that the projected rewards do not outweigh the inherent risks. Whereas you might be exceptional at working with minimum wage personnel, I might be unable to communicate effectively with younger, less-educated personnel. These are just a few of the literally hundreds of weighty considerations that you will have to evaluate before deciding to invest in a specific franchise system.

In short, one prospective franchisee will clearly not have the same life experiences, talents, God-given abilities and financial wherewithal as the next. It is therefore critical that you take what we say only as a best effort on our part to go through literally hundreds of concepts before arriving at those which, we feel, best answer our collective needs and experiences as professionals within the franchising industry.

My strong suggestion is that you take the time to read the first two chapters of the book to better understand the industry and the variables that you will have to consider in making a long-term investment decision. Even though you may already have a sense as to what type of franchise you want to purchase, maybe even a specific franchise, keep an open mind to the other options available to you. Request marketing information on all of the competing systems and rigorously evaluate each. Look at the various websites. You may be pleasantly surprised to learn that one system offers a range of benefits that better complements your experience and capabilities. Also keep in mind that, in the final analysis, it is up to you — not the franchisor — as to how successful you will be.

Remember, this is not a game: I cannot overemphasize the fact that, in most cases, you will be making a once-in-a-lifetime investment decision. It is incumbent on you to do it right at the outset. This can only be done by taking your time, properly researching all the options, realistically addressing both the "best case" and "worst case" scenarios, seeking the advice of friends and professionals and, in general, doing the due diligence required. You want to invest in a system that will take advantage of your unique talents and experiences and not take advantage of you in the process! Don't take short-cuts. Listen carefully to what the franchisor and your advisors tell you. Don't think you are so clever or independent that you can't benefit from the advice of outside professionals. Don't assume that the franchisor's required guidelines regarding the amount of investment, experience, temperament, etc., somehow don't apply to you. Don't accept any promises or "understandings" from the franchisor that are not committed in writing to the franchise agreement. Invest the additional time to talk to and/or meet with as many franchisees in the system as you can. The additional front-end investment you make, both in time and money, will pay off handsomely if it saves you from making a marginal, or poor, investment decision. This is one of the few times in business when second chances are rare. Make the extra effort to do it right the first time.

Good luck and Godspeed.

Robert Bond

Table of Contents

Introduction

Determining which franchises should be in the Top 100 (and, equally importantly, which ones should not) was a daunting task. It was difficult to choose only 100. Since franchises are so diverse, it was our intention to include at least one franchise from each industry category. Based on our comprehensive research, the 100 in this book are, in our opinion, the best in the franchising industry.

The franchising industry is a large and sometimes confusing one. There are several industry categories, each with its own characteristics and subcategories. While we will try to provide you with as meaningful an overview as we can, it is your responsibility to aggressively research every aspect of any company you're interested in. Buy a franchise much like you would a house. Whereas you can always sell a house for roughly what you bought it for, you may not be so lucky liquidating a poorly-researched franchise investment. It's a big investment and takes time.

Methodology

How did we arrive at our choices? There were several criteria that were taken into consideration. Primary among these were name recognition, product quality, litigation, total investment, on-going expenses, the company's training program, on-going support and the exclusive territory awarded to new franchisees. Many are personal choices. Is the franchise something you're interested in? Will you have the time and passion to manage it like you want to? These are questions that you'll have to answer for yourself. The information in this book will help you once you've decided what you want to do.

We chose both companies that have already established a strong brand name identity and those that are in the process of establishing a recognizable identity. ServiceMaster Clean, for example, is known the world over by millions of people. Conversely, companies like Environmental Biotech and Furniture Medic are less well-known now, but as their concepts become more and more popular, they will undoubtedly increase their name recognition in the near future.

Litigation was a silent factor in determining the Top 100 franchises. We don't have a litigation section in each profile, but while reviewing each franchisor's UFOC (Uniform Franchise Offering Circular — a required document containing 23 categories of information that must be provided by the franchisor to the prospective franchisee at least ten days prior to the execution of the franchise agreement), we most definitely took into account Item Three. This lists any relevant court cases, past and present, involving the company and tells us volumes about franchisor-franchisee relations. If a franchisor had no legal problems or a few court cases inconsequential to the reputation and operation of the company, then it was certainly a viable candidate for the Top 100.

The total investment is usually the determining factor in choosing a franchise. After all, money talks. Initially, investing in a franchise takes considerable patience. You are faced with numerous questions such as "Which items do I finance and which do I purchase?", "Are real estate costs included?", "Will the company help me with financing?", etc. We don't attempt to explore these questions in depth, but we do give you a brief overview of what you will be expected to invest. A Top 100 company may have a low total investment cost, financing assistance and a detailed account of what each item costs. We looked at all the franchisors and chose the ones which exemplified the best combination of these factors.

Before you open a franchise, one of the most critical steps is the initial training program, during which you will learn the basics about the franchise you choose. Training is usually held at the franchisor's headquarters and can last anywhere from five days to 12 weeks. The companies in this book all have strong, comprehensive training courses that include hours of both classroom and on-site training.

On-going expenses are made up of two fees: a royalty fee and an advertising fee. The royalty fee is a portion of your sales (usually four to eight percent) that you give to the franchisor in exchange for its expertise, on-going support and brand name. The advertising payment (three to five percent of sales) is also paid to the franchisor, and in return you receive advertising, marketing and promotional assistance. If these fees were within an acceptable range, then a company was a good candidate for the Top 100.

Most companies listed give exceptional on-going support to their franchisees: continual managerial aid, advertising assistance, access to the operations manual, etc. The basic tenet of franchising is, as Ray Kroc, the founder of McDonald's, said, "to be in business for yourself, not by yourself." Make sure the franchisor is going to support you over the long-term.

Another very important aspect of franchising that often gets overlooked is the franchisor's exclusive territory policy. An exclusive territory awarded by the franchisor describes the specific area or market in which you can operate your business. Why is this so important? By giving you an exclusive territory of, say, a three-mile radius surrounding your location, the franchisor is agreeing that it will not establish another location within that three-mile radius. So, logically, your business will have less competition. Most of the companies in the Top 100 have some sort of exclusive area policy.

All of these factors are important by themselves. Many companies exhibit some of them. But it's the rare few that combine the majority of these characteristics into one fluid franchising system. From those companies, we chose the Top 100.

Additional Factors to Consider

Three additional areas that clearly require serious examination before investing are 1) outstanding legal/litigation issues; 2) the current financial status of the franchisor; and 3) issues regarding renewal, termination, transfer and dispute resolution. Because the first two areas can change on a daily basis, coupled with the fact that we lack the necessary expertise to comment authoritatively on either, we have intentionally left these important responsibilities to the investor.

If there is any reason to think that an outstanding legal issue may impact the company's ability to prosper or support the franchise system, you will most likely require the interpretation of a qualified and experienced franchise attorney. Prior to signing a franchise agreement, be confident that no new or potential litigation has come up since the publication of the UFOC. The franchisor is obligated to give you an accurate status report.

Similarly, the franchisor's financial health is critical to your own success. How to determine that health? Each franchisor is required to include detailed financial statements in its UFOC. Depending upon the date of the UFOC, the information may be very current. Most likely, however, it may be outdated by 6–12 months. If this is the case, request current financials from the franchisor. If the company is publicly traded, there are numerous sources of detailed information. Go to the firm's website. If you don't have the expertise to judge the financial information, ask the advice of an accountant or financial consultant. As all of the companies included in the Top 100 have in excess of 40 operating units, they most likely are enjoying a positive cash flow from operations and, therefore, are in a much stronger financial position than smaller franchisors. This is not an excuse to avoid an investigation, however.

Item 17 of the UFOC covers "Renewal, Termination, Transfer and Dispute Resolution." These are critical areas that should be fully understood before you find out that, after you have developed a profitable business, the franchisor has the unilateral right to terminate your franchise or capriciously deny a sale to a qualified buyer. Don't get blind-sided because you were too lazy or frugal to get a legal interpretation. Again, this is the province of a qualified attorney.

The Food-Service Industry

The franchising industry contains over 2,200 different concepts. Food-service constitutes roughly one-third of the entire industry -- by far the largest. Within the food-service industry, there are several different themes: bakery/coffee, fast-food or quick-service, ice cream, sit-down, subs and sandwiches and other miscellaneous categories. Frequently, concepts are further subdivided.

For example, in the fast-food industry, there are various different segments such as pizza, hamburger, chicken, Asian, seafood and Mexican, to name a few. What does all of this mean? Simply that food-service is a large, dominant and sometimes confusing industry that has to be fully researched before settling in on a specific franchise concept.

The following table lists the 30 food-service franchises featured in Chapter 4.

Company Name	Franchise Fee	Total Investment	Royalty	Total Units
Auntie Anne's Hand-Rolled Soft Pretzels	$30K	$260,000	6.0%	785
Baskin-Robbins	$40K	$145,700–527,800	5.0–5.9%	4,500
Bennigan's Grill & Tavern	$65K	$1,400,000–2,600,000	4.0%	308
Big Apple Bagels	$25K	$174,800–349,500	5.0%	179
Blimpie Subs and Salads	$10–18K	$60,000–20,000	6.0%	1,956
Breadsmith	$30K	$200,000–400,000	7.0/6.0/5.0%	38
Carvel Ice Cream Bakery	$10K	$185,000–240,000	$1.63/Gal.	360
Churchs Chicken	$5–15K	$194,000–750,000	5.0%	1,219
Cinnabon	$35K	$150,000–250,000	5.0%	448
Cold Stone Creamery	$31–35K	$245,000–348,000	6.0%	403
Dippin' Dots Ice Cream of the Future	$12.5K	$45,600–189,800	4.0%	571
Dunkin' Donuts	$50K	$255,700–1,139,700	5.9%	5,000
Friendly's Restaurants	$30–35K	$630,000–1,900,000	4.0%	539
Fuddruckers	$50K	$740,000–1,480,000	5.0%	226
Golden Corral Family Steakhouse	$40K	$1,600,000–3,800,000	4.0%	472
Great Wraps!	$17.5K	$175,000–240,000	5.0%	52
KFC	$25K	$700,000–1,200,000	4.0%	9,638
Krystal Company, The	$32.5K	$900K–1MM	4.5%	418
Larry's Giant Subs	$19K	$110,000–170,000	6.0%	91
Long John Silver's	$15–20K	$150,000–1,000,000	5.0%	1,233
Manchu Wok (USA)	$20K	$265,500–316,750	7.0%	189
Papa Murphy's	$25K	$148,800–199,500	5.0%	648

Pizzeria Uno Chicago Bar & Grill	$35K	$900,000–1,700,000	5.0%	194
Rita's Italian Ice	$25K	$135,000–242,000	6.5%	261
Shake's Frozen Custard	$30K	$166,000–800,000	5.0%	39
Smoothie King	$20K	$120,000–220,000	5.0%	231
Subway Restaurants	$12.5K	$69,000–191,000	8.0%	17,629
Tony Roma's Famous for Ribs	$20K	Varies	4.0%	256
Wienerschnitzel	$25K	$250,000–1,200,000	5.0%	321
Wing Zone	$25K	$140,000–200,000	5.0%	38
Woody's Bar-B-Q	$35K	$250,000–450,000	4.0%	42

The Retail Industry

The franchising industry contains over 2,300 different concepts, roughly 350 of which are retail franchises. There are several different types of retail companies: Specialty retailers, clothing, athletic wear, art supplies, convenience stores, home improvement, pet products, photographic products and electronics/computer products. Like the food-service and service-based franchises, the retail industry is large and needs to be fully researched before settling in on a specific franchise concept.

The following table lists the 16 retail franchises featured in Chapter 5.

Company Name	Franchise Fee	Total Investment	Royalty	Total Units
7-Eleven, Inc.	$64K	Varies	N/A	22,648
Athlete's Foot, The	$35K	$200–650K	3.5–5.0%	686
Baby USA	$42.5K	$450–650K	3.0%	68
Batteries Plus	$25K	$173–216K	4.0%	271
Big O Tires	$25K	NR	2.0%	485
Children's Orchard	$19.5K	$69–145K	5.0%	96
EmbroidMe	$32.5K	$132–135K	5.0%	71
FastFrame USA	$25K	$93.5–131K	7.5%	214
General Nutrition Centers	$40K	$132.7–182K	6.0%	4,792
Merkinstock	$20K	$150K	6.0%	27
Merle Norman Cosmetics	$0	NR	0.0%	1,908

Metal Supermarkets International	$39.5K	$230–270K	6.0%	87
More Space Place	$22.5K	$89–166.8K	4.5%	25
Paper Warehouse/Party Universe	$35K	$184–445K	4.0%	114
Snap-On Tools	$5K	$156–248K	$50/Mo.	4,793
Wild Birds Unlimited	$18K	$75–125K	4.0%	296

The Service-Based Industry

Service-based franchises make up the remaining chunk of the franchising industry. There are several different types of service-based companies: automotive services, child development, real estate, travel, etc. The industry is large and needs to be fully researched before settling in on a specific franchise concept.

The following table lists the 54 service-based franchises featured in Chapter 6.

Company Name	Franchise Fee	Total Investment	Royalty	Total Units
Aaron's Sales & Lease Ownership	$35K	$254–559K	6.0%	647
Allegra Network LLC	$25K	$256–358.5K	3.6-6.0%	492
AlphaGraphics Printshops of the Future	$25.9K	$352–546K	1.5-8.0%	287
American Leak Detection	$55K+	$85–150K	6.0-10.0%	305
AmeriSpec Home Inspection Service	$18–26.9K	$24.6–63.5K	7.0%	369
Anago Cleaning Systems	$4.5–150K	$5–197K	5.0%	300
Century 21 Real Estate	$0–25K	$10.9–521.2K	6.0%/$500	4,196
Chem-Dry Carpet & Upholstery Cleaning	$19.5K	$6.9–27.6K	$212/Mo.	3,903
Coit Services	$25K	$100K	2.0-6.0%	70
Coldwell Banker Real Estate	$0–20.5K	$150.6–477.3K	6.0%	2,790
Crestcom International, Ltd.	$39.5K–58.5K	$47.8–78.5K	1.5%	135
Entrepreneur's Source, The	$35K	$45–50K	0.0%	195

Expetec Technology Services	$27K	$53.8–80K	5.0%	150
Express Oil Change	$17.5K	$130–1.1MM	5.0%	143
Express Personnel Services	$17.5–20.5K	$120–160K	8.0-9.0%	407
FasTracKids International Ltd.	$15K	$20.9–39.7K	1.5%	170
FASTSIGNS	$20K	$152–225K	6.0%	451
Fiducial	$12.5–25K	$44.4–115.5K	1.5-6.0%	697
FISH Window Cleaning Services	$24.5–49.5K	$60–120K	6.0-8.0%	77
Foliage Design Systems	$25–100K	$49.4–144.4K	6.0%	40
Furniture Medic	$25K	$35.5–78.9K	7.0%/$25 0 Min.	635
Gymboree Play & Music	$35K	$80–150K	6.0%	537
House Doctors Handyman Service	$12–30K	$19–46K	6.0%	225
InterContinental Hotels Group	$500/room, 40K min	Varies	5.0%	3,261
Interiors by Decorating Den	$24.9K	$40–70K	7.0-9.0%	466
Jackson Hewitt Tax Service	$25K	$47.4–75.2K	15.0%	4,316
Kinderdance International	$6.5–20K	$9–25.6K	6.0-15.0%	84
Kumon North America	$1K	$5.9–30.6K	$30000-33,800	1,360
Meineke Car Care Centers	$30K	$180–365K	3.0-7.0%	869
Merry Maids	$17–25K	$42–50K	5.0-7.0%	1,373
Midas Auto Service Experts	$20K	$360–487K	10.0%	2,714
Miracle Auto Painting & Body Repair	$35K	$215–275K	5.0%	31
Money Mailer	$25–35K	$37–71.5K	Varies	252
Mr. Electric Corp.	$19.5K	$64–157K	3.0-6.0%	117
Mr. Rooter Corp.	$22.5K	NR	3.0-6.0%	192
New Horizons Computer Learning Center	$25K–75K	$400–500K	6.0%	272
Perma-Glaze	$21.5K+	NR	6.0/5.0/4. 0%/$200 Min.	180
Pop-A-Lock	$26.1–48.9K	$8–65K	6.0%	105

PostNet Postal & Business Services	$27.9K	$120–150K	4.0%	751
PuroSystems Inc.	$25K	$76.3–119.2K	10.0-8.0%	88
Ramada Franchise Systems	$35K, $350/room	$380K–6.2MM	4.0%	945
Red Roof Inns	$30K	$2.6–3.4MM	4.5-5.0%	360
Schooley Mitchell Telecom Consultants	$37.5K	$75–100K	8.0%	160
ServiceMaster Clean	$16.9–31.5K	$18.5–90.5K	4.0-10.0%	4,488
Sign-A-Rama	$37.5K	$112–117K	6.0%	625
Sports Section, The	$10.9–30.9K	$15–45K	0.0%	165
Studio 6	$25K	$2.7–3.4MM	5.0%	37
Sylvan Learning Centers	$38–46K	$121.1–219.3K	5.0-13.0%	978
Thrifty Car Rental	Varies	$200–250K	3.0%	1,157
UPS Store, The	$29.9K	$141–240K	5.0%	4,525
Window Genie	$19.5K	$40–50K	6.0%	37
World Gym International	$13K	$300K–1MM	$6.5K/Yr.	278
World Inspection Network	$23.9K	$33.1–47.8K	7.0%	120

In closing, I'd like to emphasize that the 100 companies included in this book are here as the result of many months of intensive research and independent evaluation. We did not draw names out of a hat. We did not necessarily choose the industry "heavyweights." We did, however, pour over countless UFOCs, confer with many franchise directors and staff members, visit actual operating units and view numerous websites. In addition to studying each company's UFOC and marketing materials, we took full advantage of recent articles about each company we evaluated. We sought the opinion of friends, industry experts and existing franchisees. As we do not allow advertising in any of our publications, we do not have a built-in bias toward any of the companies selected. Nor do we have any financial or other "hidden agendas."

It is our hope that as a potential franchisee you will benefit from these efforts. In designing the format, we decided the best way to present the information would be to ask the same questions you would: "How much?", "Why are they better than their competitors?", "What do I get out of it?". Those questions and more are answered as we present what we feel are the 100 best franchises.

30 Minute Overview

In presenting this data, we have made some unilateral assumptions about our readers. The first is that you purchased the book because of the depth and accuracy of the data provided — not as a how-to manual. Chapter Three, Recommended Reading, lists several resources for anyone requiring additional background information on the franchising industry and on the process of evaluating a company. Clearly, dedication to hard work, adequate financing, commitment, good business sense and access to trusted professional counsel will determine your ultimate success as a franchisee. A strong working knowledge of the industry, however, will help ensure that you have made the best choice of franchise opportunities. I advise you to acquaint yourself with the dynamics of the industry before you initiate the evaluation and negotiation phases of selecting a franchise.

The second assumption is that you have already devoted the time necessary to conduct a detailed personal inventory. This self-assessment should result in a clear understanding of your skills, aptitudes, weaknesses, long-term personal goals, commitment to succeed and financial capabilities. Most of the books in the Recommended Reading Chapter provide worksheets to accomplish this important step.

∞

There are three primary stages to the franchise selection process: 1) the investigation stage, 2) the evaluation stage and 3) and the negotiation stage. This book is intended primarily to assist the reader in the investigation stage by providing a thorough list of the options available. Chapters One and Two include various observations based on our 15 or so years of involvement with the franchising industry. Hopefully, they will provide some insights that you will find of value.

Understand at the outset that the entire process will take many months and involve a great deal of frustration. I suggest that you set up a realistic time-line for signing a franchise agreement and that you stick with that schedule. There will be a lot of pressure on you to prematurely complete the selection and negotiation phases. Resist the temptation. The penalties are too severe for a seat-of-the-pants attitude. A decision of this magnitude clearly deserves your full attention. Do your homework!

Before starting the selection process, you would be well advised to briefly review the areas that follow.

Franchise Industry Structure

The franchising industry is made up of two distinct types of franchises. The first, and by far the larger, encompasses product and trade name franchising. Automotive and truck dealers, soft drink bottlers and gasoline service stations are included in this group. For the most part, these are essentially distributorships.

The second group encompasses business format franchisors. This book only includes information on this latter category.

Layman's Definition of Franchising

Business format franchising is a method of market expansion by which one business entity expands the distribution of its products and/or services through independent, third-party operators. Franchising occurs when the operator of a concept or system (the

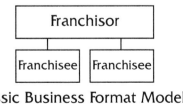

Classic Business Format Model

17

franchisor) grants an independent businessperson (the **franchisee**) the right to duplicate its entire business format at a particular location and for a specified period, under terms and conditions set forth in the contract **(franchise agreement)**. The franchisee has full access to all of the trademarks, logos, marketing techniques, controls and systems that have made the franchisor successful. In effect, the franchisee acts as a surrogate for a company-owned store in the distribution of the franchisor's goods and/or services. It is important to keep in mind that the franchisor and the franchisee are separate legal entities.

In return for a front-end **franchise fee** — which usually ranges from $15,000–35,000 — the franchisor is obligated to "set up" the franchisee in business. This generally includes assistance in selecting a location, negotiating a lease, obtaining financing, building and equipping a site and providing the necessary training, operating manuals, etc. Once the training is completed and the store is open, the new franchisee should have a carbon copy of other units in the system and enjoy the same benefits they do, whether they are company-owned or not.

Business format franchising is unique because it is a long-term relationship characterized by an on-going, mutually beneficial partnership. On-going services include research and development, marketing strategies, advertising campaigns, group buying, periodic field visits, training updates, and whatever else is required to make the franchisee competitive and profitable. In effect, the franchisor acts as the franchisee's "back office" support organization. To reimburse the franchisor for this support, the franchisee pays the franchisor an on-going **royalty fee**, generally four to eight percent of gross sales or income. In many cases, franchisees also contribute an **advertising fee** to reimburse the franchisor for expenses incurred in maintaining a national or regional advertising campaign.

For the maximum advantage, both the franchisor and the franchisees should share common objectives and goals. Both parties must accept the premise that their fortunes are mutually intertwined and that they are each better off working in a co-operative effort, rather than toward any self-serving goals. Unlike the parent/child relationship that has dominated franchising over the past 30 years, franchising is now becoming a true and productive relationship of partners.

Legal Definition of Franchising

The Federal Trade Commission (FTC) has its own definition of franchising. So do each of the 16 states that have separate franchise registration statutes. The State of California's definition, which is the model for the FTC's definition, follows:

Franchise means a contract or agreement, express or implied, whether oral or written, between two or more persons by which:

> *A franchisee is granted the right to engage in the business of offering, selling, or distributing goods or services under a marketing plan or system prescribed in substantial part by a franchisor;*

> *The operation of the franchisee's business pursuant to that plan or system as substantially associated with the franchisor's trademark, service mark, trade name, logotype, advertising, or other commercial symbol designating the franchisor or its affiliates; and*

> *The franchisee is required to pay, directly or indirectly, a franchise fee.*

Multi-Level Franchising

With franchisors continually exploring new ways to expand their distribution, the classic business format model shown above has evolved over the years. Modifications have allowed franchisors to grow more rapidly and at less cost than might have otherwise been possible.

If a franchisor wishes to expand at a faster rate than its financial resources or staff levels allow, it might choose to sell development rights in an area (state, national or international) and let the new entity do the development work. No matter which development method is chosen, the franchisee should still receive the same benefits and support provided under the standard model. The major difference is that the entity providing the training and on-going support and receiving the franchise and royalty fees changes.

Three variations of the master franchising model include: 1) master (or regional) franchising, 2) sub-franchising and 3) area development franchising.

In **master (or regional) franchising**, the franchisor sells the development rights in a particular market to a master franchisee who, in turn, sells individual franchises within the territory. In return for a front-end master franchise fee, the master franchisee has sole responsibility for developing that area under a mutually agreed upon schedule. This includes attracting, screening, signing and training all new franchisees within the territory. Once established, on-going support is generally provided by the parent franchisor.

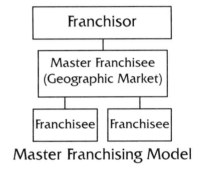

Master Franchising Model

The master franchisee is rewarded by sharing in the franchise fees and the on-going royalties paid to the parent franchisor by the franchisees within the territory.

Sub-franchising is similar to master franchising in that the franchisor grants development rights in a specified territory to a sub-franchisor. After the agreement is signed, however, the parent franchisor has no on-going involvement with the individual franchisees in the territory. Instead, the sub-franchisor becomes the focal point. All fees and royalties are paid

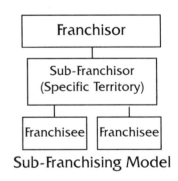

Sub-Franchising Model

directly to the sub-franchisor. It is solely responsible for all recruiting, training and on-going support, and passes on an agreed upon percentage of all incoming fees and royalties to the parent franchisor.

In a sub-franchising relationship, the potential franchisee has to be doubly careful in his or her investigation. He or she must first make sure that the sub-franchisor has the necessary financial, managerial and marketing skills to make the program work. Secondarily, the potential franchisee has to feel comfortable that the parent franchisor can be relied upon to come to his or her rescue if the sub-franchisor should fail.

The third variation is an **area development agreement**. Here again, the franchisor grants exclusive development rights for a particular geographic area to an area development investment group. Within its territory, the area developer may either develop individual franchise units for its own account or find independent franchisees to develop units. In the latter case, the area developer has a residual equity position in the profits of its "area franchisees."

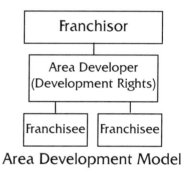

Area Development Model

In return for the rights to an exclusive territory, the area developer pays the franchisor a front-end development fee and commits to develop a certain number of units within a specified time period. (The front-end fee is generally significantly less than the sum of the individual unit fees.) Individual franchisees within the territory pay all contractual franchise, royalty and advertising fees directly to the parent franchisor. The area developer shares in neither the franchise fee nor in on-going royalty or advertising fees. Instead, the area developer shares only in the profitability of the individual franchises that it "owns." In essence, the area developer is buying multiple locations over time

Bond's Franchise Guide Annual Franchising Industry Overview (As of 8/20/2003)

Exhibit 1 CATEGORY	# of Fran- chisors	Fran- chised Units	Company- Owned Units	Total Operating Units
Automotive Products & Services	143	26,351	2,493	28,844
Auto / Truck / Trailer Rental	27	4,422	596	5,018
Building & Remodeling/Furniture/Appliance Repair	144	6,904	192	7,096
Business: Financial Services	43	11,918	6,786	18,704
Business: Advertising & Promotion	28	1,420	69	1,489
Business: Internet/Telecommunications/Misc.	70	6,478	1,866	8,344
Child Development / Education / Products	75	6,131	224	6,355
Education / Personal Development / Training	44	3,617	738	4,355
Employment & Personnel	68	5,059	3,357	8,416
Food: Donuts / Cookies / Bagels	62	12,526	1,081	13,607
Food: Coffee	30	1,497	228	1,725
Food: Ice Cream / Yogurt	43	16,637	1,050	17,687
Food: Quick Service / Take-out	351	123,354	28,138	151,492
Food: Restaurant / Family-Style	166	17,474	9,223	26,697
Food: Specialty Foods	90	9,361	863	10,224
Hairstyling Salons	31	6,581	2,340	8,921
Health / Fitness / Beauty	74	16,164	1,906	18,070
Laundry & Dry Cleaning	18	2,234	27	2,261
Lawn and Garden	22	2,432	372	2,804
Lodging	74	28,047	3,298	31,345
Maid Service & Home Cleaning	20	3,683	170	3,853
Maintenance / Cleaning / Sanitation	126	38,355	1,248	39,603
Medical / Optical / Dental Products & Services	17	1,633	318	1,951
Packaging & Mailing	18	9,112	29	9,141
Printing & Graphics	19	4,578	32	4,610
Publications	21	1,075	63	1,138
Real Estate Inspection Services	19	2,448	359	2,807
Real Estate Services	57	18,676	388	19,064
Recreation & Entertainment	32	2,267	143	2,410
Rental Services	8	2,449	564	3,013
Retail: Art, Art Supplies & Framing	12	714	30	744
Retail: Athletic Wear / Sporting Goods	14	1,551	191	1,742
Retail: Clothing / Shoes / Accessories	5	102	98	200
Retail: Convenience Stores / Supermarkets / Drugs	25	29,577	6,321	35,898

CATEGORY	# of Fran- chisors	Fran- chised Units	Company- Owned Units	Total Operating Units
Retail: Home Furnishings	38	2,490	121	2,611
Retail: Home Improvement & Hardware	12	10,936	292	11,228
Retail: Pet Products & Services	26	1,367	366	1,733
Retail: Photographic Products & Services	12	839	116	955
Retail: Specialty	94	7,393	3,577	10,970
Retail: Video / Audio / Electronics	22	4,170	8,819	12,989
Retail: Miscellaneous	10	1,342	119	1,461
Security & Safety Systems	16	954	101	1,055
Signs	11	1,872	4	1,876
Travel	15	4,563	427	4,990
Miscellaneous	123	7,693	491	8,184
Industry Total	**2,375**	**468,446**	**89,234**	**557,680**
% of Total		**84.0%**	**16.0%**	**100.0%**

Exhibit 2

Relative Size - By Number of Total Operating

Units:	#	%	Cum. %
> 5,000 Total Operating Units	13	0.5%	0.5%
1,000 - 4,999 Total Operating Units	82	3.5%	4.0%
500 - 999 Total Operating Units	91	3.8%	7.8%
250 - 499 Total Operating Units	169	7.1%	14.9%
100 - 249 Total Operating Units	331	13.9%	28.9%
50 - 99 Total Operating Units	317	13.3%	42.2%
25 - 49 Total Operating Units	308	13.0%	55.2%
15 - 24 Total Operating Units	206	8.7%	63.9%
Less Than 15 Total Operating Units	858	36.1%	100.0%
Total	**2,375**	**100.0%**	

Exhibit 3

Country of Origin:	#	%
United States	2,069	87.1%
Canada	306	12.9%
Total	**2,375**	**100.0%**

All of the data in Exhibits 1 - 3 are proprietary and should not be used or quoted without specifically acknowledging Bond's Franchise Guide as the source.

at a discount, since the franchise fee and (frequently) the royalty fee are less than the per unit rate.

Franchise Industry Statistics

The International Franchise Association (IFA) estimated that product and trade name franchising accounted for $554 billion in sales in 1992. This represents roughly 28% of all retail sales.

Business format franchising produced total sales of $249 billion in 1992, roughly 13% of all retail sales. In layman's language, this means that for every $1.00 spent at the retail level, more than $0.13 went to franchised establishments. There is no question that franchising has had a profound impact on the way business is conducted in the U.S. Most analysts anticipate that the overall numbers and market share of retail business will continue to grow well into the foreseeable future and at a faster rate than the economy in general.

According to the IFA's 1997 "Profile of Franchising (Statistical Profile of the 1997 Uniform Franchise Offering Circular Data)," 18% of the industry was concentrated in fast-food and 11% in retail, while only one percent of the concentration was in travel or printing. In terms of system size, about half of the systems analyzed had more than 50 units, with 27% (the largest concentration) having between 11 and 50 franchised units and 75% having ten or fewer company-owned units. Sixty percent of the companies had been in business 12 or more years, but only 44% had been franchising for more than eight years. Only 4% of the franchisors had an initial franchise fee of over $50,000; fast-food, which was the largest category, had an average fee of $19,999. The average total investment for most companies was under $250,000, and most had renewable franchise contracts. Although royalties varied greatly from franchise to franchise, most based it on sales/revenue and ranged from three to six percent monthly. Forty-eight percent of franchisors had an advertising fee based on percentage, usually ranging between 0.01–2%. Franchisor-sponsored financing was offered by 37% of the companies.

Exhibits 1–5, noted on the previous pages, are the result of querying our proprietary franchisor database (which has some 30 fields of information on 2,500 franchisors) and the database of some 1,200 detailed questionnaires that were returned as a result of our 2001 industry survey. You should spend some time reviewing the various Exhibits to get a better idea of the relative size, fees and investment levels required in various industry categories. If the size of the franchise fee, total investment or royalty fee fall far outside the averages noted, the franchisor should have a ready explanation as to why.

The Players

Franchisors

After extensive research, we have selected 100 of what we think are the best franchises the industry has to offer.

Selecting the most appropriate franchisor for your needs is crucial to becoming a successful franchisee. By providing general information, in addition to a detailed analysis of each company's identity, financial requirements, training, support and territory offering, we hope to aid the prospective franchisee in making the right choice.

The Regulatory Agencies

The offer and sale of franchises are regulated at both the federal and state levels. Federal requirements cover all 50 states. In addition, certain states have adopted their own requirements.

In 1979, after many years of debate, the Federal Trade Commission (FTC) implemented Rule 436. This Rule requires that franchisors provide prospective franchisees with a disclosure statement (called an offering circular) containing specific information about a company's franchise offering. The Rule has two objectives: to ensure that the potential franchisee has sufficient background information to make an educated investment decision and to provide him or her with adequate time to do so.

Certain "registration states" require additional safeguards to protect potential franchisees. Their requirements are generally more stringent than the FTC's requirements. These states include California, Florida, Hawaii, Illinois, Indiana, Maryland, Michigan, Minnesota, New York, North Dakota, Oregon, Rhode Island, South Dakota, Virginia, Washington and Wisconsin. Separate registration is also required in the province of Alberta, Canada.

For the most part, registration states require a disclosure format know as the Uniform Franchise Offering Circular (UFOC). As a matter of convenience, and because the state requirements are more demanding, most franchisors have adopted the UFOC format. This format requires that the franchisor provides a prospective franchisee with the required information at their first face-to-face meeting or at least ten business days prior to the signing of the franchise agreement, whichever is earlier. Required information includes:

1. The Franchisor and Any Predecessors.
2. Identity and Business Experience of Persons Affiliated with Franchisor.
3. Litigation.
4. Bankruptcy.
5. Franchisee's Initial Fee/Other Initial Payments.
6. Other Fees.
7. Franchisee's Initial Investment.
8. Obligations of Franchisee to Purchase or Lease from Designated Sources.
9. Obligations of Franchisee to Purchase or Lease in Accordance with Specifications or from Approved Suppliers.
10. Financing Arrangements.
11. Obligations of the Franchisor; Other Supervision, Assistance or Services.
12. Exclusive Area of Territory.
13. Trademarks, Service Marks, Trade Names, Logotypes and Commercial Symbols.
14. Patents and Copyrights.
15. Obligations of the Franchisee to Participate in the Actual Operation of the Franchise Business.
16. Restrictions on Goods and Services Offered by Franchisee.

17. Renewal, Termination, Repurchase, Modification and Assignment of the Franchise Agreement and Related Information.
18. Arrangements with Public Figures.
19. Actual, Average, Projected or Forecasted Franchise Sales, Profits or Earnings.
20. Information Regarding Franchises of the Franchisor.
21. Financial Statements.
22. Contracts.
23. Acknowledgment of Receipt by Respective Franchisee.

If you live in a registration state, make sure that the franchisor you are evaluating is, in fact, registered to sell franchises there. If not, and the franchisor has no near-term plans to register in your state, you should consider other options.

Keep in mind that neither the FTC nor any of the states has reviewed the offering circular to determine whether the information submitted is true or not. They merely require that the franchisor make representations based upon a prescribed format. If the information provided is false, franchisors are subject to civil penalties. That may not help a franchisee, however, who cannot undo a very expensive mistake.

It is up to you to read and thoroughly understand all elements of the offering circular. There is no question that it is tedious reading. Know exactly what you can expect from the franchisor and what your own obligations are. Under what circumstances can the relationship be unilaterally terminated by the franchisor? What is your protected territory? Specifically, what front-end assistance will the franchisor provide? You should have a professional review the UFOC. It would be a shame not to take full advantage of the documentation that is available to you.

The Trade Associations

The **International Franchise Association** (IFA) was established as a non-profit trade association to promote franchising as a responsible method of doing business. The IFA currently represents over 650 franchisors in the U.S. and around the world. It is recognized as the leading spokesperson for responsible franchising. For most of its 30+ years, the IFA has represented the interests of franchisors only. In recent years, however, it has initiated an aggressive campaign to recruit franchisees into its membership and represent their interests as well. The IFA's address is 1350 New York Avenue, NW, Suite 900, Washington, DC 20005. (202) 628-8000; FAX (202) 628-0812.

The **Canadian Franchise Association** (CFA), which has some 250+ members, is the Canadian equivalent of the IFA. Information on the CFA can be obtained from its offices at 5045 Orbit Dr., Bldg. 12, Unit 201, Mississauga, ON L4W 4Y4 Canada. (416) 625-2896; FAX (416) 625-9076.

The **American Association of Franchisees and Dealers** (AAFD) represents the rights and interests of franchisees and independent dealers. Formed in 1992 with the mission of "Bringing Fairness to Franchising," the AAFD represents thousands of franchised businesses, representing over 250 different franchise systems. It provides a broad range of services designed to help franchisees build market power, create legislative support, provide legal and financial support and provide a wide range of general member benefits. P.O. Box 81887, San Diego, CA 92138. (800) 733-9858, (619) 209-3775; FAX: (619) 209-3777.

Franchise Survival/Failure Rate

In order to promote the industry's attractiveness, most literature on the subject of franchising includes the same often-quoted, but very misleading, statistics that leave the impression that franchising is a near risk-free investment.

In the 1970s, the Small Business Administration produced a poorly documented report that 38% of all small businesses fail within their first year of operation and 77% fail within their first five years. With franchising, however, comparative failure rates miraculously drop to only three percent after the first year and eight percent after five years. No effort was made to define failure. Instead, "success" was defined as an operating unit still in business under the same name at the same location.

While most people would agree that the failure rates for franchised businesses are substantially lower than the failure rates for independent businesses, that assumption is not substantiated by reliable statistics. Part of the problem is definitional. Part is the fact that the industry has a vested interest in perpetuating the myth rather than debunking it.

FRANDATA, a Washington, DC-based franchise research firm, recently conducted a review of franchise terminations and renewals. It found that 4.4% of all franchisees left their franchise system each year for a variety of reasons. This figure does not include sales to third parties, however. To be fully meaningful, the data should include sales to third parties and the underlying reasons behind a sale.

The critical issue is to properly define failure and success, and then require franchisors to report changes in ownership based on these universally accepted definitions. A logical starting point in defining success should be whether the franchisee can "make an honest living" as a franchisee. A "success" would occur when the franchisee prefers to continue as a franchisee rather than sell the business. A "failure" would occur when the franchisee is forced to sell his or her business at a loss.

A reasonable measure of franchise success would be to ask franchisees "would you do it again?" If a legitimate survey were conducted of all franchisees of all systems, my guess is that the answer to this question would indicate a "success rate" well under 70% after a five-year period. Alternatively, one could ask the question "has the franchise investment met your expectations?" I estimate that fewer than 50% would say "yes" after a five-year period. These are just educated guesses.

The failure rate is unquestionably lower for larger, more mature companies in the industry that have proven their systems and carefully chosen their franchisees. It is substantially higher for smaller, newer companies that have unproven products and are less demanding in whom they accept as a franchisee.

As it now stands, the Uniform Franchise Offering Circular (UFOC) only requires the franchisor to provide the potential franchisee with the names of owners who have left the system within the past 12 months. In my opinion, this is a severe shortcoming of the regulatory process. Unless required, franchisors will not willingly provide information about failures to prospective franchisees. There is no question in my mind, however, that franchisors are fully aware of when and why past failures have occurred.

It is patently unfair that a potential investor should not have access to this critical information. To ensure its availability, I propose that the UFOC be amended to require that franchisors provide franchisee turn-over information for the most recent five-year period. Underlying reasons for a change in ownership would be provided by a departing franchisee on a universal, industry-approved questionnaire filled out during an "exit" interview. The questionnaire would then be returned to some central clearing house.

The only way to make up for this lack of information is to aggressively seek out as many previous and current franchisees as possible. Request past UFOC's to get the names of previous owners, and then contact them. Whether successful or not, these owners are an invaluable resource. Try to determine the reason for their failure and/or disenchantment. Most failures are the result of poor management or inadequate finances on the part of the departing franchisee. But people give up franchises for other reasons.

Current franchisees are even better sources of meaningful information. For systems with under 25 units, I strongly encourage you to talk to all franchisees. For those having between 25 and 100 units, I recommend talking to at least half. And for all others, interview a minimum of 50.

What Makes a Winning Franchise

Virtually every writer on the subject of franchising has his or her own idea of what determines a winning franchise. I maintain that there are five primary factors.

1. A product or service with a clear advantage over the competition. The advantage may be in brand recognition, a unique, proprietary product or 30 years of proven experience.

2. A standardized franchise system that has been time-tested. Look for a company in which most of the bugs in the system have been worked out through the cumulative experience of both company-owned and franchised units. By the time a system has 30 or more operating units, it should be thoroughly tested.

3. Exceptional franchisor support. This includes not only the initial training program, but the on-going support (research and development, refresher training, [800] help-lines, field representatives and on-site training, annual meetings, advertising and promotion, central purchasing, etc.).

4. The financial wherewithal and management experience to carry out any announced growth plans without short-changing its franchisees. Sufficient depth of management is often lacking in high-growth franchises.

5. A strong mutuality of interest between franchisor and franchisees. Unless both parties realize that their relationship is one of long-term partners, it is unlikely that the system will ever achieve its full potential. Whether they have the necessary rapport is easily determined by a few telephone calls to existing franchisees.

Financial Projections

The single most important factor in buying a franchise — or any business for that matter — is having a realistic projection of sales, expenses and profits. Specifically, how much can you expect to make after working 65 hours a week for 52 weeks a year? No one is in a better position to supply accurate information (subject to caveats) about a franchise opportunity than the franchisor itself. A potential franchisee often does not have the experience to sit down and project what his or her sales and profits will be over the next five years. This is especially true if he or she has no applied experience in that particular business.

Earnings claim statements (Item 19 of the Uniform Franchise Offering Circular) present franchisor-supplied sales, expense and/or profit summaries based on actual operating results for company-owned and/or franchised units. Since no format is prescribed, however, the data may be cursory or detailed. The only constraint is that the franchisor must be able to substantiate the data presented. Further complicating the process is the fact that providing an earnings claim statement is strictly optional. Accordingly, less than 15% of franchisors provide one.

Virtually everyone agrees that the information included in an earnings claim statement can be exceedingly helpful to a potential franchisee. Unfortunately, there are many reasons why franchisors might not willingly choose to make their actual results available to the public. Many franchisors feel that a prospective investor would be turned off if he or she had access to actual operating results. Others may not want to go to the trouble and expense of collecting the data.

Other franchisors are legitimately afraid of being sued for "misrepresentation." There is considerable risk to a franchisor if a published earnings claim statement is interpreted in any way as a "guarantee" of sales or income for new units. Given today's highly litigious society, and the propensity of courts to award large settlements to the "little guy," it's not surprising that so few franchisors provide the information.

As an assist to prospective franchisees, Source Book Publications has recently published the third edition of *"How Much Can I Make?"* It includes over 143 earnings claim statements covering a diverse group of industries. It is the only publication that contains current earnings claim statements submitted by the franchisors. Given the scarcity of industry projections, this is an invaluable resource for potential franchisees or investors in determining what he or she might make by investing in a franchise or similar business. The book is $29.95, plus $4.00 shipping. See the inside rear cover of the book for additional details on the book and the companies that have submitted earnings claim statements. The book can be obtained from Source Book Publications, P.O. Box 12488, Oakland, CA 94604 or by calling (510) 839-5471 or faxing a request to (510) 839-2401.

New vs. Used

As a potential franchisee, you have the option of becoming a franchisee in a new facility at a new location or purchasing an existing franchise. It is not an easy decision. Your success in making that choice will depend upon your business acumen and your insight into people

Purchasing a new franchise unit will mean that everything is current, clean and under warranty. Purchasing an existing franchise will probably involve a smaller investment and allow greater financial leverage. However, you will have to assess the seller's reason for selling. Is the business not performing to expectations because of poor management, poor location, poor support from the franchisor, an indifferent staff, obsolete equipment and/or facilities, etc.? The decision is further clouded because you may be working through a business broker who may or may not be giving you good information. Regardless of the obstacles, considering a "used" franchise merits your consideration. Apply the same analytical tools you would to a new franchise. Do your homework. Be thorough. Be unrelenting.

The Negotiation Process

Once you have narrowed your options down to your top two or three choices, you must negotiate the best deal you can with the franchisor. In most cases, the franchisor will tell you that the franchise agreement cannot be changed. Do not accept this explanation. Notwithstanding the legal requirement that all of a franchisor's agreements be substantially the same at any point in time, there are usually a number of variables in the equation. If the franchisor truly wants you as a franchisee, it may be willing to make concessions not available to the next applicant.

Will the franchisor take a short-term note for all or part of the franchise fee? Can you expand from your initial unit after you have proven yourself? If so, can the franchise fee be eliminated or reduced on a second unit? Can you get a right of first refusal on adjacent territories? Can the term of the agreement be extended from ten to fifteen years? Can you include a franchise cancellation right if the training and/or initial support don't meet your expectations or the franchisor's promises? The list goes on ad infinitum.

To successfully negotiate, you must have a thorough knowledge of the industry, the franchise agreement you are negotiating (and agreements of competitive franchise opportunities) and access to experienced professional advice. This can be a lawyer, an accountant or a franchise consultant. Above all else, they should have proven experience in negotiating franchise agreements. Franchising is a unique method of doing business. Don't pay someone $100+ per hour to learn the industry. Make them demonstrate that they have been through the process several times before. Negotiating a long-term agreement of this type is extremely tricky and fraught with pitfalls. The risks are extremely high. Don't be so smug as to think that you can handle the negotiations yourself. Don't be so frugal as to think you can't afford outside counsel. In point of fact, you can't afford not to employ an experienced professional advisor.

The Four Rs of Franchising

We are told as children that the three Rs of reading, 'riting, and 'rithmetic are critical to our scholastic success. Success in franchising depends on four Rs — realism, research, reserves and resolve.

Realism

At the outset of your investigation, it is important that you be realistic about your strengths and weaknesses, your goals and your capabilities. I strongly recommend that you take the time necessary to do a personal audit — possibly with the help of outside professionals — before investing your life's savings in a franchise.

Franchising is not a money machine. It involves hard work, dedication, setbacks and long hours. Be realistic about the nature of the business you are buying. What traits will ultimately determine your success? Do you have them? If it is a service-oriented business, will you be able to keep smiling when you know the client is a fool? If it is a fast-food business, will you be able to properly manage a minimum-wage staff? How well will you handle the uncertainties that will invariably arise? Can you make day-to-day decisions based on imperfect information? Can you count on your spouse's support after you have gone through all of your working capital reserves, and the future looks cloudy and uncertain?

Be equally realistic about your franchise selection process. Have you thoroughly evaluated all of the alternatives? Have you talked with everyone you can to ensure that you have left no stone unturned? Have you carefully and realistically assessed the advantages and disadvantages of the system offered, the unique demographics of your territory, near-term market trends, the financial projections, etc.? The selection process is tiring. It is easy to convince yourself that the franchise opportunity in your hand is really the best one for you. The penalties for doing so, however, are extreme.

Research

There is no substitute for exhaustive research!

It is up to you to spend the time required to come up with an optimal selection. At a minimum, you will probably be in that business for five years. More likely, you will be in it ten years or more. Given the long-term commitment, allow yourself the necessary time to ensure you don't regret having made a hasty decision. Research is a tedious, boring process. But doing it carefully and thoroughly can greatly reduce your risk and exposure. The benefits are measurable.

Based on personal experience, you may feel you already know the best franchise. Step back. Assume there is a competing franchise out there with a comparable product or service, comparable management, etc., that charges a royalty fee two percent of sales less than your intuitive choice. Over a ten-year period, that could add up to a great deal of money. It certainly justifies your requesting initial information.

A thorough analysis of the literature you receive should allow you to reduce the list of prime candidates down to six to eight companies. Aggressively evaluate each firm. Talking with current and former franchisees is the single best source of information you can get. Where possible, site visits are invaluable. My experience is that franchisees tend to be candid in their level of satisfaction with the franchisor. However, since they don't know you, they may be less candid about their sales, expenses and income. Go to the library and get studies that forecast industry growth, market saturation, industry problems, technical break-throughs, etc. Don't find out a year after becoming a franchisee of a coffee company that earlier reports suggested that the coffee market was oversaturated or that coffee was linked to some form of colon cancer.

Reserves

As a new business, franchising is replete with uncertainty, uneven cash flows and unforeseen problems. It is an imperfect world that might not bear any relation to the clean pro formas you prepared to justify getting into the business.

Any one of these unforeseen contingencies could cause a severe drain on your cash reserves. At the same time, you will have fixed and/or contractual payments that must be met on a current basis regardless of sales: rent, employee salaries, insurance, etc. Adequate back-up reserves may be in the form of savings, commitments from relatives, bank loans, etc. Just make certain that the funds are available when, and if, you need them. To be absolutely safe, I suggest you double the level of reserves recommended by the franchisor.

Keep in mind that the most common cause of business failure is inadequate working capital. Plan properly so you don't become a statistic.

Resolve

Let's assume for the time being that you have demonstrated exceptional levels of realism, research and reserves. You have picked an optimal franchise that takes full advantage of your strengths. You are in business and bringing in enough money to achieve a positive cash flow. The future looks bright. Now the fourth R — resolve — comes into play. Remember why you chose franchising in the first place: to take full advantage of a system that has been time-tested in the marketplace. Remember also what makes franchising work so well: the franchisor and franchisees maximize their respective success by working within the system for the common good. Invariably, two obstacles arise.

The first is the physical pain associated with writing that monthly royalty check. Annual sales of $250,000 and a six percent royalty fee result in a monthly royalty check of $1,250 that must be sent to the franchisor. Every month. As a franchisee, you may look for any justification to reduce this sizable monthly outflow. Resist the temptation. Accept the fact that royalty fees are simply another cost of doing business. They are also a legal obligation that you willingly agreed to pay when you signed the franchise agreement. They are the dues you agreed to pay when you joined the club.

Although there may be an incentive, don't look for loopholes in the contract that might allow you to sue the franchisor or get out of the relationship. Don't report lower sales than actual in an effort to reduce royalties. If you have received the support that you were promised, continue to play by the rules. Honor your commitment. Let the franchisor enjoy the rewards it has earned from your success.

The second obstacle is the desire to change the system. You need to honor your commitment to be a "franchisee" and to live within the franchise system. What makes franchising successful as far as your customers are concerned is uniformity and consistency of appearance, product/service quality and corporate image. The most damaging thing an individual franchisee can do is to suddenly and unilaterally introduce changes to the proven system. While these modifications may work in one market, they only serve to diminish the value of the system as a whole. Imagine what would happen to the national perception of your franchise if every franchisee had the latitude to make unilateral changes in his or her operations. Accordingly, any ideas you have on improving the system should be submitted directly to the franchisor for its evaluation. Accept the franchisor's decision on whether or not to pursue an idea.

If you suspect that you may be a closet entrepreneur, for unrestrained experimenting and tinkering, you are probably not cut out to be a franchisee. Seriously consider this question before you get into a relationship, instead of waiting until you are locked into an untenable situation.

Summary

I hope that I have been clear in suggesting that the selection of an optimal franchise is both time- and energy-consuming. Done properly, the process may take six to nine months and involve the expenditure of several thousand dollars. The difference between a hasty, gut-feel investigation and an exhaustive, well-thought out investigation may mean the difference between finding a poorly-conceived, or even fraudulent, franchise and an exceptional one.

My sense is that there is a strong correlation between the efforts you put into the investigative process and the ultimate degree of success you enjoy as a franchisee. The process is to investigate, evaluate and negotiate. Don't try to bypass any one of these critical elements.

How to Use the Data 2

The data at the beginning of each company profile is the result of a 42-point questionnaire that we send out annually to the franchising community. This information is intended as a brief overview of the company; the text that follows provides a more in-depth analysis of the company's requirements and advantages.

In some cases, an answer has been abbreviated to conserve room and to make the profiles more directly comparable. All of the data is displayed with the objective of providing as much background data as possible. In those cases where no answer was provided to a particular question within the questionnaire, an "NR" is used to signify "No Response."

Please take 20 minutes to acquaint yourself with the composition of the sample questionnaire data. Supplementary comments have been added where some interpretation of the franchisor's response is required.

છ

Blimpie Subs and Salads has been selected to illustrate how this book uses the collected data.

BLIMPIE SUBS AND SALADS
180 Interstate North Pkwy., SE, # 500
Atlanta, GA 30339
Tel: (800) 447-6256 (770) 984-2707
Fax: (770) 980-9176

E-Mail: kietha@blimpie.com
Web Site: www.blimpie.com
Mr. Keith Albright, VP Franchise Development

National submarine sandwich chain, serving fresh-sliced, high-quality meats and cheeses on fresh-baked bread. Also offering an assortment of fresh-made salads and other quality products.

BACKGROUND: IFA MEMBER
Established: 1964; 1st Franchised: 1977

Franchised Units:	1,955
Company-Owned Units	1
Total Units:	1,956
Dist.:	US-1,882; CAN-13; O'seas-61
North America:	50 States, 4 Provinces
Density:	205 in GA, 203 in FL, 121 TX
Projected New Units (12 Months):	NR
Qualifications:	4, 3, 2, 2, 2, 5
Registered:	CA,FL,HI,IL,IN,MI,MN, NY,ND,OR,RI,SD,WA,WI

FINANCIAL/TERMS:

Cash Investment:	$25-100K
Total Investment:	$60-200K
Minimum Net Worth:	$50K

Fees:	Franchise — $10-18K
	Royalty — 6%; Ad. — 4%
Earnings Claim Statement:	No
Term of Contract (Years):	20/5
Avg. # Of Employees:	4 FT, 8 PT
Passive Ownership:	Discouraged
Encourage Conversions:	Yes
Area Develop. Agreements:	Yes
Sub-Franchising Contracts:	Yes
Expand In Territory:	Yes
Space Needs:	1,200 SF; FS, SF, SC, RM

SUPPORT & TRAINING PROVIDED:

Financial Assistance Provided:	Yes(I)
Site Selection Assistance:	Yes
Lease Negotiation Assistance:	Yes
Co-Operative Advertising:	Yes
Franchisee Assoc./Member:	Yes/Yes
Size Of Corporate Staff:	109
On-Going Support:	B,C,D,E,F,G,H,I
Training:	80 Hours in Atlanta, GA; 120 Hours in Local Franchise.

SPECIFIC EXPANSION PLANS:

US:	All United States
Canada:	All Canada
Overseas:	AllCountries

Address/Contact:

1. Company name, address, telephone and fax numbers.

Comment: All of the data published in the book was current at the time the completed questionnaire was received or upon subsequent verification by phone. Over a 12-month period between annual publications, 10–15% of the addresses and/or telephone numbers become obsolete for various reasons. If you are unable to contact a franchisor at the address/telephone number listed, please give us a call at (510) 839-5471 (or fax [510] 839-2104) and we will provide you with the current address and telephone number.

2. **(800) 447-6256; (770) 984-2707**. In many cases, you may find that you cannot access the (800) number from your area. Do not conclude that the company has gone out of business. Simply call the local number.

Comment: An (800) number serves two important functions. The first is to provide an efficient, no-cost way for potential franchisees to contact the franchisor. Making the prospective franchisee foot the bill artificially limits the number of people who might otherwise make the initial contact. The second function is to demonstrate to existing franchisees that the franchisor is doing everything it can to efficiently respond to problems in the field as they occur. Many companies have a restricted (800) line for their franchisees that the general public cannot access. Since you will undoubtedly be talking with the franchisor's staff on a periodic basis, determine whether an (800) line is available to franchisees.

3. **Contact.** You should honor the wishes of the franchisor and address all initial correspondence to the contact listed. It would be counter-productive to try to reach the president directly if the designated contact is the director of franchising.

Comment: The reason for listing the president as the contact varies among franchisors. The president is the best spokesperson for his or her operation. It flatters the franchisee to talk directly with the president. There is no one else around. Regardless of the justification, it is important to determine if the operation is a one-man show in which the president does everything or if the president merely feels that having an open line to potential franchisees is the best way for him or her to sense the "pulse" of the company and the market. Convinced that the president can only do so many things well, I would want assurances that, by taking all incoming calls, he or she is not neglecting the day-to-day responsibilities of managing the business.

Description of Business:

4. Description of Business: The questionnaire provides franchisors with adequate room to differentiate their franchise from the competition. In a minor number of cases, some editing was required.

Comment: In instances where franchisors show no initiative or imagination in describing their operations, you must decide whether this is symptomatic of the company or simply a reflection on the individual who responded to the questionnaire.

Background:

5. IFA. There are two primary affinity groups associated with the franchising industry — the International Franchise Association (IFA) and the Canadian Franchise Association (CFA). Both the IFA and the CFA are described in Chapter One.

6. Established: 1964. Blimpie was founded in 1964, and, accordingly, has 39 years of experience in its primary business. It should be intuitively obvious that a firm that has been in existence for over 39 years has a greater likelihood of being around five years from now than a firm that was founded only last year.

7. 1st Franchised: 1977. 1977 was the year that Blimpie's first franchised unit(s) were established.

Comment: Almost ten years of continuous operation, both as an operator and as a franchisor, is compelling evidence that a firm has staying power. The number of years a franchisor has been in business is one of the key variables to consider in choosing a franchise. This is not to say that a new franchise should not receive your full attention. Every company has to start from scratch. Ultimately, a prospective franchisee has to be convinced that the franchise has 1) been in operation long enough, or 2) its key management personnel have adequate industry experience to have worked out the bugs normally associated with a new business. In most cases, this experience can only be gained through on-the-job training. Don't be the guinea pig that provides the franchisor with the experience it needs to develop a smoothly running operation.

8. **Franchised Units: 1,955.** As of 6/30/2002, Blimpies had 1,955 franchisee-owned and operated units.

9. **Company-Owned Units: 1**. As of 6/30/2002, Blimpie had 1 Company-owned or operated unit.

Comment: A younger franchise should prove that its concept has worked successfully in several company-owned units before it markets its "system" to an inexperienced franchisee. Without company-owned prototype stores, the new franchisee may well end up being the "testing kitchen" for the franchise concept itself.

If a franchise concept is truly exceptional, why doesn't the franchisor commit some of its resources to take advantage of the investment opportunity? Clearly, a financial decision on the part of the franchisor, the absence of company-owned units should not be a negative in and of itself. This is especially true of proven franchises, which may have previously sold their company-owned operations to franchisees.

Try to determine if there is a noticeable trend in the percentage of company-owned units. If the franchisor is buying back units from franchisees, it may be doing so to preclude litigation. Some firms also "churn" their operating units with some regularity. If the sales pitch is compelling, but the follow-through is not competitive, a franchisor may sell a unit to a new franchisee, wait for him or her to fail, buy it back for $0.60 cents on the dollar, and then sell that same unit to the next unsuspecting franchisee. Each time the unit is resold, the franchisor collects a franchise fee, plus the negotiated discount from the previous franchisee.

Alternatively, an increasing or high percentage of company-owned units may well mean the company is convinced of the long-term profitability of such an approach. The key is to determine whether a franchisor is building new units from scratch or buying them from failing and/or unhappy franchisees.

10. **Total Units: 1,956.** As of 6/30/2002, Aaron's had a total of 1,956 operating units.

Comment: Like a franchisor's longevity, its experience in operating multiple units offers considerable comfort. Those franchisors with over 15–25 operating units have proven that their system works and have probably encountered and overcome most of the problems that plague a new operation. Alternatively, the management of franchises with less than 15 operating units may have gained considerable industry experience before joining the current franchise. It is up to the franchisor to convince you that it is providing you with as risk-free an operation as possible. You don't want to be providing a company with its basic experience in the business.

11. **Distribution: US-1,882; CAN-13; O'seas-61.** As of 6/30/2002, Aaron's had 1,882 operating units in the U.S., 13 in Canada and 61 Overseas.

12. **Distribution: North America: 50 States, 4 Provinces.** As of 6/30/2002, Aaron's had operations in 50 states and 4 provinces in Canada.

Comment: It should go without saying that the wider the geographic distribution, the greater the franchisor's level of success. For the most part, such distribution can only come from a large number of operating units. If, however, the franchisor has operations in 15 states, but only 18 total operating units, it is unlikely that it can efficiently service these accounts because of geographic constraints. Other things being equal, a prospective franchisee would vastly prefer a franchisor with 15 units in New York to one with 15 units scattered throughout the U.S., Canada and overseas.

13. **Distribution: Density: GA, FL, TX.** The franchisor was asked "what three states/provinces have the largest number of operating units." As of 6/30/2002, Aaron's had the largest number of units in Georgia, Florida and Texas.

Comment: For smaller, regional franchises, geographic distribution could be a key variable in deciding whether to buy. If the franchisor has a concentration of units in your immediate geographic area, it is likely you will be well-served.

For those far removed geographically from the franchisor's current areas of operation, however, there can be problems. It is both time consuming and expensive to support a franchisee 2,000 miles away from company headquarters. To the extent that a franchisor can visit four franchisees in one area on one trip, there is no problem. If, however, your operation is the only one west of the Mississippi, you may not receive the on-site assistance you would like. Don't be a missionary who has to rely on his or her own devices to survive. Don't accept a franchisor's idle promises of support. If on-site assistance is important to your ultimate success, get assurances in writing that the necessary support will be forthcoming. Remember, you are buying into a system, and the availability of day-to-day support is one of the key ingredients of any successful franchise system.

14. **Projected New Units (12 Months): 30.** Blimpie plans to open 30 new units within the following 12 months. There was no distinction between franchised and company-owned units.

Comment: In business, growth has become a highly visible symbol of success. Rapid growth is generally perceived as preferable to slower, more controlled growth. I maintain, however, that the opposite is frequently the case. For a company of Aaron's size, adding 30 new units over a 12-month period is both reasonable and achievable. It is highly unlikely, however, that a new franchise with only five operating units can successfully attract, screen, train and bring multiple new units on-stream in a 12-month period. If it suggests that it can, or even wants to, be properly wary. You must be confident a company has the financial and management resources necessary to pull off such a Herculean feat. If management is already thin, concentrating on attracting new units will clearly diminish the time it can and should spend supporting you. It takes many months, if not years, to develop and train a second level of management. You don't want to depend upon new hires teaching you systems and procedures they themselves know little or nothing about.

15. **Qualifications: 4,3,2,2,2,5.** This question was posed to determine which specific evaluation criteria were important to the franchisor. The franchisor was asked the following: "In qualifying a potential franchisee, please rank the following criteria from Unimportant (1) to Very Important (5)." The responses should be self-explanatory.

Financial Net Worth (Rank from 1–5)
General Business Experience (Rank from 1–5)
Specific Industry Experience (Rank from 1–5)
Formal Education (Rank from 1–5)
Psychological Profile (Rank from 1–5)
Personal Interview(s) (Rank from 1–5)

16. **Registered** refers to the 16 states that require specific formal registration at the state level before the franchisor may offer franchises in that state. State registration and disclosure to the Federal Trade Commission are separate issues that are discussed in Chapter 1.

Capital Requirements/Rights:

17. **Cash Investment: $25-100K.** On average, a Blimpie franchisee will have made a cash investment of $25,000–100,000 by the time he or she finally opens the initial operating unit.

Comment: It is important that you be realistic about the amount of cash you can comfortably invest in a business. Stretching beyond your means can have grave and far-reaching consequences. Assume that you will encounter periodic set-backs and that you will have to draw on your reserves. The demands of starting a new business are harsh enough without adding the uncertainties associated with inadequate working capital. Trust the franchisor's recommendations regarding the suggested minimum cash investment. If anything, there is an incentive for setting the recommended level of investment too low, rather than too high. The franchisor will want to qualify you to the extent that you have adequate financing. No legitimate franchisor wants you to invest if there is a chance that you might fail because of a shortage of funds.

Keep in mind that you will probably not achieve a positive cash flow before you've been in business more than six months. In your discussions with the franchisor, be absolutely certain that its calculations include an adequate working capital reserve.

18. **Total Investment: $60-200K.** On average, Blimpie franchisees will invest a total of $60,000-200,000, including both cash and debt, by the time the franchise opens its doors.

Comment: The total investment should be the cash investment noted above plus any debt that you will incur in starting up the new business. Debt could be a note to the franchisor for all or part of the franchise fee, an equipment lease, building and facilities leases, etc. Make sure that the total includes all of the obligations that you assume, especially any long-term lease obligations.

Be conservative in assessing what your real exposure is. If you are leasing highly specialized equipment or if you are leasing a single-purpose building, it is naive to think that you will recoup your investment if you have to sell or sub-lease those assets in a buyer's market. If there is any specialized equipment that may have been manufactured to the franchisor's specifications, determine if the franchisor has any form of buy-back provision.

19. **Minimum Net Worth: $50K.** In this case, Blimpie feels that a potential franchisee should have a minimum net worth of $50,000. Although net worth can be defined in vastly different ways, the franchisor's response should suggest a minimum level of equity that the prospective franchisee should possess. Net worth is the combination of both liquid and illiquid assets. Again, don't think that franchisor-determined guidelines somehow don't apply to you.

20. **Fees (Franchise): $10-18K.** Blimpie requires a front-end, one-time-only payment of $10,000–18,000 to grant a franchise for a single location. As noted in Chapter One, the franchise fee is a payment to reimburse the franchisor for the incurred costs of setting the franchisee up in business — from recruiting through training and manuals. The fee usually ranges from $15,000–30,000. It

is a function of competitive franchise fees and the actual out-of-pocket costs incurred by the franchisor.

Depending upon the franchisee's particular circumstances and how well the franchisor thinks he or she might fit into the system, the franchisor may finance all or part of the franchise fee. (See Section 33 below to see if a franchisor provides any direct or indirect financial assistance.)

The franchise fee is one area in which the franchisor frequently provides either direct or indirect financial support.

Comment: Ideally, the franchisor should do no more than recover its costs on the initial franchise fee. Profits come later in the form of royalty fees, which are a function of the franchisee's sales. Whether the franchise fee is $5,000 or $35,000, the total should be carefully evaluated. What are competitive fees and are they financed? How much training will you actually receive? Are the fees reflective of the franchisor's expenses? If the fees appear to be non-competitive, address your concerns with the franchisor.

Realize that a $5,000 differential in the one-time franchise fee is a secondary consideration in the overall scheme of things. You are in the relationship for the long-term.

By the same token, don't get suckered in by an extremely low fee if there is any doubt about the franchisor's ability to follow through. Franchisors need to collect reasonable fees to cover their actual costs. If they don't recoup these costs, they cannot recruit and train new franchisees on whom your own future success partially depends.

21. **Fees (Royalty): 6%** means that six percent of gross sales (or other measure, as defined in the franchise agreement) must be periodically paid directly to the franchisor in the form of royalties. This on-going expense is your cost for being part of the larger franchise system and for all of the "back-office" support you receive. In a few cases, the amount of the royalty fee is fixed rather than variable. In others, the fee decreases as the volume of sales (or

other measure) increases (i.e., 6% on the first $200,000 of sales, 5% on the next $100,000 and so on). In others, the fee is held at artificially low levels during the start-up phase of the franchisee's business, then increases once the franchisee is better able to afford it.

Comment: Royalty fees represent the mechanism by which the franchisor finally recoups the costs it has incurred in developing its business. It may take many years and many operating units before the franchisor is able to make a true operating profit.

Consider a typical franchisor who might have been in business for three years. With a staff of five, rent, travel, operating expenses, etc., assume it has annual operating costs of $300,000 (including reasonable owner's salaries). Assume also that there are 25 franchised units with average annual sales of $250,000. Each franchise is required to pay a 6% royalty fee. Total annual royalties under this scenario would total only $375,000. The franchisor is making a $75,000 profit. Then consider the personal risk the franchisor took in developing a new business and the initial years of negative cash flows. Alternatively, evaluate what it would cost you, as a sole proprietor, to provide the myriad services included in the royalty payment.

In assessing various alternative investments, the amount of the royalty percentage is a major on-going expense. Assuming average annual sales of $250,000 per annum over a 15 year period, the total royalties at 5% would be $187,500. At 6%, the cumulative fees would be $225,000. You have to be fully convinced that the $37,500 differential is justified. While this is clearly a meaningful number, what you are really evaluating is the quality of management and the competitive advantages of the goods and/or services offered by the franchisor.

22. **Fees (Advertising): 4%.** Most national or regional franchisors require their franchisees to contribute a certain percentage of their sales (or other measure, as determined in the franchise agreement) into a corporate advertising fund. These individual advertising fees are pooled to develop a corporate advertising/marketing effort that produces great economies of scale. The end

result is a national or regional advertising program that promotes the franchisor's products and services. Depending upon the nature of the business, this percentage usually ranges from 2–6% and is in addition to the royalty fee.

Comment: One of the greatest advantages of a franchised system is its ability to promote, on a national or regional basis, its products and services. The promotions may be through television, radio, print medias or direct mail. The objective is name recognition and, over time, the assumption that the product and/or service has been "time-tested." An individual business owner could never justify the expense of mounting a major advertising program at the local level. For a smaller franchise that may not yet have an advertising program or fee, it is important to know when an advertising program will start, how it will be monitored and its expected cost.

23. **Earnings Claim Statement: No** means Blimpie does not provide an earnings claim statement to potential franchisees. Unfortunately, only 12–15% of franchisors provide an earnings claim statement in their Uniform Franchise Offering Circular (UFOC). The franchising industry's failure to require earnings claim statements does a serious disservice to the potential franchisee. See Chapter One for comments on the earnings claim statement.

24. **Term of Contract (Years): 20/5.** Blimpie's initial franchise period runs for 20 years. The first renewal period runs for an additional five years. Assuming that the franchisee operates within the terms of the franchise agreement, he or she has 25 years within which to develop and, ultimately, sell the business.

Comment: The potential (discounted) value of any business (or investment) is the sum of the operating income that is generated each year plus its value upon liquidation. Given this truth, the length of the franchise agreement and any renewals are extremely important to the franchisee. It is essential that he or she has adequate time to develop the business to its full potential. At that time, he or she will have maximized the value of the business as an on-going concern. The value of the business to a potential buyer, however, is largely a function of how long the franchise agreement runs. If there are only two years remaining before the agreement expires, or if the terms of an extension(s) are vague, the business will be worth only a fraction of the value assigned to a business with 15 years to go. For the most part, the longer the agreement and the subsequent extension, the better. (The same logic applies to a lease. If your sales are largely a function of your location and traffic count, then it is important that you have options to extend the lease under known terms. Your lease should never be longer than the remaining term of your franchise agreement, however.)

Assuming the length of the agreement is acceptable, be clear under what circumstances renewals might not be granted. Similarly, know the circumstances under which a franchise agreement might be prematurely and unilaterally canceled by the franchisor. I strongly recommend you have an experienced lawyer review this section of the franchise agreement. It would be devastating if, after spending years developing your business, there were a loophole in the contract that allowed the franchisor to arbitrarily cancel the relationship.

25. **Avg. # of Employees: 4 FT, 8 PT.** The question was asked "Including the owner/operator, how many employees are recommended to properly staff the average franchised unit?" In Blimpie's case, four full-time employees and eight part-time employees are required.

Comment: Most entrepreneurs start a new business based on their intuitive feel that it will be "fun" and that their talents and experience will be put to good use. They will be doing what they enjoy and what they are good at. Times change. Your business prospers. The number of employees increases. You are spending an increasing percentage of your time taking care of personnel problems and less and less on the fun parts of the business. In Chapter One, the importance of conducting a realistic self-appraisal was stressed. If you found that you really are not good at managing people, or you don't have the patience to manage a large minimum wage staff, cut your losses before you are locked into doing just that.

26. **Passive Ownership: Discouraged.** Depending on the nature of the business, many franchisors are indifferent as to whether you manage the business

directly or hire a full-time manager. Others are insistent that, at least for the initial franchise, the franchisee be a full-time owner/operator. Blimpie discourages franchisees from hiring full-time managers to run their outlets.

Comment: Unless you have a great deal of experience in the business you have chosen or in managing similar businesses, I feel strongly that you should initially commit your personal time and energies to make the system work. After you have developed a full understanding of the business and have competent, trusted staff members who can assume day-to-day operations, then consider delegating these responsibilities. Running the business through a manager can be fraught with peril unless you have mastered all aspects of the business and there are strong economic incentives and sufficient safeguards to ensure the manager will perform as desired.

27. **Conversions Encouraged: Yes.** This section pertains primarily to sole proprietorships or "mom and pop" operations. To the extent that there truly are centralized operating savings associated with the franchise, the most logical people to join a franchise system are sole practitioners who are working hard but only eking out a living. The implementation of proven systems and marketing clout could significantly reduce operating costs and increase profits.

Comment: The franchisor has the option of 1) actively encouraging such independent operators to become members of the franchise team, 2) seeking out franchisees with limited or no applied experience or 3) going after both groups. Concerned that it will be very difficult to break independent operators of the bad habits they have picked up over the years, many only choose course two. "They will continue to do things their way. They won't, or can't, accept corporate direction," they might say to themselves. Others are simply selective in the conversions they allow. In many cases, the franchise fee is reduced or eliminated for conversions.

28. **Area Development Agreements: Yes** means that Blimpie offers an area development agreement. Area development agreements are more fully described in Chapter One. Essentially, they allow an investor or investment group to develop an entire area or region. The schedule for development is

clearly spelled out in the area development agreement. (Note: "Var." means varies and "Neg." means negotiable.)

Comment: Area development agreements represent an opportunity for the franchisor to choose a single franchisee or investment group to develop an entire area. The franchisee's qualifications should be strong and include proven business experience and the financial depth to pull it off. An area development agreement represents a great opportunity for an investor to tie up a large geographical area and develop a concept that may not have proven itself on a national basis. Keep in mind that this is a quantum leap from making an investment in a single franchise and is relevant only to those with development experience and deep pockets.

29. **Sub-Franchising Contracts: Yes.** Blimpie grants sub-franchising agreements. (See Chapter One for a more thorough explanation.) Like area development agreements, sub-franchising allows an investor or investment group to develop an entire area or region. The difference is that the sub-franchisor becomes a self-contained business, responsible for all relations with franchisees within its area, from initial training to on-going support. Franchisees pay their royalties to the sub-franchisor, who in turn pays a portion to the master franchisor.

Comment: Sub-franchising is used primarily by smaller franchisors who have a relatively easy concept and who are prepared to sell a portion of the future growth of their business to someone for some front-end cash and a percentage of the future royalties they receive from their franchisees.

30. **Expand in Territory: Yes.** Under conditions spelled out in the franchise agreement, Blimpie will allow its franchisees to expand within their exclusive territory.

Comment: Some franchisors define the franchisee's exclusive territory so tightly that there would never be room to open additional outlets within an area. Others provide a larger area in the hopes that the franchisee will do well and have the incentive to open additional units.

There are clearly economic benefits to both parties from having franchisees with multiple units. There is no question that it is in your best interest to have the option to expand once you have proven to both yourself and the franchisor that you can manage the business successfully. Many would concur that the real profits in franchising come from managing multiple units rather than being locked into a single franchise in a single location. Additional fees may or may not be required with these additional units.

31. **Space Needs: 12,000 SF; FS, SF, SC, RM.** The average Blimpie's retail outlet will require 12,000 square feet in a Free-Standing (FS) building, Storefront (SF), Strip Center (SC) or Regional Mall (RM). Other types of leased space might be a Convenience Store (C-store) location, Executive Suite (ES), Home-Based (HB), Industrial Park (IP), Kiosk (KI), Office Building (OB), Power Center (PC), or Warehouse (WH).

Comment: Armed with the rough space requirements, you can better project your annual occupancy costs. It should be relatively easy to get comparable rental rates for the type of space required. As annual rent and related expenses can be as high as 15% of your annual sales, be as accurate as possible in your projections.

Franchisor Support and Training Provided:

32. **Financial Assistance Provided: Yes (I)** notes that Blimpie is indirectly (I) involved in providing financial assistance. Indirect assistance might include making introductions to the franchisor's financial contacts, providing financial templates for preparing a business plan or actually assisting in the loan application process. In some cases, the franchisor becomes a co-signer on a financial obligation (equipment lease, space lease, etc.). Other franchisors are (D) directly involved in the process. In this case, the assistance may include a lease or loan made directly by the franchisor. Any loan would generally be secured by some form of collateral. A very common form of assistance is a note for all or part of the initial franchise fee. Yes (B) indicates that the franchisor provides both direct and indirect financial assistance. The level of assistance will generally depend upon the relative strengths of the franchisee.

Comment: The best of all possible worlds is one in which the franchisor has enough confidence in the business and in you to co-sign notes on the building and equipment leases and allow you to pay off the franchise fee over a specified period of time. Depending upon your qualifications, this could happen. Most likely, however, the franchisor will only give you some assistance in raising the necessary capital to start the business. Increasingly, franchisors are testing a franchisee's business acumen by letting him or her assume an increasing level of personal responsibility in securing financing. The objective is to find out early in the process how competent a franchisee really is.

33. **Site Selection Assistance: Yes** means that Blimpie will assist the franchisee in selecting a site location. While the phrase "location, location, location" may be hackneyed, its importance should not be discounted, especially when a business depends upon retail traffic counts and accessibility. If a business is home- or warehouse-based, assistance in this area is of negligible or minor importance.

Comment: Since you will be locked into a lease for a minimum of three, and probably five, years, optimal site selection is absolutely essential. Even if you were somehow able to sub-lease and extricate yourself from a bad lease or bad location, the franchise agreement may not allow you to move to another location. Accordingly, it is imperative that you get it right the first time.

If a franchisor is truly interested in your success, it should treat your choice of a site with the same care it would use in choosing a company-owned site. Keep in mind that many firms provide excellent demographic data on existing locations at a very reasonable cost.

34. **Lease Negotiations Assistance: Yes.** Once a site is selected, Blimpie will be actively involved in negotiating the terms of the lease.

Comment: Given the complexity of negotiating a lease, an increasing number of franchisors are taking an active role in lease negotiations. There are far too many trade-offs that must be considered — terms, percentage rents, tenant improvements, pass-throughs, kick-out clauses, etc. This responsibility is best left to the professionals. If the franchisor doesn't have the capacity to support you directly, enlist the help of a well-recommended broker. The penalties for signing a bad long-term lease are very severe.

35. Co-operative Advertising: Yes. This refers to the existence of a joint advertising program in which the franchisor and franchisees each contribute to promote the company's products and/or services (usually within the franchisee's specific territory).

Comment: Co-op advertising is a common and mutually-beneficial effort. By agreeing to split part of the advertising costs, whether for television, radio or direct mail, the franchisor is not only supporting the franchisee, but guaranteeing itself royalties from the incremental sales. A franchisor that is not intimately involved with the advertising campaign — particularly when it is an important part of the business — may not be fully committed to your overall success.

36. Franchisee Assoc./Member: Yes/Yes. This response notes that the Blimpie system does include an active association made up of Blimpie franchisees and that the franchisor is also a member of the franchisee association.

Comment: The empowerment of franchisees has become a major rallying cry within the industry over the past three years. Various states have recently passed laws favoring franchisee rights, and the subject has been widely discussed in congressional staff hearings. Political groups even represent franchisee rights on a national basis. Similarly, the IFA is now actively courting franchisees to become active members. Whether they are equal members remains to be seen.

Franchisees have also significantly increased their clout with respect with the franchisor. If a franchise is to grow and be successful in the long term, it is critical that the franchisor and its franchisees mutually agree they are partners rather than adversaries.

37. Size of Corporate Staff: 109. Blimpie has 109 full-time employees on its staff to support its 1,956 operating units.

Comment: There are no magic ratios that tell you whether the franchisor has enough staff to provide the proper level of support. It would appear, however, that Blimpie's staff of 109 is adequate to support 1,956 operating units. Less clear is whether a staff of three, including the company president and his wife, can adequately support 15 fledgling franchisees in the field.

Many younger franchises may be managed by a skeleton staff, assisted by outside consultants who perform various management functions during the start-up phase. From the perspective of the franchisee, it is essential that the franchisor have actual in-house franchising experience, and that the franchisee not be forced to rely on outside consultants to make the system work. Whereas a full-time, salaried employee will probably have the franchisee's objectives in mind, an outside consultant may easily not have the same priorities. Franchising is a unique form of business that requires specific skills and experience — skills and experience that are markedly different from those required to manage a non-franchised business. If you are thinking about establishing a long-term relationship with a firm just starting out in franchising, you should insist that the franchisor prove that it has an experienced, professional team on board and in place to provide the necessary levels of support to all concerned.

38. On-Going Support: B,C,D,E,F,G,H,I

Like initial training, the on-going support services provided by the franchisor are of paramount importance. Having a solid and responsive team behind you can certainly make your life much easier and allow you to concentrate your energies on other areas. As is noted below, the franchisors were asked to indicate their support for nine separate on-going services:

Service Provided	Included in Fees	At Add'l. Cost	NA
Central Data Processing	A	a	NA
Central Purchasing	B	b	NA
Field Operations Evaluation	C	c	NA
Field Training	D	d	NA
Initial Store Opening	E	e	NA
Inventory Control	F	f	NA

Franchisee Newsletter	G	g	NA
Regional or National Meetings	H	h	NA
800 Telephone Hotline	I	i	NA

If the franchisor provides the service at no additional cost to the franchisee (as indicated by letters A–I), a capital letter was used to indicate this. If the service is provided, but only at an additional cost, a lower case letter was used. If the franchisor responded with a NA, or failed to note an answer for a particular service, the corresponding letter was omitted from the data sheet.

39. **Training: 80 Hours in Atlanta, GA; 120 Hours in Local Franchise.**

Comment: Assuming that the underlying business concept is sound and competitive, adequate training and on-going support are among the most important determinants of your success as a franchisee. The initial training should be as lengthy and as "hands-on" as necessary to allow the franchisee to operate alone and with confidence. Obviously, every potential situation cannot be covered in any training program. But the franchisee should come away with a basic understanding of how the business operates and where to go to resolve problems when they come up. Depending on the business, there should be operating manuals, procedural manuals, company policies, training videos, (800) help-lines, etc. It may be helpful at the outset to establish how satisfied recent franchisees are with a company's training. I would also have a clear understanding about how often the company updates its manuals and training programs, the cost of sending additional employees through training, etc.

Remember, you are part of an organization that you are paying (in the form of a franchise fee and on-going royalties) to support you. Training is the first step. On-going support is the second step.

Specific Expansion Plans:

40. **U.S.: All United States.** Blimpie is currently focusing its growth on the entire United States. Alternatively, the franchisor could have listed particular states or regions into which it wished to expand.

41. **Canada: All Canada.** Blimpie is currently seeking additional franchisees in Canada. Specific markets or provinces could have also been indicated.

42. **Overseas: Yes.** Blimpie is currently expanding overseas.

Comment: You will note that many smaller companies with less than 15 operating units suggest that they will concurrently expand throughout the U.S., Canada and internationally. In many cases, these are the same companies that foresee a 50+% growth rate in operating units over the next 12 months. The chances of this happening are negligible. As a prospective franchisee, you should be wary of any company that thinks it can expand throughout the world without a solid base of experience, staff and financial resources. Even if adequate financing is available, the demands on existing management will be extreme. New management cannot adequately fill the void until they are able to fully understand the system and absorb the corporate culture. If management's end objective is expansion for its own sake rather than by design, the existing franchisees will suffer.

Note: The statistics noted in the profiles preceding each company's analysis are the result of data provided by the franchisors themselves by way of a detailed questionnaire. Similarly, the data in the summary comparisons in the Introduction Chapter were taken from the company profile data. The figures used throughout each company's analysis, however, were generally taken from the UFOCs. In many cases, the UFOCs, which are only printed annually, contain information that is somewhat out of date. This is especially true with regard to the number of operating units and the current level of investment. A visit to our website at www.worldfranchising.com should provide current data.

∞

If you have not already done so, I would strongly encourage you to invest the modest time required to read Chapter 1 — 30 Minute Overview.

Recommended Reading

My strong sense is that every potential franchisee should be well-versed in the underlying fundamentals of the franchising industry before he or she commits to the way of life it involves. The better you understand the industry, the better prepared you will be to take maximum advantage of the relationship with your franchisor. There is no doubt that it will also place you in a better position to negotiate the franchise agreement — the conditions of which will dictate every facet of your life as a franchisee for the term of the agreement. The few extra dollars spent on educating yourself could well translate into tens of thousand of dollars to the bottom line in the years ahead.

In addition to general franchising publications, we have included several special interest books that relate to specific, but critical, parts of the start-up and on-going management process — site selection, hiring and managing minimum wage employees, preparing accurate cash flow projections, developing comprehensive business and/or marketing plans, etc.

We have also attempted to make the purchasing process easier by allowing readers to purchase the books directly from Source Book Publications, either via our 800-line or our website at www.worldfranchising.com. All of the books are currently available in inventory and are generally sent the same day an order is received. A 15% discount is available on all orders over $100.00. See page 66 for an order form. Your complete satisfaction is 100% guaranteed on all books.

Background/Evaluation

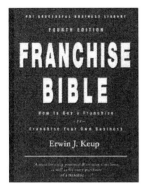

Franchise Bible: A Comprehensive Guide, 4th Edit., Keup, Oasis Press. 2000. 318 pp. $27.95.

This recently updated classic is equally useful for prospective franchisees and franchisors alike. The comprehensive guide and workbook explain in detail what the franchise system entails and the precise benefits it offers. The book features the new franchise laws that became effective January, 1995. To assist the prospective franchisee in rating a potential franchisor, Keup provides necessary checklists and forms. Also noted are the franchisor's contractual obligations to the franchisee and what the franchisee should expect from the franchisor in the way of services and support.

Tips & Traps When Buying a Franchise, Revised 2nd Edition, Tomzack, Source Book Publications. 1999. 236 pp. $19.95.

Many a green franchisee is shocked to discover that the road to success in franchising is full of hidden costs, inflated revenue promises, reneged marketing support and worse. In this candid, hard-hitting book, Tomzack steers potential franchisees around the pitfalls and guides them in making a smart, lucrative purchase. Topics include: matching a franchise with personal finances and lifestyle, avoiding the five most common pitfalls, choosing a prime location, asking the right questions, etc.

Databases

Franchisor Database, Source Book Publications. (800) 841-0873/ (510) 839-5471.

Listing of over 2,200 active North American franchisors. 24 fields of information per company: full address, telephone/800/fax numbers, Internet address, email address, contact/title/salutation, president/title/salutation, # of franchised units, # of company-owned units, # total units, IFA/CFA Member, etc. 48 industry categories. Unlimited use. Guaranteed deliverability — $0.50 rebate for any returned mailings. $1,000 for initial database, $75 per quarter for updates.

Directories

Bond's Franchise Guide — 2004 Edition, Bond, Source Book Publications, 2004. 496 pp. $29.95.

The definitive and most comprehensive franchising directory available. Over 1,000 detailed listings resulting from an exhaustive 40-point questionnaire. 45 distinct business categories. Also includes profiles of leading franchise attorneys, consultants and service providers. Excellent industry overview.

Minority Franchise Guide — 2004 Edition, Bond/Wallace, Source Book Publications, 2004. 304 pp. $19.95.

The only minority franchising directory! Contains detailed profiles and company logos of over 550 forward-looking franchisors that encourage and actively support the inclusion of minority franchisees. It also includes a listing of resources available to prospective minority franchisees.

Earnings Claims

"How Much Can I Make?", Bond, Source Book Publications. 2004. 476 pp. $29.95.

The single most important task for a prospective investor is to prepare a realistic cash flow statement that accurately reflects the economic potential of that business. *"How Much Can I Make?"* is an invaluable "insider's guide" that details historical sales, expense and/or profit data on actual franchise operations, **as provided by the franchisors themselves**. Whether you plan to buy a franchise or start your own business, these actual performance statistics will ensure that you have a realistic starting point in determining how much you can expect to make in a similar business. 132 current Earnings Claims Statements, in their entirety, are included for the 3 major industry categories. Unfortunately, less than 15% of franchisors provide such projections/guidelines to prospective franchisees. "How Much Can I Make?" includes roughly half of the total universe of earnings claim statements available. The list of companies included runs from the McDonald's and Subways of the world to newer, smaller franchises with only a few operating units. Any serious investor would be shortsighted not to take full advantage of this extraordinary resource.

International Franchising

International Herald Tribune International Franchise Guide, Bond/Thompson, Source Book Publications. 1999. 192 pp. $34.95.

This annual publication, sponsored by the International Herald Tribune, is the definitive guide to international franchising. It lists comprehensive, in-depth profiles of major franchisors who are committed (not just the usual lip service) to promote and support overseas expansion. Details specific geographic areas of desired expansion for each company, country by country — as well as the number of units in each foreign country as of the date of publication. Geared specifically to the needs and requirements of prospective international area developers, master franchisees and investors. Investors must be prepared to assume responsibility for the development of large geographic areas. Also listed are international franchise consultants, attorneys and service providers. Covers 32 distinct business categories.

Franchise Rankings

Bond's Top 50 Food-Service Franchises, Bond/Schiller, Source Book Publications, 2000. 288 pp. $19.95

In response to the constantly asked question, *"What are the best franchises?"*, Bond's new book focuses on the top 50 franchises. Over 500 food-service systems were evaluated for inclusion. Companies were analyzed on the basis of historical performance, brand identification, market dynamics, franchisee satisfaction, the level of training and on-going support, financial stability, etc. Detailed four to five page profiles on each company, as well as key statistics and industry overview. All companies are proven performers and most have a national presence. Excellent starting point for someone focusing on the food-service industry.

Bond's Top 50 Retail Franchises, Bond/Schiller/Tong, Source Book Publications, 2001. 288 pp. $19.95

In response to the constantly asked question, *"What are the best franchises?"*, Bond's new book focuses on the top 50 franchises. Over 350 retail systems were evaluated for inclusion. Companies were analyzed on the basis of historical performance, brand identification, market dynamics, franchisee satisfaction, the level of training and on-going support, financial stability, etc. Detailed four to five page profiles on each company, as well as key statistics and industry overview. All companies are proven performers and most have a national presence. Excellent starting point for someone focusing on the retail industry.

Bond's Top 50 Service-Based Franchises, Bond/Schiller, Source Book Publications, 2000. 300 pp. $19.95

In response to the constantly asked question, *"What are the best franchises?"*, Bond's new book focuses on the top 50 franchises. Over 400 service-based systems were evaluated for inclusion. Companies were analyzed on the basis of historical performance, brand identification, market dynamics, franchisee satisfaction, the level of training and on-going support, financial stability, etc. Detailed four to five page profiles on each company, as well as key statistics and industry overview. All companies are proven performers and most have a national presence. Excellent starting point for someone focusing on the service-based industry.

Site Selection

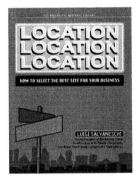

Location, Location, Location: How to Select the Best Site for Your Business, Salvaneschi, Oasis Press. 2000. 252 pp. $24.95.

Whether you are searching for a new business site or relocating an existing business, you have the power to dramatically increase your profits by choosing the right location. For any business that depends on a customer's ability to find it, location is the most important ingredient for success. Learn how to: spot the essential characteristics of the best location; understand why and how people move from one point to another; analyze and learn from your competitor's business; and learn about the retail trading zone and how to use it to capture the most customers.

The Franchise Bookstore
Order Form

Call (800) 841-0873 or (510) 839-5471; or FAX (510) 839-2104

Item #	Title	Price	Qty.	Total

Basic postage (1 Book)	$7.00
Each additional book add $4.00	
California tax @ 8.25% (if CA resident)	
Total due in U.S. dollars	
Deduct 15% if total due is over $100.00	
Net amount due in U.S. dollars	

Please include credit card number and expiration date for all charge card orders! Checks should be made payable to Source Book Publications. All prices are in U.S. dollars.

Mailing Information: All books shipped by USPS Priority Mail (2nd Day Air). Please print clearly and include your phone number in case we need to contact you. Postage and handling rates are for shipping within the U.S. Please call for international rates.

❏ Check enclosed or

Charge my:
❏ MasterCard   ❏ VISA

Card #: _____

Expiration Date: _____

Signature: _____

Name: _____

Company: _____

Address: _____

City: _____

Title: _____

Telephone No.: (___)_____

State/Prov.: _____ Zip:_____

Special Offer — Save 15%

If your total order above exceeds $100.00, deduct 15% from your bill.

Please send order to:
Source Book Publications
P.O. Box 12488, Oakland, CA 94604
Satisfaction Guaranteed. If not fully satisfied, return for a prompt, 100% refund.

Food Service 4

Auntie Anne's
Hand-Rolled Soft Pretzels

**Hand-Rolled
Soft Pretzels**

160-A, Rt. 41, P.O. Box 529
Gap, PA 17527
Tel: (717) 442-4766
Fax: (717) 442-4139
E-Mail: merrills@auntieannesinc.com
Web Site: www.auntieannesinc.com
Mr. Merrill L. Smucker, Franchise Sales/Mktg.
  Manager

As the founder and leader of what Entrepreneur Magazine calls the pretzel retailing revolution, AUNTIE ANNE'S supports over 775 locations. Customers love to watch our pretzels being rolled, twisted and baked. They choose our pretzels not only for the variety and taste, but also for our commitment to providing a nutritious snack alternative to mall treats. Our innovative mall-based concept has made AUNTIE ANNE'S one of the most sought-after franchises in the industry today.

BACKGROUND: IFA MEMBER
Established: 1988; 1st Franchised: 1989
Franchised Units: 748
Company-Owned Units: 37
Total Units: 785
Dist.:   US-744; CAN-4; O'seas-90

North America:	46 States, 2 Provinces
Density:	80 in PA, 47 in CA, 42 in NY
Projected New Units (12 Months):	50
Qualifications:	4, 2, 2, 2, 3, 5
Registered:	All States

FINANCIAL/TERMS:

Cash Investment:	$193-326K
Total Investment:	$260K
Minimum Net Worth:	$300K
Fees:	Franchise — $30K
	Royalty — 6%; Ad. — 1%
Earnings Claim Statement:	No
Term of Contract (Years):	20/5
Avg. # Of Employees:	3 FT, 10 PT
Passive Ownership:	Not Allowed
Encourage Conversions:	N/A
Area Develop. Agreements:	No
Sub-Franchising Contracts:	No
Expand In Territory:	Yes
Space Needs:	400-800 SF; RM, Airports, Train

SUPPORT & TRAINING PROVIDED:

Financial Assistance Provided:	Yes(I)
Site Selection Assistance:	Yes
Lease Negotiation Assistance:	Yes
Co-Operative Advertising:	Yes
Franchisee Assoc./Member:	No
Size Of Corporate Staff:	130
On-Going Support:	a,B,C,D,E,F,G,h
Training:	2 Weeks Gap, PA; 1 Week On-Site for Opening.

SPECIFIC EXPANSION PLANS:	Canada:	No
US: All Except PA, NJ, NY	Overseas:	All Countries

Auntie Anne's serves fresh, never frozen, pretzels (hand-rolled and twisted in full view of customers) with a 30-minute freshness guarantee, a variety of dipping sauces and three proprietary drinks—old fashioned lemonade, dutch ice frozen drinks and coffee. This variety, and the combination of sweet and savory menu items, attracts customers to Auntie Anne stores all day long. The company also sponsors the Children's Miracle Network.

Anne Beiler's pretzel-twisting began as a manager at a Maryland farmer's market in 1987. Her husband, Jonas, wanted to provide family counseling and Anne was helping him realize this dream. At another market in Downington, Pennsylvania, Anne and Jonas purchased their own stand and began to experiment with new ingredients. Soon, the couple had a pretzel "better than the best you've ever tasted!" This pretzel eventually became the only item sold at the stand and, in 1988, Auntie Anne's, Inc. was established. In 2001, it expanded its market with Anne's Cre-amo Classic Cones, a frozen custard shop.

Operating Units	12/31/2000	12/31/2001	12/31/2002
Franchised	630	671	715
% Change	--	6.0%	6.0%
Company-Owned	30	32	37
% Change	--	0.07%	14.0%
Total	660	703	752
% Change	--	6.0%	7.0%
Franchised as % of Total	95.5%	95.3%	95.1%

Investment Required
The fee for an Auntie Anne's franchise is $30,000. Franchisees who purchase additional units receive a 10% fee discount on each new unit.

Auntie Anne's provides the following range of investments required to open your initial franchise. The range assumes that all items are paid for in cash. To the extent that you choose to finance any of these expense items, your front-end investment could be substantially reduced.

Item	Established Low Range	Established High Range
Franchise Fee	$30,000	$30,000
Advertising	$500	$2,500
Equipment	$40,000	$64,000
Fixtures/Furniture/Signs	$96,500	$145,000
Insurance	$400	$2,500
Inventory	$3,300	$4,000
Lease and Utility Security Deposits	$4,000	$17,500
Training Expenses	$750	$6,000
Other Costs and Additional Funds	$17,100	$54,500
Total Investment	$192,550	$326,000

On-Going Expenses

Auntie Anne's franchisees pay royalties equaling 6% and advertising and marketing fees equaling 1% of gross revenue.

What You Get—Training and Support

The Auntie Anne's philosophy is three-fold: to provide premium products with friendly, courteous service in a sparkling clean store. To fulfill this philosophy, Auntie Anne's provides each new franchisee with four days of classroom training and two days of in-store training. Supplementary training is required for new franchisees and licensees. Upon opening, each store crew also receives seven days of on-site training.

Territory

Auntie Anne's does not grant exclusive territories.

Baskin-Robbins

14 Pacella Park Dr., P.O. Box 317
Randolph, MA 02368-0317
Tel: (800) 777-9983 (781) 961-4000
Fax: (781) 963-1215
E-Mail: apadulo@adrus.com
Web Site: www.dunkin-baskin-togos.com
Mr. Anthony Padulo, VP New Business Dev.

BASKIN-ROBBINS develops, operates and franchises retail stores that sell ice cream, frozen yogurt
and other approved services. In some markets,
BASKIN-ROBBINS, together with TOGO'S and/or
DUNKIN' DONUTS, offers multiple brand combinations of the three brands. TOGO'S, BASKIN-ROB-
BINS and DUNKIN' DONUTS are all subsidiaries
of Allied Domecq PLC.

BACKGROUND:	IFA MEMBER
Established: 1946; 1st Franchised: 1948	
Franchised Units:	4,500
Company-Owned Units	0
Total Units:	4,500
Dist.:	US-2,286; CAN-620; O'seas-1,594
North America:	41 States
Density:	554 in CA, 195 in IL, 181 NY
Projected New Units (12 Months):	27
Qualifications:	, , , , ,
Registered:	All States

FINANCIAL/TERMS:

Cash Investment:	$145.8-527.8K
Total Investment:	$145.7-527.8K
Minimum Net Worth:	$400K/unit
Fees:	Franchise — $40K
	Royalty — 5-5.9%; Ad. — 5%
Earnings Claim Statement:	Yes
Term of Contract (Years):	20
Avg. # Of Employees:	N/A
Passive Ownership:	Allowed
Encourage Conversions:	NR
Area Develop. Agreements:	Yes/3-5
Sub-Franchising Contracts:	No
Expand In Territory:	Yes
Space Needs:	NR SF; FS, SF, SC, RM

SUPPORT & TRAINING PROVIDED:

Financial Assistance Provided:	Yes(I)
Site Selection Assistance:	N/A
Lease Negotiation Assistance:	Yes
Co-Operative Advertising:	Yes
Franchisee Assoc./Member:	Yes/No
Size Of Corporate Staff:	N/A
On-Going Support:	B,C,D,G,H,I
Training:	51 Days in Randolph, MA; 3.5 Days at another Location.

SPECIFIC EXPANSION PLANS:

US:	All Regions
Canada:	All Canada
Overseas:	All Countries

Daily, Baskin-Robbins scoops more than 2.2 million ice cream cones,
each one topped with one of their 31 ever-changing flavors—one for
every day of the month. With so many choices, there is sure to be the
right taste to satisfy each and every snack and dessert craving. Baskin-
Robbins was the originator of the legendary Jamoca Almond Fudge and
Pralines and Cream ice cream flavors, both of which are now internationally known in both Baskin-Robbins franchises and the greater frozen
dessert world.

Irv Robbins and Burt Baskin opened the first Baskin-Robbins in 1947. From that one California shop, Irv and Burt's establishment has spread throughout the United States and across the globe from Belgium and Moscow to Japan and Australia.

Along with its sister companies Dunkin' Donuts and Togo's, Baskin-Robbins is one of Allied Domecq's Quick Service Restaurants. The Allied Domecq family bears more than 130 years of business experience and manages and operates 10,000 restaurants around the world. The company's Complementary Daypart Branding Strategy offers each of its franchise concepts as co-brands with the others. With three different concepts whose peak selling hours correlate to three distinct times of day, respectively, Allied Domecq presents franchisees with a schedule-proof earning opportunity—Dunkin' Donuts's coffee and pastries in the morning, Togo's sandwiches and salads for lunch and Baskin-Robbins's desserts and snacks throughout the afternoon and evening.

Operating Units	8/31/2000	8/31/2001	8/31/2002
Franchised	2,152	1,363	1,257
% Change	--	-36.7%	-7.8%
Company-Owned	10	4	0
% Change	--	-60.0%	-100.0%
Total	2,162	1,367	1,257
% Change	--	-36.8%	-8.0%
Franchised as % of Total	99.5%	99.7%	100.0%

Investment Required
The fee for a Baskin-Robbins franchise varies, ranging from $30,000 to $60,000, depending upon the market in which the unit is located. The company works with a group of preferred lenders to offer competitive and flexible financing options to franchisees.

Baskin-Robbins provides the following range of investments required to open your initial franchise. The range assumes that all items are paid for in cash. To the extent that you choose to finance any of these expense items, your front-end investment could be substantially reduced. The following figures apply to the opening of a new, single-brand store.

Item	Established Low Range	Established High Range
Franchise Fee	$30,000	$60,000
Equipment/Fixtures/Signs	$31,500	$158,700
Insurance	$4,500	$15,000
Marketing Start-Up Fee	$3,000	$3,000
Opening Inventory	$5,000	$8,000
Real Estate	$13,975	$165,975
Training Expenses	$1,000	$20,500
Uniforms	$400	$800
Other Costs and Additional Funds (for 3 months)	$42,850	$115,800
Total Investment	$132,225	$547,775

On-Going Expenses

Baskin-Robbins franchisees pay continuing franchise fees equaling 5 to 5.9% and advertising fees equaling 5% of gross revenue.

What You Get—Training and Support

Baskin-Robbins and Allied Domecq have a lot of successful franchisees behind them, and they want to put that to work for you. The first service offered to franchisees by Allied Domecq is site selection and market analysis. Always seeking sites with strong business potential, the company's market optimization model (MOM) evaluates the quality of the retail and demographic conditions in each market to find the intersections that are most like already open, booming locations.

Once the ideal site is found, the Baskin-Robbins concept can be adapted to suit many venues and geographic locations. Each new location's development process is staffed by a design team whose members include personnel from operations, retail technology services, design, construction services and multi-branding development. Among other things, they provide brand-consistent floor plans and assistance in selecting which store layout and what equipment will optimize efficiency. Decisions take into account customer traffic patterns, points of ingress and egress and street access.

For training, Baskin-Robbins franchisees study the Baskin-Robbins brand itself at a certified training store and attend classroom managerial training. Both segments of training are followed by real time practice in a real store. Training, however, doesn't stop there. At Allied Domecq, follow-up training is the key to success. Market-specific regional training consultants conduct on-going training, district meetings house new product training sessions and i-Train CD-ROMs, operations manuals and manager training guides fill in any holes. Furthermore, the need for quality training isn't limited to the franchisee alone. The "Off To A Great Start" crew member training and orientation program is provided to all franchisees and can be tailored to meet any store's specific training needs.

For on-going support to complement their on-going training, franchisees receive access to and advice from a myriad of field support professionals—franchise licensing managers, development managers, construction managers, business consultants, operations consultants, field marketing managers, field marketing specialists and regional training managers; and corporate resources—the QSR Navigator, a toll-free representative network, bargain purchasing power and efficient supply distribution, marketing campaigns, local advertising assistance, operations systems, product development and quality assurance.

Baskin-Robbins marketing aims to build brand awareness and increase store traffic through national brand support as well as store- and market- specific activities and events. Examples of national marketing efforts include radio, television and print advertisements; tie-ins with sporting events and movie premieres and new product launches. Field marketing specialists and managers work directly with franchisees to develop local marketing and advertising. Local drives include grand opening activities, direct mail campaigns, community event sponsorships, radio and local cable television advertising, coupon programs and promotions. Each market is also serviced by an advertising committee that oversees the market's advertising and evaluates its promotional success.

Territory
Baskin-Robbins does not grant exclusive territories.

Bennigan's Grill & Tavern

6500 International Pkwy., # 1000
Plano, TX 75093
Tel: (972) 588-5654
Fax: (972) 588-5806
E-Mail: lmckee@metrogroup.com
Web Site: www.bennigans.com
Ms. Lynette McKee, VP Franchise Development

BENNIGAN'S is a leading casual restaurant chain known for the warm hospitality of an Irish pub and the great taste of fun American foods. Established in 1976, BENNIGAN'S has expanded beyond its original tavern image to become more food-focused. Today, each restaurant serves a wide assortment of moderately-priced, quality food, as well as a wide selection of beverages.

BACKGROUND: IFA MEMBER
Established: 1976; 1st Franchised: 1995
Franchised Units: 127
Company-Owned Units: 181
Total Units: 308
Dist.: US-285; CAN-0; O'seas-23
  North America: 34 States
  Density: 61 in TX, 44 in FL, 23 in IL
Projected New Units (12 Months): 28
Qualifications: 5, 5, 4, 4, 4, 5

Registered: All States
FINANCIAL/TERMS:
Cash Investment: $NR
Total Investment: $1.4-2.6MM
Minimum Net Worth: $3MM
Fees: Franchise — $65K
  Royalty — 4%; Ad. — 4%
Earnings Claim Statement: Yes
Term of Contract (Years): 15/NR
Avg. # Of Employees: 5 FT, 65 PT
Passive Ownership: Not Allowed
Encourage Conversions: No
Area Develop. Agreements: No
Sub-Franchising Contracts: No
Expand In Territory: Yes
Space Needs: 6,689 SF; FS, SC

SUPPORT & TRAINING PROVIDED:
Financial Assistance Provided: No
Site Selection Assistance: No
Lease Negotiation Assistance: No
Co-Operative Advertising: Yes
Franchisee Assoc./Member: Yes/NA
Size Of Corporate Staff: 23
On-Going Support: A,B,C,D,E,F,G,H,I
Training: 13 Weeks at a Certified Training Restaurant.

SPECIFIC EXPANSION PLANS:
US: NW, SW, SE, HI
Canada: All Canada
Overseas: Germany, Italy, Portugal, Spain, Caribbean, Brazil, China

To own a Bennigan's franchise is to run your own neighborhood tavern. Offering a full line of spirits, wine and beers, as well as a full line of entrees, desserts, appetizers, soups and salads, including specialties such as Fire Roasted Salsa Shrimp, Death by Chocolate and light and tasty Health Club selections, Bennigan's has something for everyone.

While the locations of any given Bennigan's may be on opposite sides of the globe, two things remain constant. Every Bennigan's serves great American food and provides a customer-oriented atmosphere with rewards for all involved.

Bennigan's namesake, D. Bennigan, left his native Ireland during the great potato famine of the early 1900s. Initially a bartender, during the Great Depression, Bennigan added entrepreneur to his resume, turning an old bank building into Bennigan's Irish American Grill and Tavern. As Bennigan both worked and lived in the old bank, he welcomed customers to his restaurant and into his home, always sponsoring the local bowling and softball teams and decorating the walls with the photos of local heroes. The first Bennigan's franchise opened in Atlanta in 1976 with the same cozy atmosphere as the original and constructed with the polished brass of old banks and eclectic artifacts.

Operating Units	12/31/2000	12/31/2001	12/31/2002
Franchised	94	96	104
% Change	--	2.1%	8.3%
Company-Owned	170	183	181
% Change	--	7.6%	-1.1%
Total	264	279	285
% Change	--	5.7%	2.1%
Franchised as % of Total	35.6%	34.4%	36.5%

Investment Required
The fee for a Bennigan's franchise is $65,000 per unit, which funds franchise system organization, trademark registration and protection and franchisee selection. Multi-unit costs vary.

Bennigan's provides the following range of investments required to open your initial franchise. The range assumes that all items are paid for in cash. To the extent that you choose to finance any of these expense items, your front-end investment could be substantially reduced.

Item	Established Low Range	Established High Range
Franchise Fee	$65,000	$65,000
Equipment/Fixtures/Real Estate/Signs	$1,175,000	$2,155,000
Exclusive Territory Fee (if Development Agreement)	$65,000	$287,500
Insurance	$60,000	$150,000
Inventory	$30,000	$50,000
Liquor License	$1,500	$600,000
Real Estate	$12,500	$56,250
Training Expenses	$15,000	$30,000
Other Costs and Additional Funds (for 3 months)	$131,075	$165,925
Total Investment	$1,555,075	$3,559,675

On-Going Expenses

Bennigan's franchisees pay royalties equaling 4%, system-wide advertising production contributions equaling 1% and local and regional advertising fees equaling 3% of gross revenue.

What You Get—Training and Support

Bennigan's training program takes place in the classroom and the restaurant and covers restaurant operations, crew and financial management and marketing.

Furthermore, Bennigan's supplies all franchisees with a franchise consultant who assists in all aspects of the restaurant's operation and can bring each franchisee the know-how and insight of 350 peers in 35 specialties to aid in construction, including prototype restaurant plans, personnel visits and modification recommendations, remodeling, equipment selection, permit review and preferred lenders.

The Bennigan's marketing department assists franchisees with planning and marketing, in addition to creating advertising guidelines and promotional material samples to serve all Bennigan's markets, whether international, national or local. The purchasing department negotiates services and price agreements with suppliers and distributors for all companies within the Metromedia Restaurant Group, to which Bennigan's belongs, combining the purchasing power acquired by nearly 1000 restaurants with $250 million of products.

All franchisees are also stocked with frequently updated, easy-to-use, authoritative manuals that cover every lesson taught in Bennigan's training and more.

Territory
Bennigan's grants exclusive territories of a one-mile radius.

Big Apple Bagels

8501 W. Higgins Rd., # 320
Chicago, IL 60631
Tel: (800) 251-6101 (773) 380-6100
Fax: (773) 380-6183
E-Mail: tcervini@babcorp.com
Web Site: www.babcorp.com
Mr. Anthony S. Cervini, Dir. Franchise Development

Bakery-café featuring three brands, fresh-from-scratch Big Apple Bagels and My Favorite Muffin, and freshly roasted Brewster's specialty coffee. Our product offering covers many day parts with a delicious assortment of made-to-order gourmet sandwiches, salads, soups, espresso beverages, and fruit smoothies. Franchisees can develop beyond their stores with corporate catering and gift basket opportunities, as well as wholesaling opportunities within their market area.

BACKGROUND:	IFA MEMBER
Established: 1992; 1st Franchised: 1993	
Franchised Units:	173
Company-Owned Units	6

Total Units:	179
Dist.:	US-171; CAN-0; O'seas-8
North America:	26 States
Density:	33 in MI, 23 in WI, 23 in IL
Projected New Units (12 Months):	20
Qualifications:	3, 4, 3, 3, 3, 5
Registered:	All States

FINANCIAL/TERMS:	
Cash Investment:	$60K
Total Investment:	$174.8-349.5K
Minimum Net Worth:	$250K
Fees:	Franchise — $25K
	Royalty — 5%; Ad. — 1%
Earnings Claim Statement:	No
Term of Contract (Years):	10/10
Avg. # Of Employees:	3 FT, 11 PT
Passive Ownership:	Allowed
Encourage Conversions:	Yes
Area Develop. Agreements:	Yes/Varies
Sub-Franchising Contracts:	No
Expand In Territory:	Yes
Space Needs:	1,500-1,800 SF; SC

SUPPORT & TRAINING PROVIDED:	
Financial Assistance Provided:	No
Site Selection Assistance:	Yes
Lease Negotiation Assistance:	Yes
Co-Operative Advertising:	No

Franchisee Assoc./Member:	No	SPECIFIC EXPANSION PLANS:	
Size Of Corporate Staff:	23	US:	All United States
On-Going Support:	C,D,E,F,G,H,I	Canada:	All Canada
Training:	2 Weeks Milwaukee, WI.	Overseas:	All Countries

Big Apple Bagels combines three proprietary product families—Big Apple bagels, My Favorite Muffin gourmet muffins and Brewster's brewed coffees and specialty drinks—into one franchise. Big Apple Bagels locations also serve sandwiches and salads, and bagels are topped with their exclusive cream cheese recipes. The diversity of Big Apple Bagels's offerings allow them to appeal to many customers at all different times of the day. It also allows them to tap into three separate, yet all booming, food industries, the $2.5 billion bagel market, the $3 billion sandwich market and the $2 billion coffee market.

Since Big Apple Bagels is not a full service restaurant, its hours of operation, generally six a.m. to six p.m., more closely match those of a traditional work-day. As each location is also a bakery, franchisees are responsible for the manufacturing of the proprietary products. However, don't let this prospect daunt you! Prior food experience is not necessary. Moreover, this production aspect of Big Apple Bagels expands your range of revenue potential; their freshly-baked bagels are also sold through wholesale distribution to other businesses, such as corporate clients, restaurants and convenience stores.

Operating Units	11/26/2000	11/25/2001	11/30/2002
Franchised	170	167	176
% Change	--	-1.8%	5.4%
Company-Owned	12	5	3
% Change	--	-58.3%	-40.0%
Total	182	172	179
% Change	--	-5.5%	4.1%
Franchised as % of Total	93.4%	97.1%	98.3%

Investment Required
The fee for a Big Apple Bagels franchise varies depending on store type. For a standard production store, the fee is $25,000. For a satellite store, the fee is

$15,000. A kiosk is $10,000. A cart is $5,000. Additional units for standard franchises cost $20,000, or $15,000 within an area development agreement, which is available for qualified applicants.

Big Apple Bagels provides the following range of investments required to open your initial franchise. The range assumes that all items are paid for in cash. To the extent that you choose to finance any of these expense items, your front-end investment could be substantially reduced. The following quotes apply to the opening of a Big Apple Bagels production store.

Item	Established Low Range	Established High Range
Franchise Fee	$25,000	$25,000
Equipment/Fixtures/Signs	$60,000	$135,000
Insurance	$5,200	$7,200
Inventory/Supplies	$6,000	$9,000
Opening, Promotion	$3,000	$3,000
Real Estate	$62,000	$135,500
Training	$1,600	$3,200
Other Costs and Additional Funds (for 3 months)	$12,000	$31,600
Total Investment	$174,800	$349,500

On-Going Expenses
Big Apple Bagels franchisees pay royalties equaling 5%, marketing fund contributions (funding ad slicks for placement in local media and point of purchase materials for store use) equaling 1% of gross revenue and local advertising fees equaling 2% of gross revenue. A local coop fee may also apply.

What You Get—Training and Support
Big Apple Bagels will train two people in every phase of store operation. Franchisees learn marketing techniques, how to hire, train and retain quality employees and financial management. Pre-opening operational training at each franchisee's shop complements the classroom lessons.

In addition to training, franchisees receive guidance in site evaluation and BAB's design consultants draft an individual site plan to suit the specific location selected. Franchisees also receive assistance with store layout, purchasing coordination, equipment and merchandise acquisition at negotiated rates, and a grand opening marketing campaign. Finally, a field operations consultant will keep an eye on everything taking place before and during opening, ensuring that nothing slips through the cracks.

After opening, franchisees benefit from full seasonal marketing strategies, with compact discs to facilitate local advertising and marketing material production.

The system's E-mail bulletin program keeps franchisees abreast of breaking news and allows them to submit company feedback, and a password-protected intranet site gives franchisees access to online sales reporting, resource centers, management tools and downloads. In addition, if and when franchisees decide to expand within the Big Apple Bagels system, the company will work with them to determine which growth options best suit their resources.

Territory
Big Apple Bagels grants exclusive territories to franchisees with area development agreements.

Blimpie Subs & Salads

SUBS & SALADS

180 Interstate North Pkwy., SE, # 500
Atlanta, GA 30339
Tel: (800) 447-6256 (770) 984-2707
Fax: (770) 980-9176
E-Mail: kietha@blimpie.com
Web Site: www.blimpie.com
Mr. Keith Albright, VP Franchise Development

National submarine sandwich chain, serving fresh-sliced, high-quality meats and cheeses on fresh-baked bread. Also offering an assortment of fresh-made salads and other quality products.

BACKGROUND:	IFA MEMBER
Established: 1964; 1st Franchised: 1977	
Franchised Units:	1,955
Company-Owned Units	1
Total Units:	1,956
Dist.:	US-1,882; CAN-13; O'seas-61
North America:	50 States, 4 Provinces
Density:	205 in GA, 203 in FL, 121 TX
Projected New Units (12 Months):	NR
Qualifications:	4, 3, 2, 2, 2, 5

Registered:	CA,FL,HI,IL,IN,MI,MN,NY, ND,OR,RI,SD,WA,WI	Space Needs:	1,200 SF; FS, SF, SC, RM
		SUPPORT & TRAINING PROVIDED:	
FINANCIAL/TERMS:		Financial Assistance Provided:	Yes(I)
Cash Investment:	$25-100K	Site Selection Assistance:	Yes
Total Investment:	$60-200K	Lease Negotiation Assistance:	Yes
Minimum Net Worth:	$50K	Co-Operative Advertising:	Yes
Fees:	Franchise — $10-18K	Franchisee Assoc./Member:	Yes/Yes
	Royalty — 6%; Ad. — 4%	Size Of Corporate Staff:	109
Earnings Claim Statement:	No	On-Going Support:	B,C,D,E,F,G,H,I
Term of Contract (Years):	20/5	Training: 80 Hours in Atlanta, GA; 120 Hours in
Avg. # Of Employees:	4 FT, 8 PT		Local Franchise.
Passive Ownership:	Discouraged		
Encourage Conversions:	Yes	**SPECIFIC EXPANSION PLANS:**	
Area Develop. Agreements:	Yes	US:	All United States
Sub-Franchising Contracts:	Yes	Canada:	All Canada
Expand In Territory:	Yes	Overseas:	All Except Anti-American

A Blimpie shop provides franchisees with win-win circumstances—the sub sandwich restaurant serves top quality, fresh food, but requires no cooking. The restaurant is simple to operate and requires little overhead, producing less waste and using less equipment than most quick service restaurants. The Blimpie's concept is flexible and can be tailored to nearly any location, whether shopping center, commercial mall, convenience store, free-standing, sports arena, hospital, college, kiosk or vending machine.

Blimpie prides itself upon its proven business model, but the company isn't one to settle. Recently, the sub shop embarked on The Next Great Step program, which aims to enhance Blimpie's merchandise and atmosphere and expand the menu variety of Blimpie restaurants to improve the company's service to both the consumer and the franchisees those consumers support.

The beauty of Blimpie's—the finest quality meats, cheeses and toppings on freshly baked bread right before the customer's eyes—is the brainchild of Tony Conza, two high school friends and $2,000. Their first store opened on Washington Street in Hoboken, New Jersey in 1964.

Operating Units (US only)	6/30/2000	6/30/2001	6/30/2002
Franchised	1,933	1,894	1,821
% Change	--	-2.0%	-3.8%

Company-Owned	0	1	0
% Change	--	N/A	-100.0%
Total	1,933	1,895	1,821
% Change	--	-2.0%	-3.9%
Franchised as % of Total	100.0%	99.9%	100.0%

Investment Required

The fee for a Blimpie franchise in a traditional location is $18,000. The fee for a nontraditional location is $10,000. Additional units can be purchased at a reduced fee.

Blimpie provides the following range of investments required to open your initial franchise. The range assumes that all items are paid for in cash. To the extent that you choose to finance any of these expense items, your front-end investment could be substantially reduced. The following quotes apply to the opening of a traditional restaurant.

Item	Established Low Range	Established High Range
Franchise Fee	$1	$18,000
Deposits	$4,100	$9,300
Equipment	$40,500	$112,500
Grand Opening and Initial Program	$5,000	$5,000
Inventory	$5,000	$10,000
Real Estate	$21,000	$144,500
Training Expenses	$950	$2,500
Uniforms	$270	$1,400
Other Costs and Additional Funds (for 3 months)	$16,500	$35,000
Total Investment	$93,321	$338,200

On-Going Expenses

Blimpie franchisees pay continuing fees equaling 6% and advertising contributions equaling 4% of gross revenues. Other expenses may include regional advertising association fees or additional training.

What You Get—Training and Support

Blimpie's three-part training program begins with 80 hands-on hours working at a local Blimpie location and transitions into two weeks of formal classroom training at the Blimpie University in Atlanta, Georgia. This second leg of training includes instruction on marketing, accounting, hiring policies and procedures, cost management and customer relations. Finally, Blimpie training comes full circle with another 40 hours of local restaurant experience, allowing franchisees to gain additional hands-on experience to complement and test their new knowledge. Despite all the training, Blimpie doesn't abandon its new franchisees just yet, a representative or subfranchisor assists at all restaurant openings to ensure the best start for each and every franchisee.

Additional Blimpie services include business consulting from a Blimpie representative, a national franchise advisory council that gives franchisees a clear voice at the corporate level, monthly newsletters, operating manuals, computer-based communication systems, site evaluation, lease negotiation assistance, national purchasing power and marketing and advertising on the national, regional and local level.

Territory

Blimpie does not grant exclusive territories.

Breadsmith

BREADSMITH®
HAND MADE. HEARTH BAKED.™

409 E. Silver Spring Dr.
Whitefish Bay, WI 53217
Tel: (888) BREADS-1 (414) 962-1965
Fax: (414) 962-5888
E-Mail: alhasse@breadsmith.com

Web Site: www.breadsmith.com
Mr. Albert Hasse, President

Award-winning, European, hearth-bread bakery, featuring fresh-from-scratch crusty breads, scones, muffins, gourmet jams and oils. Open kitchen concept reveals a six-ton, stone hearth oven imported from Europe used to bake the hand-crafted loaves each morning. BREAD-SMITH has been ranked by Bon Appetit, Best in 11 cities across the country.

BACKGROUND: IFA MEMBER	

BACKGROUND: IFA MEMBER
Established: 1993; 1st Franchised: 1994
Franchised Units: 37
Company-Owned Units 1
Total Units: 38
Dist.: US-38; CAN-0; O'seas-0
 North America: 10 States
 Density: 10 in MI, 7 in IL
Projected New Units (12 Months): 5
Qualifications: 4, 4, 2, 4, 4, 5
Registered: CA,FL,IL,IN,MI,MN,NY,OR
 ,SD,VA,WA,WI

FINANCIAL/TERMS:
Cash Investment: $100-250K
Total Investment: $200-400K
Minimum Net Worth: $500K
Fees: Franchise — $30K
 Royalty — 7/6/5%; Ad. — 0%
Earnings Claim Statement: Yes
Term of Contract (Years): 15/15
Avg. # Of Employees: 6 FT, 12 PT

Passive Ownership: Not Allowed
Encourage Conversions: N/A
Area Develop. Agreements: Varies
Sub-Franchising Contracts: No
Expand In Territory: Yes
Space Needs: 1,800 SF; FS, SF, SC

SUPPORT & TRAINING PROVIDED:
Financial Assistance Provided: Yes(I)
Site Selection Assistance: Yes
Lease Negotiation Assistance: Yes
Co-Operative Advertising: Yes
Franchisee Assoc./Member: Yes
Size Of Corporate Staff: 10
On-Going Support: C,D,E,F,G,H,I
Training: 4 Weeks Corporate Store; 1 Week Franchisee Store.

SPECIFIC EXPANSION PLANS:
US: All United States
Canada: All Canada
Overseas: No

Breadsmith peddles European style, artisan breads, rolls, croutons, muffins and cookies made from scratch, in front of customers, everyday. The wide variety of breads and baked goods offered by Breadsmith ensures that it can successfully serve any demographic. From hard crust to soft crust, Breadsmith offers 14 varieties of bread each day, all chosen from over 85 rotating recipes. Not only does this provide something for everyone and every taste, but also always something new and exciting, which customers are urged to sample. Breadsmiths strives to create a warm, inviting atmosphere and the company seeks community-minded franchisees.

Operating Units	12/31/1999	12/31/2000	12/31/2001
Franchised	43	41	37
% Change	--	-4.6%	-9.8%
Company-Owned	2	1	1
% Change	--	-50.0%	0.0%
Total	45	42	38
% Change	--	-6.7%	-9.5%
Franchised as % of Total	95.5%	97.6%	97.4%

Investment Required

The fee for a Breadsmith franchise is $30,000. Breadsmith does provide assistance with third-party franchising.

Breadsmith provides the following range of investments required to open your initial franchise. The range assumes that all items are paid for in cash. To the extent that you choose to finance any of these expense items, your front-end investment could be substantially reduced.

Item	Established Low Range	Established High Range
Franchise Fee	$30,000	$30,000
Delivery Vehicle	$0	$25,000
Equipment/Fixtures/Signs	$88,500	$110,000
Inventory	$2,500	$4,000
Promotion	$5,000	$10,000
Real Estate	$59,500	$169,000
Training	$3,500	$6,000
Other Costs and Additional Funds (for 3 months)	$28,500	$62,000
Total Investment	$217,500	$416,000

On-Going Expenses

Breadsmith franchisees pay royalties equaling 5 to 7% of gross revenue.

What You Get—Training and Support

Breadsmith's four-week training consists of two weeks at the corporate training center in Milwaukee and two weeks at the franchisee's store site.

Breadsmith also offers assistance with site selection, layout and design, equipment procurement, recipe development, marketing and on-going operational support.

Territory

Breadsmith grants designated territories of a one-mile radius.

Carvel

We're Creamy. We're Crunchy. We're Carvel.™

200 Glenridge Point Pkwy.
Atlanta, GA 30342
Tel: (800) 227-8353 (404) 255-3250
Fax: (440) 255-4978
E-Mail: ghill@carvel.com
Web Site: www.carvel.com
Mr. Geoff Hill, VP Franchise Sales

CARVEL ICE CREAM BAKERIES manufacture and sell ice cream and no-fat desserts through retail stores. CARVEL ICE CREAM cakes are designed to compete not only in the frozen dessert markets, but in the $13 billion dollar retail bakery market. Franchise operators can open additional branch units in malls, tourist areas and stadiums for no additional licensing fee. Franchisee can also purchase a license to sell products to supermarket through CARVEL Branded-Products Program.

BACKGROUND:

Established: 1934; 1st Franchised: 1947	
Franchised Units:	360
Company-Owned Units	0
Total Units:	360
Dist.:	US-392; CAN-3; O'seas-29
North America:	12 States, 1 Province
Density:	220 in NY, 63 in NJ, 37 FL
Projected New Units (12 Months):	20

Qualifications:	5, 5, 3, 3, 3, 5
Registered:	CA,MD,NY,RI,VA
FINANCIAL/TERMS:	
Cash Investment:	$100-125K
Total Investment:	$185-240K
Minimum Net Worth:	$100K
Fees:	Franchise — $10K
Royalty — $1.63/Gal.; Ad. — $1.42/Gal.	
Earnings Claim Statement:	No
Term of Contract (Years):	10/5/5
Avg. # Of Employees:	2 FT, 6 PT
Passive Ownership:	Not Allowed
Encourage Conversions:	Yes
Area Develop. Agreements:	Yes
Sub-Franchising Contracts:	No
Expand In Territory:	Yes
Space Needs:	1,200-1,500 SF; FS, SF, RM
SUPPORT & TRAINING PROVIDED:	
Financial Assistance Provided:	Yes(I)
Site Selection Assistance:	Yes
Lease Negotiation Assistance:	Yes
Co-Operative Advertising:	Yes
Franchisee Assoc./Member:	Yes/Yes
Size Of Corporate Staff:	50
On-Going Support:	A,B,C,D,E,G,H,I
Training:	11 Days Farmington, CT.
SPECIFIC EXPANSION PLANS:	
US:	East Coast
Canada:	All Canada

The Carvel "experience" has a long history of expertise, unique marketing and industry revolutions. By combining the highest quality, freshest milks, creams and butterfat, in-store, every day, Carvel makes the "creamiest" ice cream on the market and maintains itself as the fourth largest ice cream chain in the United States. The company, however, has no intention of settling for number four. Supplying the number one comfort food for men and women, the ice cream industry has experienced the highest growth of any food industry since 1999 and is consumed by 95% of American households.

Since its debut in Hartsdale, New York, Carvel has been at the forefront of the ice cream industry. Founded in 1934 by the inventor of the ice cream cake, Carvel was one of the very first ice cream chains and, in 1947, it became the first franchise in the ice cream industry. In addition, Carvel was the first to market soft ice cream and uniquely shaped specialty character cakes, such as the legendary Fudgie the Whale. The Carvel brand has been behind the introduction of more than 300 trademarks, copyrights, registrations and designs and is even featured in the American History Museum at the Smithsonian Institute.

Operating Units	12/31/2000	12/31/2001	12/31/2002
Franchised	382	359	369
% Change	--	-6.0%	2.8%
Company-Owned	4	0	0
% Change	--	-100.0%	0.0%
Total	386	359	369
% Change	--	-7.0%	2.8%
Franchised as % of Total	99.0%	100.0%	100.0%

Investment Required

Carvel maintains two franchising concepts: the ice cream store, which can stand alone or be placed in a strip center and offers a full menu of products including cakes and soft and hard ice cream; and the Carvel express, which primarily appears in co-branded and limited square footage locations and offers a reduced menu of products. The fee for an ice cream store is $25,000, while the fee for an express store is $15,000.

Carvel provides the following range of investments required to open your initial franchise. The range assumes that all items are paid for in cash. To the extent that you choose to finance any of these expense items, your front-end investment could be substantially reduced.

Item	Established Low Range	Established High Range
Franchise Fee	$25,000	$25,000
Construction	$45,500	$105,500
Equipment/Signs	$85,320	$98,250
Inventory	$8,424	$8,424
Training Expenses	$1,000	$2,000
Other Costs and Additional Funds	$12,300	$21,800
Total Investment (does not include real property)	$177,544	$260,974

On-Going Expenses

Carvel franchisees pay royalties equaling $1.74 and advertising fees equaling $1.53 per liquid gallon of mix purchased. Royalties and advertising contributions must equal an annual minimum of $11,310 and $9,945 respectively.

What You Get—Training and Support

Carvel franchisees attend a two-week ice cream training school.

Support includes site and market evaluation and selection assistance, a field support team, a development network of real estate brokers, architects, lenders and contractors, quality assurance review and a toll-free franchise resource support hotline.

Territory

Carvel does not grant exclusive territories.

Church's Chicken

980 Hammond Dr. NE, # 1100, Bldg. # 2
Atlanta, GA 30328
Tel: (866) 345-6788 (770) 350-3800
Fax: (770) 512-3922
E-Mail: hmyers@afce.com
Web Site: www.churchs.com
Mr. Hannibal Myers, Worldwide Development Officer

CHURCHS is the 2nd largest chicken restaurant chain in the country. CHURCHS offers Southern fried chicken with signature side items such as fried okra, corn-on-the-cob, jalapenos and honey butter biscuits. CHURCHS has a proven business system niche customer base, low square footage require-ments (as little as 750 square feet) and world class franchise support.

BACKGROUND: IFA MEMBER
Established: 1952; 1st Franchised: 1972

Franchised Units:	761
Company-Owned Units	468
Total Units:	1,219
Dist.:	US-1,032; CAN-80; O'seas-107
North America:	28 States

Density:	416 in TX, 103 in GA, 74 CA
Projected New Units (12 Months):	125
Qualifications:	5, 4, 3, 3, 3, 5
Registered:	All States

FINANCIAL/TERMS:

Cash Investment:	$200K
Total Investment:	$194-750K
Minimum Net Worth:	$400K
Fees:	Franchise — $5-15K
	Royalty — 5%; Ad. — 4%
Earnings Claim Statement:	No
Term of Contract (Years):	20/10
Avg. # Of Employees:	15 FT, 6 PT
Passive Ownership:	Discouraged
Encourage Conversions:	Yes
Area Develop. Agreements:	Yes/Varies
Sub-Franchising Contracts:	No
Expand In Territory:	Yes
Space Needs:	750-22,000 SF; FS, C-Store

SUPPORT & TRAINING PROVIDED:

Financial Assistance Provided:	No
Site Selection Assistance:	Yes
Lease Negotiation Assistance:	Yes
Co-Operative Advertising:	Yes
Franchisee Assoc./Member:	Yes/Yes
Size Of Corporate Staff:	70
On-Going Support:	C,D,E,F,G,h,I
Training:	6 Weeks Regional.

SPECIFIC EXPANSION PLANS:

US:	All United States
Canada:	All Canada
Overseas:	Europe, Asia, Middle East, Australia

Church's specializes in large, marinated portions of fried chicken and a full line of side items. However, as time has passed, Church's has expanded their menu to meet more culinary demands, offering a full breakfast menu, additional side items, sandwiches and frequent limited time offers.

A Church's franchise offers franchisees: highly efficient facilities, a simple operating system for quick and easy food preparation, optimal production, purchasing power and limited labor requirements that keep costs down and labor productivity high, with easy, universal training and a diverse menu that feeds a growing customer base.

Church's also offers friendly international development, allowing for flexibility in venue selection and often modifying the traditional menu to match local tastes.
Across the street from the Alamo in San Antonio, Texas, the first Church's Chicken was opened in 1952. Church's is now a division of AFC Enterprises, which was established in 1992 and operates over 3,800 restaurants, bakeries and cafes in 33 countries. Outreach work through participation in local and national philanthropic and volunteer organizations and initiatives is a Church's Chicken priority.

Operating Units	12/31/1999	12/31/2000	12/31/2001
Franchised	687	760	843
% Change	--	10.6%	10.9%
Company-Owned	497	466	397
% Change	--	-6.2%	-14.8
Total	1184	1226	1240
% Change	--	3.5%	1.1%
Franchised as % of Total	58.0%	62.0%	68.0%

Investment Required
The fee for a Church's franchise is generally $15,000. However, the fee varies according to store type. Reduced fees apply to additional franchise units.

Church's also offers a multi-unit development plan that requires aggressive restaurant growth to establish brand presence. Experience in multi-unit management, retail services, franchising, business development or other related business experience and/or commercial holdings is preferred for applicants for this license.

Church's Chicken provides the following range of investments required to open your initial franchise. The range assumes that all items are paid for in cash. To the extent that you choose to finance any of these expense items, your front-end investment could be substantially reduced.

Item	Established Low Range	Established High Range
Franchise Fee	$15,000	$15,000
Development Fee	$10,000	$10,000
Equipment/Signs/Supplies	$134,500	$210,000
Insurance	$7,500	$10,000
Training	$15,000	$30,000
Utility Deposits	$2,500	$5,000
Other Costs and Additional Funds (for 3 months)	$20,300	$30,600
Total Investment	$204,800	$310,600

On-Going Expenses

Church's Chicken franchisees pay royalties equaling 5% and advertising fees equaling 4% of gross revenue. Franchisees may also be responsible for co-op advertising costs. If so, Church's will adjust your system advertising fees accordingly.

What You Get—Support and Training

Church's support comes in four main forms: business services, development services, product management and marketing.

Business services are delivered by international directors of operations who speak the local language and help franchisees with site selection, operations, training, product quality and marketing.

Development services include assistance with the construction process, whether a new construction or a conversion, development and design guidance, site selection, design, kitchen layout, and material and supplier recommendations.

Product management services organize supply acquisition. Every attempt is made to find supplies within each Church's country of operation. Local ingredients may be used to complement proprietary ingredients.

Marketing services are administered by the international marketing team, which works with each franchise to plan advertising, sales promotions and merchandising.

Finally, Church's Chicken's membership in AFC Enterprises, a family of franchise brands including Cinnabon and Popeyes Chicken and Biscuits, increases the number and scope of people and resources working to expand the success and presence of Church's Chicken worldwide. AFC also strives to make the world a better place and has built 316 Habitat for Humanity houses on four continents and in 45 cities.

Territory
Church's will grant exclusive territory rights.

Cinnabon

\6 Concourse Pkwy., # 1700
Atlanta, GA 30328-6117
Tel: (800) 639-3826 (770) 353-3271
Fax: (770) 353-3093
E-Mail: whaas@afce.com
Web Site: www.cinnabon.com
Ms. Wanda M. Haas, Specialist, New Business Devel

Commitment to premium ingredients and quality baking - served hot. No more than 30 minutes out of oven.

BACKGROUND:

Established: 1985; 1st Franchised: 1986	
Franchised Units:	364
Company-Owned Units:	84
Total Units:	448
Dist.:	US-444; CAN-23; O'seas-149
North America:	NR
Density:	34 in CA, 28 in FL, 24 in OH

Projected New Units (12 Months):	50
Qualifications:	5, 5, 5, 4, 4, 5
Registered:	HI,IL,MD,MN,ND,RI,SD,VA ,WA,WI

FINANCIAL/TERMS:

Cash Investment:	$300K-3 Units
Total Investment:	$150-250K
Minimum Net Worth:	$600K
Fees: Franchise —	$35K
Royalty — 5%;	Ad. — 1.5%
Earnings Claim Statement:	No
Term of Contract (Years):	10/5
Avg. # Of Employees:	6 FT
Passive Ownership:	Not Allowed
Encourage Conversions:	Yes
Area Develop. Agreements:	Yes
Sub-Franchising Contracts:	No
Expand In Territory:	Yes
Space Needs:	850 SF; RM

SUPPORT & TRAINING PROVIDED:

Financial Assistance Provided:	NA
Site Selection Assistance:	Yes
Lease Negotiation Assistance:	Yes
Co-Operative Advertising:	Yes
Franchisee Assoc./Member:	Yes/Yes

Size Of Corporate Staff:	52	SPECIFIC EXPANSION PLANS:	
On-Going Support:	E,G	US:	LA, NY, AL, MS, AR, MO
Training:	CRT Location 4 Weeks.	Canada:	No
		Overseas:	All Countries

Cinnabon offers three formats—the bakery stand, the kiosk bakery and the in-line bakery—from which to sell its famous cinnamon rolls—which are served fresh and hot out of the oven. Cinnabon can be found in malls, airports, transportation centers, casinos, universities, theme parks and hospitals. Since its inception, the Cinnabon menu has expanded to include signature beverages, an expanded array of delicious bakery items, and other snacks, including Cinnabonstix and frequent limited time offers and promotions.

From a single store at the SeaTac Mall in Seattle, Washington, Cinnabon has found international recognition in the cinnamon roll industry. In the last three years, the company has expanded from locations in three countries to venues in 21 countries. The company was acquired by AFC Enterprises, which was established in 1992 and operates over 4,071 restaurants, bakeries and cafes in 33 countries, in October 1998.

Operating Units	12/31/2000	12/31/2001	12/31/2002
Franchised	201	266	364
% Change	--	32.3%	36.8%
Company-Owned	186	152	84
% Change	--	-18.3%	-44.7%
Total	387	418	448
% Change	--	8.0%	7.2%
Franchised as % of Total	51.9%	63.6%	81.3%

Investment Required

Most Cinnabon agreements are for at least three retail bakeries within an exclusive territory. The fee for a Cinnabon franchise is $30,000 for the first location, $20,000 for the second and third and $15,000 for the fourth and each subsequent. There is a $5,000 development fee per location.

Multi-unit territory development opportunities are also offered. For these licensees, Cinnabon seeks people around the world with established operational and financial strength and experience in food service operations, multi-unit management, franchising and business.

Cinnabon provides the following range of investments required to open your initial franchise. The range assumes that all items are paid for in cash. To the extent that you choose to finance any of these expense items, your front-end investment could be substantially reduced. The following figures apply to the opening of a bakery location.

Item	Established Low Range	Established High Range
Franchise Fee	$30,000	$30,000
Development Fee	$5,000	$5,000
Advertising	$3,000	$3,000
Equipment/Fixtures/Signs/ Supplies	$65,000	$104,000
Insurance	$2,000	$5,000
Real Estate	$130,000	$170,000
Training	$3,500	$9,000
Other Costs and Additional Funds (for 3 months)	$8,500	$17,000
Total Investment (does not include real estate)	$247,000	$343,000

On-Going Expenses
Cinnabon franchisees pay royalties equaling 5% and advertising fees equaling 1.5 to 3% of gross revenue.

What You Get—Training and Support
In addition to its simple operating systems, Cinnabon builds its name through the reading rewards program that partners Cinnabon bakeries with local schools and libraries to endorse reading. Cinnabon has also formed strategic alliances in film and licensed merchandise promotion and media—and the

company has appeared twice in *Time* magazine.

Cinnabon's membership in AFC Enterprises, a family of franchise brands including Church's Chicken and Popeyes Chicken and Biscuits, increases the number and scope of people and resources working to expand the success and presence of Cinnabon worldwide. AFC also strives to make the world a better place and has built 316 Habitat for Humanity houses on four continents and in 45 cities.

Territory
Cinnabon grants limited, exclusive or non-exclusive territories.

Cold Stone Creamery

16101 N. 82nd St., # A-4
Scottsdale, AZ 85260
Tel: (888) 218-3349 (480) 348-1704
Fax: (480) 348-1718
E-Mail: lmichaels@coldstonecreamery.com
Web Site: www.coldstonecreamery.com
Ms. Lindsey Michaels, Brand Manager

The COLD STONE CREAMERY team is made up of seasoned professionals who deliver a proven system for providing the world's best ice cream experience to more people more often. Making our franchisee's successful is our number one priority. Our super-premium ice cream, yogurt, sorbet and waffle cones are made fresh daily right in our stores. Fresh-baked brownies and brand-name mix-ins like Snickers and M&Ms are blended on our frozen granite stones to make every dessert pure delight.

BACKGROUND: IFA MEMBER
Established: 1988; 1st Franchised: 1995
Franchised Units: 400
Company-Owned Units 3

Total Units:	403
Dist.:	US-403; CAN-0; O'seas-0
North America:	34 States
Density:	135 in CA, 30 in AZ, 6 in NV
Projected New Units (12 Months):	360
Qualifications:	2, 3, 1, 1, 3, 5
Registered:	All States

FINANCIAL/TERMS:	
Cash Investment:	$50K
Total Investment:	$245-348K
Minimum Net Worth:	$NR
Fees:	Franchise — $31-35K
	Royalty — 6%; Ad. — 3%
Earnings Claim Statement:	No
Term of Contract (Years):	10/5/5/5
Avg. # Of Employees:	3 FT, 9 PT
Passive Ownership:	Discouraged
Encourage Conversions:	NR
Area Develop. Agreements:	Yes
Sub-Franchising Contracts:	No
Expand In Territory:	Yes
Space Needs:	1,200 SF; SC

SUPPORT & TRAINING PROVIDED:	
Financial Assistance Provided:	No
Site Selection Assistance:	Yes
Lease Negotiation Assistance:	Yes
Co-Operative Advertising:	Yes
Franchisee Assoc./Member:	No

Size Of Corporate Staff:	106	**SPECIFIC EXPANSION PLANS:**	
On-Going Support:	C,D,E,G,H	US:	All United States
Training:	10 Days Scottsdale, AZ.	Canada:	All Canada
		Overseas:	All Countries

Cold Stone Creamery sells ice cream to meet the demands of today's consumers, a diverse group of people who want things their way, fast. Each individual Cold Stone store prepares its proprietary ice cream, yogurt, sorbet, waffle cones and brownies on-site everyday. Customers select their desired ice cream, yogurt or sorbet, which is placed on a frozen granite (16 degree Fahrenheit "cold") stone, where the mix-ins (more than 40 nationally branded candy, fruits and nuts) of their choice are added. The resulting "ultimate ice cream experience" is served in a waffle cone or bowl or formed into a personalized cake or pie, delivering "ice cream, entertainment and an experience all in one," and creating loyal, happy customers.

Cold Stone is the nation's fastest growing concept in the fastest growing segment of the food franchise industry. The first Cold Stone Creamery opened in Tempe, Arizona in 1988 and founders Don and Susan Sutherland began franchising their business in 1995. The company boasts proven stability, growth and success and has become a treasured destination in many neighborhoods and communities.

Cold Stone seeks to have 1,000 profitable stores in operation by the year 2004. Opportunities are available in current markets and new markets for both experienced multi-concept operators and other motivated business professionals.

Operating Units	12/31/2000	12/31/2001	12/31/2002
Franchised	116	185	322
% Change	--	59.5%	74.1%
Company-Owned	3	4	4
% Change	--	33.3%	0.0%
Total	119	189	326
% Change	--	58.8%	72.5%
Franchised as % of Total	97.5%	97.9%	98.8%

Investment Required

In most states, the fee for a Cold Stone Creamery is $31,000. The fee for franchises located in California or Hawaii is $35,000. Additional units carry a fee of $21,000 or $25,000 respectively. Franchisees are also responsible for a development fee amounting to 1 to 10% of each location's build-out cost.

Cold Stone provides the following range of investments required to open your initial franchise. The range assumes that all items are paid for in cash. To the extent that you choose to finance any of these expense items, your front-end investment could be substantially reduced.

Item	Established Low Range	Established High Range
Franchise Fee	$31,000	$35,000
Advertising	$2,000	$2,000
Cake Decorating Course	$35	$70
Equipment/Signs/Uniforms	$94,500	$105,300
Insurance	$250	$1,000
Inventory	$6,000	$6,000
Real Estate	$100,750	$181,500
Training Expenses	$500	$3,500
Additional Funds (for 3 months)	$10,000	$10,000
Total Investment	$245,035	$344,370

On-Going Expenses

Cold Stone franchisees pay royalties equaling 6%, advertising fees equaling 3%, finance fees equaling 2 to 5% and equipment fees equaling 1 to 10% of gross revenue.

What You Get—Training and Support

The Cold Stone Creamery franchise fee confers franchisees with use of the Cold Stone brand name and logo, proprietary ice cream, yogurt, sorbet and waffle cone secret formulas and a proven successful system. Franchisees also receive lease and contract negotiation assistance, store design, construction consultations and décor standards.

Each franchisee and one other key person in the franchisee's unit attend a two-week training program at the Ice Cream University, where they will learn how to own and operate their creamery.

Cold Stone support is available from on-site visits, telephone correspondence, Scoops Reports, operation manuals and marketing toolkits and the Internet and E-mails, as well as other franchise newsletters and reports. The company also maintains an in-house creative services unit, system-wide and local marketing and sales programs, on-going product development and volume pricing to make its franchises more efficient and more profitable.

Territory
Cold Stone does not grant exclusive territories.

Dippin' Dots

P.O. Box 9207, 5110 Charter Oak Dr.
Paducah, KY 42003
Tel: (270) 575-6990
Fax: (270) 575-6997
E-Mail: vanril@dippindots.com
Web Site: www.dippindots.com
Ms. Vanessa Riley, Franchise Dev. Specialist

DIPPIN' DOTS are those tiny beads of ice cream that are super-cold, creamy, and delicious. Here's your invitation to look at our exciting alternative to traditional ice cream, yogurt, and flavored ice products.

BACKGROUND:	IFA MEMBER
Established: 1988; 1st Franchised: 1999	
Franchised Units:	569
Company-Owned Units	2
Total Units:	571

Dist.:	US-571; CAN-0; O'seas-0
North America:	42 States
Density:	49 in TX, 37 in CA, 29 in FL
Projected New Units (12 Months):	Unknown
Qualifications:	5, 4, 2, 3, 3, 5
Registered:	All States

FINANCIAL/TERMS:	
Cash Investment:	$75K
Total Investment:	$45.6-189.8K
Minimum Net Worth:	$250K
Fees:	Franchise — $12.5K
	Royalty — 4%; Ad. — .05%
Earnings Claim Statement:	No
Term of Contract (Years):	5/5/5
Avg. # Of Employees:	1 FT
Passive Ownership:	Discouraged
Encourage Conversions:	No
Area Develop. Agreements:	No
Sub-Franchising Contracts:	No
Expand In Territory:	Yes
Space Needs:	100 SF; RM

SUPPORT & TRAINING PROVIDED:		On-Going Support:	B,C,D,E,G,H
Financial Assistance Provided:	No	Training: 2 Days in Paducah, KY; 2 Days On-Site.	
Site Selection Assistance:	Yes	SPECIFIC EXPANSION PLANS:	
Lease Negotiation Assistance:	Yes	US:	All United States
Co-Operative Advertising:	No	Canada:	No
Franchisee Assoc./Member:	No	Overseas:	No
Size Of Corporate Staff:	130		

A one-of-a-kind product, Dippin' Dots's name says it all. The company sells "the ice cream of the future," a treat made entirely of small, cryogenically frozen sphere-shaped ice cream, sherbet or flavored-ice "dots," and whose individuality has garnered a lot of product publicity and subsequent brand recognition. Dippin' Dots can be found in stores, fairs, festivals, theme parks and other attractions throughout the United States and across the world.

Dippin' Dots are the result of a seven-step laboratory process, which passes USDA and FDA inspections and produces a food that is kosher and pareve certified. The product is shipped to its retail locations in special freezers and containers that maintain the ice cream at the necessary, very low temperature; the unique constitution of Dippin Dots ensures that any untimely melting is easily evident. Curt Jones began his career as a cryogenics-specializing microbiologist at a Lexington, Kentucky biotechnical laboratory. Jones became taken with the idea of flash-freezing ice cream and, after a year of experimentation, he sold his first Dippin' Dots in 1988. The company incorporated in Grand Chain, Illinois in 1988, received its first amusement park account in 1989 and acquired Japan as its first major international licensee in 1994. The first Dippin' Dots franchise was offered in 2000.

Operating Units	12/31/1999	12/31/2000	12/31/2001
Franchised	0	526	555
% Change	--	N/A	5.5%
Company-Owned	0	1	2
% Change	--	N/A	100.0%
Total	0	527	557
% Change	--	N/A	5.7%
Franchised as % of Total	N/A	99.8%	99.6%

Investment Required
The fee for a Dippin' Dots franchise $12,500. Additional units are available at a reduced fee.

Dippin' Dots provides the following range of investments required to open your initial franchise. The range assumes that all items are paid for in cash. To the extent that you choose to finance any of these expense items, your front-end investment could be substantially reduced.

Item	Established Low Range	Established High Range
Franchise Fee	$12,500	$12,500
Advertising	$500	$500
Build-Out/Equipment	$11,000	$114,050
Inventory	$1,650	$5,600
Printing/Signs/Supplies	$1,750	$3,500
Real Estate	$500	$9,400
Training Expenses	$1,250	$3,250
Other Costs and Additional Funds (for 6 months)	$18,000	$41,000
Total Investment	$47,150	$189,800

On-Going Expenses
Dippin' Dots franchisees pay royalties equaling 4%, advertising fee equaling 2% and regional advertising fees equaling no more than 2% of gross revenue.

What You Get—Training and Support
The Dippin' Dots customer service department conducts initial staff training and orientation on serving and handling Dippin' Dots products.

On-site, franchisees and workers have the benefit of reference manuals, on-site instruction and a full-time call center that specializes in customer support and problem resolution. Customer service field representatives also monitor each franchise to ensure that proper selling techniques are used and to train and re-train staff when necessary.

Territory
Dippin' Dots awards exclusive territories encompassing a 30-foot radius around each unit.

Dunkin' Donuts

14 Pacella Park Dr., P.O. Box 317
Randolph, MA 02368-0317
Tel: (800) 777-9983 (781) 961-4000
Fax: (781) 963-1215
E-Mail: apadulo@adrus.com
Web Site: www.dunkin-baskin-togos.com
Mr. Anthony Padulo, VP New Business Dev.

DUNKIN' DONUTS is the world's largest coffee and doughnut chain. We offer a full array of quick-service menu items, including muffins, bagels and donuts. In some markets DUNKIN' DONUTS, together with TOGO's and/or BASKIN-ROBBINS, offers multiple brand combinations of the three brands. TOGO's, BASKIN-ROBBINS, and DUNKIN' DONUTS are all subsidiaries of Allied Domecq PLC.

BACKGROUND:	IFA MEMBER
Established: 1950; 1st Franchised: 1955	
Franchised Units:	5,000
Company-Owned Units	0
Total Units:	5,000
Dist.:	US-3,390; CAN-500; O'seas-1,110
North America:	39 States
Density:	490 in MA, 359 in NY, 237 IL
Projected New Units (12 Months):	350
Qualifications:	5, 4, 2, 2, 5, 4
Registered:	CA,FL,IL,IN,MD,MI,MN,NY, OR,RI,VA,WA,WI,DC

FINANCIAL/TERMS:	
Cash Investment:	$200K
Total Investment:	$255.7-1139.7K
Minimum Net Worth:	$400K/unit
Fees:	Franchise — $50K
	Royalty — 5.9%; Ad. — 5%
Earnings Claim Statement:	Yes
Term of Contract (Years):	20
Avg. # Of Employees:	NR
Passive Ownership:	Allowed
Encourage Conversions:	Yes
Area Develop. Agreements:	Yes/3-5
Sub-Franchising Contracts:	No
Expand In Territory:	Yes
Space Needs:	NR SF; FS, SF, SC, RM

SUPPORT & TRAINING PROVIDED:	
Financial Assistance Provided:	Yes(I)
Site Selection Assistance:	N/A
Lease Negotiation Assistance:	Yes
Co-Operative Advertising:	Yes
Franchisee Assoc./Member:	Yes/No
Size Of Corporate Staff:	NR
On-Going Support:	B,C,E,G,H,I
Training:	51 Days in Randolph, MA; 3.5 Days in another Location.

SPECIFIC EXPANSION PLANS:	
US:	All Regions
Canada:	PQ, ON
Overseas:	All Countries

Dunkin' Donuts is the largest coffee, bagel and donut chain in the world, selling 52 varieties of donuts to customers from Boston to Bangkok. In fact, the quantity of business Dunkin' Donuts generates is so great that the amount of coffee sold by its franchises in one year alone weighs more than one million elephants.

Bill Rosenberg opened the first Dunkin' Donuts in Quincy, Massachusetts in 1950. The famous shop has sold more than 20 billion cups of coffee in its fifty-three year career.

Along with its sister companies Baskin-Robbins and Togo's, Dunkin' Donuts is one of Allied Domecq's Quick Service Restaurants. The Allied Domecq family bears more than 130 years of business experience and manages and operates 10,000 restaurants around the world. The company's Complementary Daypart Branding Strategy offers each of its franchise concepts as co-brands with the others. With three different concepts whose peak selling hours correlate to three distinct times of day, respectively, Allied Domecq presents franchisees with a schedule-proof earning opportunity—Dunkin' Donuts's coffee and pastries in the morning, Togo's sandwiches and salads for lunch and Baskin-Robbins's desserts and snacks throughout the afternoon and evening.

Operating Units	8/26/2000	8/25/2001	8/31/2002
Franchised	3,732	3,101	3,183
% Change	--	-16.9%	2.6%
Company-owned	2	0	0
% Change	--	-100.0%	N/A
Total	3,734	3,101	3183
% Change	--	-16.9%	2.6%
Franchised as % of Total	99.9%	100.0%	100.0%

Investment Required
The fee for a Dunkin' Donuts franchise varies, ranging from $40,000 to $60,000, depending upon the market in which the unit is located. The company works with a group of preferred lenders to offer competitive and flexible financing options to franchisees.

Dunkin' Donuts provides the following range of investments required to open your initial franchise. The range assumes that all items are paid for in cash. To the extent that you choose to finance any of these expense items, your front-end investment could be substantially reduced. The following figures apply to the opening of a new, single-brand store.

Item	Established Low Range	Established High Range
Franchise Fee	$40,000	$60,000
Equipment/Fixtures/Signs	$70,000	$356,700
Insurance	$4,500	$15,000
Inventory	$6,400	$25,500
Marketing Start-Up Fee	$5,000	$5,000
Real Estate	$13,975	$569,475
Training Expenses	$2,000	$35,500
Uniforms	$400	$800
Other Costs and Additional Funds (for 3 months)	$101,350	$221,300
Total Investment	$243,625	$1,289,275

On-Going Expenses

Dunkin' Donuts franchisees pay continuing franchise fees equaling 5 to 5.9% and advertising fees equaling 5% of gross revenue.

What You Get—Training and Support

Dunkin' Donuts and Allied Domecq have a lot of successful franchisees behind them, and they want to put that to work for you. The first service offered to franchisees by Allied Domecq is site selection and market analysis. Always seeking sites with strong business potential, the company's market optimization model (MOM) evaluates the quality of the retail and demographic conditions in each market to find the intersections that are most like already open, booming locations.

Once the ideal site is found, the Dunkin' Donuts concept can be adapted to suit many venues and geographic locations. Each new location's development process is staffed by a design team whose members include personnel from operations, retail technology services, design, construction services and multi-branding development. Among other things, they provide brand-consistent floor plans and assistance in selecting which store layout and what equipment will optimize efficiency. Decisions take into account customer traffic patterns, points of ingress and egress and street access.

For training, Dunkin' Donuts franchisees study the Dunkin' Donuts brand itself at a certified training store and attend classroom managerial training. Both segments of training are followed by real time practice in a real store. Training, however, doesn't stop there. At Allied Domecq, follow-up training is the key to success. Market-specific regional training consultants conduct on-going training, district meetings house new product training sessions and i-Train CD-ROMs, operations manuals and manager training guides fill in any holes. Furthermore, the need for quality training isn't limited to the franchisee alone. The "Off To A Great Start" crew member training and orientation program is provided to all franchisees and can be tailored to meet any store's specific training needs.

For on-going support to complement their on-going training, franchisees receive access to and advice from a myriad of field support professionals— franchise licensing managers, development managers, construction managers, business consultants, operations consultants, field marketing managers, field marketing specialists and regional training managers; and corporate resources—the QSR Navigator, a toll-free representative network, bargain purchasing power and efficient supply distribution, marketing campaigns, local advertising assistance, operations systems, product development and quality assurance.

Dunkin' Donuts marketing aims to build brand awareness and increase store traffic through national brand support as well as store- and market- specific activities and events. Examples of national marketing efforts include radio, television and print advertisements; tie-ins with sporting events and movie premieres and new product launches. Field marketing specialists and managers work directly with franchisees to develop local marketing and advertising. Local drives include grand opening activities, direct mail campaigns, community event sponsorships, radio and local cable television advertising, coupon programs and promotions. Each market is also serviced by an advertising committee that oversees the market's advertising and evaluates its promotional success.

Territory

Dunkin' Donuts does not grant exclusive territories.

Friendly's Restaurants

1855 Boston Rd.
Wilbraham, MA 01095
Tel: (800) 576-8088 (413) 543-2400
Fax: (413) 543-2820
E-Mail: laurel.adams@friendlys.com
Web Site: www.friendlys.com
Ms. Laurel Adams, Manager Franchise Development

FRIENDLY'S is a full-service restaurant chain with ice cream a key point of difference. FRIENDLY'S has enjoyed 9 quarters of comparable store sales increases. The franchisee will receive support, including training, marketing, site selection, store openings and on-going operational assistance.

BACKGROUND:	IFA MEMBER
Established: 1935; 1st Franchised: 1997	
Franchised Units:	156
Company-Owned Units	383
Total Units:	539
Dist.:	US-539; CAN-0; O'seas-0
North America:	16 States
Density:	122 in MA, 114 in NY, 45 CT
Projected New Units (12 Months):	10
Qualifications:	, , , , ,
Registered:	FL,IL,IN,MD,NY,RI,VA

FINANCIAL/TERMS:

Cash Investment:	$400-500K
Total Investment:	$630K-1.9MM
Minimum Net Worth:	$1.5MM-650Liq
Fees:	Franchise — $30-35K
	Royalty — 4%; Ad. — 3%
Earnings Claim Statement:	Yes
Term of Contract (Years):	20/10-20
Avg. # Of Employees:	40 FT, 35 PT
Passive Ownership:	Allowed
Encourage Conversions:	Yes
Area Develop. Agreements:	Yes
Sub-Franchising Contracts:	No
Expand In Territory:	Yes
Space Needs:	4,100-5,000 SF; FS

SUPPORT & TRAINING PROVIDED:

Financial Assistance Provided:	No
Site Selection Assistance:	Yes
Lease Negotiation Assistance:	No
Co-Operative Advertising:	No
Franchisee Assoc./Member:	No
Size Of Corporate Staff:	400
On-Going Support:	A,b,C,d,E,F,G,h
Training:	12 Weeks at the Corporate Training Center and in Individual Training Units.

SPECIFIC EXPANSION PLANS:

US:	SE, NE, Mid-Atlantic
Canada:	No
Overseas:	No

Friendly's Restaurants strive to provide a place where there's something for everyone, from soups and salads to burgers and fajitas, to cater to guests of all ages and provide a backdrop for memories. Logically, families fit well into the Friendly's vision; more than half of all parties that visit a Friendly's include kids.

The first Friendly's opened in Springfield, MA in 1935. The shop committed itself to being a place for families, offering great food, great ice cream, courteous service and reasonable prices. The name Friendly's was, and is, a reminder of this commitment. Even today, Friendly's Restaurants still make their own ice cream from freshly delivered milk, hot fudge from imported Dutch chocolate and whipped topping from fresh cream—every day. There is one difference between these products at the original Friendly's and current Friendly's; you can find them in your supermarket.

Operating Units	12/31/2000	12/31/2001	12/31/2002
Franchised	122	161	156
% Change	--	32.0%	-3.1%
Company-Owned	449	393	387
% Change	--	-12.5%	-1.5%
Total	571	554	543
% Change	--	-3.0%	-2.0%
Franchised as % of Total	21.4%	29.1%	28.7%

Investment Required
The fee for a first and second Friendly's franchise is $35,000. Third and subsequent units are available for a reduced fee of $30,000. Friendly's also offers exclusive agreements for qualified current restaurant owners and operators who are willing to develop a minimum of five Friendly's restaurants.

Friendly's Restaurants provides the following range of investments required to open your initial franchise. The range assumes that all items are paid for in cash. To the extent that you choose to finance any of these expense items, your front-end investment could be substantially reduced.

Item	Established Low Range	Established High Range
Franchise Fee	$30,000	$35,000
Construction	$76,500	$1,055,000
Equipment/Furniture/Signs	$226,700	$326,500
Grand Opening Fee	$10,000	$10,000

Inventory	$32,000	$50,000
Training Expenses	$12,000	$57,500
Other Costs and Additional Funds (for 3 months)	$190,000	$275,000
Total Investment	$577,200	$1,809,000

On-Going Expenses

Friendly's franchisees pay royalties equaling 4% and marketing fees equaling 3% of gross revenue.

What You Get—Training and Support

At the start, Friendly's franchisees receive system assistance with real estate selection and evaluation, construction planning and development, the product purchasing program and staff training resources. Other services available at start-up, as well as throughout the life of a Friendly's franchise, include professional marketing, advertising and public relations support; on-going operational support; bulk purchasing power (although proprietary products are received from Friendly's itself); equipment, methods and technology research; menu development and a cost-efficient distribution system.

Also, the company regularly searches each marketplace for the most effective solutions or improvements to existing, upcoming or even non-existent problems.

However, each franchisee is not left alone to navigate through and utilize these various forms of support. Each franchisee is assigned an area franchise consultant who will help him or her take full advantage of the company's resources, maximize brand recognition within the trade area and help run each Friendly's with the high quality and efficiency that the system demands.

Territory

Friendly's grants exclusive territories to area developers, but not to standard franchisees.

Fuddruckers

4407 Monterey Oaks Blvd., Bldg. 1, # 100
Austin, TX 78749
Tel: (512) 275-0426
Fax: (512) 275-0670
E-Mail: dino.chavez@fuddruckers.com
Web Site: www.fuddruckers.com
Mr. Dino Chavez, Franchise Sales Manager

It's an exciting time at FUDDRUCKERS. Our relentless commitment to freshness makes us "Home of the World's Greatest Hamburgers". Our in-house butcher shops and bakeries provide our guests with the freshest products available. FUDDRUCKERS' menu includes not only our famous 1/3 and 1/2 pound hamburgers but now features a 1-lb. burger. We have also added Big Bowl salads, new Steakhouse Platters and fantastic desserts like our Brownie Blast Sundae. We also have a new 50's and 60's rock and roll image.

BACKGROUND: IFA MEMBER
Established: 1980; 1st Franchised: 1983
Franchised Units: 110
Company-Owned Units: 111
Total Units: 226
Dist.: US-204; CAN-1; O'seas-21
  North America: 30 States, 1 Province
  Density: 44 in TX, 16 in CA, 12 in VA
Projected New Units (12 Months): 30
Qualifications: 5, 5, 4, 3, 2, 5

Registered: CA,FL,HI,IL,IN,MD,MI,MN, NY,ND,RI,SD,VA,WA,DC

FINANCIAL/TERMS:
Cash Investment: $550K
Total Investment: $740K-1.48MM
Minimum Net Worth: $1.5MM
Fees: Franchise — $50K
  Royalty — 5%; Ad. — 0-4%
Earnings Claim Statement: Yes
Term of Contract (Years): 10 & 20
Avg. # Of Employees: 15 FT, 30 PT
Passive Ownership: Discouraged
Encourage Conversions: Yes
Area Develop. Agreements: Yes/Varies
Sub-Franchising Contracts: No
Expand In Territory: Yes
Space Needs: 6,200-7,000 SF; FS

SUPPORT & TRAINING PROVIDED:
Financial Assistance Provided: No
Site Selection Assistance: Yes
Lease Negotiation Assistance: No
Co-Operative Advertising: Yes
Franchisee Assoc./Member: No
Size Of Corporate Staff: 70
On-Going Support: C,D,E,G,H
Training: 6-8 Weeks at Regional Training Locations.

SPECIFIC EXPANSION PLANS:
US: All United States
Canada: All Canada
Overseas: All Countries

Fuddruckers sells "The World's Greatest Hamburgers," specializing in high quality burgers cooked to order from only the freshest ingredients. Each Fuddruckers restaurant is fully contained, housing a butcher shop where meat is prepared fresh daily and a bakery where bread and desserts are baked every day. Visitors create their own ideal burger at the "fixin's" bar, stocked with fresh produce and condiments.

Over the years, Fuddruckers has expanded its scope, offering not only beer and burgers, but chicken, salads, steaks, hot dogs, kid's meals, baked goods and desserts as well. But, while the décor and menu has been recently revamped, Fuddruckers' motto remains the same: "If it ain't great, we don't do it!" While not necessary, prior restaurant experience is beneficial to Fuddruckers franchisees.

Phil Romano couldn't find a place to get a great, fresh hamburger. So, he took matters into his own hands, opening the first Fuddruckers in San Antonio, Texas in 1980.

Operating Units	10/1/2000	9/30/2001	9/29/2002
Franchised	91	88	90
% Change	--	-3.3%	2.3%
Company-Owned	106	106	110
% Change	--	0.0%	3.8%
Total	197	194	200
% Change	--	-1.5%	3.1%
Franchised as % of Total	46.2%	45.4%	45.0%

Investment Required

The fee for a single Fuddruckers franchise is $50,000. Multiple territories are available and the more units operated by the franchisee, the lower the fees for additional units. Fudds Express Restaurants are available for a fee of $25,000 and Fudds in the City Restaurants for a fee of $35,000.

Fuddruckers provides the following range of investments required to open your initial franchise. The range assumes that all items are paid for in cash. To the extent that you choose to finance any of these expense items, your front-end investment could be substantially reduced. The following figures apply to the opening of a standard restaurant.

Item	Established Low Range	Established High Range
Franchise Fee	$35,000	$50,000
Advertising and Promotion	$5,000	$10,000
Equipment/Fixtures/Signs	$315,000	$385,000

Insurance	$15,000	$25,000
Inventory	$15,000	$15,000
Real Estate	$250,000	$900,000
Training Expenses	$20,000	$25,000
Other Costs and Additional Funds (for 3 months)	$70,000	$70,000
Total Investment (does not include real estate and liquor license costs)	$725,000	$1,480,000

On-Going Expenses

Fuddruckers franchisees pay royalties equaling 4 to 5% and advertising fees equaling up to 4% of gross revenue.

What You Get—Training and Support

Fuddruckers requires that all franchisees must have three certified managers attend a six- to eight-week training course. The training is covered in the franchise fee, however, franchisees are responsible for all travel and living expenses.

Territory

Fuddruckers grants exclusive territories during your development term. After the development term, all exclusivity is null.

Golden Corral Buffet and Grill

P.O. Box 29502
Raleigh, NC 27626-0502
Tel: (800) 284-5673 (919) 881-5128
Fax: (919) 881-5252
E-Mail: tsullivan@goldencorral.net
Web Site: www.goldencorral.net
Mrs. Tammy Sullivan, Franchise Development

Golden Corral family restaurants feature 'steaks, buffet and bakery.' The 'Golden Choice Buffet' offers 140 hot and cold items. A special feature is 'The Brass Bell Bakery' which prepares made-from-scratch rolls, cookies, muffins, brownies and pizza. Steak, chicken and fish entrees are also available. Value-driven concept with a $6.97 per person check average in 2001. Open lunch and dinner - 7 days; Breakfast Buffet - weekends or holidays.

BACKGROUND: IFA MEMBER
Established: 1973; 1st Franchised: 1986

Franchised Units:	350	Encourage Conversions:		No
Company-Owned Units	122	Area Develop. Agreements:		Yes/Varies
Total Units:	472	Sub-Franchising Contracts:		No
Dist.:	US-472; CAN-0; O'seas-0	Expand In Territory:		Yes
North America:	40 States	Space Needs:		7,700-11,500 SF; FS
Density:	TX, OK, NC			
Projected New Units (12 Months):	25	**SUPPORT & TRAINING PROVIDED:**		
Qualifications:	, , , , ,	Financial Assistance Provided:		No
Registered:	All States Exc. HI	Site Selection Assistance:		Yes
		Lease Negotiation Assistance:		No
FINANCIAL/TERMS:		Co-Operative Advertising:		Yes
Cash Investment:	$300K	Franchisee Assoc./Member:		NR
Total Investment:	$1.6-3.8MM	Size Of Corporate Staff:		190
Minimum Net Worth:	$1.5MM	On-Going Support:		C,D,E,G
Fees:	Franchise — $40K	Training:	12 Weeks Headquarters and Field.	
	Royalty — 4%; Ad. — 2%			
Earnings Claim Statement:	Yes	**SPECIFIC EXPANSION PLANS:**		
Term of Contract (Years):	15/5	US:		All United States
Avg. # Of Employees:	80 FT, 40 PT	Canada:		All Canada
Passive Ownership:	Not Allowed	Overseas:		Mexico, Puerto Rico

In the mid-1980s, Golden Corral guests decided that they wanted additional entrees and an expanded salad bar. They got their wish—the Golden Corral Buffet and Grill, which includes 150 hot and cold items, a carving station and The Brass Bell Bakery. In 2001, flame-broiled USDA sirloin was added to the line-up and Golden Corral is continuing to prepare for the demands of the future with Strata, a dining concept that puts food preparation in full view of the dining area to emphasize freshness and quality. As this new concept has tested well most new Golden Corrals will be Stratas.

Golden Corral's diverse menu provides something for everyone and helps its restaurants retain their value throughout recessions and booms. As the company's market priority has changed from small towns to large population centers, so has the décor. Rather than resembling a ranch of dark wood, Golden Corral is now bright and open. New products are always heavily tested, with as many as 20 in development at any time. In 2001, Golden Corral had 147,797,000 patrons, likely lured by promotions such as Fisherman's Fridays and All You Can Eat Steak and Shrimp Wednesdays. Each restaurant processed average checks of $6.97. Franchisees must have restaurant experience.

The first Golden Corral was located in Fayetteville, North Carolina and opened for business in 1973.

Operating Units	1999	2000	2001
Franchised	311	332	343
% Change	--	6.7%	3.3%
Company-Owned	141	120	122
% Change	--	-14.9%	1.7%
Total	452	452	465
% Change	--	0.0%	2.9%
Franchised as % of Total	68.8%	73.4%	73.8%

Investment Required
The fee for a Golden Corral franchise is $40,000. Financing is available.

Golden Corral provides the following range of investments required to open your initial franchise. The range assumes that all items are paid for in cash. To the extent that you choose to finance any of these expense items, your front-end investment could be substantially reduced. The following figures apply to the opening of a GC-10 franchise.

Item	Established Low Range	Established High Range
Franchise Fee	$40,000	$40,000
Advertising	$10,000	$15,000
Equipment/Furniture/Signs	$590,000	$736,000
Insurance	$14,000	$25,000
Inventory	$30,000	$70,000
On-Site Assistance Costs	$21,000	$78,400
Real Estate	$1,460,000	$2,650,000
Training	$42,600	$95,600
Other Costs and Additional Funds (for 3 months)	$38,000	$176,400
Total Investment	$2,245,600	$3,886,400

On-Going Expenses

Golden Corral franchisees pay royalties equaling 4% and advertising fees equaling 2 to 6% of gross revenue.

What You Get—Training and Support

Golden Corral training for franchisees and managers lasts for 12 weeks and earns participants a phase 3 certification. The first ten weeks are spent in certified training and the last two in the corporate center.

Golden Corral will also assist in site selection and construction plans for design, furniture, fixtures, equipment, leasehold improvements and signs. Grand opening assistance provides advertising, marketing, new employee training and a team of certified senior co-workers and crew leaders (from company units) to help guide you smoothly through the opening.

In addition, the advertising agency and support center marketing department provide year-round advertising and support, with television and radio commercials, print ads, billboard ads, local store marketing programs and television marketing in 25 markets.

Franchisees also benefit from the training manuals, videos and interactive computer-based training programs, field operations support from service consultants, Golden Corral's purchasing power and research, development and testing of new products, processes and promotions.

Golden Corral also maintains an advisory council that meets twice a year with corporate support staff, senior management and the Golden Corral CEO.

Territory

Golden Corral does not grant exclusive territories.

Great Wraps

4 Executive Park E., # 315
Atlanta, GA 30329
Tel: (888) 489-7277 (404) 248-9900
Fax: (404) 248-0180
E-Mail: ckoestner@greatwraps.com
Web Site: www.greatwraps.com
Ms. Chris Koestner, Director Franchise Development

GREAT WRAPS! is the #1 Hot Wrapped Sandwich & Cheesesteak Franchise, and is experiencing rapid growth. That's because we offer a franchise opportunity that is different and proven . . . and provides tremendous growth potential. We feature a powerful menu that is fresher and tastier than traditional fast food . . .like the Santa Fe Chicken Wrap, our signature GyroWrap, Grilled (hot deli) Rollers, etc. The operation is extremely efficient and is so simple to learn, you don't even need prior food experience.

BACKGROUND:	IFA MEMBER
Established: 1978; 1st Franchised: 1986	
Franchised Units:	51
Company-Owned Units	1
Total Units:	52
Dist.:	US-52; CAN-0; O'seas-0
North America:	13 States
Density:	26 in GA, 6 in FL, 4 in TX
Projected New Units (12 Months):	35

Qualifications:	5, 3, 3, 3, 4, 4
Registered:	CA,IL,MI,NY,VA

FINANCIAL/TERMS:

Cash Investment:	$60-80K
Total Investment:	$175-240K
Minimum Net Worth:	$250K
Fees:	Franchise — $17.5K
	Royalty — 5%; Ad. — 0.5%
Earnings Claim Statement:	No
Term of Contract (Years):	10/10
Avg. # Of Employees:	5 FT, 6 PT
Passive Ownership:	Discouraged
Encourage Conversions:	Yes
Area Develop. Agreements:	Yes/Varies
Sub-Franchising Contracts:	No
Expand In Territory:	Yes
Space Needs:	600-1,500 SF; RM, SC, Airport, Univer.

SUPPORT & TRAINING PROVIDED:

Financial Assistance Provided:	Yes(I)
Site Selection Assistance:	Yes
Lease Negotiation Assistance:	Yes
Co-Operative Advertising:	Yes
Franchisee Assoc./Member:	Yes
Size Of Corporate Staff:	11
On-Going Support:	B,C,D,E,G,H
Training:	3 Weeks Atlanta, GA.

SPECIFIC EXPANSION PLANS:

US:	NE, SE, SW, MW
Canada:	No
Overseas:	No

Great Wraps is a refreshing change for those bored with burgers and fries and those looking for healthier food. With something for everyone, the Great Wraps menu includes Pita Wraps, Tortilla Wraps, Grilled Hot Deli Rollers, Philly Cheesesteaks and frozen Smoothies. In addition, a Great Wraps franchise is easy to operate and labor efficient. No previous food experience is necessary.

In the late 1970s, Great Wraps began to sell its hot wrapped sandwiches, including unique offerings like the Gyro or Teriyaki Chicken Wrap. In 1989,

Mark Kaplan and Bob Solomon, former Coca-Cola executives with more than 20 years of business experience, acquired the company and built Great Wraps into the largest wrap chain in the country.

Operating Units	12/31/2000	12/31/2001	12/31/2002
Franchised	38	40	45
% Change	--	5.3%	12.5%
Company-Owned	0	0	0
% Change	--	0.0%	0
Total	38	40	45
% Change	--	5.3%	12.5%
Franchised as % of Total	100.0%	100.0%	100%

Investment Required

The fee for a Great Wraps franchise is $17,500. The fee for additional franchises is $12,500.

Great Wraps provides the following range of investments required to open your initial franchise. The range assumes that all items are paid for in cash. To the extent that you choose to finance any of these expense items, your front-end investment could be substantially reduced.

Item	Established Low Range	Established High Range
Franchise Fee	$17,500	$17,500
Equipment/Furniture/Signs	$63,000	$73,000
Insurance	$3,000	$3,000
Inventory	$4,000	$4,000
Real Estate	$89,000	$151,000
Training Expenses	$3,000	$3,000
Additional Funds (for 2 months)	$5,000	$5,000
Total Investment	$184,500	$256,500

On-Going Expenses
Great Wraps franchisees pay royalties equaling 5% and advertising fees equaling 0.5 to 2% of gross revenue.

What You Get—Training and Support
Great Wraps training consists of 11 days in Atlanta and five to seven days on-site. The Great Wraps system believes that a well-trained franchisee is a confident and successful franchisee. Additional training is provided with all major product changes and new product rollouts.

Other support includes site selection, lease negotiation, store opening and marketing, all with an emphasis on long-term success and expansion.

Territory
Great Wraps grants exclusive territories to franchisees under a Master Franchising/Area Development program.

KFC

1441 Gardiner Ln.
Louisville, KY 40213
Tel: (800) 544-5774 (502) 872-2021
Fax: (502) 874-5306
E-Mail: steve.provost@tricon-yum.com
Web Site: www.kfc.com
Mr. Steve Provost, SVP Franchising

World's largest quick-service restaurant with a chicken-dominant menu. KFC offers full-service restaurants and non-traditional express units for captive markets.

BACKGROUND:
Established: 1954; 1st Franchised: 1959
Franchised Units: 6,663

Company-Owned Units	2,975
Total Units:	9,638
Dist.:	US-3,122; CAN-3,555; O'seas-3,192
North America:	50 States, 10 Provinces
Density:	CA, TX, IL
Projected New Units (12 Months):	100
Qualifications:	5, 4, 5, 3, 3, 5
Registered:	All States

FINANCIAL/TERMS:

Cash Investment:	$500K
Total Investment:	$700K-1.2MM
Minimum Net Worth:	$1MM
Fees:	Franchise — $25K
	Royalty — 4%; Ad. — 4.5%
Earnings Claim Statement:	No
Term of Contract (Years):	20/10
Avg. # Of Employees:	2 FT, 22 PT
Passive Ownership:	Not Allowed
Encourage Conversions:	No
Area Develop. Agreements:	No
Sub-Franchising Contracts:	No
Expand In Territory:	Yes

Space Needs:	2,000-3,000 SF; FS	On-Going Support:	C,d,E,G,h,I
SUPPORT & TRAINING PROVIDED:		Training:	14 Weeks at Varied Sites.
Financial Assistance Provided:	No		
Site Selection Assistance:	Yes	SPECIFIC EXPANSION PLANS:	
Lease Negotiation Assistance:	No	US:	All United States
Co-Operative Advertising:	Yes	Canada:	All Canada
Franchisee Assoc./Member:	Yes/Yes	Overseas:	All Countries
Size Of Corporate Staff:	820		

KFC sells more chicken than any other quick service restaurant in the world and commands more than 50% of its market share. Every day, more than eight million customers savor the Colonel's famous specialties, such as Original Recipe and Extra Crispy chicken, the Colonel's crispy chicken strips, Twister and many homestyle sides.

The world's largest chicken restaurant is a YUM! Brand and, hence, a member of the world's largest restaurant company. With more than 32,000 restaurants in more than 10 countries and territories, four of YUM!'s five internationally-recognized brands command the highest market share in the chicken, pizza, Mexican and seafood markets.

As a result of this powerful coalition, KFC franchisees have many multi-branding options at their disposal. Not only do multi-brand franchisees have more menu variety to attract more customers, but they leverage their initial and marketing investments, sharing resources, space and labor amongst multiple profit centers, to get more for their money. YUM! currently focuses on multi-branding as a major vehicle for future expansion.

Operating Units	12/31/2000	12/31/2001	12/31/2002
Franchised	3,980	4,099	4,150
% Change	--	3.0%	1.2%
Company-Owned	1,338	1,271	1,308
% Change	--	-5.0%	2.9%
Total	5,318	5,370	5,458
% Change	--	1.0%	1.6%
Franchised as % of Total	74.8%	76.3%	76.0%

Investment Required

The fee for a KFC franchise is $25,000.

KFC provides the following range of investments required to open your initial franchise. The range assumes that all items are paid for in cash. To the extent that you choose to finance any of these expense items, your front-end investment could be substantially reduced. The following quotes apply to the opening of a free-standing restaurant.

Item	Established Low Range	Established High Range
Franchise Fee	$25,000	$25,000
Advertising	$5,000	$5,000
Equipment/Signs	$250,000	$300,000
Inventory	$10,000	$10,000
Real Estate	$832,000	$1,357,000
Training	$2,300	$2,300
Other Costs and Additional Funds	$18,000	$33,000
Total Investment (does not include development services fee)	$1,142,300	$1,732,300

On-Going Expenses

KFC franchisees pay royalties equaling 4%, or $600 per month, local advertising fees equaling 3% and national co-op advertising fees equaling 2% of gross revenue.

What You Get—Training and Support

The YUM! Brands family treats each franchisee to a team of "customer maniacs," whose purpose is to ensure that every customer receives the best service they can get.

Operations and quality assurance systems also provide KFC's franchisees with extensive training and food safety, performance and compliance audits.

Territory

KFC grants protected territories the smaller of a one-and-one-half mile radius or a population of 30,000.

The Krystal Company

1 Union Square, 10th Fl.
Chattanooga, TN 37402-2505
Tel: (800) 458-5912 (423) 757-1381
Fax: (423) 757-5644
E-Mail: jschmidt@krystalco.com
Web Site: www.krystal.com
Mr. Jamie Schmidt, Dir. Franchise Development

The KRYSTAL COMPANY, a 'cultural icon' in the Southeast, is a unique brand with 70 years of success As a niche franchisor, we provide quality service and thoughtful leadership to our franchise partners. We have made major changes in re-engineering and reducing the size of the initial investment. We offer a protected development territory, requiring a minimum 3-restaurant development agreement, minimum liquidity of $600K and a net worth of $1.2 million. KRYSTAL, fresh, hot, small and square.

BACKGROUND:

Established: 1932; 1st Franchised: 1990	
Franchised Units:	172
Company-Owned Units	246
Total Units:	418
Dist.:	US-418; CAN-0; O'seas-0
North America:	15 States
Density:	104 in GA, 105 in TN, 53 AL

Projected New Units (12 Months):	45
Qualifications:	5, 4, 5, 2, 2, 5
Registered:	FL, VA

FINANCIAL/TERMS:

Cash Investment:	$200-300K
Total Investment:	$900K-1MM
Minimum Net Worth:	$1.2MM
Fees:	Franchise — $32.5K
	Royalty — 4.5%; Ad. — 4%
Earnings Claim Statement:	No
Term of Contract (Years):	20/20
Avg. # Of Employees:	14 FT, 15 PT
Passive Ownership:	Allowed
Encourage Conversions:	Yes
Area Develop. Agreements:	Yes/10
Sub-Franchising Contracts:	No
Expand In Territory:	Yes
Space Needs:	1,300-2,200 SF; FS,SC,C-Store

SUPPORT & TRAINING PROVIDED:

Financial Assistance Provided:	No
Site Selection Assistance:	Yes
Lease Negotiation Assistance:	No
Co-Operative Advertising:	Yes
Franchisee Assoc./Member:	Yes/No
Size Of Corporate Staff:	100
On-Going Support:	A,B,C,D,E,F,G,H,I
Training:	4 Weeks Company Store; 1 Week Corporate Computer Center.

SPECIFIC EXPANSION PLANS:

US:	SE, TX, OK, VA, NC,SC, MO,WV
Canada:	No
Overseas:	No

Since 1932, each Krystal restaurant has served the same fresh, hot, small and square burger, "the little food with the big taste." The Krystal franchise system is built on state-of-the-art, labor-efficient buildings and a unique product with a true niche. While well-known in the southeast, the second oldest quick service restaurant in the United States offers a benefit its over-represented competitors can't—they haven't saturated as many markets and thus offer more and better franchise opportunities. Exclusive multi-unit territories in major metropolitan areas—for franchisees interested in opening at least three Krystal locations—are also currently available.

In September of 1997, after 65 years of business as a public company, Krystal was acquired by Port Royal Holdings, Inc. Under new management for the first time, Krystal has since decided to focus on its roots and unite the best of the past with the benefits and trends of the present. New restaurant designs recall traditional Krystals while providing management and consumers with more efficient construction and equipment, and a streamlined menu, concentrating on the original Krystal burger to strengthen the company's brand and service mark position, has also expanded to meet new tastes and demands, such as the Krystal Chik and Chik'n'Bites.

Operating Units	12/31/2000	12/31/2001	12/31/2002
Franchised	138	166	176
% Change	--	20.3%	6.0%
Company-Owned	252	246	245
% Change	--	-2.4%	-0.4%
Total	390	412	421
% Change	--	5.6%	2.2%
Franchised as % of Total	35.4%	40.3%	41.8%

Investment Required
The fee for a Krystal franchise is $32,500.

Krystal provides the following range of investments required to open your initial franchise. The range assumes that all items are paid for in cash. To the extent that you choose to finance any of these expense items, your front-end investment could be substantially reduced. The following figures apply to the opening of a full-service, conventional restaurant.

Item	Established Low Range	Established High Range
Franchise Fee	$32,500	$32,500
Advertising	$5,000	$5,000
Construction	$224,900	$392,000
Development	$101,500	$295,000
Equipment/Fixtures	$149,100	$208,000
Inventory	$12,500	$15,500
Training Expenses	$14,000	$18,000
Other Costs and Additional Funds (for 2 months)	$21,000	$23,000
Total Investment (does not include land)	$560,500	$989,000

On-Going Expenses

Krystal franchisees pay royalties equaling 4 to 5% and advertising fees equaling 4% of gross revenue.

What You Get—Training and Support

A new franchisee has a lot to think about, and a lot to do. Krystal knows that and wants to help. With the company's pre-construction management program, new franchisees are assigned an experienced development manager who will arrange for and oversee tasks like soil testing, line surveys, site architecture and engineering and contractor bid solicitation and review. The program is designed to provide franchisees with a timely and efficient beginning to their Krystal career. For the program, the franchisee makes one deposit, which covers all costs involved. From the start, Krystal also provides site selection and design consultation assistance.

All franchisees and their managers receive comprehensive introductory training, on-going field support and corporate updates. In addition, throughout a franchisee's relationship with Krystal, each restaurant is serviced with local marketing strategies and materials and broadcast and print advertisements to increase consumer traffic.

Territory

Krystal grants exclusive territories to franchisees with development contracts.

Larry's Giant Subs

8616 Baymeadows Rd.
Jacksonville, FL 32256
Tel: (800) 358-6870 (904) 739-9069
Fax: (904) 739-1218
E-Mail: bigone@larryssubs.com
Web Site: www.larryssubs.com
Mr. Mitchell Raikes, Vice President

Upscale submarine sandwich franchise, featuring top-quality foods, such as USDA choice roast beef, oven-roasted turkey, white meat chicken salad, store décor, custom table tops, laser logo steel chairs and huge ape display.

BACKGROUND:

Established: 1982; 1st Franchised: 1986	
Franchised Units:	88
Company-Owned Units	3
Total Units:	91
Dist.:	US-91; CAN-0; O'seas-0
North America:	6 States
Density:	53 in FL, 28 in GA, 2 in TX
Projected New Units (12 Months):	15
Qualifications:	3, 3, 3, 3, 3, 5

Registered:	FL
FINANCIAL/TERMS:	
Cash Investment:	$25-40K
Total Investment:	$110-170K
Minimum Net Worth:	$150K
Fees:	Franchise — $19K
	Royalty — 6%; Ad. — 2%
Earnings Claim Statement:	No
Term of Contract (Years):	10/10
Avg. # Of Employees:	6 FT, 10 PT
Passive Ownership:	Discouraged
Encourage Conversions:	No
Area Develop. Agreements:	Yes/2
Sub-Franchising Contracts:	Yes
Expand In Territory:	Yes
Space Needs:	1,400 SF; FS, SC

SUPPORT & TRAINING PROVIDED:

Financial Assistance Provided:	No
Site Selection Assistance:	Yes
Lease Negotiation Assistance:	Yes
Co-Operative Advertising:	Yes
Franchisee Assoc./Member:	No
Size Of Corporate Staff:	10
On-Going Support:	A,B,C,D,E,F,G,H,I
Training:	30 Days at Corporate Office; 1 - 2 Weeks Franchise Store.

SPECIFIC EXPANSION PLANS:

US:	Southeast
Canada:	No
Overseas:	No

At Larry's Giant Subs, quality is on display. Arrayed in six-foot deli cases, each Larry's restaurant stocks only the highest quality products, such as USDA choice extra lean Angus roast beef, imported hams, caramel roasted Golden Supreme turkey breast and real provolone cheese. Moreover, right before the customers' eyes, all meats and cheeses are sliced and all sub rolls are baked daily. Every sandwich ingredient is fresh every day and nothing is ever frozen. All foods, chosen from 50 varieties of New York-style submarine sandwiches, deli sandwiches, salads, soups, hotdogs and desserts, are made to order. Prior restaurant experience is not necessary.

Larry's Giant Subs has been doing "everything in a Big Way" since 1982 and currently serves approximately ten million sandwiches a year.

Operating Units	1/1/1999	1/1/2000	1/1/2001
Franchised	49	56	73
% Change	--	14.3%	30.3%
Company-Owned	2	2	2
% Change	--	0.0%	0.0%
Total	51	58	75
% Change	--	13.7%	29.3%
Franchised as % of Total	96.1%	96.5%	97.3%

Investment Required
The fee for a Larry's Giant Subs franchise is $20,000.

Larry's Giant Subs provides the following range of investments required to open your initial franchise. The range assumes that all items are paid for in cash. To the extent that you choose to finance any of these expense items, your front-end investment could be substantially reduced.

Item	Established Low Range	Established High Range
Franchise Fee	$20,000	$20,000
Décor/Equipment	$50,000	$69,400
Inventory	$2,500	$3,500
Real Estate	$37,000	$69,500
Signs	$2,200	$5,800
Training Expenses	$0	$2,200
Other Costs and Additional Funds	$13,170	$20,550
Total Investment	$124,870	$190,950

On-Going Expenses

Larry's Giant Subs franchisees pay royalties equaling 6% and national and regional advertising fees equaling 2% of gross revenue.

What You Get—Training and Support

Training takes place at corporate headquarters and at each franchisee's location. All unit managers are required to complete the three-week, 120-hour program. To ensure the highest quality, all trainees must display mastery of sandwich-making and other key operating elements. For further training, franchisees also have access to training videos, a 24-hour emergency hotline, Larry's confidential operations manual detailing all aspects of the system and the guidance of Larry and Mitchell Raikes, president and vice president of Larry's Giant Subs.

Larry's Giant Subs also assists franchisees with site location, design, equipment purchasing and lease negotiations. Through Larry's national vendor contracts, franchisees also receive price breaks on needed equipment and supplies.

Territory

Larry's Giant Subs grants exclusive territories of a two-mile radius.

Long John Silver's

101 Yorkshire Blvd.
Lexington, KY 40579-1988
Tel: (800) 545-8360 (859) 543-6000
Fax: (859) 543-6190
E-Mail: bryon.stephens@yum.com
Web Site: www.ljsilvers.com
Mr. Bryon Stephens

LONG JOHN SILVER'S is the largest, quick-service seafood restaurant chain in the world. We continue to aggressively grow with new units and sales. Opportunities are available in new and existing markets and with our sister brand, A & W in our new co-brand facilities.

BACKGROUND:	IFA MEMBER
Established: 1969; 1st Franchised: 1970	
Franchised Units:	491
Company-Owned Units:	742
Total Units:	1,233
Dist.:	US-1,233; CAN-0; O'seas-18
North America:	35 States
Density:	185 in TX, 114 in OH, 101 IN
Projected New Units (12 Months):	NR
Qualifications:	5, 5, 3, 4, 5, 5

Registered:	All	Financial Assistance Provided:	No
		Site Selection Assistance:	Yes
FINANCIAL/TERMS:		Lease Negotiation Assistance:	NR
Cash Investment:	$150-250K	Co-Operative Advertising:	Yes
Total Investment:	$150K-1MM	Franchisee Assoc./Member:	Yes
Minimum Net Worth:	$250K	Size Of Corporate Staff:	300
Fees:	Franchise — $15-20K	On-Going Support:	C,D,E,G,h,I
	Royalty — 5%; Ad. — 5%	Training:	24 Days of Training.
Earnings Claim Statement:	NR		
Term of Contract (Years):	10-20-5	**SPECIFIC EXPANSION PLANS:**	
Avg. # Of Employees:	NR	US:	All United States
Passive Ownership:	Allowed	Canada:	All Canada
Encourage Conversions:	NR	Overseas: Asia, Europe, Caribbean, Latin America,	
Area Develop. Agreements:	NR		Middle East
Sub-Franchising Contracts:	No		
Expand In Territory:	Yes		
Space Needs: NR SF; FS, C-Store, Food Court			
SUPPORT & TRAINING PROVIDED:			

Long John Silver's has offered customers its special batter-dipped fish, chicken and shrimp for over 30 years. It commands 50% of its market and offers multiple franchise opportunities.

Co-branding development, which leverages real estate costs and creates more franchise locations and opportunities, is available with another Yorkshire franchise, A&W Restaurants. They are great complements in daypart and menu—seafood provides the perfect alternative to the pizzas, sandwiches and hamburgers.

Although Long John Silver's is an established franchise, it has recently undergone many changes and offers many new perks. It has a new logo, image and building design and offers new products. It is aggressively growing, with limitless development opportunities in a variety of locations. Franchisees can now purchase convenience store licenses for Long John Silver's and take advantage of customer demographics both businesses share.

Long John Silver's, inspired by the villainous cook of Robert Louis Stevenson's legendary Treasure Island, has been serving fish and chips for more than 30 years. Yorkshire Restaurants purchased the franchise in 1999.

Operating Units	1999	2000	2001
Franchised	455	457	451
% Change	--	0.4%	-1.3%
Company-Owned	793	747	745
% Change	--	-5.8%	-0.3%
Total	1,248	1,204	1,196
% Change	--	-3.5%	-0.7%
Franchised as % of Total	36.4%	37.9%	37.7%

Investment Required

The fee for a Long John Silvers franchise is usually $15,000. The fee for a strip center location with a drive-thru is $20,000. If you choose to open additional units, a reduced fee applies.

Long John Silver's provides the following range of investments required to open your initial franchise. The range assumes that all items are paid for in cash. To the extent that you choose to finance any of these expense items, your front-end investment could be substantially reduced. The following figures apply to the opening of a traditional freestanding restaurant.

Item	Established Low Range	Established High Range
Franchise Fee	$20,000	$20,000
Advertising Fee	$3,000	$5,000
Décor/Equipment/ Furniture/Signs	$195,000	$380,000
Inventory	$10,000	$20,000
Real Estate	$425,000	$1,000,000
Training Expenses	$10,000	$25,000
Other Costs and Additional Funds (for 3 months)	$103,000	$230,000
Total Investment	$766,000	$1,680,000

On-Going Expenses

Long John Silver's franchisees pay royalties equaling 5% and marketing fees equaling 5% of gross revenue.

What You Get—Training and Support

Long John Silver's franchisee support includes marketing and operations managers that can assist in daily marketing and operations, site and facility development, a technology team and a proprietary system of training and procedural assistance.

Territory

Long John Silver's grants protected territories.

Manchu Wok (USA)

816 S. Military Trail, # 6
Deerfield Beach, FL 33442
Tel: (800) 423-4009 (954) 481-9555
Fax: (954) 481-9670
E-Mail: alec_hudson@manchuwok.com
Web Site: www.manchuwok.com
Mr. Alec Hudson, Franchise Sales Mgr.

MANCHU WOK is one of the largest Chinese quick service franchises in North America. MANCHU WOK operates in over 225 food court locations in large regional malls. MANCHU WOK franchisees are enjoying profitable growth; many owning multiple locations.

BACKGROUND:	IFA MEMBER
Established: 1980; 1st Franchised: 1980	
Franchised Units:	142
Company-Owned Units	47
Total Units:	189
Dist.:	US-111; CAN-76; O'seas-2
North America:	28 States,10 Provinces
Density:	45 in ON, 14 in FL, 13 in IL

Projected New Units (12 Months):	40
Qualifications:	4, 4, 4, 3, 4, 4
Registered:	All States and AB

FINANCIAL/TERMS:	
Cash Investment:	$100-150K
Total Investment:	$265.5-316.75K
Minimum Net Worth:	$100-150K
Fees:	Franchise — $20K
	Royalty — 7%; Ad. — 1%
Earnings Claim Statement:	Yes
Term of Contract (Years):	5/5
Avg. # Of Employees:	2-3 FT, 6-10 PT
Passive Ownership:	Discouraged
Encourage Conversions:	Yes
Area Develop. Agreements:	Yes
Sub-Franchising Contracts:	No
Expand In Territory:	Yes
Space Needs:	800 SF; RM

SUPPORT & TRAINING PROVIDED:	
Financial Assistance Provided:	Yes(I)
Site Selection Assistance:	Yes
Lease Negotiation Assistance:	Yes
Co-Operative Advertising:	N/A
Franchisee Assoc./Member:	Yes
Size Of Corporate Staff:	500
On-Going Support:	B,C,D,E,F,G,H,I
Training:	3-4 Weeks Corporate Site.

SPECIFIC EXPANSION PLANS:		Canada:	All Canada
US:	Northeast, Southeast	Overseas:	No

With a menu inspired by four different Chinese cuisines and serving more than 30 special dishes, Manchu Wok is one of only two oriental quick service restaurants; the market for Manchu Wok franchisees is wide. Together, the Manchu Wok corporate team has over 100 years of restaurant and business experience and corporate locations keep them in the business, just like their franchisees, and aware of what's happening and what needs to be done to help and improve their franchises.

Manchu Wok was first opened in 1980 and has more than twenty years of experience in food courts, regional malls, office complexes, colleges and airports.

Operating Units	4/30/1999	9/28/2000	9/2/2001
Franchised	80	93	85
% Change	--	16.3%	-8.6%
Company-Owned	31	28	21
% Change	--	-9.7%	-25.0%
Total	111	121	106
% Change	--	9.0%	-12.4%
Franchised as % of Total	72.1%	76.9%	80.2%

Investment Required
The fee for a Manchu Wok franchise is $20,000. The company does run a finance program.

Manchu Wok provides the following range of investments required to open your initial franchise. The range assumes that all items are paid for in cash. To the extent that you choose to finance any of these expense items, your front-end investment could be substantially reduced.

Item	Established Low Range	Established High Range
Franchise Fee	$20,000	$20,000
Equipment/Fixtures	$77,000	$77,000
Inventory/Supplies	$5,000	$5,000
Real Estate	$128,500	$179,250
Other Costs and Additional Funds (for 3 months)	$35,050	$35,500
Total Investment	$265,550	$316,750

On-Going Expenses

Manchu Wok franchisees pay royalties equaling 7% and advertising fees equaling 1% of gross revenue.

What You Get—Training and Support

At the beginning of a franchisee's relationship with Manchu Wok, they receive assistance with lease negotiation, coordinate drawings, design and equipment layout. In addition, the franchisee's Manchu Wok location is a turn-key operation—they will provide you with a completed restaurant.

Training lasts for three weeks and takes place at the company's training restaurant in Toronto, Canada. A field training manager guides all franchisees through pre-opening and initial hiring and training and remains on-site for as long as necessary to get the business up and running smoothly.

Seminars throughout the year address the needs of a changing marketplace and keep franchisees on their toes, operating manuals provide instant insight and district managers provide direct links to the corporate side of the Manchu Wok system. Franchisees will host planned and unplanned visits, as well as assistance with profit optimization, cost control, labor scheduling, staff competency, employee productivity, quality assurance and operational procedures, recipe management and local marketing (including a grand opening package), national promotions and local marketing kits, point of sale materials and an annual promotion calendar.

Manchu Wok's approved proprietary items not only keep costs down, but maintain consistency in the products and quality of all Manchu Wok locations, further strengthening the identity of the Manchu Wok brand.

Franchisees will also benefit from research into and development of new products and equipment, group insurance rates and an accounting system.

Territory
Manchu Wok does not grant exclusive territories.

Papa Murphy's

TAKE 'N' BAKE PIZZA

8000 NE Parkway Dr., # 350
Vancouver, WA 98662
Tel: (800) 257-7272 (360) 260-7272
Fax: (360) 260-0500
E-Mail: frankg@papamurphys.com
Web Site: www.papamurphys.com
Mr. Frank Gunderson, VP Development

PAPA MURPHY'S produces a great pizza made from top-quality ingredients. Letting customers bake it themselves is smart business. Put the 2 together and you get the largest, fastest-growing Take 'N' Bake franchise in the world. PAPA MURPHY'S now has 565 stores with another 175 stores expected to open in 2000.

BACKGROUND: IFA MEMBER
Established: 1981; 1st Franchised: 1982
Franchised Units: 636
Company-Owned Units 12
Total Units: 648
Dist.: US-640; CAN-0; O'seas-0
   North America: 22 States
   Density: 163 in CA, 117 in WA, 85 in OR
Projected New Units (12 Months): 175
Qualifications: 4, 3, 2, 3, 3, 5
Registered: CA,IL,IN,MI,MN,ND,OR,SD
,WA,WI

FINANCIAL/TERMS:
Cash Investment: $80K
Total Investment: $148.8-199.5K
Minimum Net Worth: $250K
Fees: Franchise — $25K
   Royalty — 5%; Ad. — 1%
Earnings Claim Statement: No
Term of Contract (Years): 10/5
Avg. # Of Employees: 2 FT, 8-10 PT
Passive Ownership: Not Allowed
Encourage Conversions: Yes
Area Develop. Agreements: No
Sub-Franchising Contracts: No
Expand In Territory: Yes
Space Needs: 1,200-1,400 SF; FS, SF, SC

SUPPORT & TRAINING PROVIDED:
Financial Assistance Provided: Yes(I)
Site Selection Assistance: Yes
Lease Negotiation Assistance: Yes
Co-Operative Advertising: Yes
Franchisee Assoc./Member: Yes/No
Size Of Corporate Staff: 106
On-Going Support: B,C,D,E,G,H,I
Training: 3 Days/30 Hours in the Closest Training Store; 6 Weeks in Store; 6 Days Corporate Office.

SPECIFIC EXPANSION PLANS:
US: Midwest
Canada: No
Overseas: No

Papa Murphy's offers its customers the best of both worlds—made-to-order, fresh pizza hot from their own oven and a great value. Ingredients at Papa Murphy's undergo a thorough selection process that results in the finest, most expensive varieties, but it's worth it to ensure that its franchisees have the best quality and the highest quantity (the Papa Murphy's Family Combo weighs over five pounds) to offer their customers. The chain's dough recipe, created from premium flour, was chosen from more than 200 tested recipes and all cheeses, shredded fresh daily, are made from Grade A pasteurized milk and aged for full, rich flavor. The "take 'n' bake" business is an incredible value not only for its customers, but also for its franchisees, boasting a low initial investment, limited space requirements, minimum labor requirements and a simple equipment package.

Operating Units	12/31/2000	12/31/2001	12/31/2002
Franchised	628	698	736
% Change	--	11.1%	5.4%
Company-Owned	12	12	12
% Change	--	0.0%	0.0%
Total	640	710	748
% Change	--	10.9%	5.3%
Franchised as % of Total	98.1%	98.3%	98.4%

Investment Required
The fee for a Papa Murphy's franchise is $25,000. Additional units cost $15,000.

Papa Murphy's provides the following range of investments required to open your initial franchise. The range assumes that all items are paid for in cash. To the extent that you choose to finance any of these expense items, your front-end investment could be substantially reduced.

Item	Established Low Range	Established High Range
Franchise Fee	$25,000	$25,000
Advertising Fees and Expenses	$10,000	$10,000

Employee Training	$500	$1,500
Insurance	$700	$1,000
Inventory	$4,000	$6,000
Opening Package (including Equipment and Supplies)/ Materials/Supplies/Signs	$54,500	$80,000
Real Estate	$35,900	$59,400
Additional Funds	$10,000	$20,000
Total Investment	$140,600	$202,900

On-Going Expenses

Papa Murphy's franchisees pay continuing service fees and royalties equaling 5%, advertising fees equaling 1% (which could be raised to 2% at the sole discretion of Papa Murphy's) and local advertising, promotion and regional co-op advertising fees equaling the greater of 5% or $500 of gross revenue.

What You Get—Training and Support

Just like its toppings, Papa Murphy's training focuses on quantity and quality. The Papa Murphy's training program is a series of six phases—store orientation, skill development, management duties, shift certification, owners' class and additional training—designed to train franchisees to "make a difference" in the marketplace. The entire program lasts 38 days.

The Papa Murphy's real estate department and broker network provides all franchisees with site selection and lease negotiation assistance. Other opening support comes as preliminary layouts, construction bid review and negotiation, a project manager who guides the construction of each restaurant to keep it on-time and on-budget and grand opening marketing design and implementation. Franchisees may also receive on-site assistance during opening. Comprehensive marketing support persists following a Papa Murphy's opening. Each local store receives the aid of a field marketing staff, graphics and production resources (such as menus, point-of-sale materials and personal ads) and advertising co-ops in more than 40 television markets.

All franchisees also receive the assistance of district operations managers and franchise consultants who provide a host of services through a host of avenues: quick responses to questions and problems through a company 800-number, store visits, visitation reports and reviews, operations manuals, monthly newsletters, franchisee conventions, workshops and advisory board meetings, food cost tracking, food and labor cost control and breakeven business analysis.

Territory

Papa Murphy's does not grant exclusive territories, except in large population metropolitan markets.

Pizzeria Uno
Chicago Bar & Grill

100 Charles Park Rd.
Boston, MA 02132-4985
Tel: (617) 218-5325
Fax: (617) 218-5376
E-Mail: randy.clifton@unos.com
Web Site: www.unos.com
Mr. Randy M. Clifton, Senior VP, Franchise

A full-service casual theme restaurant with a brand name signature product - UNO's Original Chicago Deep Dish Pizza. A full varied menu with broad appeal featuring steak, shrimp and pasta. A flair for fun including a bar and comfortable décor in a facility that attracts guests of all ages.

BACKGROUND: IFA MEMBER

Established: 1943; 1st Franchised: 1979	
Franchised Units:	76
Company-Owned Units	118
Total Units:	194
Dist.:	US-187; CAN-0; O'seas-7
North America:	32 States
Density:	28 in MA, 24 in NY, 14 in VA
Projected New Units (12 Months):	18
Qualifications:	5, 5, 5, 3, 4, 4
Registered:	All States

FINANCIAL/TERMS:

Cash Investment:	$500K
Total Investment:	$900K-1.7MM
Minimum Net Worth:	$2MM
Fees:	Franchise — $35K
	Royalty — 5%; Ad. — 1%
Earnings Claim Statement:	Yes
Term of Contract (Years):	20/10
Avg. # Of Employees:	30 FT, 35 PT
Passive Ownership:	Allowed
Encourage Conversions:	No
Area Develop. Agreements:	Yes
Sub-Franchising Contracts:	No
Expand In Territory:	Yes
Space Needs:	5,500 SF; FS, SC

SUPPORT & TRAINING PROVIDED:

Financial Assistance Provided:	Yes(I)
Site Selection Assistance:	Yes
Lease Negotiation Assistance:	Yes
Co-Operative Advertising:	Yes
Franchisee Assoc./Member:	Yes/Yes
Size Of Corporate Staff:	135
On-Going Support:	a,B,C,D,E,F,G,H,I
Training:	12 Weeks in a Training Restaurant; 2 Weeks On-Site Staff Training.

SPECIFIC EXPANSION PLANS:

US:	All United States
Canada:	All Canada
Overseas:	Asia, South and Central America, Europe

Pizzeria Uno is a world-famous pizzeria and restaurant whose full-range menu offers much more than pizza, broadening the restaurant's appeal and impact.

The original Pizzeria Uno was located in Chicago at the corner of Ohio and Wabash and opened in 1943. It was a full-service pizza place, a rare combination, that received more guests than it could handle. Pizzeria Due was opened one block away to handle the overflow. The owner of the two world-celebrated pizzerias was hesitant to franchise his business, but in 1979 he gave in. The first franchise belonged to Aaron Spencer, now chairman of the board. The company is now based in Boston.

Operating Units	9/30/1999	9/30/2000	9/30/2001
Franchised	61	63	69
% Change	--	3.3%	9.5%
Company-Owned	98	110	113
% Change	--	12.2%	2.7%
Total	159	173	182
% Change	--	8.8%	5.2%
Franchised as % of Total	38.4%	36.4%	37.9%

Investment Required
The fee for a Pizzeria Uno franchise is $35,000.

Pizzeria Uno provides the following range of investments required to open your initial franchise. The range assumes that all items are paid for in cash. To the extent that you choose to finance any of these expense items, your front-end investment could be substantially reduced.

Item	Established Low Range	Established High Range
Franchise Fee	$35,000	$35,000
Advertising and Promotion	$1,000	$5,000
Equipment/ Fixtures	$281,000	$478,000
Insurance	$12,000	$20,000
Inventory	$10,000	$20,000

Real Estate	$377,000	$985,000
Other Costs and Additional Funds (for 3 months)	$62,500	$160,000
Total Investment (does not include liquor license)	$778,500	$1,703,000

On-Going Expenses

Pizzeria Uno franchisees pay royalties equaling 5%, or $4,000 per month, business co-op fees equaling 1%, local advertising expenses equaling 2% and additional advertising fees equaling at least 1% of gross revenue.

What You Get—Training and Support

Pizzeria Uno franchisees receive the following marketing and advertising support: quarterly promotions, periodic secondary marketing programs, on-going appetizer, drink and dessert merchandising pieces, turnkey local store marketing programs, a database program designed to build customer loyalty, newspaper inserts, semi-annual menus, guest satisfaction survey supports, primary and secondary research studies, media buying and analysis, in-house art department support and radio and television spots. However, the franchise fee does not include all of the above services.

Pizzeria Uno's Manager-in-Training workbooks and training systems that allow students to learn at their own pace in a comfortable environment of their choosing.

Territory

Pizzeria Uno grants exclusive territories.

Rita's Italian Ice

1525 Ford Rd.
Bensalem, PA 19020-4505

Tel: (800) 677-7482 (215) 633-9899
Fax: (215) 633-9922
E-Mail: s.miele@ritascorp.com
Web Site: www.ritasice.com
Mr. Steve Miele, Franchise Licensing Manager

Retail outlets selling Italian ices.

BACKGROUND:	IFA MEMBER
Established: 1984; 1st Franchised: 1989	
Franchised Units:	260
Company-Owned Units	1
Total Units:	261
Dist.:	US-261; CAN-0; O'seas-0
North America:	9 States
Density:	PA, NJ, MD
Projected New Units (12 Months):	35
Qualifications:	5, 3, 2, 3, 5, 5
Registered:	RI,MD,NY,VA

FINANCIAL/TERMS:	
Cash Investment:	$75K
Total Investment:	$135-242K
Minimum Net Worth:	$250K
Fees:	Franchise — $25K
	Royalty — 6.5%; Ad. — 2.5%
Earnings Claim Statement:	Yes
Term of Contract (Years):	10/10
Avg. # Of Employees:	1 FT, 9 PT
Passive Ownership:	Discouraged

Encourage Conversions:	Yes
Area Develop. Agreements:	Yes
Sub-Franchising Contracts:	No
Expand In Territory:	Yes
Space Needs:	600-1,500 SF; FS

SUPPORT & TRAINING PROVIDED:	
Financial Assistance Provided:	Yes(I)
Site Selection Assistance:	Yes
Lease Negotiation Assistance:	Yes
Co-Operative Advertising:	Yes
Franchisee Assoc./Member:	No
Size Of Corporate Staff:	35
On-Going Support:	B,C,D,E,G,h
Training:	6 Days Corporate Office; 2-4 Days On-Site.

SPECIFIC EXPANSION PLANS:	
US:	FL,MD,OH,VA,PA,NY,SC,WV,CT
Canada:	No
Overseas:	No

If I have seen further it is by standing on the shoulders of giants.
-Isaac Newton, Letter to Robert Hooke, February 5, 1675

Rita's Italian Ice invites franchisees to stand on their shoulders so that they can see farther and achieve more. Made daily from the highest quality fresh fruit and other wholesome ingredients, Rita's fat- and cholesterol-free Italian Ice is an ideal product for the health-conscious twenty-first century.

In May 1984, Robert Tumolo and his mother Elizabeth opened a family business—Rita's Water Ice in Bensalem, Pennsylvania. In 1985, brother John signed on and the family opened the second Rita's location in 1987. The chain franchised in 1989 and is currently the largest Italian ice chain in existence.

Operating Units	12/31/1999	12/31/2000	12/31/2001
Franchised	277	299	320
% Change	--	7.9%	7.0%
Company-Owned	3	2	1
% Change	--	33.3%	50.0%
Total	280	301	321

% Change	--	7.5%	
Franchised as % of Total	98.9%	99.3%	99.7%

Investment Required

The fee for a Rita's Italian Ice franchise is $25,000.

Rita's Italian Ice provides the following range of investments required to open your initial franchise. The range assumes that all items are paid for in cash. To the extent that you choose to finance any of these expense items, your front-end investment could be substantially reduced. The following figures apply to the opening of a traditional location.

Item	Established Low Range	Established High Range
Franchise Fee	$22,500	$25,000
Advertising	$1,900	$1,900
Equipment/Signs	$60,700	$80,000
Insurance	$1,500	$1,500
Inventory	$4,800	$6,000
Real Estate	$32,000	$108,600
Training	$250	$2,000
Additional Funds (for 3 months)	$9,500	$17,400
Total Investment	$133,150	$242,400

On-Going Expenses

Rita's franchisees pay royalties equaling 6.5%, advertising fees equaling 2.5%, or $100 a week and an advisory council fee equaling $120 a year of gross revenue. Any additional training costs $600 and employee certification costs $100 per day.

What You Get—Training and Support

Franchising with Rita's Italian Ice guarantees brand recognition, operation specifications for quality and uniformity and access to Rita's proprietary products.

Rita's training, beginning with 6 days of training at the corporate training center and ending with two to four days of personalized opening support, covers everything from product preparation and services to store operations and policies. Following training, franchise services imparts on-going lessons as needed.

In addition, Rita's franchisees receive personal attention and support from a tight-knit franchise family run by the original franchise founder and product inventor. Rita's support system includes store development services to guide franchisees through the real estate selection and construction process, marketing and advertising and research development.

Territory
Rita's grants exclusive territories.

Shake's Frozen Custard

244 W. Dickson St.
Fayetteville, AR 72701-5221
Tel: (866) 742-5648 (479) 587-9115
Fax: (479) 587-0780
E-Mail: clarawhite@shakesfrozencustard.com
Web Site: www.shakesfrozencustard.com
Ms. Clara White, Franchise Development

SHAKE'S FROZEN CUSTARD is where friends gather, couples fall in love, and people of all ages come to enjoy the vibrant nostalgic atmosphere of the 50's. Featuring an extensive menu consisting of our one-of-a-kind, delicious frozen custard and a wide variety of innovative concepts, SHAKE'S is a rapidly growing franchise system. With intensive training and continuous support, we will always ensure your business is operating to its maximum potential.

BACKGROUND: IFA MEMBER
Established: 1991; 1st Franchised: 1999
Franchised Units:	37
Company-Owned Units:	2
Total Units:	39
Dist.:	US-39; CAN-0; O'seas-0
North America:	8 States
Density:	12 in AR, 8 in MO, 7 in TX
Projected New Units (12 Months):	25
Qualifications:	4, 4, 2, 1, 3, 5
Registered:	FL,IL,IN,VA,WI

FINANCIAL/TERMS:
Cash Investment:	$50-250K
Total Investment:	$166-800K
Minimum Net Worth:	$250K
Fees:	Franchise — $30K
	Royalty — 5; Ad. — 3%
Earnings Claim Statement:	Yes
Term of Contract (Years):	15/5
Avg. # Of Employees:	3 FT, 12 PT
Passive Ownership:	Discouraged
Encourage Conversions:	No
Area Develop. Agreements:	Yes/15
Sub-Franchising Contracts:	No

Expand In Territory:	Yes	Size Of Corporate Staff:	10
Space Needs:	1,200 SF; FS	On-Going Support:	A,B,C,D,E,F,G,h
		Training:	2 Weeks in Fayetteville, AR.
SUPPORT & TRAINING PROVIDED:			
Financial Assistance Provided:	Yes(I)	**SPECIFIC EXPANSION PLANS:**	
Site Selection Assistance:	Yes	US:	South, SE, SW, Midwest
Lease Negotiation Assistance:	Yes	Canada:	No
Co-Operative Advertising:	Yes	Overseas:	No
Franchisee Assoc./Member:	Yes		

Shake's Frozen Custard is the fastest-growing franchise system in the mid-south and the most successful organization in the frozen custard industry. Shake's signature product is a smooth and creamy homemade ice cream, reminiscent of the hand-cranked ice cream of the past, with no added air or fillers, made from the highest quality and all natural ingredients. "Let Us Take You Back To The Way Ice Cream Was Meant To Taste."

When you think of Shake's think of James Dean, Elvis Presley, Marilyn Monroe, poodle skirts and rock 'n' roll. With no inside seating and fast, friendly "service with a smile," Shake's is like the drive-ins of the 1940s and 1950s.

Co-founder Debbie Osborne put years of research and experimentation into the theme, menu and recipes that would shape Shake's Frozen Custard. The first Shake's was in Joplin, Missouri and opened on August 2, 1991 by founders looking for a friendly, service-oriented family business. The first franchised unit came eight years later, in Neosho, Missouri in June 1999.

Operating Units	12/31/2000	12/31/2001	12/31/2002
Franchised	11	25	37
% Change	--	127.3%	48%
Company-Owned	3	3	2
% Change	--	0.0%	-33.3%
Total	14	28	39
% Change	--	100.0%	39.3%
Franchised as % of Total	78.6%	89.3%	94.9%

Investment Required

The fee for a Shake's franchise is $30,000.

Shake's Frozen Custard provides the following range of investments required to open your initial franchise. The range assumes that all items are paid for in cash. To the extent that you choose to finance any of these expense items, your front-end investment could be substantially reduced.

Item	Established Low Range	Established High Range
Franchise Fee	$30,000	$30,000
Equipment/Signs	$100,000	$155,000
Inventory/Supplies	$7,000	$20,000
Other Costs and Additional Funds (for 3 months)	$25,000	$65,000
Total Investment (does not include real estate)	$162,000	$270,000

On-Going Expenses

Shake's franchisees pay royalties equaling 5%, marketing fees equaling 1.5% and local marketing fees equaling 1.5% of gross revenue. There is also a 50-cent per gallon fee for the special label custard mix served in Shake's specialties.

What You Get—Training and Support

The Shake's corporation provides intensive training, corporate support, building layouts, and site acquisition assistance, in addition to field operations support.

Training takes place in Fayetteville, Arkansas and takes the form of a two-week program during which franchisees learn how to operate and maintain their Shake's unit. All owners may bring two additional managers or employees to the training sessions, but travel, food and lodging are at the franchisee's expense. Here, franchisees learn how to make Shake's custard and other recipes. They also learn how to order needed supplies and services.

Shake's also provides on-site assistance for five to seven days when the unit opens. Future assistance is provided continuously through the field operations department. Each franchisee receives visits from their personal Shake's operations consultant at least once a quarter. A jointly conducted franchise partnership assessment will be performed by you and your operations consultant. These assessments can be conducted at any time, and may be requested by the franchisee.

Shake's franchises receive periodic deliveries of Shake's frozen custard mixes, exclusive toppings, paper goods and other products, and qualify for volume pricing discounts and exclusive products.

Territory
Shake's Frozen Custard grant protected territories within a three-mile radius around each store. Shake's recommends that each trade territory have a population of at least 40,000 people.

Smoothie King

2400 Veterans Blvd., # 110
Kenner, LA 70062
Tel: (800) 577-4200 (504) 467-4006 + 232
Fax: (504) 469-1274
E-Mail: mikep@smoothieking.com
Web Site: www.smoothieking.com
Mr. Michael C. Powers, EVP Franchise Development
SMOOTHIE KING is the original nutritional smoothie bar and health marketplace since 1973. Our brand is recognized by Entrepreneur Magazine as being # 1 in our category for 11 consecutive years and has steadily grown to 264 stores. Brand loyalty and recognition, corporate support and innovation are some reasons why SMOOTHIE KING is in the front of the industry.

BACKGROUND:	IFA MEMBER
Established: 1973; 1st Franchised: 1989	
Franchised Units:	230
Company-Owned Units	1
Total Units:	231
Dist.:	US-165; CAN-0; O'seas-0
North America:	10 States
Density:	37 in LA, 28 in TX, 14 in FL
Projected New Units (12 Months):	75
Qualifications:	3, 3, 3, 3, 4, 4
Registered:	All States

FINANCIAL/TERMS:	
Cash Investment:	$40K
Total Investment:	$120-220K
Minimum Net Worth:	$100K
Fees:	Franchise — $20K
	Royalty — 5%; Ad. — 1%
Earnings Claim Statement:	No
Term of Contract (Years):	10/10
Avg. # Of Employees:	2 FT, 6 PT
Passive Ownership:	Discouraged
Encourage Conversions:	Yes

Area Develop. Agreements:	Yes	Franchisee Assoc./Member:	No
Sub-Franchising Contracts:	No	Size Of Corporate Staff:	16
Expand In Territory:	Yes	On-Going Support:	C,D,E,F,G,h,I
Space Needs:	800-1,000 SF; SC	Training:	7 Days New Orleans, LA.
SUPPORT & TRAINING PROVIDED:		**SPECIFIC EXPANSION PLANS:**	
Financial Assistance Provided:	N/A	US:	All United States
Site Selection Assistance:	Yes	Canada:	No
Lease Negotiation Assistance:	Yes	Overseas:	No
Co-Operative Advertising:	No		

Smoothie King is a franchise catered to serve busy schedules and increase nutritional awareness and the need for convenient sources of nutritional meals at any time of day. Part of the $53 billion nutrition industry, Smoothie King's flagship product is the smoothie. Each Smoothie King franchise houses a smoothie bar offering 40 different flavors, each custom made with real fruit and other natural ingredients, and a nutrition center stocking nutritional supplements, vitamins, snacks, sports nutrition and diet products.

They have sold more than 157 million smoothies since 1973, and with 290 stores in 33 states, Smoothie King is reaching for national recognition.

Operating Units	12/31/1999	12/31/2000	12/31/2001
Franchised	206	227	264
% Change	--	10.2%	16.3%
Company-Owned	6	2	2
% Change	--	-6.67%	0.0%
Total	212	229	266
% Change	--	8.0%	16.2%
Franchised as % of Total	97.2%	99.1%	99.2%

Investment Required
The fee for a Smoothie King franchise is $25,000.

Smoothie King provides the following range of investments required to open your initial franchise. The range assumes that all items are paid for in cash. To the extent that you choose to finance any of these expense items, your front-end investment could be substantially reduced.

Item	Established Low Range	Established High Range
Franchise Fee	$25,000	$25,000
Equipment/Fixtures/Signs	$20,000	$50,000
Insurance	$500	$2,500
Inventory/Start-up Supplies	$4,000	$15,000
Opening Advertising	$1,000	$2,500
Real Estate	$52,000	$65,500
Training Expenses	$500	$2,500
Other Costs and Additional Funds (for 3 months)	$9,750	$26,000
Total Investment	$112,750	$189,000

On-Going Expenses

Smoothie King franchisees pay royalties equaling 6%, local advertising fees equaling 2% and an advertising fund contribution equaling up to 2% of gross revenue.

What You Get—Training and Support

While previous small business experience may be helpful in the development of a Smoothie King franchise, the step-by-step training provided by the franchisor will make up for any lack of know-how. This training occurs at both the company research center in New Orleans and the franchisee's own site and covers operations, marketing, nutrition, customer service and support manual use and understanding. Trainees also receive hands-on training and experience at the smoothie bar and on the retail sales floor.

In addition, what Smoothie King franchisees get: an established franchise system, training, marketing and advertising support, on-going home office support and volume buying power. Franchise conference seminars and workshops provide additional training and insights and contribute to the synergy of the entire Smoothie King concept. Smoothie King wants its franchisees to feel that they, while independent franchisees, are part of a larger family working for the good of the whole and not just the part.

Territory
Smoothie King does not guarantee protected territories.

Subway Restaurants

325 Bic Dr.
Milford, CT 06460-3072
Tel: (800) 888-4848 (203) 877-4281
Fax: (203) 783-7325
E-Mail: franchise@subway.com
Web Site: www.subway.com
Mr. Donald Fertman, Franchise Director

For more than 37 years, SUBWAY RESTAURANTS has been offering entrepreneurs a chance to build and succeed in their own business through a proven, well-structured sandwich franchise. In 2003, Entrepreneur Magazine again chose SUBWAY as the overall number one franchise in all categories, making that 11 out of the past 15 years. With more than 17,500 independently-owned locations in 74 countries, SUBWAY continues to inspire partnerships worldwide.

BACKGROUND: IFA MEMBER
Established: 1965; 1st Franchised: 1974
Franchised Units: 17,628
Company-Owned Units 1
Total Units: 17,629
Dist.: US-14,584; CAN-1,686; O'seas-1,359
 North America: All States & Provinces
 Density: 1,200 CA, 1,000 TX, 800 FL
Projected New Units (12 Months): 1,000+
Qualifications: 5, 4, 3, 4, 3, 3
Registered: All States

FINANCIAL/TERMS:
Cash Investment: $NR
Total Investment: $69-191K
Minimum Net Worth: $NR
Fees: Franchise — $12.5K
 Royalty — 8%; Ad. — 3.5%
Earnings Claim Statement: No
Term of Contract (Years): 20/20
Avg. # Of Employees: 2-3 FT, 6-10 PT
Passive Ownership: Not Allowed
Encourage Conversions: N/A
Area Develop. Agreements: Yes/20
Sub-Franchising Contracts: No
Expand In Territory: Yes
Space Needs: 300-2,000 SF; FS, SF, SC, RM, C-Store

SUPPORT & TRAINING PROVIDED:
Financial Assistance Provided: Yes(D)
Site Selection Assistance: Yes
Lease Negotiation Assistance: Yes
Co-Operative Advertising: No
Franchisee Assoc./Member: Yes/Yes
Size Of Corporate Staff: 600
On-Going Support: A,B,C,D,E,F,G,H,I
Training: 2 Weeks Hands-On Training in Milford, CT, Miami, FL, Sidney, AU, China or Germany.

SPECIFIC EXPANSION PLANS:
US: All United States
Canada: All Canada
Overseas: All Countries

Subway's concept—to serve made-to-order sandwiches (and salads) on freshly baked gourmet breads—is simple. Likewise, Subway's pitch to franchisees is simple. They serve great food, have a simple, proven operating system with efficient methods of control, extensive franchisee support and flexible location options with little investment necessary. The facilities are compact and the décor simple, thus, franchisees finance few leasehold improvements.

In 2002, the healthier fast food alternative had more open and operating North America locations than the omnipresent McDonalds. However, McDonalds still dominates in some markets, leaving many opportunities in which Subway still needs to step in and take the lead. In fact, the company lists two main objectives. Number one? Customer satisfaction. Number two? To surpass McDonalds in all markets. Subway is also a great franchise for franchisees seeking to expand their franchise investment into multiple franchises. More than 65% of Subway's new franchises in the year 2002 were purchased by existing Subway franchisees.

The first Subway opened in Bridgeport, Connecticut on August 28, 1965. The proprietors were 17-year-old Fred DeLuca and his family friend, Dr. Peter Buck. DeLuca had approached Buck for advice about financing his college education. Buck gave him $1,000 and told him to open a sandwich shop. The shop franchised in 1974.

Operating Units	12/31/2000	12/31/2001	12/31/2002
Franchised	12,353	13,196	14,477
% Change	--	6.8%	9.7%
Company-Owned	4	2	2
% Change	--	-50.0%	0.0%
Total	12,357	13,198	14,479
% Change	--	6.8%	9.7%
Franchised as % of Total	100.0%	100.0%	100.0%

Investment Required
The fee for a Subway franchise is $12,500. Additional franchises cost $6,000 and satellites cost $1,500. Financing is available.

Subway provides the following range of investments required to open your initial franchise. The range assumes that all items are paid for in cash. To the extent that you choose to finance any of these expense items, your front-end investment could be substantially reduced. The following figures apply to the opening of a traditional location.

145

Item	Established Low Range	Established High Range
Franchise Fee	$12,500	$12,500
Advertising	$2,000	$2,500
Equipment/Signs/Supplies	$5,000	$11,500
Insurance	$800	$2,500
Inventory	$2,500	$5,000
Real Estate	$42,000	$112,000
Training Expenses	$1,500	$3,000
Other Costs and Additional Funds (for 3 months)	$20,000	$64,500
Total Investment	$86,300	$213,500

On-Going Expenses

Subway franchisees pay royalties equaling 8% and advertising fund fees equaling 3.5% (soon to be 4.5%) of gross revenue.

What You Get—Training and Support

Training for Subway franchisees usually takes place at company headquarters in Milford, Connecticut. Training sessions are also held in Miami, Florida, Australia, Germany and China. Franchisees can obtain additional training through instructional videos and additional class time.

At the beginning of the franchise development process, franchisees also receive site selection and equipment ordering assistance and floor plans for their restaurant's design. Additional support comes from Subway's operations manual, field consultants who help with restaurant openings as well as with **on-going** operational evaluations, a personal franchisee services coordinator at the main office who is just a phone call or E-mail away, research and development into new and better food products and newsletters, e-mails and voice-mails.

Subway's extensive advertising is yet another advantage reaped by its franchisees. With $244,959,980 in media spending in 2002, Subway is the largest advertiser among sub sandwich franchises.

The Subway Franchisee Advertising Fund Trust, the Independent Purchasing Co-op and the North American Association of Subway Franchisees are all franchisee-run councils that contribute to Subway's success and are always available to fellow franchisees. For example, an Ad Advisor from the SFAFT is always available to answer questions about its local and national advertising materials and promotions.

Territory

Subway grants exclusive territories to franchisees enrolled in the area development program.

Tony Roma's Famous for Ribs

9304 Forest Ln., # 200
Dallas, TX 75243-8953
Tel: (800) 286-7662 (214) 343-7800
Fax: (214) 343-9203
E-Mail: kenm@romacorp.com
Web Site: www.tonyromas.com
Mr. Kenneth L. Myres, VP Franchise Development

At TONY ROMA'S, we are committed to 'World Wide - World Class.' With intense guest focus, high integrity and Great Food! Providing for a great business opportunity. We started out with one restaurant in Miami FL, and today there are 280 TONY ROMA'S on six continents. We owe our phenomenal growth to one thing - Great People! TONY ROMA'S franchisee partners are a cut above the rest and we are always looking for more people to join our success.

BACKGROUND:	IFA MEMBER
Established: 1972; 1st Franchised: 1979	
Franchised Units:	213
Company-Owned Units:	43
Total Units:	256

Dist.:	US-111; CAN-23; O'seas-79
North America:	42 States, 3 Provinces
Density:	37 in CA, 14 in AB, 15 in MX
Projected New Units (12 Months):	NR
Qualifications:	5, 5, 5, 4, 4, 5
Registered:	CA,FL,IN,MD,MI,MN,NY,N
	D,RI,SD,WA,WI

FINANCIAL/TERMS:

Cash Investment:	$Varies
Total Investment:	$Varies
Minimum Net Worth:	$3MM
Fees:	Franchise — $20K
	Royalty — 4%; Ad. — .5%
Earnings Claim Statement:	No
Term of Contract (Years):	20/10
Avg. # Of Employees:	NR
Passive Ownership:	Allowed
Encourage Conversions:	Yes
Area Develop. Agreements:	Yes/Var
Sub-Franchising Contracts:	No
Expand In Territory:	Yes
Space Needs:	6,500 SF; FS, SC

SUPPORT & TRAINING PROVIDED:

Financial Assistance Provided:	No
Site Selection Assistance:	Yes
Lease Negotiation Assistance:	No
Co-Operative Advertising:	Yes
Franchisee Assoc./Member:	No
Size Of Corporate Staff:	35

On-Going Support:	C,D,E,h,I	SPECIFIC EXPANSION PLANS:	
Training:	8 1/2 Weeks.	US:	All United States
		Canada:	Yes
		Overseas:	Yes

Tony Roma's offers diners flame-grilled ribs, steaks, chicken and seafood, using only premium, meatier and more tender rack cuts specially prepared to seal in smoked flavor. The first Tony Roma's restaurant was in North Miami, Florida. It specialized in grilled burgers and steaks, but one weekend, on a whim, they decided to grill some ribs using Chef Dave Smith's secret barbecue recipe. The ribs were a hit and business boomed. Finally, Dallas Cowboys owner Clint Murchison, Jr. found that he couldn't get to North Miami often enough to satiate his Tony Roma's appetite. He bought the concept and began building Tony Roma's restaurants in Texas, California, New York, Hawaii and Tokyo.

Operating Units	2001	2002	2003
Franchised	162	197	240
% Change	--	21.6%	21.8%
Company-Owned	60	56	43
% Change	--	-6.7%	23.2%
Total	222	253	283
% Change	--	14.0%	11.9%
Franchised as % of Total	73.0%	77.9%	84.8%

Investment Required
The fee for a Tony Roma's franchise is $20,000.

Tony Roma's provides the following range of investments required to open your initial franchise. The range assumes that all items are paid for in cash. To the extent that you choose to finance any of these expense items, your front-end investment could be substantially reduced. The following quotes refer to the opening of a newly constructed freestanding location.

Item	Established Low Range	Established High Range
Franchise Fee	$35,000	$35,000
Décor/Equipment/Furniture /Signs	$333,000	$585,000
Insurance	$7,500	$17,000
Management Training	$2,050	$3,050
Opening Team Expenses	$30,000	$35,000
Other Costs and Additional Funds	$70,500	$140,000
Real Estate	$785,000	$1,115,000
Total Investment	$1,263,050	$1,930,050

On-Going Expenses

Tony Roma's franchisees pay royalties equaling 4%, joint marketing accounts fees equaling 0.5%, minimum marketing expenditures equaling 4% and, if such a fund is established, special advertising assessment fees equaling no more than 1% of gross revenue. Cooperative advertising fees equaling up to 2% may partially offset the required franchisee marketing expenditure of 4% of gross revenue.

What You Get—Training and Support

Tony Roma's strives to meet each and every franchisee need throughout development and operation. To this end, Tony Roma's provides support in site selection, restaurant construction, recruitment, training, marketing and on-going operations.

Training is hands-on and classroom-based and includes restaurant operations, crew and financial management and marketing.

A team of operations personnel staffs each opening to assist franchisees with training, organization, inventory planning and overall restaurant control. Furthermore, each Tony Roma's franchise is assigned a Director of Franchise Operations (DFO), who assists with all operational aspects and will be the franchisee's key resource, providing insight from personal experience, the franchise community and Tony Roma's Global Support Center staff.

New franchisees receive the expertise of Tony Roma's research and development department, which will assist with menu development to create the menu that will fit guest tastes to maximize sales for your specific location; purchasing department, which negotiates service and price agreements with approved suppliers and distributors and provides franchisees with volume buying power and marketing department, which provides guidelines for advertising and marketing implementation.

Tony Roma's franchisees also have access to print and broadcast materials to aid in the development of advertising cooperatives in multiple-unit markets.

Territory
Tony Roma's franchisees receive a three-mile protected territory.

Wienerschnitzel

4440 Von Karman Ave., # 222
Newport Beach, CA 92660
Tel: (800) 764-9353 (949) 851-2609
Fax: (949) 851-2618
E-Mail: fcoyle@galardigroup.com
Web Site: www.wienerschnitzel.com
Mr. Frank R. Coyle, Franchise Sales Dir.

WIENERSCHNITZEL is the world's largest quick service hot dog restaurant chain with over 300 locations selling 90 million hot dogs annually. We are interested in developing new locations throughout California, the Southwest and Pacific Northwest.

BACKGROUND:

Established: 1961; 1st Franchised: 1965	
Franchised Units:	321
Company-Owned Units:	0
Total Units:	321
Dist.:	US-316; CAN-0; O'seas-0
North America:	11 States
Density:	220 in CA, 30 in TX, 7 in NM
Projected New Units (12 Months):	35
Qualifications:	4, 3, 3, 2, 1, 4
Registered:	CA,IL,OR,WA

FINANCIAL/TERMS:

Cash Investment:	$100-200K
Total Investment:	$250K-1.2MM
Minimum Net Worth:	$150K
Fees:	Franchise — $25K
	Royalty — 5%; Ad. — 3-5%
Earnings Claim Statement:	No
Term of Contract (Years):	20/1-20

Avg. # Of Employees:	1-3 FT, 25-30 PT	Co-Operative Advertising:	Yes
Passive Ownership:	Discouraged	Franchisee Assoc./Member:	Yes/Yes
Encourage Conversions:	Yes	Size Of Corporate Staff:	48
Area Develop. Agreements:	Yes/1	On-Going Support:	A,B,C,d,E,F,G,H,I
Sub-Franchising Contracts:	No	Training: 30 Days Plano, TX; 30 Days Gilroy, CA;	
Expand In Territory:	Yes		7 Days Corporate Office.
Space Needs:	20,000 SF; FS, RM		
		SPECIFIC EXPANSION PLANS:	
SUPPORT & TRAINING PROVIDED:		US:	NW, SW, SE, NE
Financial Assistance Provided:	Yes(I)	Canada:	No
Site Selection Assistance:	Yes	Overseas:	No
Lease Negotiation Assistance:	No		

At the age of 19, John Galardi got a 50-cent-an-hour job at a tiny taco restaurant owned by Glen Bell. Two years later, Galardi bought one of Bell's restaurants. However, when he was offered an additional restaurant site next door to another Taco Bell location, Galardi was forced to break with Mexican food. He chose to build his new restaurant menu around hot dogs and considered naming it John's Hot Dogs. Mrs. Bell suggested Wienerschnitzel.

The first Der Wienerschitzel opened in 1961 along the Pacific Coast Highway. It sold 15-cent hot dogs and 10-cent cokes. By 1968, Wienerschnitzel was operating out of more than 200 units, and in 1977 the chain simplified, dropping the "Der" from its name. The chain would go on to be one of the first quick service restaurants to utilize drive-thrus, originally in an attempt to solve loitering problems, and later Galardi would add the Original Hamburger Stand to his franchise concept, begin selling 39-cent burgers and incite the Burger Price Wars.

Operating Units	1999	2000	2001
Franchised	250	257	269
% Change	--	2.8%	4.7%
Company-Owned	0	0	0
% Change	--	N/A	N/A
Total	250	257	269
% Change	--	2.8%	4.7%
Franchised as % of Total	100.0%	100.0%	100.0%

Investment Required
The fee for a Wienerschnitzel franchise is $25,000. Additional locations carry a fee of $15,000. Franchisees also have the option of co-branding a Wienerschnitzel franchise with a Tastee Freeze franchise.

Wienerschnitzel provides the following range of investments required to open your initial franchise. The range assumes that all items are paid for in cash. To the extent that you choose to finance any of these expense items, your front-end investment could be substantially reduced.

Item	Established Low Range	Established High Range
Franchise Fee	$2,500	$25,000
Advertising Fee (for 3 months)	$3,600	$18,000
Equipment/Fixtures	$112,500	$175,000
Insurance	$4,000	$5,800
Inventory	$5,000	$8,000
Real Estate	$3,500	$805,500
Training	$2,000	$4,500
Other Costs	$3,000	$3,000
Total Investment	$136,100	$1,044,800

On-Going Expenses
Wienerschnitzel franchisees pay service fees equaling 5%, national advertising fees equaling 1% and local advertising fees equaling 3 to 5% of gross revenue. Additional training is available at a cost of $2,000 per manager trained.

What You Get—Training and Support
Wienerschnitzel provides the following initial support services: site approval; referenced vendors for kitchen design, equipment and sign packages; prototype drawings for buildings; comprehensive training and an opening support operations team. Following opening, franchisees benefit from company management programs, marketing materials, an established national distribution system, a semi-annual national seminar and regional

meetings. Also, a franchise area director is designated for every 30 to 40 Wienerschnitzel locations.

Wienerschnitzel training is comprehensive and intensive. While in training, franchisees can expect to work 10 hours a day, 6 days a week. The Galardi Group training program teaches basic restaurant operations and aims to prepare all franchisees to operate their restaurant effectively and independently. Lessons cover production and service floor skills, paperwork, ordering and receiving, labor laws, team training, payroll and checkbook procedures, sanitation, inventory and food cost control, maximizing profits, balance sheet and income statement interpretation, scheduling, customer complaint handling, interviewing and hiring, marketing and preventive maintenance. Trainees are responsible for homework assignments and exams. Training takes place in the Newport Beach classrooms and at the franchisee's restaurant.

Territory
Wienerschnitzel grants exclusive territories with a radius of a half-mile, or one-mile if the other unit is to be located on the same street.

Wing Zone

1720 Peachtree St., NW, # 940
Atlanta, GA 30309-2452
Tel: (877) 333-9464 (404) 875-5045
Fax: (404) 875-6631
E-Mail: stan@wingzone.com
Web Site: www.wingzone.com
Mr. Stan Friedman, Executive Vice President

Take-out/delivery of fresh, jumbo, cooked-to-order, Buffalo wings with 25 taste-tempting sauces. Grilled or fried chicken sandwiches and strips, 1/2 lb. burgers, salads, onion rings, fries, appetizers and desserts. A great opportunity in urban and suburban markets, near campuses, bases or hospitals and offices.

BACKGROUND: IFA MEMBER

Established: 1991; 1st Franchised: 1999	
Franchised Units:	34
Company-Owned Units	4
Total Units:	38
Dist.:	US-38; CAN-0; O'seas-0
North America:	14 States
Density:	8 in TX, 5 in FL, 4 in LA
Projected New Units (12 Months):	17
Qualifications:	5, 5, 5, 5, 1, 5
Registered:	FL,MD,MI,NY,OR,RI,VA, WA,DC
FINANCIAL/TERMS:	
Cash Investment:	$50-75K
Total Investment:	$140-200K
Minimum Net Worth:	$150K
Fees:	Franchise — $25K
	Royalty — 5%; Ad. — 0.5%
Earnings Claim Statement:	No
Term of Contract (Years):	10/10
Avg. # Of Employees:	5 FT, 10 PT
Passive Ownership:	Not Allowed

Encourage Conversions:	No	Co-Operative Advertising:	No
Area Develop. Agreements:	No	Franchisee Assoc./Member:	Yes/Yes
Sub-Franchising Contracts:	No	Size Of Corporate Staff:	7
Expand In Territory:	Yes	On-Going Support:	B,C,D,E,F,G,H,I
Space Needs:	1,200 SF; SF, SC	Training: 10 Days Atlanta, GA; 7 Days In-Store.	
SUPPORT & TRAINING PROVIDED:		**SPECIFIC EXPANSION PLANS:**	
Financial Assistance Provided:	Yes(I)	US:	SE, NE, MW, SW
Site Selection Assistance:	Yes	Canada:	Near Border
Lease Negotiation Assistance:	Yes	Overseas:	No

While the name may focus on wings, Wing Zone's menu offers much more. With offerings of sandwiches, salads, chicken fingers, mozzarella sticks, waffle fries, egg rolls and buffalo shrimp, in addition to jumbo buffalo wings doused with a selection of 25 sauces, such as mild, medium, hot, hotter, nuclear, garlic parmesan, honey mustard, sweet and sour, teriyaki, Cajun and lemon pepper, it's no wonder that Wing Zone has been a hit in both its original college markets and standard residential areas. Wing Zone's lunch, dinner and late night offerings are a welcome alternative to the pizza-saturated take out and delivery food market, and an ideal business in today's busy world, where the number of home-prepared meals continues to decline. The company also caters.

Wing Zone opened in a fraternity house kitchen in 1991. Although originally funded by a mere $500—spent on a telephone line and publicity—within three weeks, founders Matt Friedman and Adam Scott found themselves with a successful storefront operation. Six locations later, the fraternity brothers franchised and, after graduation, Wing Zone spread throughout Florida and Georgia. In 1999, Wing Zone's Atlanta headquarters opened and the WZ Franchise Corporation was founded.

Operating Units	9/30/2000	9/30/2001	9/30/2002
Franchised	8	16	27
% Change	--	100.0%	68.7%
Company-Owned	5	6	5
% Change	--	20.0%	-16.7%
Total	13	22	32
% Change	--	69.2%	45.4%
Franchised as % of Total	61.5%	72.7%	84.4%

Investment Required

The fee for a Wing Zone franchise is $25,000.

Wing Zone provides the following range of investments required to open your initial franchise. The range assumes that all items are paid for in cash. To the extent that you choose to finance any of these expense items, your front-end investment could be substantially reduced.

Item	Established Low Range	Established High Range
Franchise Fee	$25,000	$25,000
Computer/Equipment/Signs	$667,000	$79,000
Grand Opening	$5,000	$5,000
Insurance	$2,000	$2,500
Inventory	$3,500	$3,500
Marketing	$4,000	$4,000
Real Estate	$26,000	$73,500
Training Expenses	$500	$2,000
Additional Funds	$10,000	$10,000
Total Investment	$144,500	$204,500

On-Going Expenses

Wing Zone franchisees pay royalties equaling 5% and marketing development fees equaling 0.5% of gross revenue. Refresher training classes cost $400 a day.

What You Get—Training and Support

Wing Zone trains new franchisees, at its corporate training center and on-site, in food preparation, delivery procedures and point-of-sale computers. Franchisees also receive comprehensive operating manuals as an additional training resource.

Wing Zone's initial franchisee support focuses on territory demographics, site selection, lease negotiations, staffing, architectural and build out requirements, signage and menu creation. Additional services include assistance with national food procurement contracts, equipment packages, insurance, public relations and franchisee-specific advertising and marketing. As needed, Wing Zone will continue to provide consulting and marketing support after opening.

Territory
Wing Zone grants exclusive territories.

Woody's Bar-B-Q

WOODY'S

Bar B-Q®

4745 Sutton Park Ct., # 301
Jacksonville, FL 32224
Tel: (904) 992-0556 + 12
Fax: (904) 992-0551
E-Mail: admin@woodysbarbq.com
Web Site: www.woodysbarbq.com
Mr. Fred Rhoden, Dir. Franchising/Real Estate

WOODY'S BAR-B-Q is a full-service family restaurant, serving 'southern classic' ribs, chicken, pork and beef since 1981. WOODY'S support system includes full training, purchasing, site selection, marketing, opening team and field support. WOODY'S roadhouse décor is generally located in shopping center sites and is a great conversion at a low entry cost.

BACKGROUND:

Established: 1981; 1st Franchised: 1989	
Franchised Units:	40
Company-Owned Units	2
Total Units:	42
Dist.:	US-40; CAN-0; O'seas-0
North America:	3 States
Density:	37 in FL, 2 in GA, 1 in AL
Projected New Units (12 Months):	8
Qualifications:	4, 3, 4, 3, 1, 5

Registered:	FL

FINANCIAL/TERMS:

Cash Investment:	$100-175K
Total Investment:	$250-450K
Minimum Net Worth:	$250K
Fees:	Franchise — $35K
	Royalty — 4%; Ad. — 1%
Earnings Claim Statement:	No
Term of Contract (Years):	10/10
Avg. # Of Employees:	10 FT, 14 PT
Passive Ownership:	Allowed
Encourage Conversions:	Yes
Area Develop. Agreements:	Yes/Varies
Sub-Franchising Contracts:	No
Expand In Territory:	Yes
Space Needs:	4,000 SF; FS, SC

SUPPORT & TRAINING PROVIDED:

Financial Assistance Provided:	Yes(I)
Site Selection Assistance:	Yes
Lease Negotiation Assistance:	Yes
Co-Operative Advertising:	Yes
Franchisee Assoc./Member:	No
Size Of Corporate Staff:	9
On-Going Support:	B,C,d,E,G,H
Training:	6 Weeks Jacksonville, FL.

SPECIFIC EXPANSION PLANS:

US:	Southeast
Canada:	No
Overseas:	No

When Woody and Yolanda Mills first opened Woody's Bar-B-Q, they had no intention of becoming restaurant franchisors. They did, however, open several locations, all of which thrived and kept customers begging for more of their "classic southern" ribs, chicken, pork and beef. Woody and Yolanda finally surrendered in the late 1980s. Through its dedication, innovation—since its inception, Woody's has instituted a catering service and low calorie and special diet items—consistency, cordiality, aggressive marketing, and thorough franchisee support, Woody's Bar-B-Qs can be found all over the Southeast, from the mountains of North Carolina to the beaches of Southern Florida.

Operating Units	12/31/2000	12/31/2001	12/31/2002
Franchised	27	34	39
% Change	--	25.9%	14.7%
Company-Owned	3	2	2
% Change	--	-33.3%	0.0%
Total	30	36	41
% Change	--	20.0%	13.9%
Franchised as % of Total	90.0%	94.4%	95.1%

Investment Required

The fee for a Woody's Bar-B-Q franchise is $35,000.

Woody's Bar-B-Q provides the following range of investments required to open your initial franchise. The range assumes that all items are paid for in cash. To the extent that you choose to finance any of these expense items, your front-end investment could be substantially reduced.

Item	Established Low Range	Established High Range
Franchise Fee	$35,000	$35,000
Advertising	$3,000	$6,000
Equipment/Furniture/Signs	$165,000	$210,000
Insurance (for 6 months)	$2,000	$3,000
Inventory/Supplies	$4,000	$6,000
Real Estate	$172,000	$251,000
Training Expenses	$9,500	$11,000
Other Costs and Additional Funds	$29,000	$38,500
Total Investment	$419,500	$560,500

On-Going Expenses

Woody's Bar-B-Q franchisees pay royalties equaling 4%, advertising and promotion fees equaling 1% and national advertising fund fees equaling 1% of gross revenue. Franchisees are also required to spend at least 3% of gross revenue on local advertising.

What You Get—Training and Support

In training, Woody's instructs franchisees on the basics of restaurant operation and management, covering food purchasing and preparation, customer service, employee hiring, training and management.

To ensure that each restaurant projects the appropriate Woody's image and achieves its due success, franchisees also receive assistance with site selection and layout, equipment selection and design, decorating, grand opening plans, marketing, advertising and menus. If desired, Woody's provides an on-hand team to assist with start-up. Franchisees are also assisted by operating and marketing manuals, regular visits and phone-accessible advice from franchise service representatives.

Realizing the importance of franchise consistency for name identity and customer loyalty and referrals, Woody's also maintains established product vendors and proprietary recipes and procedures.

Territory

Woody's Bar-B-Q grants protected territories.

7-Eleven, Inc.

2711 N. Haskell Ave., P.O. Box 711
Dallas, TX 75204-2911
Tel: (800) 255-0711 (214) 828-7764
Fax: (214) 841-6776
E-Mail: jwebbj@7-11.com
Web Site: www.7-eleven.com
Ms. Joanne Webb-Joyce, National Franchise Mgr.

7-ELEVEN stores were born from the simple concept of giving people 'what they want, when and where they want it.' This idea gave rise to the entire convenience store industry. While this formula still works today, customers' needs are changing at an accelerating pace. We are meeting this challenge with an infrastructure of daily distribution of fresh perishables, regional production of fresh foods and pastries and an information system that greatly improves ordering and merchandising decisions.

BACKGROUND: IFA MEMBER
Established: 1927; 1st Franchised: 1964
Franchised Units: 19,992
Company-Owned Units: 2,656
Total Units: 22,648
Dist.: US-5,771; CAN-499; O'seas-16,378
  North America: 36 States, 5 Provinces
  Density: 1,183 in CA, 613 VA, 547 FL
Projected New Units (12 Months): 150

Qualifications: 4, 4, 3, 3, 5, 5
Registered: CA,IL,IN,MD,MI,NY,OR,RI,
VA,WA,WI

FINANCIAL/TERMS:
Cash Investment: $81K
Total Investment: $Varies
Minimum Net Worth: $12.5K
Fees: Franchise — $64K
Royalty — N/A; Ad. — N/A
Earnings Claim Statement: No
Term of Contract (Years): 10
Avg. # Of Employees: 4 FT, 4 PT
Passive Ownership: Not Allowed
Encourage Conversions: N/A
Area Develop. Agreements: No
Sub-Franchising Contracts: No
Expand In Territory: No
Space Needs: 2,400 SF; FS, SC

SUPPORT & TRAINING PROVIDED:
Financial Assistance Provided: Yes(D)
Site Selection Assistance: N/A
Lease Negotiation Assistance: N/A
Co-Operative Advertising: No
Franchisee Assoc./Member: Yes/Yes
Size Of Corporate Staff: 1,000
On-Going Support: A,B,C,D,E,F,G,H,I
Training: 6 Weeks at Various Training Stores
throughout US.

SPECIFIC EXPANSION PLANS:
US: NW,SW,MW,NE, Great Lakes
Canada: No
Overseas: No

159

In more than 75 years of business and nearly 40 years of franchising, 7-11, "the friendly little store that's just around the corner," has matured into the world's largest convenience store operator and franchisor. Most famous for its around-the-clock provisions of everything from soft drinks and salty snacks to wines and candy bars, 7-11s across the globe serve millions of customers each day. To maintain its reputation for fast, reliable and convenient service, each 7-11 strives to meet a variety of needs within each store and amongst all stores, ensuring that each neighborhood 7-11 stocks the perfect mix of products and services for its community. In addition, 7-11 takes the groundwork out of site selection; franchisees select their desired location from a list of stores available in the city of their choice.

When you decide to become a 7-11 franchisee, you join a company that has built a single concept into the largest convenience store system in the world. 7-11 knows how to succeed.

Operating Units	12/31/2000	12/31/2001	12/31/2002
Franchised	3,118	3,173	3,276
% Change	--	1.8%	3.2%
Company-Owned	2,392	2,441	2,276
% Change	--	2.0%	-6.7%
Total	5,510	5,614	5,552
% Change	--	1.9%	-1.1%
Franchised as % of Total	56.6%	56.5%	59.0%

Investment Required

The fee for a 7-11 franchise varies depending on the past total gross profit (excluding gasoline sales if applicable) experienced by each individual store during a 12-month cycle, i.e. franchisees pay more for more successful locations. The fee for a store with sales less than $200,000 in 12 months is fixed at $10,000. For stores with sales of $200,001 to $250,000, the fee equals 5% of the store's historical sales volume, generally between $10,000 and $12,500. Stores with sales between $250,001 and $300,000 come at a fee of 10% of past sales volume, or $25,000 to $30,000. Franchisees taking over a store with sales exceeding $300,000, pay a 15% franchise fee of $45,000 or more. Some fees run as high as

$231,000. Fees for brand new store locations are determined by the high gross profits of other locations. Financing is available.

7-11 provides the following range of investments required to open your initial franchise. The range assumes that all items are paid for in cash. To the extent that you choose to finance any of these expense items, your front-end investment could be substantially reduced.

Item	Established Low Range	Established High Range
Franchise Fee	$0	$194,800
Cash Register Fund	$250	$10,000
Inventory	$29,000	$86,600
Licenses/Permits	$100	$3,000
Supplies	$250	$2,000
Training Expenses	$0	$2,930
Additional Funds (for 3 months)	$133,860	$471,540
Total Investment (does not include equipment and real estate)	$163,460	$770,870

On-Going Expenses
7-11 franchisees pay on-going fees equaling 52% of gross revenues. The fee includes the 7-11 service mark and system, the facilities' lease and continuing services and pays for property, building and equipment rent; property taxes; heat, cooling, electricity and water; national advertising; bookkeeping, auditing and financial reports; merchandising, product selection and price recommendations; point-of-sale materials; general business advisory assistance and local and national franchisee advisory councils. Franchisees may also be responsible for varying advertising fees.

What You Get—Training and Support
A 7-11 franchise is essentially a turnkey business, including an internationally recognized service mark and image, modern equipment, training, field counseling, book-

keeping, auditing, financial reports, advertising and merchandising assistance, and a ready-to-operate store centered at a carefully selected location.

Territory

7-11 does not grant exclusive territories.

Aaron's Sales & Lease Ownership

Aaron's

309 E. Paces Ferry Rd., N. E.
Atlanta, GA 30305-2377
Tel: (800) 551-6015 (678) 402-3500
Fax: (678) 402-3540
E-Mail: kim.vanwagner@aaronrents.com
Web Site: www.aaronsfranchise.com
Mr. Kim VanWagner, Dir. Franchise Development

AARON'S SALES & LEASE OWNERSHIP is one of the fastest-growing retail companies in the U.S., specializing in furniture, electronics and appliances. AARON'S SALES & LEASE OWNERSHIP offers franchisees the expertise, advantages and support of a well-established company, plus the opportunity to realize a significant financial return in a booming market segment.

BACKGROUND: IFA MEMBER
Established: 1955; 1st Franchised: 1992

Franchised Units:	240
Company-Owned Units	407
Total Units:	647
Dist.:	US-647; CAN-0; O'seas-0
North America:	43 States
Density:	TX, FL, GA
Projected New Units (12 Months):	60
Qualifications:	5, 5, 1, 4, 5, 5
Registered:	CA,FL,HI,IL,IN,MI,NY,ND,

OR,RI,SD,VA,WA,WI

FINANCIAL/TERMS:

Cash Investment:	$250K
Total Investment:	$254-559K
Minimum Net Worth:	$450K
Fees:	Franchise — $35K
	Royalty — 6%; Ad. — 2.5%
Earnings Claim Statement:	Yes
Term of Contract (Years):	10/10
Avg. # Of Employees:	6 FT
Passive Ownership:	Allowed
Encourage Conversions:	N/A
Area Develop. Agreements:	Yes/Varies
Sub-Franchising Contracts:	No
Expand In Territory:	Yes
Space Needs:	8,000 SF; SC

SUPPORT & TRAINING PROVIDED:

Financial Assistance Provided:	Yes(I)
Site Selection Assistance:	Yes
Lease Negotiation Assistance:	Yes
Co-Operative Advertising:	Yes
Franchisee Assoc./Member:	Yes
Size Of Corporate Staff:	3,500
On-Going Support:	A,B,C,D,E,F,H,I
Training:	3 Weeks Corporate Headquarters; 2 Weeks Minimum On-Site; On-Going Varies.

SPECIFIC EXPANSION PLANS:

US:	All United States
Canada:	All Canada
Overseas:	Yes

Aaron's is a leasing industry leader that can fulfill any need—whether the customer wants to lease, buy, lease to buy or return an item. Unlike many lease to buy services, the ultimate price of the desired item varies little, if at all, from the original. Aaron's also offers many products at a price lower than other lessors, thanks to their own manufacturing and purchasing power.

Whether incomes are rising or dropping, there is always a demand for ways to obtain quality merchandise at low costs and through convenient means. Today, the need to lease big-ticket consumer goods is rising and the consumer durable goods market is valued at nearly five billion dollars. However, despite the potential, few people have yet to enter this market.

The recent bankruptcies of several major credit furniture retailers whose annual revenues totalled approximately $3.5 billion has created a $3.5 billion industry vacancy that Aaron's is poised to fill. In 2001, Aaron's converted more than 80 liquidated furniture units into Aaron's Sales and Lease Ownership stores. By doing so, Aaron's not only expanded its market share, but also leveraged the company's advertising, purchasing and leveraging capabilities.

Operating Units	12/31/1999	12/31/2000	12/31/2001
Franchised	155	193	209
% Change	--	24.5%	8.3%
Company-Owned	213	262	364
% Change	--	23.0%	38.9%
Total	368	455	573
% Change	--	23.6%	25.9%
Franchised as % of Total	42.1%	42.4%	36.5%

Investment Required
The fee for an Aaron's franchise is $35,000.

Aaron's provides the following range of investments required to open your initial franchise. The range assumes that all items are paid for in cash. To the extent that you choose to finance any of these expense items, your front-end investment could be substantially reduced.

Item	Established Low Range	Established High Range
Franchise Fee	$35,000	$35,000
Advertising	$2,000	$5,000
Delivery Vehicle	$1,100	$5,500
Equipment/Fixtures/Signs	$12,570	$17,680
Insurance	$6,500	$11,000
Inventory	$120,000	$160,000
Real Estate	$6,000	$141,000
Training Expenses	$500	$3,800
Additional Funds (for 6 to 15 months)	$70,000	$180,000
Total Investment	$253,670	$558,980

On-Going Expenses

Aaron's franchisees pay royalties equaling 6%, advertising production fees equaling 0.5%, or $3,750 per year, and regional media fees equaling the lesser of $15,000 per year or 2% of gross revenue. Additional fees payable by the franchisee include advertising agency funding and consulting services.

What You Get—Training and Support

Aaron's provides new franchisees with many goods and services, including: site selection, personnel selection, training, computer software systems, marketing and ad support, inventory financing, volume purchasing, network communications, on-going support, lease negotiation, design, business plan drafting assistance, pre-opening advertising, vendor relationships, initial inventory, operational forms, fleet rates and a decal kit for your company vehicles.

Aaron's University travels. Each week, a team of trainers arrives in a different city to conduct a series of in-depth, beginner and advanced training sessions. Franchise principals are required to attend one session a month. Before opening their Aaron's, they must have attended three. Each franchisee receives one week of on-site job training from a franchise field consultant.

Benefits of the Aaron's package include Aaron's Customer Tracking System, which records sales information and produces operational control reports, a technical support help line, inventory financing assistance and an advertising committee and an in-house advertising agency, both of which provide point-of-purchase, print, radio and television advertisements.

Territory
Aaron's grants exclusive territories.

The Athlete's Foot

1950 Vaughn Rd.
Kennesaw, GA 30144-7005
Tel: (800) 524-6444 (770) 514-4523
Fax: (770) 514-4843
E-Mail: pfranetovich@theathletesfoot.com
Web Site: www.theathletesfoot.com
Mr. Peter Franetovich, Director Franchise Sales

THE ATHLETE'S FOOT, with more than 700 stores in 45 countries, is the leading international franchisor of name-brand athletic footwear. As a franchisee, you will benefit from headquarters' support, including training, advertising, product selection, special vendor discount programs, continual footwear research and much more.

BACKGROUND:	IFA MEMBER
Established: 1971; 1st Franchised: 1972	
Franchised Units:	521
Company-Owned Units:	165
Total Units:	686
Dist.:	US-351; CAN-2; O'seas-333
North America:	47 States, 1 Province
Density:	NR
Projected New Units (12 Months):	120
Qualifications:	4, 5, 3, 3, 2, 5
Registered:	All States

FINANCIAL/TERMS:	
Cash Investment:	$75-125K
Total Investment:	$200-650K
Minimum Net Worth:	$300K
Fees:	Franchise — $35K Single St
	Royalty — 3.5 - 5%; Ad. — 0.6%
Earnings Claim Statement:	No
Term of Contract (Years):	10/5
Avg. # Of Employees:	2 FT, 6 PT
Passive Ownership:	Discouraged
Encourage Conversions:	Yes
Area Develop. Agreements:	Yes/10
Sub-Franchising Contracts:	Yes
Expand In Territory:	Yes
Space Needs:	1,200 SF; FS, SF, SC, RM

SUPPORT & TRAINING PROVIDED:	
Financial Assistance Provided:	Yes(I)
Site Selection Assistance:	Yes
Lease Negotiation Assistance:	Yes
Co-Operative Advertising:	No
Franchisee Assoc./Member:	Yes/Yes
Size Of Corporate Staff:	180
On-Going Support:	B,C,D,E,f,G,H,I
Training:	1 Week at Headquarters in Atlanta; 1 Wk. Prior to and during Opening on Location; On-Going.

SPECIFIC EXPANSION PLANS:	
US:	All United States
Canada:	All Canada
Overseas:	All Countries

If you want a franchise with a proven track record and years of experience, The Athlete's Foot may be the one for you. The world's first franchisor of athletic footwear, The Athlete's Foot's continued success owes much to the franchise's on-going shoe research and development and access to exclusive styles at global vendor discounts.

The "first athletic footwear specialty store of its kind," Robert and David Lando opened the first The Athlete's Foot in Pittsburgh, Pennsylvania in 1971. Oshkosh, Wisconsin was the site of the first Athlete's Foot franchise in America and, in 1978, Adelaide, Australia became the site of the first international location. The Athlete's Foot can now be found in more than 50 countries.

Operating Units	12/31/1999	12/31/2000	12/31/2001
Franchised	171	172	179
% Change	--	0.6%	4.1%
Company-Owned	264	269	182
% Change	--	1.9%	-32.3%
Total	435	441	361
% Change	--	1.4%	-18.1%
Franchised as % of Total	39.3%	39.0%	49.6%

Investment Required
The fee for an Athlete's Foot franchise is $35,000. The fee for additional stores is discounted according to your personal plans.

The Athlete's Foot provides the following range of investments required to open your initial franchise. The range assumes that all items are paid for in cash. To the extent that you choose to finance any of these expense items, your front-end investment could be substantially reduced. The following quotes apply to the opening of a traditional location.

Item	Established Low Range	Established High Range
Franchise Fee	$35,000	$35,000
Advertising Fee (for 3 months)	$500	$5,000
Equipment/Signs	$53,750	$124,300
Inventory	$50,000	$200,000
Real Estate	$22,850	$206,500
Training Expenses	$1,000	$2,000
Other Costs and Additional Funds (for 3 months)	$58,500	$112,800
Total Investment	$221,600	$685,600

On-Going Expenses

The Athlete's Foot franchisees pay royalties equaling 5% of their net sales. Six-tenths of one percent of these royalties constitute a Marketing Support Fund that provides select visual merchandising and local marketing materials to owners. Master franchisees pay royalties equaling 2.5 to 5% of net sales.

What You Get—Training and Support

The Athlete's Foot's initial training instructs new franchisees in the arts of inventory control, purchasing philosophy and retail sales.

Furthermore, all The Athlete's Foot associates must be certified "Fit Technicians." Administered at the store level, this certification ensures the associate's knowledge of shoe fit and The Athlete Foot's product line. Advanced training leads to the certification of a "Master Fit Technician."

In-store support includes visits from operations managers to evaluate and reinforce store efficiency and success, visual marketing support to maintain a fresh image, and research into and development of state-of-the-art technology and new store systems.

Territory

The Athlete's Foot grants exclusive territories.

Baby USA

857 N. Larch Ave.
Elmhurst, IL 60126
Tel: (630) 832-9880 + 27
Fax: (630) 832-0139
E-Mail: jimcourtney@usababy.com
Web Site: www.usababy.com
Mr. James L. Courtney, Sr. Mgr. Franchise Dev.

USA BABY is North America's leading specialty retailer of infant and juvenile furniture and accessories. Franchisees receive market evaluation, site selection, store design, financing, opening, advertising, merchandising and on-going operational support. Exclusive territories and substantial single, multi-unit and area development opportunities exist for candidates with a passion for serving customers, developing employee teams and participating in a proven retail environment.

BACKGROUND: IFA MEMBER
Established: 1975; 1st Franchised: 1986

Franchised Units:	68
Company-Owned Units	0
Total Units:	68
Dist.:	US-64; CAN-0; O'seas-4
North America:	22 States
Density:	8 in IL, 7 in NY, 6 in OH
Projected New Units (12 Months):	12
Qualifications:	4, 4, 1, 3, 2, 5

Registered: CA,FL,HI,IL,IN,MD,MI,MN, NY,VA,WA,WI

FINANCIAL/TERMS:

Cash Investment:	$120-170K
Total Investment:	$450-650K
Minimum Net Worth:	$180K
Fees:	Franchise — $42.5K
	Royalty — 3%; Ad. — 5%
Earnings Claim Statement:	Yes
Term of Contract (Years):	10/10
Avg. # Of Employees:	5 FT, 4 PT
Passive Ownership:	Not Allowed
Encourage Conversions:	Yes
Area Develop. Agreements:	Yes/Varies
Sub-Franchising Contracts:	No
Expand In Territory:	Yes
Space Needs:	12,000 SF; SC

SUPPORT & TRAINING PROVIDED:

Financial Assistance Provided:	Yes(I)
Site Selection Assistance:	Yes
Lease Negotiation Assistance:	Yes
Co-Operative Advertising:	N/A
Franchisee Assoc./Member:	Yes/Yes
Size Of Corporate Staff:	15
On-Going Support:	C,D,E,G,H,I
Training:	14 Days Corporate Office/Store; 4 Days Pre-Opening; 4 Days Opening; 4-5 Days Post-Opening.

SPECIFIC EXPANSION PLANS:

US:	All United States
Canada:	All Canada
Overseas:	No

Baby USA sells baby furniture by making their stores parent-friendly. Designer room vignettes attractively display merchandise and Baby USA's liberal product return and layaway, competitive pricing and product availability, helpful employee and safety information, baby shower registry, financing, delivery and setup make it easy for parents to purchase the items necessary to recreate these scenes in their own homes.

There are 10,000 babies born every day. Over eight million people buy baby furniture every year. Some figures even claim that new parents spend nearly $8,000 on supplies and comforts for their first child and the U.S. Bureau of Labor has estimated that child-related businesses will remain among the top 15 through the year 2005.

Alan Levine became a door-to-door salesman in 1975 and had a revelation—he was really good at selling baby furniture. He moved his family to Chicago where he opened his own baby furniture chain, which he franchised in 1986. Within a few years, the franchise outgrew Levine's original chain.

Operating Units	12/31/1999	12/31/2000	12/31/2001
Franchised	40	52	59
% Change	--	30.0%	13.5%
Company-Owned	8	0	0
% Change	--	-100.0%	0.0%
Total	48	52	59
% Change	--	8.3%	13.5%
Franchised as % of Total	83.3%	100.0%	100.0%

Investment Required

Baby USA offers three different franchise licenses. The start-up agreement includes one store with an exclusive territory. The conversion agreement for those who want to convert an existing store into a Baby USA franchise is similar to the start-up agreement, but includes the possibility for substantial credits. The area development license can be purchased in conjunction with the others and bestows licensees with a protected metropolitan area within which they can develop multiple Baby USA units. Depending on population, the fee for a Baby USA franchise ranges from $23,400 to $60,200. Financing is available.

Baby USA provides the following range of investments required to open your initial franchise. The range assumes that all items are paid for in cash. To the extent that you choose to finance any of these expense items, your front-end investment could be substantially reduced.

Item	Established Low Range	Established High Range
Franchise Fee	$23,400	$60,200
Computer/Equipment/ Fixtures/Signs	$73,000	$132,000
Insurance	$2,000	$4,000
Inventory/Supplies	$150,000	$250,000
Real Estate	$43,500	$100,500
Training	$2,000	$3,000
Additional Funds (for 3 months)	$50,000	$100,000
Total Investment	$343,900	$649,700

On-Going Expenses
Baby USA franchisees pay royalties equaling 1.5 to 3%, advertising and development fund fees equaling 0.5%, local advertising fees equaling 5% and a co-op advertising fee equaling no more than 5% of gross revenue.

What You Get—Training and Support
The Baby USA system provides franchisees with the following start-up services: site selection and lease negotiation, exterior and interior design, two weeks of training in advertising, merchandising, sales, freight, store layout, and employee recruiting and leading, lessons from the Chief Merchandising Officer about strategic planning and merchandise placement, targeted local advertising and media selections and on-site start-up assistance and employee training.

Continuing support exists through one-on-one franchise health checks; three annual franchisee meetings—one annual company event, one with the Juvenile Products Manufacturer's Association and one with vendors; buying power; exclusive products; superior advertising; proven growth and exit strategies.

Territory
Baby USA grants protected territories determined by population.

Batteries Plus

BatteriesPlus.

925 Walnut Ridge Dr., # 100
Hartland, WI 53029-9389
Tel: (262) 369-0690
Fax: (262) 369-0680
E-Mail: franchising@batteriesplus.com
Web Site: www.batteriesplus.com
Mr. Rod Tremelling, Franchise Sales

BATTERIES PLUS is America's Battery Experts (TM), providing 1,000's of batteries for 1,000's of items, serving both retail and commercial customers. The $19 billion battery market, growing 6.5% annually, is driven by technology and lifestyles. BATTERIES PLUS is a unique opportunity in this growth industry not yet saturated with competitors. Our turn-key program includes a unique store design, graphics, signage and product brands and proven operating methods.

BACKGROUND: IFA MEMBER
Established: 1988; 1st Franchised: 1992
Franchised Units: 255
Company-Owned Units: 16
Total Units: 271
Dist.: US-271; CAN-0; O'seas-0
  North America: 41 States
  Density: 16 in WI, 15 in MN, 14 in MI
Projected New Units (12 Months): 35

Qualifications: 5, 5, 2, 3, 2, 3
Registered: All Except HI

FINANCIAL/TERMS:
Cash Investment: $100K
Total Investment: $173-216K
Minimum Net Worth: $400K
Fees: Franchise — $25K
  Royalty — 4%; Ad. — 1%
Earnings Claim Statement: No
Term of Contract (Years): 10/10
Avg. # Of Employees: 3-4 FT
Passive Ownership: Not Allowed
Encourage Conversions: No
Area Develop. Agreements: Yes
Sub-Franchising Contracts: No
Expand In Territory: No
Space Needs: 1,800-2,000 SF; FS, SF, SC

SUPPORT & TRAINING PROVIDED:
Financial Assistance Provided: Yes(I)
Site Selection Assistance: Yes
Lease Negotiation Assistance: Yes
Co-Operative Advertising: No
Franchisee Assoc./Member: No
Size Of Corporate Staff: 65
On-Going Support: C,D,E,F,G,I
Training: 3 Weeks Corporate Training Center; 2
  Weeks On-Site Franchisee's Store.

SPECIFIC EXPANSION PLANS:
US: All United States
Canada: No
Overseas: No

It may be hard to believe that something as small as a battery could constitute an entire retail market, but don't be fooled by its size—its earning potential is huge. With three major market customer categories—retail, commercial and Tech Center—Batteries Plus franchisees never want for clients, and with products and services like common, specialty, made-to-order and rechargeable batteries, superior product knowledge, conditioning, maintenance and delivery, those clients always find what they need.

In Green Bay, Wisconsin in 1998, Batteries Plus became the first to corner the replacement battery market. The store is now the largest and most comprehensive retail and business-to-business chain serving battery users. However, despite its success, Batteries Plus still offers franchisees substantial opportunities in the unsaturated and ever-growing battery market. The company strives for "an integrated network of 400 successful Batteries Plus stores by 2007."

Operating Units	12/31/2000	12/31/2001	12/31/2002
Franchised	152	162	191
% Change	--	6.6%	17.9%
Company-Owned	21	23	15
% Change	--	9.5%	-34.8%
Total	173	185	206
% Change	--	6.9%	11.3%
Franchised as % of Total	87.9%	87.6%	92.7%

Investment Required

The fee for a Batteries Plus franchise in a market with a population between 30,000 and 50,000 people is $15,000. The fee for all other markets is $25,000.

Batteries Plus provides the following range of investments required to open your initial franchise. The range assumes that all items are paid for in cash. To the extent that you choose to finance any of these expense items, your front-end investment could be substantially reduced.

Item	Established Low Range	Established High Range
Franchise Fee	$15,000	$25,000
Advertising and Promotion	$12,000	$20,000
Equipment/Signs	$54,000	$64,000
Inventory/Supplies	$52,000	$60,000
Leasehold Improvements	$20,000	$60,000
Van or Panel Truck	$0	$35,000
Other Costs and Additional Funds (for 3 months)	$23,000	$64,000
Total Investment	$176,000	$328,000

On-Going Expenses
Batteries Plus franchisees pay royalty and service fees equaling 4%, national marketing and promotional fees equaling 4% and local and coop advertising expenses equaling 4% of gross revenue.

What You Get—Training and Support
Batteries Plus training and support starts and remains big. The three-week training program, conducted at the corporate training center, consists of classroom instruction and hands-on operations experience covering general business practices, store operations, financial management, products and technology, information technology systems, sales and marketing. Franchisees interested in opening a Tech Center, offering build-to-suit batteries and related services, also receive a week of certified training on Tech Center operation.

Meanwhile, Batteries Plus provides market analysis and site selection services, site and design-floor plans, a list of approved fixtures and other merchandising standards aimed to preserve the consistent look and feel of Batteries Plus franchises. Franchisees are also assisted with equipment and product ordering, merchandising tools, retail floor and storage organization and pre-opening preparations.

Batteries Plus support is far from over once official business begins. Throughout operation, franchisees benefit from competitive pricing and the highest-quality, most innovative products available, management software that shares, analyzes and updates data across the entire Batteries Plus network, professionally produced television and radio commercials, a graphics library, ad layout services and consultation, an intranet site, national and regional meetings, a franchisee advisory council, a national marketing fund council, web-based ordering and processing for commercial accounts and company stores that refine and test merchandising and store operation methods.

Territory
Batteries Plus grants protected territories of a three-mile radius.

Big O Tires

BIG O TIRES
12650 E. Briarwood Ave., # 2D
Englewood, CO 80112-6734
Tel: (800) 321-2446 (303) 728-5500
Fax: (303) 728-5700
E-Mail: dboeke@bigotires.com
Web Site: www.bigotires.com
Mr. David Boeke, Director of Franchising

BIG O TIRES is the fastest-growing retail tire and under-car service center franchisor in North America. We offer over 30 years' experience and proven success, site selection assistance, comprehensive training and on-going field support, protected territory, exclusive product lines, consistent product supply, unique marketing programs, contemporary building designs, effective advertising support, and proven business systems.

BACKGROUND: IFA MEMBER
Established: 1962; 1st Franchised: 1967
Franchised Units: 485
Company-Owned Units: 0
Total Units: 485
Dist.: US-484; CAN-1; O'seas-0
  North America: 20 States, 1 Province
  Density: 175 in CA, 56 in AZ, 44 CO
Projected New Units (12 Months): 40
Qualifications: 5, 5, 1, 2, 1, 5

Registered: NR

FINANCIAL/TERMS:
Cash Investment: $100K
Total Investment: $NR
Minimum Net Worth: $300K
Fees: Franchise — $25K
Royalty — 2%; Ad. — 4%
Earnings Claim Statement: No
Term of Contract (Years): 10
Avg. # Of Employees: NR
Passive Ownership: Discouraged
Encourage Conversions: Yes
Area Develop. Agreements: Yes/Varies
Sub-Franchising Contracts: Yes
Expand In Territory: Yes
Space Needs: NR SF; FS

SUPPORT & TRAINING PROVIDED:
Financial Assistance Provided: Yes(I)
Site Selection Assistance: Yes
Lease Negotiation Assistance: Yes
Co-Operative Advertising: Yes
Franchisee Assoc./Member: NR
Size Of Corporate Staff: 100
On-Going Support: A,B,C,d,E,F,G,h,I
Training: 5 Weeks Littleton, CO.

SPECIFIC EXPANSION PLANS:
US: All United States
Canada: BC and AB
Overseas: No

Big O Tires sells a complete line of Big O brand passenger, light truck and RV tires along with related automotive products, brake alignment and front-end repair services and a complete line of Monroe Auto Equipment shocks and struts. Big O prides itself on its commitment to customer service. Its motto is "A Reputation You Can Ride On." Big O Tires provides free tire mounting and balancing and free rotations and repairs for the life of the tire.

Big O Tires was established in 1962.

Operating Units	12/31/1999	12/31/2000	12/31/2001
Franchised	438	452	497
% Change	--	3.2%	10.0%
Company-Owned	16	10	7
% Change	--	-37.5%	-30.0%
Total	454	462	504
% Change	--	1.8%	9.1%
Franchised as % of Total	96.5%	97.8%	98.6%

Investment Required

The fee for a Big O Tires franchise is $25,000. Financing is available.

Big O Tires provides the following range of investments required to open your initial franchise. The range assumes that all items are paid for in cash. To the extent that you choose to finance any of these expense items, your front-end investment could be substantially reduced.

Item	Established Low Range	Established High Range
Franchise Fee	$0	$25,000
Advertising/Inventory	$55,000	$95,000
Equipment/Signs	$45,000	$172,500
Insurance	$12,000	$19,000
Real Estate	$4,000	$266,000
Training Expenses	$0	$3,600
Other Costs and Additional Funds (for 3 months)	$23,000	$85,000
Total Investment	$139,000	$666,100
Total Investment (when purchasing and building store site)	$570,000	$1,830,000

On-Going Expenses

Big O Tires franchisees pay royalties equaling 2%, local fund fees equaling 4%

and national advertising fees equaling 0.15% of gross revenue.

What You Get—Training and Support
At Big O, you get whatever you need.

For five weeks at the Big O University in Denver, Colorado, new franchisees learn about product lines, personnel management, accounting, advertising and business skills.

Professionals design all advertising and merchandising and provide franchisees with the materials and ideas necessary to maximize their store's appearance and sales.

On-going support includes visits from Area Managers, the latest advertising and marketing, sales and service training and personnel and accounting business assistance. Big O also provides product logistics support by maintaining product distribution to ensure that each location has what it needs, when it's needed and, yet, incurs minimum expenses. The Big O carrier system provides next day service for most products at ninety percent of all Big O stores.

Big O has a host of other resources at a franchisee's disposal, including: a national company website as well as a personalized store homepage for each location, video certification, express lube certification, three-day basic tire technician training, two-week store manager training, one-week multi-store training workshops, alignment technician training, brake technician training and self-training guides.

Big O bases their business upon four pillars of strength, encompassing exclusive product offerings in addition to Michelin, Goodyear and BFGoodrich so that customers find exactly what they're looking for, unique retail programs, the shared experience and success of many put to work for one and all, regional meetings and annual conventions and input in sales development and marketing.

Territory
Big O Tires grants exclusive territories. There can be no more than one unit for every 50,000 people.

Children's Orchard

CHILDREN'S ORCHARD

2100 S. Main St., # B
Ann Arbor, MI 48103-6432
Tel: (800) 999-5437 (734) 994-9199
Fax: (734) 994-9323
E-Mail: whamilton@childorch.com
Web Site: www.childrensorchard.com
Mr. Walter F. Hamilton, Jr., President/CEO

Upscale children's retail/resale stores, featuring clothing, toys, furniture, equipment, books and parenting products. We buy top-brand items from area families by appointment, and re-sell in lovely stores, along with top-quality new children's items from over 100 suppliers. These are large volume stores selling thousands of items per week.

BACKGROUND:

Established: 1980; 1st Franchised: 1985	
Franchised Units:	95
Company-Owned Units	1
Total Units:	96
Dist.:	US-96; CAN-0; O'seas-0
North America:	24 States
Density:	20 in CA, 15 in MA, 7 in MI
Projected New Units (12 Months):	9
Qualifications:	5, 3, 2, 4, 2, 5
Registered:	All Except HI,MN,ND,SD

FINANCIAL/TERMS:

Cash Investment:	$30-35K
Total Investment:	$69-145K
Minimum Net Worth:	$150K
Fees: Franchise —	$19.5K
Royalty — 5%;	Ad. — 1.0%
Earnings Claim Statement:	No
Term of Contract (Years):	10/5
Avg. # Of Employees:	1 FT, 3 PT
Passive Ownership:	Discouraged
Encourage Conversions:	Yes
Area Develop. Agreements:	Yes/Open
Sub-Franchising Contracts:	No
Expand In Territory:	No
Space Needs:	2,000 SF; SF, SC

SUPPORT & TRAINING PROVIDED:

Financial Assistance Provided:	Yes(I)
Site Selection Assistance:	Yes
Lease Negotiation Assistance:	Yes
Co-Operative Advertising:	Yes
Franchisee Assoc./Member:	Yes/Yes
Size Of Corporate Staff:	7
On-Going Support:	B,C,D,E,F,G,H,I
Training:	2 Weeks in Ann Arbor, MI; 2 Weeks in Lake Forest, CA.

SPECIFIC EXPANSION PLANS:

US:	All United States
Canada:	No
Overseas:	No

To ensure a full selection of all items, Children's Orchard sells used, and some new, children's apparel and products for the newborn through seven-year-old age group. There are nearly 40 million kids under the age of nine in the United States and by the age of two, their parents have already spent $5,300 to $6,300 on their living and clothing needs. Children's Orchard answers their need to make the most of their money by offering them the items they need at prices 50-80% lower than retail. In 2001, system-wide Children's Orchard sales amounted to $28.1 million.

Children's Orchard is also the public service sponsor for the Family Builder's

Adoption Network, the first national adoption agency network devoted to facilitating and promoting the adoption of abused, neglected and special needs children.

The first Children's Orchard opened in Newburyport, Massachusetts in 1980.

Operating Units	12/31/1999	12/31/2000	12/31/2001
Franchised	92	97	97
% Change	--	5.4%	0.0%
Company-Owned	2	2	1
% Change	--	0.0%	-50.0%
Total	94	99	98
% Change	--	5.3%	-1.0%
Franchised as % of Total	97.9%	98.0%	99.0%

Investment Required

The fee for a Children's Orchard franchise is $19,500. Additional units can be purchased at a reduced fee.

Children's Orchard provides the following range of investments required to open your initial franchise. The range assumes that all items are paid for in cash. To the extent that you choose to finance any of these expense items, your front-end investment could be substantially reduced.

Item	Established Low Range	Established High Range
Franchise Fee	$19,500	$19,500
Equipment/Fixtures/ Signs/Supplies	$13,500	$20,250
Inventory	$15,000	$30,000
Marketing	$4,000	$6,000
Real Estate	$15,250	$42,250
Training Expenses	$1,200	$1,950
Additional Funds (for 12 months)	$1,000	$25,000
Total Investment	$69,450	$144,950

On-Going Expenses

Children's Orchard franchisees pay royalties equaling 5% and advertising fees equaling 1% of gross revenue.

What You Get—Training and Support

Training starts with two weeks learning acquisition methods, computer systems, products, market surveying, vendor and seasonal arrangements, Children's Orchard's ten-point business system and more. Each franchisee then undergoes at least five more days of training on-site.

To achieve the "crisp, clean, high-style décor" of each Children's Orchard store, experts help design each store. Franchisees are also provided with professionally produced point-of-purchase displays, signage and merchandising programs.
In addition, Children's Orchard offers its franchisees: advertising materials, a local marketing manual, information about and assistance with legal and regulatory issues, staff training leadership and motivation guidance, comprehensive manuals, regional meetings, business executive management consulting, store and trend analysis and a private company internet site.

Territory

Children's Orchard grants exclusive territories.

EmbroidMe

1801 Australian Ave. S.
West Palm Beach, FL 33409
Tel: (800) 727-6720 (561) 478-4340
Fax: (561) 640-6062
E-Mail: csimnick@embroidme.com
Web Site: www.embroidme.com
Mr. Christopher Simnick, VP Franchise Development

The custom apparel and merchandise industry is exploding and embroidery is everywhere. To capitalize on this explosion, EMBROIDME has launched a revolution in the custom embroidery industry. At EMBROIDME, we are 'casually dressing America,' not only in our retail showrooms and through our corporate marketing program, but across the internet as well. We invite you to learn more about our unique, turn-key EMBROIDME concept, system and cutting edge franchise. Call 800/727-6720 or www.EmbroidMe.com.

BACKGROUND:		IFA MEMBER
Established: 2000; 1st Franchised: 2001		
Franchised Units:		71
Company-Owned Units		0
Total Units:		71
Dist.:		US-69; CAN-1; O'seas-1
North America:		21 States, 1 Province

Density:	11 in CA, 9 in IL, 8 in FL	Space Needs:	1,300-1,500 SF; SC
Projected New Units (12 Months):	85		
Qualifications:	3, 3, 2, 2, 1, 4	**SUPPORT & TRAINING PROVIDED:**	
Registered:	All States	Financial Assistance Provided:	Yes(I)
		Site Selection Assistance:	Yes
FINANCIAL/TERMS:		Lease Negotiation Assistance:	Yes
Cash Investment:	$35-40K	Co-Operative Advertising:	Yes
Total Investment:	$132-135K	Franchisee Assoc./Member:	No
Minimum Net Worth:	$40K	Size Of Corporate Staff:	30
Fees:	Franchise — $32.5K	On-Going Support:	C,D,E,F,G,H,I
	Royalty — 5%; Ad. — 1%	Training: 2 Weeks West Palm Beach, FL; 2 Weeks	
Earnings Claim Statement:	No	Franchisee's Location (1 Wk. Technical, 1 Wk.	
Term of Contract (Years):	35/35	Mktng.)	
Avg. # Of Employees:	3 FT		
Passive Ownership:	Discouraged	**SPECIFIC EXPANSION PLANS:**	
Encourage Conversions:	Yes	US:	All United States
Area Develop. Agreements:	Yes/Varies	Canada:	All Canada
Sub-Franchising Contracts:	No	Overseas:	
Expand In Territory:	Yes		All Countries

EmbroidMe supplies small and large businesses and organizations with customized apparel and promotional accessories. Clients include retail, service, professional, corporate and athletic groups, including restaurants, schools, clubs, churches, real estate offices, auto service stations, special events, hair salons, trade shows, car dealerships, bars and sport teams. Not only is the potential customer base for an EmbroidMe franchise substantial, but it is ever-increasing as the corporate casual revolution continues. Resources like EmbroidMe's products are perfect for promoting corporate identities despite more relaxed professional wardrobes. Each EmbroidMe's on-site production facilities make the process easy and fast, yet the turnkey operation provided in the Franchise Agreement requires no previous related experience. EmbroidMe showrooms, available both on-site and on the web, stock the highest quality apparel and accessory brands.

EmbroidMe's founder, Ray Titus, began his franchising affair in the printing and signs industry and has been franchising multiple concepts across the world for more than 30 years. The first full-service EmbroidMe opened in West Palm Beach, Florida in April of 2000. The store franchised five months later and went on to open 20 stores in 11 states in its first year as a franchise.

Operating Units	12/31/1999	12/31/2000	12/31/2001
Franchised	0	0	18
% Change	--	0.0%	N/A
Company-Owned	0	1	0
% Change	--	N/A	-100.0%
Total	0	1	18
% Change	--	N/A	1700.0%
Franchised as % of Total	N/A	0.0%	100.0%

Investment Required

The fee for an EmbroidMe franchise is $32,500. The fee for a second store is $19,500. Financing is available.

EmbroidMe provides the following range of investments required to open your initial franchise. The range assumes that all items are paid for in cash. To the extent that you choose to finance any of these expense items, your front-end investment could be substantially reduced.

Item	Established Low Range	Established High Range
Franchise Fee	$19,500	$32,500
Equipment Package	$104,221	$109,420
Insurance	$750	$2,000
Inventory	$1,600	$2,900
Licenses/Security and Utility Deposits	$500	$3,000
Training Expenses	$210	$490
Yellow Page Advertisement (for first 6 months)	$300	$1,500
Additional Funds (for 6 months)	$20,000	$55,000
Total Investment (leasing equipment)	$41,660	$136,281
Total Investment (purchasing equipment)	$188,741	$343,091

On-Going Expenses

EmbroidMe franchisees pay royalties equaling 5% and marketing fees equaling 1% of gross revenue.

What You Get—Training and Support

EmbroidMe franchisees benefit from on-site training as the company's field representatives will train all franchisees on their own equipment, which the field representatives set up for them in their own store. From the start, franchisees also receive one-on-one marketing assistance and printing and other promotional materials to build an immediate presence in the community. EmbroidMe also distributes regular newsletters, holds national conferences, and provides assistance on-site as well as through a toll-free phone number and company website.

Territory

EmbroidMe grants exclusive territories.

FASTFRAME USA

EXPERT PICTURE FRAMING

1200 Lawrence Dr., # 300
Newbury Park, CA 91320-1234
Tel: (888) TO-FRAME (805) 498-4463
Fax: (805) 498-8983
E-Mail: brenda@FASTFRAME.com
Web Site: www.FASTFRAME.com
Ms. Brenda Hales, Franchise Development

Over the past 14 years, FASTFRAME USA has captured its share of the market with its 200+ franchises within the US, along with affiliates in Brazil, Japan and Australia. FASTFRAME has emerged as a leader in the custom picture framing industry. FASTFRAME has built its foundation and reputation by providing high-quality craftsmanship, in a variety of products, at competitive prices, with immediate turn-around capabilities while guaranteeing customer satisfaction.

BACKGROUND: IFA MEMBER

Established: 1986; 1st Franchised: 1987

Franchised Units:	207
Company-Owned Units	7
Total Units:	214
Dist.:	US-207; CAN-7; O'seas-214
North America:	24 States
Density:	95 in CA, 21 in IL, 13 in TX
Projected New Units (12 Months):	60
Qualifications:	5, 4, 1, 1, 1, 5
Registered:	CA,FL,HI,IL,IN,MD,MI,MN, NY,OR,RI,VA,WA,WI,DC

FINANCIAL/TERMS:

Cash Investment:	$30-40K
Total Investment:	$93.5-131K
Minimum Net Worth:	$150K
Fees: Franchise —	$25K
Royalty — 7.5%;	Ad. — 3%
Earnings Claim Statement:	No
Term of Contract (Years):	10/10
Avg. # Of Employees:	1 FT, 2 PT
Passive Ownership:	Allowed
Encourage Conversions:	Yes

Area Develop. Agreements:	Yes/5	Franchisee Assoc./Member:	Yes/Yes
Sub-Franchising Contracts:	N/A	Size Of Corporate Staff:	18
Expand In Territory:	Yes	On-Going Support:	A,B,C,D,E,G,H,I
Space Needs:	1,200-1,500 SF; FS, SF, SC	Training:	2 Weeks at Corporate Headquarters; 1 Week at On Site Store.

SUPPORT & TRAINING PROVIDED:

Financial Assistance Provided:	Yes(I)	**SPECIFIC EXPANSION PLANS:**	
Site Selection Assistance:	Yes	US:	All United States
Lease Negotiation Assistance:	Yes	Canada:	No
Co-Operative Advertising:	Yes	Overseas:	No

The first FASTFRAME was opened in 1986, blending modern technology with the custom trade of picture framing and outpacing competitors in the six billion dollar framing market. FASTFRAMEs require minimal staffing, are easy to administer and operate during typical office business hours.

FASTFRAME offers many program options. The standard franchise program allows franchisees to open up to three FASTFRAMEs. The satellite program licenses storeroom-only locations that use other production facilities. The managing partner program allows franchisees to own additional locations without direct involvement in the daily operation of each unit. These licensees are partnered with existing owners and are often those with talent and drive, but not the required capital. The conversion program converts an existing framing business into one of the FASTFRAME fleet. The regional development program bestows upon the licensee the responsibility of recruiting new franchisees for a specified territory. This developer then acts as a liaison between the region's units and the corporate FASTFRAME and benefits from the investments and earnings of these new locations.

Operating Units	9/30/1999	9/30/2000	9/30/2001
Franchised	188	198	205
% Change	--	5.3%	3.5%
Company-Owned	5	6	5
% Change	--	20.0%	-16.7%
Total	193	204	210
% Change	--	5.7%	2.9%
Franchised as % of Total	97.4%	97.1%	97.6%

Investment Required

The typical fee for a FASTFRAME franchise is $25,000. There is no fee for a satellite store. FASTFRAME does provide financial advice.

FASTFRAME provides the following range of investments required to open your initial franchise. The range assumes that all items are paid for in cash. To the extent that you choose to finance any of these expense items, your front-end investment could be substantially reduced. The following figures apply to the opening of a full service FASTFRAME outlet.

Item	Established Low Range	Established High Range
Franchise Fee or Administrative Fee	$2,500	$25,000
Computer System, Equipment	$18,500	$19,500
Displays/Fixtures/ Leasehold Improvements/ Signs/Store Opening Costs	$8,000	$34,000
Inventory/Supplies	$8,000	$9,000
Marketing	$5,000	$9,000
Opening Fee	$5,000	$8,500
Training Expenses	$1,000	$2,000
Other Costs and Additional Funds (for 3 months)	$15,500	$24,000
Total Investment	$63,500	$131,000

On-Going Expenses

FASTFRAME franchisees pay royalties equaling 7.5%, marketing services fees equaling 3% and co-op campaign services fees equaling 2% of gross revenue.

What You Get—Training and Support

Franchisees receive complete turn-key opening assistance, meaning that all decisions will be made by FASTFRAME experts, but with your consent; the presence of a training department member for the first week of operation; in-house marketing; purchasing power; advertising materials and programs and online web offers to entice customers to your location.

During construction, FASTFRAME franchisees attend an 11-day training session where they learn framing operations, business management and marketing, so they can get a fresh start and can open shop immediately upon construction completion.

FASTFRAME strives for constructive communication to improve and sustain their franchises. Support includes a company intranet site with access to the interactive Franchise Support System, national and regional conferences, local franchisee in-store meetings, scheduled visits from support staff and FAST-FRAME's franchise advisory council.

Territory
FASTFRAME grants exclusive territories.

General
Nutrition Centers

300 Sixth Ave.
Pittsburgh, PA 15222-2514
Tel: (800) 766-7099 (412) 402-7121
Fax: (412) 402-7105
E-Mail: jsorrenti@gncfranchising.com
Web Site: www.gncfranchising.com
Mr. J. J. Sorrenti, SVP General Manager

GNC is the leading national specialty retailer of vitamins, minerals, herbs and sports nutrition supplements and is uniquely positioned to capitalize on the accelerating self-care trend. As the leading provider of products and information for personal health enhancement, the company holds the largest specialty-retail share of the nutritional supplement market. GNC was ranked America's #1 retail franchise for 14 consecutive years.

BACKGROUND:

Established: 1935; 1st Franchised: 1988	
Franchised Units:	1,941
Company-Owned Units	2,851
Total Units:	4,792
Dist.:	US-4,075; CAN-145; O'seas-572
North America:	50 States, 9 Provinces
Density:	409 in CA,376 in FL,309 TX
Projected New Units (12 Months):	NR
Qualifications:	5, 5, 1, 1, 1, 4
Registered:	All States

FINANCIAL/TERMS:

Cash Investment:	$65K
Total Investment:	$132.7-182K
Minimum Net Worth:	$100K
Fees:	Franchise — $40K
	Royalty — 6%; Ad. — 3%
Earnings Claim Statement:	Yes
Term of Contract (Years):	10/5
Avg. # Of Employees:	1 FT, 3-5 PT
Passive Ownership:	Not Allowed
Encourage Conversions:	NR
Area Develop. Agreements:	Yes/Varies

Sub-Franchising Contracts:	No	Size Of Corporate Staff:	600
Expand In Territory:	Yes	On-Going Support:	A,b,D,E,F,G,H,L
Space Needs: 1,402 (avg.) SF; SF, SC, RM		Training: 1 Wk. On-Site in Local Corporate Store; 1 Wk. in Pittsburgh, PA; 1 Wk. Opening Assistance.	
SUPPORT & TRAINING PROVIDED:			
Financial Assistance Provided:	Yes(D)		
Site Selection Assistance:	Yes	**SPECIFIC EXPANSION PLANS:**	
Lease Negotiation Assistance:	Yes	US:	All United States
Co-Operative Advertising:	No	Canada:	All Canada
Franchisee Assoc./Member:	Yes/Yes	Overseas:	All Countries

General Nutrition Centers, a specialty retailer of high-quality vitamin and mineral supplements, sports nutrition, herbal products and personal care, was the health industry's first business dedicated solely to nutritional health. All GNC multivitamins and minerals are thoroughly evaluated and submitted to 150 quality checks that even the FDA does not require.

The retail supplement market garners $17.4 billion in revenue a year and the rising costs of medical care and an emphasis on prevention can only contribute to this figure. What's more, three out of every four vitamin consumers are over the age of 35. By 2005, this demographic will number 150 million.

The first GNC opened in 1935. Over a nearly seventy-year career, GNC has grown to 4,800 locations in 32 countries and all 50 states. They have become well-known for quality nutritional supplements and other health products. They command the majority of the nutritional health market.

Operating Units	12/31/1999	12/31/2000	12/31/2001
Franchised	1326	1405	1354
% Change	--	5.9%	-3.6%
Company-Owned	2708	2736	2845
% Change	--	1.0%	4.0%
Total	4034	4141	4199
% Change	--	2.6%	1.4%
Franchised as % of Total	32.9%	33.9%	32.2%

Investment Required

The fee for a GNC franchise is $40,000. Financing, both direct and indirect, is available. Additional units are available at a fee of $30,000.

General Nutrition Centers provides the following range of investments required to open your initial franchise. The range assumes that all items are paid for in cash. To the extent that you choose to finance any of these expense items, your front-end investment could be substantially reduced. The following quotes apply to the opening of a new franchise.

Item	Established Low Range	Established High Range
Franchise Fee	$20,000	$40,000
Construction Costs/Site Selection Assistance	$19,500	$64,000
Equipment/Fixtures/Signs	$36,431	$46,831
Insurance	$1,000	$2,000
Inventory	$46,500	$46,500
Promotion	$1,250	$1,250
Training	$1,500	$3,000
Other Costs and Additional Funds	$4,000	$8,000
Total Investment	$130,181	$211,581

On-Going Expenses

GNC franchisees pay royalties equaling 6% of gross revenue.

What You Get—Training and Support

GNC support comes in three forms and phases.

The first is start-up assistance. This covers financing, real estate, construction and the GNC point of sale cash register system.

The second is opening support, which includes your grand opening, in-store and classroom training and field support.

The third and most elaborate is on-going support. On-going support comes from corporate and division business specialists, toll-free phone lines and in-store field consultations. GNC also provides updated manuals, sales and customer service training and interactive in-store training. Communications with the franchise system are kept up-to-date through franchiser meetings, the national advisory council, conventions, publications and the intranet. Franchisees also have access to discounts on insurance and supplies, multi-million dollar national advertising and promotion materials and two of the largest and most sophisticated manufacturing facilities of its kind.

Territory
GNC grants protected territories, but for a specified, and variable, length of time. The size of each territory varies depending on each franchise's specific location.

Merkinstock

P.O. Box 12488
Oakland, CA 94604
Tel: (510) 839-5462
Fax: (510) 839-2104
E-Mail: sourcebook@earthlink.net
Web Site: www.merkinstock.com
Ms. Sidney E. Anning, President

World's largest selection of merkins — natural and synthetic. Over 35 models, 15 colors. Custom fitting and dyeing in discrete environment. Guaranteed satisfaction. 15 stores in Far East and Europe prove concept is ripe for aggressive U.S. expansion. market. Looking for entrepreneurs who want to succeed.

BACKGROUND:

Established: 1992; 1st Franchised: 1995	
Franchised Units:	21
Company-Owned Units	6

Total Units:	27
Dist.:	US-3; CAN-2; O'seas-15
North America:	2 States, 1 Province
Density:	2 in CA, 1 in NV
Projected New Units (12 Months):	10
Qualifications:	3, 5, 4, 2, 3, 5
Registered:	CA

FINANCIAL/TERMS:

Cash Investment:	$90K
Total Investment:	$150K
Minimum Net Worth:	$250K
Fees:	Franchise — $20K
	Royalty — 6%; Ad. — 2%
Earnings Claim Statement:	Yes
Term of Contract (Years):	15/15
Avg. # Of Employees:	2 FT
Passive Ownership:	Not Allowed
Encourage Conversions:	Yes
Area Develop. Agreements:	Yes/15
Sub-Franchising Contracts:	Yes
Expand In Territory:	No
Space Needs:	1,200 SF; FS, SC, RM

SUPPORT & TRAINING PROVIDED:

Financial Assistance Provided:	Yes(D)
Site Selection Assistance:	Yes
Lease Negotiation Assistance:	Yes

Co-Operative Advertising:	Yes	SPECIFIC EXPANSION PLANS:	
Franchisee Assoc./Member:	No	US:	All United States
Size Of Corporate Staff:	4	Canada:	All Canada
On-Going Support:	a,B,C,D,E,f,G,I	Overseas:	All Countries
Training: 3 Weeks Headquarters; 2 Weeks On-Site; On-Going.			

Merkinstock has brought back the popular usage of merkins as a decorative form of self-expression and personality, rather than simply a physical necessity. Merkinstock currently possesses the largest variety of colors, materials and designs in the industry with styles to suit any personality and need.

The Merkinstock brand is widely associated with personal creativity and customization, allowing customers to pick and choose their own combinations of available merkin models. The company invests tremendously in customer service, providing sales representatives sensitive and discrete enough to make any customer feel comfortable.

In 1992, founders Sidney and Bob Anning invented a line of merkins that added more spunk and inspiration to the drab, conservative merkins traditionally offered. The Annings began franchising in 1995, and have led a merkin revolution in the process. Market response to this new retail segment has been astounding in Europe and Asia and American markets show promising increases in the number of operating units and revenue gross. Now, with the popularity of body piercings and tattoos waning, merkins are perched to become the next big thing in body decoration and personalization the world over.

Operating Units	12/31/2000	12/31/2001	12/31/2002
Franchised	67	75	93
% Change	--	11.9%	24.0%
Company-Owned	0	0	0
% Change	--	N/A	N/A
Total	67	75	93
% Change	--	11.9%	24.0%
Franchised as % of Total	100.0%	100.0%	100.0%

Investment Required

The fee for a Merkinstock franchise is $20,000.

Merkinstock provides the following range of investments required to open your initial franchise. The range assumes that all items are paid for in cash. To the extent that you choose to finance any of these expense items, your front-end investment could be substantially reduced.

Item	Established Low Range	Established High Range
Franchise Fee	$20,000	$20,000
Advertising and Promotion	$2,500	$5,000
Computer Installation and Training	$6,000	$8,000
Insurance	$3,500	$5,000
Inventory	$2,000	$3,600
Real Estate	$5,000	$15,000
Training Expenses	$0	$5,000
Additional Funds (for 3 months)	$37,500	$55,000
Total Investment	$76,500	$116,600

On-Going Expenses

Merkinstock franchisees pay royalties equaling 6% and advertising contributions equaling 2.9% of gross revenue.

What You Get—Training and Support

As Merkinstock values its customer service orientation, the company provides a comprehensive training program designed to familiarize you with basic business management, merkin history and the Merkinstock product line. The program is free, but all travel, lodging and meal expenses must be paid by the franchisee. The program lasts approximately three weeks. Successful completion of the program is based upon the customization of your own merkin and your ability to properly attach, adjust and clean the merkin in the presence of a trained Merkinstock employee.

Merkinstock's support system is both strong and loving. Each year, a large convention brings franchisees together in a weekend bonding event. During the convention, franchisees share their opinions on the latest merkin models as well as tips on how to better serve their customers' needs. Merkinstock also encourages franchisees to submit their ideas for new models. In addition to the annual convention, franchisees receive support and assistance from their assigned Merkinstock experts, who will periodically visit their stores to evaluate the business's performance and product quality.

The company relies primarily upon foot traffic, word-of-mouth recommendations and gossip to gain exposure and promotion. While relaxing social rules may accommodate the emergence of merkins into the conventional marketplace, Merkinstock's marketing department believes that national advertising campaigns in major media forms would upset the delicate balance between the need for and acceptance of merkins as a major retail item and the private nature of their use. Accordingly, advertising funds are focused solely on the printing of catalogues, accompanying instructions and point-of-sale and store design displays.

Territory
Merkinstock grants exclusive territories.

Merle Norman Cosmetics

and 'try before you buy' complete customer satisfaction methods of selling.

9130 Bellanca Ave.
Los Angeles, CA 90045-4710
Tel: (800) 421-6648 (310) 641-3000
Fax: (310) 337-2370
E-Mail: claporta@merlenorman.com
Web Site: www.merlenorman.com
Ms. Carol LaPorta, VP Studio Development

MERLE NORMAN COSMETICS is a specialty retail store, selling scientifically-developed, state-of-the-art cosmetic products, using the 'free make over'

BACKGROUND:	IFA MEMBER
Established: 1931; 1st Franchised: 1989	
Franchised Units:	1,899
Company-Owned Units	9
Total Units:	1,908
Dist.:	US-1,802; CAN-90; O'seas-16
North America:	50 States, 1 Province
Density:	256 in TX, 100 in GA, 95 AL
Projected New Units (12 Months):	88
Qualifications:	3, 4, 3, 3, 4, 4
	Registered: All States

191

FINANCIAL/TERMS:		SUPPORT & TRAINING PROVIDED:	
Cash Investment:	$NR		
Total Investment:	$NR	Financial Assistance Provided:	Yes(I)
Minimum Net Worth:	$NR	Site Selection Assistance:	Yes
Fees:	Franchise — $0	Lease Negotiation Assistance:	Yes
Royalty — 0%; Ad. — 0%		Co-Operative Advertising:	Yes
Earnings Claim Statement:	Yes	Franchisee Assoc./Member:	No
Term of Contract (Years):	Unlimited	Size Of Corporate Staff:	630
Avg. # Of Employees:	2 FT, 2-5 PT	On-Going Support:	a,B,C,D,E,F,G,H,I
Passive Ownership:	Discouraged	Training:	2 Weeks Los Angeles, CA.
Encourage Conversions:	No		
Area Develop. Agreements:	No	SPECIFIC EXPANSION PLANS:	
Sub-Franchising Contracts:	No	US:	All United States
Expand In Territory:	Yes	Canada:	All Canada
Space Needs: 450-800 SF; SC, RM		Overseas:	No

The new Merle Norman offers customers make-up and skin care products in a new environment with dramatic lighting, easy-to-use displays and an informal, yet sophisticated setting. Makeovers are performed at the consultation tables and sampling counters offer customers the latest colors to test.

The first Merle Norman, selling products developed by Merle Norman and her nephew J.B. Nethercutt, opened in Santa Monica in 1931. This was long before the working woman revolution, but Merle Norman forged ahead, encouraging other women to open one of her "try before you buy" studios. Since 1931, Merle Norman has marketed an exclusive and complete line of cosmetics in more than 2,000 studios in the United States and Canada. Its legendary before-and-after makeovers and "try before you buy" policy have built up high brand loyalty, with most Merle Norman customers averaging 14 years of devotion to the company's products.

Operating Units	12/31/1999	12/31/2000	12/31/2001
Franchised	1852	1816	1795
% Change	--	-1.9%	-1.1%
Company-Owned	4	11	11
% Change	--	175.0%	0.0%
Total	1856	1827	1806
% Change	--	-1.6%	-1.1%
Franchised as % of Total	99.8%	99.4%	99.4%

Investment Required
There is no fee for a Merle Norman franchise, but all franchisees must purchase the initial Merle Norman package of cosmetics and supplies.

Merle Norman provides the following range of investments required to open your initial franchise. The range assumes that all items are paid for in cash. To the extent that you choose to finance any of these expense items, your front-end investment could be substantially reduced.

Item	Established Low Range	Established High Range
Initial Package of Inventory and Supplies	$12,000	$21,500
Computer Equipment	$1,800	$4,900
Construction/Fixtures/ Signs	$21,836	$94,369
Training Expenses	$1,500	$3,000
Advertising, Deposits, Insurance and Additional Funds (for 3 months)	$12,800	$29,300
Total Investment (does not include real estate costs)	$49,936	$153,069

On-Going Expenses
Merle Norman franchisees pay a variable amount to the advertising co-op and $300 a year for annual software upgrades and support.

What You Get—Training and Support
Merle Norman franchisees receive the support of the Merle Norman system in many ways. Initially, franchisees receive site selection, lease review and studio design assistance, training, grand opening assistance from a regional sales consultant and grand opening promotion materials, such as signage, posters, direct mail and ad slicks.

Training consists of two weeks at the Los Angeles home office learning everything from makeup artistry to business management.

Other areas of support include marketing, training and management. Marketing support comes in the form of professional television and radio spots, ad slicks, direct mail and product brochures. Through co-op programs, Merle Norman reimburses 60% of approved media costs. Training support features field training on staffing, recruiting, selling skills and make-up artistry, one-week seminars and annual conventions. Management support comes from regional sales consultants, a personal home office regional specialist (a direct contact for daily help) and point-of-sale software to track customer data, sales and inventory.

Territory
Merle Norman does not grant exclusive territories.

Metal Supermarkets International

Metal Supermarkets
The Convenience Stores of the Metal Industry™

METAL SUPERMARKETS INTERNATIONAL
170 Wilkinson Rd., # 17/18
Brampton, ON L6T 4Z5 CANADA
Tel: (905) 459-0466
Fax: (905) 459-3690
E-Mail: aarminen@metalsupermarkets.com
Web Site: www.metalsupermarkets.com
Mr. Andrew Arminin, VP Franchise Division

METAL SUPERMARKETS is a highly specialized supplier of small quantities of virtually all types and forms of metal. Customers are maintenance departments of all types of industries. As 'convenience stores of the metal industry,' we have no minimum order We offer fast delivery, custom cutting and can source rare metals.

BACKGROUND:	IFA MEMBER
Established: 1985; 1st Franchised: 1987	
Franchised Units:	65
Company-Owned Units	22

Total Units:	87
Dist.:	US-44; CAN-30; O'seas-13
North America:	24 States, 7 Provinces
Density:	13 in ON, 3 in FL, 3 in PA
Projected New Units (12 Months):	12
Qualifications:	5, 3, 3, 3, 3, 5
Registered:	All States

FINANCIAL/TERMS:	
Cash Investment:	$100K
Total Investment:	$230-270K
Minimum Net Worth:	$300K
Fees:	Franchise — $39.5
	Royalty — 6%; Ad. — 0%
Earnings Claim Statement:	No
Term of Contract (Years):	10/10
Avg. # Of Employees:	3 FT, 1 PT
Passive Ownership:	Discouraged
Encourage Conversions:	Yes
Area Develop. Agreements:	Yes/10
Sub-Franchising Contracts:	No
Expand In Territory:	Yes
Space Needs:	4,000 SF; Industrial Park

SUPPORT & TRAINING PROVIDED:	
Financial Assistance Provided:	No

Site Selection Assistance:	Yes	Training:	1 Week in Toronto, ON; 2 Weeks Corporate Store; 2 Weeks Own Store.
Lease Negotiation Assistance:	Yes		
Co-Operative Advertising:	No	**SPECIFIC EXPANSION PLANS:**	
Franchisee Assoc./Member:	Yes/Yes	US:	All United States
Size Of Corporate Staff:	15	Canada:	PQ
On-Going Support:	C,D,E,F,G,h,I	Overseas:	Europe

Metal Supermarkets is a highly specialized metal distributor that offers fast access to small amounts of all types and forms of metal, whether common, rare or exotic. The primary customers of a Metal Supermarket are manufacturing maintenance departments, machine shops, tool and die shops, recreational facilities, hospitals, universities and government departments, but the draw of homeowners, artists and hobbyists is increasing. The average order placed at Metal Supermarkets amounts to $150 and franchisees enjoy retail margins with low capital and overheads.

Recognizing a market niche by realizing that companies needing small quantities of metal were not well-served by large metal distributors, the first Metal Supermarket was built in Mississauga, a suburb of Toronto, Canada, in 1985. The store depended upon the fact that customers would pay premium prices for small quantities of custom-cut metal, quickly delivered and not subject to minimum orders. The store's foundation proved sound and a second store opened in Toronto. In 1987, Metal Supermarkets franchised. The store can now be found in Canada, the United States, the United Kingdom and Austria.

Operating Units	1999	2000	2001
Franchised	20	23	28
% Change	--	15.0%	21.7%
Company-Owned	2	7	9
% Change	--	250.0%	28.6%
Total	22	30	37
% Change	--	36.4%	23.3%
Franchised as % of Total	90.9%	76.7%	75.7%

Investment Required
The fee for a Metal Supermarkets franchise is $39,500.

Metal Supermarkets provides the following range of investments required to open your initial franchise. The range assumes that all items are paid for in cash. To the extent that you choose to finance any of these expense items, your front-end investment could be substantially reduced.

Item	Established Low Range	Established High Range
Franchise Fee	$39,500	$39,500
Advertising	$3,000	$6,000
Equipment/Fixtures/Signs	$47,000	$65,000
Insurance	$2,000	$3,000
Inventory	$40,000	$50,000
Real Estate	$16,000	$28,000
Training Expenses	$5,000	$10,000
Additional Funds (for 3 months)	$40,000	$70,000
Total Investment (does not include real estate and related costs)	$192,500	$271,500

On-Going Expenses

Metal Supermarkets franchisees pay royalties equaling 6% of gross revenue. There are currently no marketing or advertising fees.

What You Get—Training and Support

Training takes place in Toronto, Canada and lasts three weeks.

Metal Supermarkets also provide franchisees with: support group services to organize setup and opening, a database of potential customers within their territory, an initial fax and mailer program to build a customer base, two weeks of opening assistance from an on-location field supervisor, a comprehensive store start-up manual, an operations manual, site selection, lease negotiations, store layout, software with one year of maintenance, a supplier source manual, initial sales and marketing materials, preferred pricing on store equipment and a salary subsidy program for franchisees that choose to hire an outside sales representative.

Territory
Metal Supermarkets grants protected territories.

More Space Place

We Make Room For Living®

12555 Enterprise Blvd., # 101
Largo, FL 33773
Tel: (888) 731-3051 (727) 539-1611
Fax: (727) 524-6382
E-Mail: mjuarez@morespaceplace.com
Web Site: www.morespaceplace.com
Mr. Marty Juarez, Vice President Franchising

MORE SPACE PLACE is the largest Murphy bed and closet systems retailer in America. We create beautifully-designed, professionally-installed, space saving solutions. At MORE SPACE PLACE, amazing innovations can convert bedrooms into offices or dens, and then back into a bedroom again when you need it. We conquer clutter in closets, entertainment centers, utility rooms and garages, and turn spare bedrooms into multi-purpose rooms.

BACKGROUND: IFA MEMBER
Established: 1989; 1st Franchised: 1993

Franchised Units:	22
Company-Owned Units	3
Total Units:	25
Dist.:	US-25; CAN-0; O'seas-0
North America:	3 States
Density:	23 in FL, 1 in MI, 1 in NC
Projected New Units (12 Months):	12
Qualifications:	4, 4, 1, 3, 2, 5

Registered:	FL,MI
FINANCIAL/TERMS:	
Cash Investment:	$30-166.8K
Total Investment:	$89-166.8KK
Minimum Net Worth:	$250K
Fees:	Franchise — $22.5K
	Royalty — 4.5%; Ad. — 2.5%
Earnings Claim Statement:	No
Term of Contract (Years):	10/10
Avg. # Of Employees:	3 FT, 1 PT
Passive Ownership:	Allowed
Encourage Conversions:	Yes
Area Develop. Agreements:	Yes/10
Sub-Franchising Contracts:	No
Expand In Territory:	Yes
Space Needs:	1,400-2,400 SF; FS, SF, SC
SUPPORT & TRAINING PROVIDED:	
Financial Assistance Provided:	Yes(I)
Site Selection Assistance:	Yes
Lease Negotiation Assistance:	Yes
Co-Operative Advertising:	Yes
Franchisee Assoc./Member:	Yes
Size Of Corporate Staff:	30
On-Going Support:	B,C,D,E,F,G,H,I
Training:	1 Week Headquarters Largo, FL; 4 Days On-Site.
SPECIFIC EXPANSION PLANS:	
US:	All United States
Canada:	No
Overseas:	No

The More Space Place markets "better ways to utilize space you have." The space-maximizing movement may have begun with closets, but the market has since expanded to cater to home-based businesses, empty nesters who want to reclaim space while accommodating guests, the hospitality industry, interior designers, house remodelers, downsizers and many more. The More Space Place sells multiple purpose living spaces, with an emphasis on Murphy and

Panel Beds, home office designs, custom closets, entertainment centers, utility rooms and garages.

Operating Units	6/30/2000	6/30/2001	6/30/2002
Franchised	14	19	23
% Change	--	35.7%	21.1%
Company-Owned	1	1	1
% Change	--	0.0%	0.0%
Total	15	20	24
% Change	--	33.3%	20.0%
Franchised as % of Total	93.3%	95%	95.8%

Investment Required

The fee for a More Space Place franchise is $22,500. Additional units are available at a reduced fee of $15,000.

The More Space Place provides the following range of investments required to open your initial franchise. The range assumes that all items are paid for in cash. To the extent that you choose to finance any of these expense items, your front-end investment could be substantially reduced.

Item	Established Low Range	Established High Range
Franchise Fee	$15,000	$22,500
Advertising	$3,000	$7,500
Equipment/Signs/Supplies	$7,600	$19,000
Insurance	$600	$1,800
Inventory	$12,000	$35,000
Real Estate	$22,800	$44,500
Training Expenses	$1,000	$2,000
Other Costs and Additional Funds (for 3 months)	$28,000	$37,000
Total Investment	$90,000	$169,300

On-Going Expenses

More Space Place franchisees pay royalties equaling the greater of 4.5%, or $500 a month, national advertising contributions of 2.5%, or $250 a month, regional advertising fees of 2.5%, or $500 a month, and local advertising fees of 7%, or $2,500 a month, of gross revenue.

What You Get—Training and Support

The turnkey operation offered by The More Space Place includes site selection, start-up support and advertising and promotional materials.

Included perks and advantages include a simple ordering and inventory system, minimal standing inventory, consistent quality control, a single source supplier, new product development and acquisition, group purchasing power and manufacturer product guarantees. In addition, most products are designed, packaged and shipped in ready to complete units.

Territory

The More Space Place grants territories with estimated populations of 150,000 people and development territories to franchisees qualified to open multiple units.

Paper Warehouse/ Party Universe

7630 Excelsior Blvd.
Minneapolis, MN 55426-4504
Tel: (800) 229-1792 (952) 936-1000
Fax: (952) 352-9091
E-Mail: mike.anderson@paperwarehouse.com
Web Site: www.paperwarehouse.com
Mr. Mike Anderson, VP Franchising

PAPER WAREHOUSE specializes in party supplies and paper goods. They operate under the names PAPER WAREHOUSE, PARTY UNIVERSE and www.paperwarehouse.com. PAPER WAREHOUSE stores offer an extensive assortment of special occasion, seasonal and everyday party and entertainment supplies, gift wrap, greeting cards and catering supplies at everyday low prices.

BACKGROUND:	IFA MEMBER
Established: 1983; 1st Franchised: 1987	
Franchised Units:	52
Company-Owned Units	62
Total Units:	114
Dist.:	US-113; CAN-1; O'seas-0
North America:	24 States
Density:	23 in MN, 12 in MO, 11 in CO
Projected New Units (12 Months):	6
Qualifications:	5, 3, 3, 3, 3, 3
Registered:	All States Except Hawaii

FINANCIAL/TERMS:		SUPPORT & TRAINING PROVIDED:	
		Financial Assistance Provided:	Yes(I)
Cash Investment:	$75-100K	Site Selection Assistance:	Yes
Total Investment:	$184-445K	Lease Negotiation Assistance:	Yes
Minimum Net Worth:	$450K+	Co-Operative Advertising:	No
Fees:	Franchise — $35K	Franchisee Assoc./Member:	Yes/IFA
	Royalty — 4%; Ad. — 0%	Size Of Corporate Staff:	35
Earnings Claim Statement:	No	On-Going Support:	A,C,D,E,G,I
Term of Contract (Years):	10/10	Training:	1 Week in Minneapolis, MN.
Avg. # Of Employees:	5-6 FT		
Passive Ownership:	Allowed	SPECIFIC EXPANSION PLANS:	
Encourage Conversions:	Yes	US:	All United States
Area Develop. Agreements:	Yes/10	Canada:	All Canada
Sub-Franchising Contracts:	No	Overseas:	No
Expand In Territory:	N/A		
Space Needs:	7,200 SF; SC		

Paper Warehouse and Party Universe sell special occasion, seasonal and everyday paper products like party supplies, gift wrap, greeting cards and catering supplies.

Impressed the success they've found in their special retail market, many Paper Warehouse franchisees run more than one location. The steady cycle of holidays and events throughout the year, every year, keep Paper Warehouse/Party Universe business up year-round. Every month, there's another reason for a celebration, whether it's a birthday, a good-bye party, Thanksgiving or a business get-together. Everyone, of every profession, lifestyle and background, is a potential customer.

The first Paper Warehouse/Party Universe store opened in 1983. The Paper Warehouse/Party Universe franchise system was created in 1987.

Operating Units	1/28/2000	2/2/2001	2/1/2002
Franchised	47	49	52
% Change	--	4.2%	6.1%
Company-Owned	102	98	100
% Change	--	-3.9%	2.0%
Total	149	147	152
% Change	--	-1.3%	3.4%
Franchised as % of Total	31.5%	33.3%	34.2%

Investment Required

The fee for a Paper Warehouse/Party Universe franchise is $35,000. Additional units are available for a reduced fee.

The system is also looking for individuals and organizations, such as investor and management firms with a strong financial position and management team, interested in and qualified for multi-store development, a cluster of stores in one market or a chain of stores in several small cities within a defined region. There are several top 50 markets still open.

Paper Warehouse/Party Universe provides the following range of investments required to open your initial franchise. The range assumes that all items are paid for in cash. To the extent that you choose to finance any of these expense items, your front-end investment could be substantially reduced. The following figures apply to the opening of a standard store.

Item	Established Low Range	Established High Range
Franchise Fee	$35,000	$35,000
Equipment/Fixtures/Signs	$38,000	$102,000
Inventory	$75,000	$100,000
Promotion	$5,000	$5,000
Real Estate	$3,800	$15,800
Other Costs and Additional Funds (for 3 months)	$27,600	$34,100
Total Investment	$184,400	$291,900

On-Going Expenses

Paper Warehouse/Party Universe franchisees pay royalties equaling 4% of gross revenue. There is no system-wide advertising fee, but advertising co-op and other local advertising expenses may apply.

What You Get—Training and Support

Prior to opening, Paper Warehouse/Party Universe franchisees receive business planning, site selection and setup, advertising and public relations guidance, as well as training in how to operate a Paper Warehouse/Party Universe franchise.

On-going support includes the guidance of a field representative, a toll-free direct phone line, direct factory purchasing, merchandise management and advertising and promotions, such as full-color circulars and print and radio advertisements that can be customized for each individual store.

Each Paper Warehouse/Party Universe store also receives professional display design assistance and discount pricing.

Territory
Paper Warehouse/Party Universe grants exclusive trade areas.

Snap-On Tools

Snap-on.

2801 80th St.
Kenosha, WI 53141-1410
Tel: (800) 786-6600 (262) 656-6516
Fax: (262) 656-5088
E-Mail: ray.moore@snapon.com
Web Site: www.snapon.com
Mr. M. Raymond Moore, Dir. Franchise Operations

The premier solutions provider to the vehicle service industry. Premium quality products, delivered and sold with premium service. We are proud of our heritage and are boldly addressing the future needs of our customers with improved efficiency, creating products and services from hand tools to data and management systems. Contact us today for discussion.

BACKGROUND:	IFA MEMBER
Established: 1920; 1st Franchised: 1991	
Franchised Units:	4,708
Company-Owned Units	85
Total Units:	4,793
Dist.:	US-3,622; CAN-357; O'seas-814
North America:	All States & Provinces
Density:	373 in CA, 245 in TX, 202 PA

Projected New Units (12 Months):	682
Qualifications:	3, 4, 2, 2, 5, 5
Registered:	All States
FINANCIAL/TERMS:	
Cash Investment:	$Low Cost
Total Investment:	$156-248K
Minimum Net Worth:	$NR
Fees:	Franchise — $5K
	Royalty — $50/Mo.; Ad. — 0%
Earnings Claim Statement:	Yes
Term of Contract (Years):	10/5
Avg. # Of Employees:	1 FT
Passive Ownership:	Not Allowed
Encourage Conversions:	Yes
Area Develop. Agreements:	No
Sub-Franchising Contracts:	No
Expand In Territory:	Yes
Space Needs:	NR SF; N/A
SUPPORT & TRAINING PROVIDED:	
Financial Assistance Provided:	Yes(D)
Site Selection Assistance:	N/A
Lease Negotiation Assistance:	N/A
Co-Operative Advertising:	N/A
Franchisee Assoc./Member:	No
Size Of Corporate Staff:	NR

On-Going Support: A,B,C,D,E,F,G,h,I Training: 1 Week at Branch or Regional Office; 1 Week at Branch; 3 Weeks On-the-Job.	SPECIFIC EXPANSION PLANS: US: All United States Canada: All Canada Overseas: Japan, UK, Germany, Australia, New Zealand, S. Africa

Snap-On sells high-quality tools and equipment with an outstanding reputation for quality, service and innovation. As a Snap-On franchisee, you become one of 4,000 Snap-On dealers who buy Snap-On's products and sell them to assigned accounts. Currently, there are limited Snap-On franchise opportunities available nationwide.

Snap-On produced the first interchangeable socket wrench in 1920 and has gone on to become a leader in tools and equipment for professional technicians. The company was also at the forefront of the implementation of direct sales and service to merchants and credit programs that allow customers to acquire the tools needed to build a business.

Operating Units	1/1/2000	12/30/2000	12/29/2001
Franchised	3,458	3,508	3,973
% Change	--	1.4%	13.2%
Company-Owned	23	26	28
% Change	--	13.0%	7.7%
Total	3,481	3,534	4,001
% Change	--	1.5%	13.2%
Franchised as % of Total	99.3%	99.3%	99.3%

Investment Required
The fee for a Snap-On franchise is $5,000. The Franchise Expansion Program allows you to add an additional van to your existing route or to add another franchise altogether. Snap-On does provide financing assistance.

Snap-On provides the following range of investments required to open your initial franchise. The range assumes that all items are paid for in cash. To the extent that you choose to finance any of these expense items, your front-end investment could be substantially reduced.

Item	Established Low Range	Established High Range
Franchise Fee	$5,000	$5,000
Acquisition and Development of Revolving Accounts	$45,000	$45,000
Equipment/Fixtures	$4,500	$4,500
Inventory	$83,750	$83,750
Training Expenses	$1,000	$2,000
Vehicle Expenses	$6,250	$71,075
Other Costs and Additional Funds (for 3 months)	$10,005	$16,354
Total Investment	$155,505	$227,679

On-Going Expenses

Snap-On charges no royalty or advertising fees, but does require a monthly license fee of $50.

What You Get—Training and Support

The first two weeks of Snap-On franchisee training covers record keeping, the computer sales system, policies and procedures, product knowledge, sales, van (the franchisee's showroom- and office-on-wheels) display and credit program management. The next three weeks are on the job, but with the accompaniment of a field manager. Meanwhile, franchisees are immediately assigned to a field group, which brings them together with other dealers to learn and share.

To help accommodate accounts, Snap-On provides credit and financing by buying credit accounts from its franchisees and offering extended credit accounts, open accounts and equipment leases to Snap-On customers.

Sales and marketing support, on which millions is spent each year, is provided through media and trade publications, professional racing, customer newsletters, sales contests and promotions, national accounts, industry trade shows, business aids and electronic and print catalogs.

The Snap-On/Sun Tech Systems staff, which works out of branch offices, assists dealers with diagnostic equipment sales, traveling with them to demonstrate the equipment's features and operations to customers.

Territory
Snap-On does not grant exclusive territories.

Wild Birds Unlimited

Wild Birds Unlimited®
Your Backyard Birdfeeding Specialist®
www.wbu.com

11711 N. College Ave., # 146
Carmel, IN 46032-5634
Tel: (888) 730-7108 (317) 571-7100 + 135
Fax: (317) 571-7110
E-Mail: pickettp@wbu.com
Web Site: www.wbu.com
Mr. Paul E. Pickett, Dir. Franchise Development

WILD BIRDS UNLIMITED is North America's original and largest group of retail stores catering to the backyard birdfeeding and nature enthusiast. We currently have over 290 stores in the U. S. and Canada. Stores provide birdseed, feeders, houses, optics and nature-related gifts. Additionally, stores provide extensive educational programs regarding backyard birdfeeding. Franchisees are provided an all-inclusive support system.

BACKGROUND:
Established: 1981; 1st Franchised: 1983	
Franchised Units:	296
Company-Owned Units	0
Total Units:	296
Dist.:	US-284; CAN-12; O'seas-0
North America:	42 States, 3 Provinces
Density:	23 in TX, 17 in MI, 15 in IL
Projected New Units (12 Months):	15

Qualifications:	5, 5, 1, 3, 2, 5
Registered:	CA,FL,IL,IN,MD,MI,MN,NY, OR,RI,VA,WA,WI,DC

FINANCIAL/TERMS:
Cash Investment:	$25-35K
Total Investment:	$75-125K
Minimum Net Worth:	$150K
Fees:	Franchise — $18K
	Royalty — 4%; Ad. — 1%
Earnings Claim Statement:	Yes
Term of Contract (Years):	10/5
Avg. # Of Employees:	2 FT, 4 PT
Passive Ownership:	Not Allowed
Encourage Conversions:	N/A
Area Develop. Agreements:	No
Sub-Franchising Contracts:	No
Expand In Territory:	Yes
Space Needs:	1,400-1,800 SF; FS, SC

SUPPORT & TRAINING PROVIDED:
Financial Assistance Provided:	Yes(I)
Site Selection Assistance:	Yes
Lease Negotiation Assistance:	Yes
Co-Operative Advertising:	No
Franchisee Assoc./Member:	Yes/Yes
Size Of Corporate Staff:	45
On-Going Support:	C,D,E,F,G,H,I
Training:	6 Days in Indianapolis, IN; 1 Day at Store Site.

SPECIFIC EXPANSION PLANS:
US:	All United States
Canada:	All Canada
Overseas:	No

The draw of Wild Birds Unlimited, a birdfeeding hobby store, is greater than one might think. Birdfeeding is easy to do and brings quick satisfaction. It's educational for children and one in three families does it. It is a hobby without barriers—it is year-round and not limited to a select age, income or sex—and it is a hobby that can be as elaborate or simple as you wish, ranging from a lone birdfeeder to a complete habitat with food, water, plantings and nesting spots.

On the world wide web, Wild Birds Unlimited was the first to feature real-time birdfeeder cams, allowing website visitors to view live footage of Wild Bird Center products, and nature, at work.

Wild Birds Unlimited first joined people with nature in 1981. The stores are designed to be customer friendly and loyal and seek to provide both a shopping environment and a community knowledge resource.

Operating Units	12/31/1999	12/31/2000	12/31/2001
Franchised	259	265	277
% Change	--	2.3%	4.5%
Company-Owned	0	0	0
% Change	--	N/A	N/A
Total	259	265	277
% Change	--	2.3%	4.5%
Franchised as % of Total	100.0%	100.0%	100.0%

Investment Required
The fee for a Wild Birds Unlimited franchise is $18,000. Additional franchises are available for half of the initial franchise fee. Initial training costs $2,000.

Wild Birds Unlimited provides the following range of investments required to open your initial franchise. The range assumes that all items are paid for in cash. To the extent that you choose to finance any of these expense items, your front-end investment could be substantially reduced.

Item	Established Low Range	Established High Range
Franchise Fee	$18,000	$18,000
Advertising/Equipment/ Fixtures/Signs	$16,185	$28,293
Insurance	$250	$1,000
Inventory	$20,070	$26,994
Real Estate	$7,383	$21,583
Training	$3,000	$4,500
Other Costs and Additional Funds (for 3 months)	$8,738	$23,108
Total Investment	$73,626	$123,478

On-Going Expenses

Wild Birds Unlimited franchisees pay royalties equaling 4%, local advertising fees equaling 2%, regional and local advertising cooperative fees equaling 2% and advertising fund contributions equaling 1% of gross revenue.

What You Get—Training and Support

Wild Birds Unlimited support starts right at the beginning of the franchising process. The company assists franchisees with site selection using market research that focuses on population age, income, family type and lifestyle.

Training includes professional retail management, inventory forecasting, system trends, understanding financial statements, profit and cash flow forecasting, information systems, marketing, merchandising and advertising, product purchasing, human resources, regional retail operations and birdfeeding education. Training also includes an observation of each franchisee's store opening.

Franchisees can also turn to the franchise support center and the Franchise Advisory Council, which is elected by peers and increases communication between the franchisees and the corporate offices.

Wild Birds Unlimited provides extensive information systems (back office hardware and software, the WBU accounting system, electronic cash registers, daily and monthly sales summaries, purchase orders, the WBU intranet), marketing assistance (national and local synergy, market research, advertising and media objectives and strategies, print advertising, direct mail, television and radio commercials, outdoor advertisements, yellow page advertisements, public relations assistance, strategic alliances, in-store marketing and visual merchandising, customer literature, logos, artwork and illustrations), regional retail operations (field visits, marketing programs, product purchasing programs, market research, merchandising programs, monthly newsletters, annual and regional meetings, vendor program development, strategic alliances, a toll-free phone number for the franchise support center), human resources (certified birdfeeding specialists, store manager training, eagle sales training), branded products (exclusive bird seed blends and private label products), purchasing (volume buying, vendor mart, product development, pricing guidelines, product education), and store design and layout strategy.

Territory
Wild Birds Unlimited grants exclusive territories.

Allegra Print & Imaging

1800 W. Maple Rd.
Troy, MI 48084-7104
Tel: (888) 258-2730 (248) 614-3700
Fax: (248) 614-3719
E-Mail: meredithz@allegranetwork.com
Web Site: www.allegranetwork.com
Mrs. Meredith Zielinski, Development Program
    Manager

Our owners operate full-service communications centers, marketing a range of products including high-speed duplicating, color copying, desktop publishing, 2-4 color printing and digital capabilities. Our franchisees set themselves apart through exceptional personalized customer service. Printers Plan and PrintSmith order entry software are used in the centers.

BACKGROUND:	IFA MEMBER
Established: 1976; 1st Franchised: 1977	
Franchised Units:	492
Company-Owned Units	0
Total Units:	492
Dist.:	US-448; CAN-33; O'seas-11
North America:	42 States, 3 Provinces
Density:	68 in MI, 3 in MN, 37 in IL
Projected New Units (12 Months):	0

Qualifications:	5, 2, 1, 2, 2, 2
Registered:	All States

FINANCIAL/TERMS:	
Cash Investment:	$50-100K
Total Investment:	$256-358.5K
Minimum Net Worth:	$N/A
Fees:	Franchise — $25K
	Royalty — 3.6-6%; Ad. — 1-2%
Earnings Claim Statement:	No
Term of Contract (Years):	20/20
Avg. # Of Employees:	3 FT, 1 PT
Passive Ownership:	Not Allowed
Encourage Conversions:	Yes
Area Develop. Agreements:	No
Sub-Franchising Contracts:	Yes
Expand In Territory:	Yes
Space Needs:	1,500 SF; FS, SF, SC

SUPPORT & TRAINING PROVIDED:	
Financial Assistance Provided:	Yes
Site Selection Assistance:	Yes
Lease Negotiation Assistance:	Yes
Co-Operative Advertising:	Yes
Franchisee Assoc./Member:	Yes/Yes
Size Of Corporate Staff:	57
On-Going Support:	C,D,E,F,G,h,I
Training:	2 Weeks at Home Office; 1 Week On-Site; On-Going

SPECIFIC EXPANSION PLANS:	
US:	All United States
Canada:	All Canada
Overseas:	No

Allegra is a full-service communications provider, offering services such as high-speed duplicating, color copying, desktop publishing, two- to four-color printing, website services, online file transfers, high-volume copying, multi-color printing, stationery and graphic design. The Allegra network serves the $90 billion printing industry through several brands, including Allegra Print & Imaging, American Speedy Printing Centers and Insty-Prints. The benefits of owning an Allegra franchise include standard workday business hours, low inventory costs and a growing market. Allegra often offers existing franchises for sale, allowing franchisees to skip all the toil and expense of starting a franchise from scratch. The elimination of this hassle, however, does not eliminate the essential need for people skills in this service-heavy industry that receives most of its business from repeat visitors and through word-of-mouth recommendations.

Allegra was founded in 1976 and franchised in 1977. In 2002, the Allegra system's nearly 500 centers garnered $286.9 million in sales.

Operating Units	1/31/2000	1/31/2001	1/31/2002
Franchised	320	301	493
% Change	--	-6.3%	63.8%
Company-Owned	0	0	0
% Change	--	--	--
Total	320	301	493
% Change	--	6.3%	63.8%
Franchised as % of Total	100.0%	100.0%	100.0%

Investment Required
The fee for an Allegra franchise is $25,000.

Allegra provides the following range of investments required to open your initial franchise. The range assumes that all items are paid for in cash. To the extent that you choose to finance any of these expense items, your front-end investment could be substantially reduced.

Item	Established Low Range	Established High Range
Franchise Fee	$25,000	$25,000
Equipment/Fixtures/Signs	$155,000	$216,000
Insurance	$1,200	$2,000
Paper Inventory	$3,500	$4,500
Real Estate	$7,600	$16,500
Additional Funds (for 12 months)	$50,000	$75,000
Total Investment	$242,300	$339,000

On-Going Expenses

Allegra franchisees pay royalties equaling 3.6 to 6%, marketing fees equaling 1 to 2% of gross revenue. Once an individual franchisee's revenue reaches a certain, a royalty rebate may apply.

What You Get—Training and Support

The Allegra franchise fee includes name and logo use, trademarks and business methods.

Allegra training lasts for two intensive weeks in Troy, Michigan and one week on-site.

Franchisees also gain access to preferred vendors, a toll-free support line, technical support (for pre-press, printing and bindery operations, equipment selection, supplies, pricing, computer systems and more), marketing and public relations support, such as turn-key material and program production to build brand awareness, account development and name recognition. The in-house sales group also hires, trains and manages the sales consultants and account managers that help franchisees run their centers. Half of all national marketing fund contributions are returned to the franchisees to fund local marketing. Further support comes in bi-annual international conventions and regional field directors that act as business consultants and also organize bi-annual performance group meetings. Support also includes a technical staff that evaluates new products, distributes technical bulletins, manuals, newsletter articles and training materials and maintains company websites.

Territory
Allegra does not grant exclusive territories.

AlphaGraphics PrintShops of the Future

alphagraphics®

DESIGN ■ COPY ■ PRINT

268 S. State St., # 300
Salt Lake City, UT 84111
Tel: (800) 528-4885 (801) 595-7270
Fax: (801) 595-7271
E-Mail: opportunity@alphagraphics.com
Web Site: www.alphagraphics.com
Mr. Keith M. Gerson, VP Global Development

ALPHAGRAPHICS PRINTSHOPS OF THE FUTURE are the leading providers of print-related and digital publishing services for business worldwide. Our mission is to enable our customers to easily and effectively communicate in any publishing medium - anywhere in the world, any time. Our franchisees enjoy the industry's highest reported average annual sales. Services include design, high-speed duplication, single and multi-color printing, digital large format publishing, binding, CD-ROM and Web site services.

BACKGROUND:	IFA MEMBER
Established: 1970; 1st Franchised: 1980	
Franchised Units:	287
Company-Owned Units	0
Total Units:	287
Dist.:	US-231; CAN-0; O'seas-56
North America:	42 States
Density:	27 in IL, 26 in AZ, 25 in TX
Projected New Units (12 Months):	24
Qualifications:	4, 5, 1, 3, 3, 5

Registered:	All States
FINANCIAL/TERMS:	
Cash Investment:	$100-150K
Total Investment:	$352-546K
Minimum Net Worth:	$350K
Fees:	Franchise — $25.9K
	Royalty — 1.5-8%; Ad. — 2.5%
Earnings Claim Statement:	Yes
Term of Contract (Years):	20/20
Avg. # Of Employees:	5 FT
Passive Ownership:	Not Allowed
Encourage Conversions:	Yes
Area Develop. Agreements:	Yes/N/A
Sub-Franchising Contracts:	No
Expand In Territory:	Yes
Space Needs:	2,200-3,000 SF; FS, SC, SC
SUPPORT & TRAINING PROVIDED:	
Financial Assistance Provided:	Yes(I)
Site Selection Assistance:	Yes
Lease Negotiation Assistance:	No
Co-Operative Advertising:	Yes
Franchisee Assoc./Member:	No/No
Size Of Corporate Staff:	94
On-Going Support:	b,C,D,E,G,H,I
Training:	4 Weeks Salt Lake City, UT Service Center
SPECIFIC EXPANSION PLANS:	
US:	All United States
Canada:	All Canada
Overseas:	Spain, Italy, France, Germany, Benelux, Austria

AlphaGraphics is a one-stop source for designing, copying, printing and digital publishing needs. The company is driven by customer needs and with franchises across the globe, customers can expect and find the same Alpha-Graphics quality anywhere they need it. AlphaGraphics hopes that its customers will see the company as their "personal conduit for global distribution of published communications."

AlphaGraphics began in 1970 as a single store in Tucson, Arizona. It franchised in 1980.

Operating Units	6/30/2000	6/30/2001	6/30/2002
Franchised	262	249	242
% Change	--	-5.0	-2.8
Company-Owned	0	0	0
% Change	--	0	0
Total	262	249	242
% Change	--	-5.0	-2.8
Franchised as % of Total	100.0%	100.0%	100.0%

Investment Required
The fee for an AlphaGraphics franchise is $25,900. Initial franchise and development fees may differ if a development agreement is signed. If additional franchises are established outside the franchisee's protected area, there is a $10,000 franchise fee.

AlphaGraphics provides the following range of investments required to open your initial franchise. The range assumes that all items are paid for in cash. To the extent that you choose to finance any of these expense items, your front-end investment could be substantially reduced.

Item	Established Low Range	Established High Range
Franchise Fee	$25,900	$25,900
Advertising Contribution	$15,000	$15,000
Equipment/Fixtures/ Inventory/Signs	$155,000	$155,000
Insurance	$1,600	$4,000

ISO Certification/ Other Fees	$5,000	$5,000
Real Estate	$32,000	$126,000
Training and Marketing Fee	$24,000	$24,000
Other Costs and Additional Funds (for 12 months)	$93,500	$191,000
Total Investment	$352,000	$545,900

On-Going Expenses

AlphaGraphics franchisees pay royalties equaling 1.5 to 8%, local marketing fees equaling 1 to 2%, regional marketing fees up to 2%, multi-regional marketing fees equaling 0.5% and national advertising fees equaling 3% of gross revenue. Any additional training or assistance desired costs $750 to $900 a day.

AlphaGraphics offers a special franchise agreement that includes reduced royalty levels, a unique royalty credit system for obtaining customized marketing and training programs and the opportunity to buy out of the franchise agreement within certain timeframes.

What You Get—Training and Support

AlphaGraphics's four weeks of training cover every facet of the business. At the corporate headquarters, new franchisees learn how to manage their business, build their customer base and handle daily operations. They will receive on-going support through regional seminars, audio, video and computer-based instruction, telephone support and field consultant site visits.

AlphaGraphics Integrated Marketing uses software-powered customer analysis and prospecting, plus direct mail, sales and marketing support to focus on business print and copy buyers and to build long-term relationships that will bring them back to AlphaGraphics again and again. To meet this goal and other marketing objectives, Alpha-Graphics' off-the-shelf materials, such as radio scripts, full-color products and services catalogs, brochures, point of purchase displays, posters, postcards and self-mailers, are available for use by franchisees.

Each AlphaGraphics also utilizes an operating system that packages everything the franchise will need into one product. In 1997, AlphaGraphics became the first quick-print shop to earn an ISO 9002 certification for meeting international quality management and assurance standards with its operating and performance measurement systems.

Furthermore, each AlphaGraphics franchisee and employee benefits from succession planning, which allows employees to earn up to $39,920 in credits to purchase their own shop and, consequently, provides franchisees with a committed and hard-working staff.

Territory
AlphaGraphics grants protected territories encompassing 1,200 to 2,500 businesses.

American
Leak Detection

888 Research Dr., # 100, P.O. Box 1701
Palm Springs, CA 92263-1701
Tel: (800) 755-6697 (760) 320-9991
Fax: (760) 320-1288
E-Mail: sbangs@americanleakdetection.com
Web Site: www.americanleakdetection.com

Ms. Sheila T. Bangs, Dir. Franchise Sales/Marketing
Electronic detection of water, drain, waste, sewer and gas leaks under concrete slabs of homes, commercial buildings, pools, spas, fountains, etc. with equipment commissioned/ manufactured by company.

BACKGROUND:	IFA MEMBER
Established: 1974; 1st Franchised: 1985	
Franchised Units:	303
Company-Owned Units	2
Total Units:	305
Dist.:	US-223; CAN-8; O'seas-72
North America:	38 States, 3 Provinces
Density:	63 in CA, 34 in FL, 15 in TX
Projected New Units (12 Months):	6

Qualifications:	3, 3, 2, 2, 2, 3
Registered:	CA,FL,HI,IL,IN,MD,MI,MN,NY,OR,RI ,VA,WA,WI,DC,AB

FINANCIAL/TERMS:	
Cash Investment:	$58-120K
Total Investment:	$85-150K
Minimum Net Worth:	$Varies
Fees:	Franchise — $55K+
	Royalty — 6-10%; Ad. — N/A
Earnings Claim Statement:	No
Term of Contract (Years):	10/10
Avg. # Of Employees:	1-4 FT, 2 PT
Passive Ownership:	Discouraged
Encourage Conversions:	N/A
Area Develop. Agreements:	No
Sub-Franchising Contracts:	No
Expand In Territory:	Yes
Space Needs:	NR SF; NR

SUPPORT & TRAINING PROVIDED:	
Financial Assistance Provided:	Yes(D)
Site Selection Assistance:	N/A
Lease Negotiation Assistance:	N/A
Co-Operative Advertising:	Yes

215

Franchisee Assoc./Member:	Yes/Yes	SPECIFIC EXPANSION PLANS:	
Size Of Corporate Staff:	37	US:	Northeast, Midwest
On-Going Support:	a,B,C,D,f,G,H,I	Canada:	MB, SK, AB
Training:	6-10 Weeks Palm Springs, CA.	Overseas:	Western Europe, Far East, South America

American Leak Detection's mission is simple: "Leak detection without destruction," using "non-invasive, efficient and environmentally sound" techniques and to "give prompt, professional and courteous service to all customers." ALD uses proprietary technology to locate leaks in any piping system that carries fluid or gaseous materials, locate and trace lines in preparation for construction or remodeling and inspect sewer lines. The endeavor sounds more difficult than it is. "If you are mechanically inclined," ALD says, "and have a 'good ear,' you will be able to find and repair leaks." Meanwhile, you're also helping to conserve water and prevent contamination.

The first American Leak Detection began business in 1974 and has since revolutionized leak detection and become the recognized world leader in the detection of hidden leaks of any kind—water, sewer or gas. They are the "original leak specialists."

Operating Units	9/30/1999	9/30/2000	9/30/2001
Franchised	142	144	140
% Change	--	1.4%	-2.8%
Company-Owned	2	2	2
% Change	--	0.0	0.0
Total	144	146	142
% Change	--	1.4%	-2.7%
Franchised as % of Total	98.6%	98.6%	98.6%

Investment Required

The usual fee for an American Leak Detection franchise in the United States is $57,500. If you have good credit, American Leak Detection can provide up to

50% financing. International master franchises vary by country.

American Leak Detection provides the following range of investments required to open your initial franchise. The range assumes that all items are paid for in cash. To the extent that you choose to finance any of these expense items, your front-end investment could be substantially reduced.

Item	Established Low Range	Established High Range
Franchise Fee	$57,500	$100,000
Business Licenses/Taxes	$0	$2,250
Insurance	$750	$3,000
Supplies	$375	$6,300
Vehicle	$0	$20,000
Other Costs and Additional Funds (for 3 months)	$12,630	$23,500
Total Investment	$71,255	$155,050

On-Going Expenses
American Leak Detection franchisees pay royalties equaling 6 to 10% of gross revenue.

What You Get—Training and Support
The franchise fee for an American Leak Detection franchise provides the franchisee with the following: the franchise license and a protected territory; federally protected service marks; trademarks, name and symbol copyrights; six weeks of technical, marketing, accounting and management training at the ALD corporate office; public relations and marketing support to secure local, regional and national newspaper, television and radio coverage; national advertising; follow-up on-site training; a complete electronic leak and line location equipment package that is continually updated and improved; on-staff troubleshooters; team and customer service training; a company website and an annual four-day convention.

A primary focus of ALD's continuing support is helping you keep your overhead down.

Territory
American Leak Detection grants protected territories.

AmeriSpec Home Inspection Service

AMERISPEC®
HOME INSPECTION SERVICE
Number One in North America

889 Ridge Lake Blvd.
Memphis, TN 38120-9421
Tel: (800) 426-2270 (901) 820-8500
Fax: (901) 820-8520
E-Mail: jsullivan@amerispec.net
Web Site: www.amerispecfranchise.com
Mr. Jim Sullivan, VP Sales/Operations

AMERISPEC delivers productivity enhancing tools to our owners like feature-rich personal websites, branded e-mail accounts, secure web delivery for reports and contact management software specifically designed to manage a home inspection business. A private intranet permits two-way communication with and among our owners. Consider our extensive training, the acclaimed and recognized 'AMERISPEC REPORT,' our on-going educational support and the package is complete.

BACKGROUND: IFA MEMBER
Established: 1987; 1st Franchised: 1988
Franchised Units: 367
Company-Owned Units 2
Total Units: 369
Dist.: US-287; CAN-80; O'seas-0
  North America: 48 States, 8 Provinces
  Density: 24 in CA, 16 in FL, 11 in IL
Projected New Units (12 Months): 25

Qualifications: 3, 3, 3, 3, 1, 5
Registered: All States

FINANCIAL/TERMS:
Cash Investment: $10-15K
Total Investment: $24.6-63.5K
Minimum Net Worth: $25K
Fees: Franchise — $18-26.9K
  Royalty — 7%; Ad. — 3%
Earnings Claim Statement: No
Term of Contract (Years): 5/5
Avg. # Of Employees: 1 FT, 2 PT
Passive Ownership: Allowed
Encourage Conversions: Yes
Area Develop. Agreements: No
Sub-Franchising Contracts: No
Expand In Territory: Yes
Space Needs: N/A SF; HB

SUPPORT & TRAINING PROVIDED:
Financial Assistance Provided: Yes(D)
Site Selection Assistance: N/A
Lease Negotiation Assistance: N/A
Co-Operative Advertising: Yes
Franchisee Assoc./Member: No
Size Of Corporate Staff: 45
On-Going Support: C,D,E,G,h,I
Training: 2 Weeks Memphis, TN.

SPECIFIC EXPANSION PLANS:
US: All United States
Canada: All Canada
Overseas: No

AmeriSpec performs one of the most widely recommended home services on the market today—home inspections for homeowners, prospective home owners and realtors.

The first AmeriSpec franchise was offered in 1988 and the system has gone on to perform more than 1.5 million home inspections. In 1996, it joined ServiceMaster's Consumer Service Division, which was founded in 1952 and now has more than 5,000 franchise partners on 4 continents. As an Ameri-Spec franchisee, you reap the rewards of the ServiceMaster family, with the resources of each franchise used to develop and enhance the training and marketing of all. Today there are more than 350 AmeriSpec locations in the United States and Canada that conduct more than 150,000 home inspections each year.

Operating Units	12/31/2000	12/31/2001	12/31/2002
Franchised	282	291	287
% Change	--	3.2%	-1.4%
Company-Owned	1	2	2
% Change	--	100.0%	0.0%
Total	283	293	289
% Change	--	3.5%	-1.4%
Franchised as % of Total	99.6%	99.3%	99.3%

Investment Required

The fee for an AmeriSpec franchise ranges from $18,000 to $26,900. Members of the military or federal employees may qualify for a franchise fee discount of 10%. Financing assistance is also available through a Service Master Acceptance Company initial financing investment of 20%. Additional units are available at discounted fees.

AmeriSpec provides the following range of investments required to open your initial franchise. The range assumes that all items are paid for in cash. To the extent that you choose to finance any of these expense items, your front-end investment could be substantially reduced.

Item	Established Low Range	Established High Range
Franchise Fee	$16,200	$26,900
Advertising	$1,900	$4,000
AmeriSpec Report and Field Inspection System	$450	$4,000

Computer System/ Equipment/Furniture	$700	$6,500
Training Expenses	$750	$1,250
Additional Funds (for 3 months)	$500	$12,000
Total Investment	$20,500	$54,650

On-Going Expenses

AmeriSpec franchisees pay an earned service fee equaling at least $250, or 7%, of gross revenue.

What You Get—Training and Support

During Pre-Management Institute, which occurs two to four weeks before the Management Institute, AmeriSpec introduces franchisees to their business consultants, originating a relationship that will persist throughout the initial development and opening processes, and helps franchisees determine personal business and training objectives.

With these tasks out of the way no time is wasted in the Management Institute, a two-week intensive training course at the AmeriSpec Training Center in Memphis, Tennessee. Week one focuses on conducting home inspections (executed in a state-of-the-art full-scale, working home model), including report formatting and presentation and use of technical tools, such as the home inspector software. Week two is about marketing and management. You will analyze your market, develop marketing and risk management strategies, choose your target audience and determine pricing. Additionally, participants learn to use the Phoenix DX business management software and various other technology tools.

In addition to the live training you receive in the management institutes, AmeriSpec provides a technical home study system featuring ten modules composed of more than 4,000 pages of information and 1,500 illustrations, and more than 17 hours of videos, tests and field exercises to make anyone an expert in the art of home inspection. AmeriSpec's Smart Start® program provides weekly game plans that outline the steps to take to minimize or avoid the typical, and often expensive, start-up errors that plague franchisees.

In addition to training, AmeriSpec utilizes the following tools to aid in the administration of a new AmeriSpec business: The AmeriSpec Report, home inspection software, AmeriSpec intranet site, personalized AmeriSpec website, AmeriSpec e-mail address, business model application, Phoenix DX Business Management software and Quick Books Pro Accounting Software and the AmeriSpec Local and National Marketing Gameplan.

On-going support with AmeriSpec comes in many forms. Regional conferences held four times a year offer insight into both technical aspects of your business as well as management issues. The annual international convention allows you to touch base with AmeriSpec administration as well as your fellow franchisees from around the world and provides you with your first glimpse of the marketing plan for the upcoming year. An AmeriSpec business consultant works closely with you to help you with your specific AmeriSpec business, marketing and risk management concerns.

AmeriSpec's association with the ServiceMaster franchises also allow for periodic cross-selling and joint marketing ventures.

Territory

AmeriSpec grants Standard territories encompassing approximately 400,000 people, or 4,000 real estate transactions and Alternate territories encompassing approximately 100,000 to 200,000 people, or between 1,000 to 2,000 real

Anago Cleaning Systems

Cleaning Systems

1515 University, # 203
Coral Springs, FL 33071
Tel: (800) 213-5857 (954) 745-0193
Fax: (954) 656-1014
E-Mail: khirst@anagousa.net
Web Site: www.goanago.com

Ms. Kathy Hirst, Director Franchise Sales

We are the digital generation of cleaning franchises. We provide you with customers!!! Plus invoicing and collection services. We provide complete training, progressive business development, equipment package and start-up. Master franchises available for select locations, as well as local unit franchises.

BACKGROUND:
Established: 1995; 1st Franchised: 2001

Franchised Units:	300	Area Develop. Agreements:	Yes/10
Company-Owned Units	0	Sub-Franchising Contracts:	Yes
Total Units:	300	Expand In Territory:	Yes
Dist.:	US-300; CAN-0; O'seas-0	Space Needs:	1,200 SF; FS
North America:	8 States		
Density:	120 in FL, 35 in OH,31 in GA	**SUPPORT & TRAINING PROVIDED:**	
Projected New Units (12 Months):	200	Financial Assistance Provided:	Yes(I)
Qualifications:	3, 3, 3, 2, 2, 2	Site Selection Assistance:	Yes
Registered:	CA,FL,IL,VA,DC	Lease Negotiation Assistance:	Yes
FINANCIAL/TERMS:		Co-Operative Advertising:	NA
Cash Investment:	$1-25K	Franchisee Assoc./Member:	No
Total Investment:	$5-197K	Size Of Corporate Staff:	10
Minimum Net Worth:	$2K	On-Going Support:	A,b,c,D
Fees:	Franchise — $4.5-150K	Training: 2 Weeks for Master in FL Corp. Office; 75	
	Royalty — 5%; Ad. — 2%	Hours for Unit Franchise - Master Office.	
Earnings Claim Statement:	No		
Term of Contract (Years):	10/10	**SPECIFIC EXPANSION PLANS:**	
Avg. # Of Employees:	4 FT, 4 PT	US:	All United States
Passive Ownership:	Discouraged	Canada:	All Canada
Encourage Conversions:	Yes	Overseas:	All Countries

estate transactions.

Anago, a commercial cleaning service, is expanding throughout the global market and experiencing incredible growth from taking a proven concept to a new level through technological designed support programs. Unlike other franchise opportunities, Anago grants its licensees the right to become a franchisor themselves by selling unit franchises to others. The licensee is in charge of building a network of franchises in the U.S. metropolitan territories or countries. With the state-of-the-art technology and processing systems Anago has developed, the Master Licensee does not have to worry about paperwork or administrative details. These sophisticated systems distinguish Anago from its competitors and are the key to Anago's success.

Anago's founder, David R. Povlitz, is the creator of a variable 5- and 10-step cleaning system and a special task analysis system for inventorying any site needing cleaning easily and clearly. Armed with these tools, success found Povlitz as a young man. Bored with the cleaning world, Povlitz took time off. However, Povlitz quickly bored of the non-working life. It was then that he discovered the beauty of franchising and transformed Anago into the cleaning force it now is.

Operating Units	7/31/2000	7/31/2001	7/31/2002
Franchised	126	157	200
% Change	--	24.6%	27.4%
Company-Owned	0	0	0
% Change	--	0.0%	0.0%
Total	126	157	200
% Change	--	24.6%	27.4%
Franchised as % of Total	100.0%	100.0%	100.0%

Investment Required

The fee for an Anago franchise ranges from $125,000 to $900,000.

Anago provides the following range of investments required to open your initial franchise. The range assumes that all items are paid for in cash. To the extent that you choose to finance any of these expense items, your front-end investment could be substantially reduced.

Item	Established Low Range	Established High Range
Franchise Fee	$100,000	$900,000
Equipment/Fixtures/Supplies	$19,500	$33,500
Insurance	$15,000	$15,000
Legal Expenses	$3,500	$7,500
Real Estate/Licenses/Permits	$2,725	$9,500
Site Development Services Fee	$1,000	$2,500
Training Expenses	$1,500	$3,500
Vehicle Operating Expenses	$7,200	$12,000
Other Costs and Working Capital (for 6 months)	$81,900	$118,500
Total Investment	$232,325	$1,102,000

On-Going Expenses

Anago master franchisees pay monthly royalty fees equaling 5% of the unit's gross revenues, with a minimum payment of $2,000 per month after one year. Franchisees who expand their businesses and territories are responsible for additional commission fees relative to growth.

What You Get—Training and Support

The purchase of an Anago master franchise gives the franchisee: master franchisor rights to the tradename, Anago; the right to sell unit franchises; assistance with site selection; intensive training and support; on-call advice and mentoring and trade secrets and proprietary systems to help recruit franchisees, track finances, develop, manage and administer your franchise.

Territory

Anago grants exclusive territories.

Century 21 Real Estate

1 Campus Dr.
Parsippany, NJ 07054
Tel: (877) 221-5737 (973) 428-9700
Fax: (973) 496-5806
E-Mail: david.hardy@cendant.com
Web Site: www.century21.com
Mr. David Hardy, SVP Franchise Development

The franchise offered is for the operation of a real estate borkerage office, including services such as the listing and sale of properties, property management and other services generally provided by a licensed real estate broker. Century 21 Real Estate Corporation is a subsidiary of Cendant Corportion (NYSE: CD). Cendant is the world's premier provider of business and consumer services.

BACKGROUND: IFA MEMBER
Established: 1972; 1st Franchised: 1972

Franchised Units:	4,196
Company-Owned Units	0
Total Units:	4,196
Dist.:	US-3,931; CAN-265; O'seas-1,442
North America:	All States & Provinces
Density:	486 in CA, 328 in FL, 263 TX
Projected New Units (12 Months):	417
Qualifications:	4, 4, 5, 4, 4, 4
Registered:	All States

FINANCIAL/TERMS:

Cash Investment:	$0-25K
Total Investment:	$10.9-521.2K
Minimum Net Worth:	$25K
Fees:	Franchise — $0-25K
	Royalty — 6%/$500; Ad. — 2%/$289
Earnings Claim Statement:	No
Term of Contract (Years):	10/5-10
Avg. # Of Employees:	Varies
Passive Ownership:	Not Allowed
Encourage Conversions:	Yes
Area Develop. Agreements:	No
Sub-Franchising Contracts:	No
Expand In Territory:	Yes
Space Needs:	1,000 SF; FS, SF, SC

SUPPORT & TRAINING PROVIDED:		Training:	5 Days in Parsippany, NJ; 3-7 Sessions
Financial Assistance Provided:	No		on Telephone; 1 Day On-Site.
Site Selection Assistance:	No		
Lease Negotiation Assistance:	No	**SPECIFIC EXPANSION PLANS:**	
Co-Operative Advertising:	Yes	US:	All United States
Franchisee Assoc./Member:	Yes/Yes	Canada:	All Canada
Size Of Corporate Staff:	176	Overseas:	All Countries
On-Going Support:	A,C,D,E,G,H,I		

The goal of Century 21, the world's largest residential real estate sales organization: Provide full-service real estate transactions with professional and knowledgeable customer service.

Century 21 began as a small California real estate office opened by Art Bartlett and Marsh Fisher in 1971. While they started small, they always thought big and they took their first step towards creating the national real estate sales organization of their dreams when they affiliated their first broker at the end of that first year. By 1975, Century 21's sales exceeded one billion dollars and the company went public in 1977. In 1995, Hospitality Franchise Systems, Inc. acquired the company, and, from there, the system later became Cendant Corporation, an international franchisor of hotels, travel, real estate, vehicle and financial services.

Operating Units	12/31/2000	12/31/2001	12/31/2002
Franchised	4,260	4,180	4,099
% Change	--	-1.9%	-1.9%
Company-Owned	0	0	0
% Change	--	N/A	N/A
Total	4,260	4,180	4,099
% Change	--	-1.9%	-1.9%
Franchised as % of Total	100.0%	100.0%	100.0%

Investment Required
The fee for a Century 21 franchise is $25,000. The fee for additional units is $10,000.

Century 21 provides the following range of investments required to open your initial franchise. The range assumes that all items are paid for in cash. To the extent that you choose to finance any of these expense items, your front-end investment could be substantially reduced.

Item	Established Low Range	Established High Range
Franchise Fee	$0	$25,000
Advertising (for 3 months)	$0	$28,600
Brokers Council Fees and Assessments (for 3 months)	$105	$1,500
Equipment/Fixtures	$0	$122,332
Service Fees (for 3 months)	$1,500	$170,129
Signs	$5,000	$24,000
Supplies	$3,200	$19,700
Training	$237	$33,100
Other Costs	$48	$98,000
Total Investment (does not include real estate)	$10,090	$522,361

On-Going Expenses
Century 21 franchisees pay royalties equaling 6% and national advertising fund fees equaling 2% of gross revenue. Franchisees may also be responsible for broker council fees, which vary, and tuition for the International Management Academy, which is free to new franchisees.

What You Get—Training and Support
In a company with the operating size and global scope of Century 21, service, support and other organizational perks are extensive and numerous.

Examples of Century 21's numerous communication and technological tools:
— A free virtual classroom with training and professional, long-term development for brokers, agents and management. Curricula is accredited to achieve and maintain professional certifications.
— Homestore Suite, which includes the brokernet intranet that keeps employees up to date on daily events in their office and the industry, Century 21 e-mail, Hometour 360—which allows visitors to view homes online—online

advertising, a personalized website and lead generation.

— Century 21 resource center, which includes online support, news, workshops and brainstorming, training, recruiting, awards status, national events calendar, access to special vendor deals to improve profit and reduce costs on supplies like telephones, computers and office machinery, marketing, advertising, an image library and promotions.

— Merrill net: Prospective, professional marketing supplies to increase publicity and lead generation.

— Century 21 Global Referral Network, the largest network of its kind providing instant two-way communication with more than 8,000 of Cendant's participating offices nationwide, 24 hours a day.

— Home buyer resources including listings, financing information and neighborhood statistics.

— Home owner services including virtual home planning and shopping.

— Specialty marketing programs, complete with appropriate training, tools and materials, for all property types.

— An electronic quality service survey sent to all customers at the close of a transaction that provides service feedback and substantiates marketing claims for national award recognition.

— Broker tools including a fully-supported back office management and accounting software system.

— Sales associate tools including a powerful contact system, a personalized business solutions database, automated listings and closing management and employee management software.

At the national and corporate level, Century 21 boasts many highly publicized cross-marketing relationships, especially with the Major League Baseball Association. In fact, Century 21 was the title sponsor of the league's Home Run Derby competition, ESPN's most-watched, non-football sporting event. The company has also teamed with the Ladies Professional Golf Association and the National Hot Rod Association and sponsored the Ringo Starr and His All-Star Band tour in 2000.

Territory
Century 21 grants protected territories of a quarter-mile radius. However, no franchisee is prohibited from seeking listings or buyers in any area.

Chem-Dry Carpet & Upholstery Cleaning

ChemDry®

1530 N. 1000 West
Logan, UT 84093
Tel: (800) CHEMDRY (877) 307-8233
Fax: (435) 755-0021
E-Mail: sfinn@chemdry.com
Web Site: www.chemdry.com
Mr. Scott Finn, Dir. New Franchise Licensing

CHEM-DRY has: 1-2 hour dry times (carpet & upholstery cleaning); hot carbonating cleaning solution (safe); uses 80% less water than steam cleaning; and no harsh chemicals.

BACKGROUND:

Established: 1977; 1st Franchised: 1977	
Franchised Units:	3,903
Company-Owned Units	0
Total Units:	3,903
Dist.:	US-2,495; CAN-124; O'seas-1,330
North America	50 States, 11 Provinces
Density:	421 in CA, 166 in TX, 146 FL
Projected New Units (12 Months):	2200
Qualifications:	4, 3, 1, 1, 1, 5
Registered:	All States

FINANCIAL/TERMS:

Cash Investment:	$10.0-14.9K
Total Investment:	$6.9-27.6K
Minimum Net Worth:	$10K
Fees:	Franchise — $19.5K
	Royalty — $212/Mo.; Ad. — 0%
Earnings Claim Statement:	No
Term of Contract (Years):	5/5
Avg. # Of Employees:	1 FT
Passive Ownership:	Not Allowed
Encourage Conversions:	N/A
Area Develop. Agreements:	No
Sub-Franchising Contracts:	No
Expand In Territory:	No
Space Needs:	N/A SF; Home Based

SUPPORT & TRAINING PROVIDED:

Financial Assistance Provided:	Yes(D)
Site Selection Assistance:	N/A
Lease Negotiation Assistance:	No
Co-Operative Advertising:	No
Franchisee Assoc./Member:	No
Size Of Corporate Staff:	70
On-Going Support:	B,C,D,G,H,I
Training:	5 Days Logan, UT.

SPECIFIC EXPANSION PLANS:

US:	Northeast,Cenrtral,Southeast
Canada:	All Canada
Overseas:	Most Countries

Chem-Dry's hot carbonated carpet cleaning methods are sophisticated enough to protect expensive and natural fibers, yet simple enough to allow Chem-Dry franchisees to focus on customer service, sales and profits rather than technology. Chem-Dry's commitment to simplicity and franchisee success is evident throughout its system. The company's royalty fees are not calculated according to gross revenue; franchisees pay one flat rate each month. Franchisees can work from home and the business doesn't require additional employees. However, there are no extra fees for expansion, and some franchisees maintain more than ten vans, making additional employees a necessity. In this case, the Chem-Dry video training program can train them on-site in just two days.

Operating Units	1/31/2003	1/31/2002	1/31/2001
Franchised	2,473	2,433	2,446
% Change	--	-1.6%	-0.5%
Company-Owned	0	0	0
% Change	--	N/A	N/A
Total	2,473	2,433	2,446
% Change	--	-1.6%	-0.5%
Franchised as % of Total	100.0%	100.0%	100.0%

Investment Required

The fee for a Chem-Dry franchise package ranges from $20,950 to $36,950. Financing is available.

Chem-Dry provides the following range of investments required to open your initial franchise. The range assumes that all items are paid for in cash. To the extent that you choose to finance any of these expense items, your front-end investment could be substantially reduced.

Item	Established Low Range	Established High Range
Franchise Fee	$9,950	$9,950
Advertising/Equipment Package	$11,900	$31,500
Computer System	$800	$2,000
Insurance	$600	$2,000
Rent (for 3 months)	$0	$3,000
Training Expenses	$0	$1,000
Van	$0	$30,000
Other Costs and Additional Funds (for 3 months)	$975	$4,800
Total Investment	$24,225	$84,250

On-Going Expenses

Chem-Dry franchisees pay royalties equaling $212.87 a month. Franchisees must also meet a yearly minimum purchase requirement of $2,000. There are also additional fees for the administration and equipment for additional franchise services, such as water damage restoration and leather and vinyl cleaning.

What You Get—Training and Support

Chem-Dry training comes from three sources: a five-day hands-on program in cleaning methods and marketing at company headquarters in Logan, Utah, 10 hours of videotape instruction and numerous operation manuals. Furthermore, as new products and techniques are discovered and developed, a company crew travels the world to bring educational seminars and training classes to Chem-Dry franchisees. On-going training is supplemented by system newsletters, technical bulletins, marketing tips and annual conventions.

The purchase of a Chem-Dry franchise includes: state-of-the-art equipment; tested and proven cleaning products and supplies worth $10,000; technical support (even about specific stains); continuing research into and development of cleaning solutions; a 300-page Media Center Kit containing radio scripts, four-color brochures, newspaper and Yellow Page advertisements, on-line advertising and artwork libraries, coupon mailers, flyers and door hangers; and a business start-up kit containing stationery, business cards, uniforms and sign layouts and designs.

Territory

Chem-Dry does not grant exclusive territories.

Coit Services

Experience You Can Trust

897 Hinckley Rd.
Burlingame, CA 94010-1502

Tel: (800) 243-8797 (650) 697-5471
Fax: (650) 697-6117
E-Mail: nick@coit.com
Web Site: www.coit.com
Mr. Nick Granato, Chief Operating Officer

Granting large, exclusive territories, COIT SER-

VICES provides a proven opportunity in the carpet, upholstery, drapery, area rug air-duct cleaning and hard surface renewal business. COIT franchisees enjoy use of a universal 800# (1-800-FOR-COIT), along with successful marketing and business development that have been developed in 50 years of operational experience.

BACKGROUND: IFA MEMBER
Established: 1950; 1st Franchised: 1963

Franchised Units:	60
Company-Owned Units	10
Total Units:	70
Dist.:	US-66; CAN-3; O'seas-1
North America:	26 States, 2 Provinces
Density:	16 in CA, 4 in WA, 4 in OH
Projected New Units (12 Months):	51
Qualifications:	3, 5, 4, 3, 1, 5
Registered:	All States

FINANCIAL/TERMS:

Cash Investment:	$40-60K
Total Investment:	$100K
Minimum Net Worth:	$No Minimum
Fees:	Franchise — $25K
	Royalty — 2-6%; Ad. — 0%

Earnings Claim Statement:	Yes
Term of Contract (Years):	10/10
Avg. # Of Employees:	2 FT, 1 PT
Passive Ownership:	Discouraged
Encourage Conversions:	Yes
Area Develop. Agreements:	No
Sub-Franchising Contracts:	No
Expand In Territory:	Yes
Space Needs:	1,000 SF; Industrial

SUPPORT & TRAINING PROVIDED:

Financial Assistance Provided:	Yes(D)
Site Selection Assistance:	Yes
Lease Negotiation Assistance:	Yes
Co-Operative Advertising:	Yes
Franchisee Assoc./Member:	Yes/Yes
Size Of Corporate Staff:	19
On-Going Support:	A,a,B,C,D,E,G,H,I
Training:	7 Days Corporate Headquarters; 1-2 Weeks in Field.

SPECIFIC EXPANSION PLANS:

US:	Northeast, Southeast, Midwest
Canada:	All Canada
Overseas:	All Countries

Coit has been in business for more than 50 years and—thanks to customer trust, satisfaction and loyalty and the increasing number of households seeking professional cleaning services—is still growing. Contributing to Coit's success is the company's proven operating strategies and techniques; franchisee network; large, protected territories, enabling the development of multi-truck and multi-profit center franchisees; and royalty reductions correlated to volume increases, providing each franchisee with an incentive to grow.

Over the years, Coit has expanded the number of services it offers to meet growing demand and increase its profit centers. Coit services include carpet, upholstery, drapery, area rug and air duct cleaning; hard surface treatment; new drapery and carpet sales; mini-blind cleaning and sales. In addition to this wide range of services, Coit also provides peace of mind. No matter what the service or product provided, each is backed by a satisfaction guarantee. If the customer isn't happy, Coit promises to reclean, repair or refund.

Operating Units	12/31/2000	12/31/2001	12/31/2002
Franchised	59	60	56
% Change	--	1.7%	-6.7%
Company-Owned	13	13	11
% Change	--	0.0%	-15.4
Total	72	73	67
% Change	--	1.4%	-8.2%
Franchised as % of Total	81.9%	82.2%	83.6%

Investment Required

The fee for a Coit franchise is $20,000 plus 4 cents per each household located in the franchisee's territory.

Coit provides the following range of investments required to open your initial franchise. The range assumes that all items are paid for in cash. To the extent that you choose to finance any of these expense items, your front-end investment could be substantially reduced. The following figures apply to the opening of an on-location service franchise.

Item	Established Low Range	Established High Range
Franchise Fee	$24,000	$40,000
Advertising and Promotions	$3,000	$8,000
Equipment/Fixtures	$6,000	$15,000
Real Estate	$0	$4,200
Training Expenses	$1,000	$2,000
Vehicle	$1,000	$20,000
Other Costs and Additional Funds	$10,125	$26,125
Total Investment	$45,125	$115,325

On-Going Expenses

Coit franchisees pay royalties equaling 6% of gross revenue. Franchisees also pay software usage fees equaling $125 for a single user or $225 for multiple users.

What You Get—Training and Support

Coit training consists of customized initial lessons, on-going field training and advanced learning. Topics covered in a franchisee's two weeks of initial training include computer systems, advertising, sales calls, selling techniques, customer service, business planning and development, employee training, cleaning techniques, fabrics, human resources and financial planning and management. After initial training concludes, franchisees are aided by Performance Academy advanced learning classes, international conventions, field and certification training and on-site visits.

Other franchisee resources include "image-building" professional marketing programs and materials (including television, radio, print and internet exposure, strategy and research, direct mail, public relations and yellow pages listings) and Coit's business management system and proprietary software (featuring order entry, marketing evaluations, customer tracking, employee productivity reports, accounting and statistical reports).

In addition, Coit offers franchisees strength from numbers. The company offers national account pricing on equipment and services (reducing costs and trouncing competition), on-going research and development, a nationwide hotline for customer inquiries, a franchise advisory council and, where available, commercial accounts.

Territory

Coit grants exclusive territories.

Coldwell Banker
Real Estate

1 Campus Dr.
Parsippany, NJ 07054
Tel: (973) 428-8600
Fax: (973) 496-7217
E-Mail: david.hardy@cendant.com
Web Site: www.coldwellbanker.com

Mr. David Hardy, SVP Franchise Development	Royalty — 6%; Ad. — 2.5%/$245

The franchise is a real estate brokerage office offering defined real estate brokerage services from a specified location under the registered name Coldwell Banker. Coldwell Banker Real Estate Corporation is a subsidiary of Cendant Corportion (NYSE: CD). Cendant is the world's premier provider of business and consumer services.

Earnings Claim Statement:	No
Term of Contract (Years):	10/10
Avg. # Of Employees:	NR
Passive Ownership:	Not Allowed
Encourage Conversions:	Yes
Area Develop. Agreements:	No
Sub-Franchising Contracts:	No
Expand In Territory:	Yes
Space Needs:	1,000 SF; FS, SF, SC

BACKGROUND: IFA MEMBER
Established: 1902; 1st Franchised: 1982

Franchised Units:	2,790
Company-Owned Units	0
Total Units:	2,790
Dist.:	US-2,225; CAN-224; O'seas-0
North America:	50 States,11 Provinces
Density:	238 in CA, 155 in TX, 142 NY
Projected New Units (12 Months):	225
Qualifications:	4, 4, 5, 3, 2, 4
Registered:	All States

FINANCIAL/TERMS:

Cash Investment:	$23.5-65.6K
Total Investment:	$150.6-477.3K
Minimum Net Worth:	$25K
Fees:	Franchise — $0-20.5K

SUPPORT & TRAINING PROVIDED:

Financial Assistance Provided:	Yes(D)
Site Selection Assistance:	No
Lease Negotiation Assistance:	No
Co-Operative Advertising:	Yes
Franchisee Assoc./Member:	Yes
Size Of Corporate Staff:	136
On-Going Support:	C,d,G,h,I
Training:	4 Days in Parsippany, NJ

SPECIFIC EXPANSION PLANS:

US:	All United States
Canada:	All Canada
Overseas:	All Countries

In the wake of the 1906 San Francisco earthquake, Colbert Coldwell responded to his city's need for honest, ethical and professional real estate services. Seven years later, Coldwell discovered that Benjamin Arthur, one of his salesmen, shared similar values and business sense. Arthur became Coldwell's partner in 1914 and they opened their first residential real estate office in 1925. Over nearly a century of real estate transactions, Coldwell Banker has established itself throughout the world with its performance and associations with big name companies, such as Sears, Roebuck and Co., to which it belonged in 1981, further entrenching Coldwell Banker in the retail and commercial real estate market. The company began to expand internationally in the 1990s. Now, Coldwell Banker is part of Cendant Corporation, the world's largest hotel and real estate brokerage franchisor.

Operating Units	12/31/2000	12/31/2001	12/31/2002
Franchised	2,780	2,909	3,092
% Change	--	4.6%	6.3%
Company-Owned	0	0	0
% Change	--	N/A	N/A
Total	2,780	2,909	3,092
% Change	--	4.6%	6.3%
Franchised as % of Total	100.0%	100.0%	100.0%

Investment Required

The fee for a Coldwell Banker franchise ranges from $13,000 to $20,500, depending on the franchise's market. The fee for a second and each subsequent location is reduced to $10,000 and $7,500, respectively.

Coldwell Banker provides the following range of investments required to open your initial franchise. The range assumes that all items are paid for in cash. To the extent that you choose to finance any of these expense items, your front-end investment could be substantially reduced.

On-Going Expenses

Coldwell Banker franchisees pay royalties equaling 6% and advertising fees equaling 2.5% of gross revenues.

Item	Established Low Range	Established High Range
Franchise Fee	$13,000	$20,500
Computer Equipment	$1,000	$4,000
Insurance	$300	$1,000
Name Badges/Printed Materials/Signs	$8,850	$34,050
Training Expenses	$200	$2,700
Other Costs and Additional Funds (for 3 months)	$250	$3,500
Total Investment	$23,600	$65,750

What You Get—Training and Support

Coldwell Banker presents franchisees with a host of tools to boost business and save them time and money. A sampling of these tools includes:

—The Coldwell Banker Concierge program, which supplies members, whether franchisees, employees or their clients, with money-saving deals at international businesses.

—An extensive website housing resource on marketing, special markets, bilingual materials and markets, an image and logo library, flyers, statistics, press releases, PowerPoint presentations, promotions, customizable newsletters and advertisements and the Mortgage Resource Center.

—Live online training classes.

—A comprehensive marketing packet for each special market, such as the Coldwell Banker Previews International program, which focuses on luxury homes across the globe.

—This Week on CBNet, an e-mailed newsletter sent to sales associates every two weeks and brokers every week to update them on industry news and services, training and management procedures.

In addition, Coldwell Banker puts each franchisee's advertising fee to good use through the development of national advertising and the establishment of identity standards to create and maintain a strong, consistent presence for the Coldwell Banker brand. Advertising support includes proper usage and specifications rules, network and cable television advertising, local radio and television advertisements, postcards, brochures and display ads. Coldwell Banker's marketing program also develops and presents to franchisees a number of theme promotions that they may choose to implement in their communities. Recent promotions include Celebrate America, which can be staged year round or associated with a holiday like the 4th of July or Veterans' Day; Be Fire Safe!, which takes place each November and builds relationships and recognition with local fire departments and schools; Spring Open House, which taps into the peak home-buying and -selling season; and Helping Others Throughout the Holiday Season, which benefits homeless shelters, inner-city schools and nursing homes.

Territory

Coldwell Banker does not grant exclusive territories.

Crestcom International, Ltd.

6900 E. Belleview Ave., # 300
Greenwood Village, CO 80111-1619
Tel: (888) 273-7826 (303) 267-8200
Fax: (303) 267-8207
E-Mail: kelly.kraus@crestcom.com
Web Site: www.crestcom.com
Mr. Kelly Krause, Dir. International Marketing

Recognized by Entrepreneur and Success magazines as the #1 management/sales training franchise, CRESTCOM INTERNATIONAL offers business executives and professionals the opportunity to put their experience to work for themselves as the CEO of their own training company. CRESTCOM training combines live-facilitated instruction by franchisees and videos featuring internationally known business experts.

BACKGROUND: IFA MEMBER
Established: 1987; 1st Franchised: 1992
Franchised Units: 135
Company-Owned Units 0
Total Units: 135
Dist.: US-51; CAN-10; O'seas-74
  North America: 25 States, 4 Provinces
  Density: NR
Projected New Units (12 Months): 35

Qualifications: 4, 5, 2, 4, 5, 5
Registered: All States

FINANCIAL/TERMS:
Cash Investment: $39.5-58.5K
Total Investment: $47.8-78.5K
Minimum Net Worth: $NR
Fees: Franchise — $39.5-58.5K
  Royalty — 1.5%; Ad. — N/A
Earnings Claim Statement: Yes
Term of Contract (Years): 7/7/7
Avg. # Of Employees: 2-5 FT
Passive Ownership: Discouraged
Encourage Conversions: N/A
Area Develop. Agreements: No
Sub-Franchising Contracts: No
Expand In Territory: Yes
Space Needs: NR SF; SF, HB

SUPPORT & TRAINING PROVIDED:
Financial Assistance Provided: Yes
Site Selection Assistance: N/A
Lease Negotiation Assistance: N/A
Co-Operative Advertising: No
Franchisee Assoc./Member: Yes
Size Of Corporate Staff: 15
On-Going Support: D,G,H
Training: 7-10 Days Denver, CO, Phoenix, AZ or Sacramento, CA.

SPECIFIC EXPANSION PLANS:
US: All United States
Canada: All Canada
Overseas: All Countries

Recent surveys indicate that workplace performance and retention are heavily impacted by the relationships that employees have with their immediate supervisor. So what's the problem? Another recent survey found that more than half of business professionals would fire their boss if they were given the chance. Crestcom International, Ltd. has turned this business problem into a worldwide franchise opportunity.

Crestcom International licensees deliver video-based, live-facilitated management and sales training to thousands of business executives to help them become better, more effective leaders. Crestcom® was founded in the late 1980s and is now a growing network of more than 135 distributors and franchisees that have been appointed in more than 50 countries. Each year, Crestcom® graduates more business professionals from its Bullet Proof® Manager program than were graduated from Harvard, Yale and Stanford Business Schools *combined.*

An important part of Crestcom's® success is the screening/evaluation process for new distributors and franchisees. Before prospects acquire a license, the company is willing to make an investment in qualified applicants by putting them through an intensive Initial Training course. This allows prospects to determine whether Crestcom® is right for them.

Operating Units	12/31/2000	12/31/2001	12/31/2002
Franchised	39	42	47
% Change	--	7.7%	11.9%
Company-Owned	0	0	0
% Change	--	0.0%	0.0%
Total	39	42	47
% Change	--	7.7%	11.9%
Franchised as % of Total	100.0%	100.0%	100.0%

Investment Required

The fee for a Crestcom franchise ranges from $39,500 to $58,500 in the United States. Fees are typically higher for international locations. Master franchises are available in some areas.

Crestcom International provides the following range of investments required to open your initial franchise. The range assumes that all items are paid for in cash. To the extent that you choose to finance any of these expense items, your front-end investment could be substantially reduced.

Item	Established Low Range	Established High Range
Franchise Fee	$39,500	$58,500
Equipment/Supplies	$675	$3,230
Insurance	$600	$1,800
Inventory/Shipping Costs	$200	$800
Real Estate	$0	$400
Training Expenses	$1,120	$2,550
Other Costs and Additional Funds (for 3 months)	$5,700	$11,175
Total Investment	$47,795	$78,455

On-Going Expenses

Crestcom franchisees pay royalties equaling 1.5%. Distribution fees vary by franchise type.

What You Get—Training and Support

Crestcom franchisees are backed by a strong and proven system of support, fellow franchisees and home staff who shared the same problems and opportunities. The Crestcom program provides franchisees with international training materials available in more than 20 languages, including a new version of the Crestcom flagship, the BULLET PROOF Manager program, every five years.

Territory

Crestcom territories are based on population.

The
Entrepreneur's Source

THE
ENTREPRENEUR'S
©SOURCE *"Your success is our only business"*

900 Main St. S., Bldg. # 2
Southbury, CT 06488
Tel: (800) 289-0086 (203) 264-2006
Fax: (203) 264-3516
E-Mail: info@theesource.com

Web Site: www.franchisesearch.com	Royalty — 0%; Ad. — $350/Mo.
Mr. Chris Otter, Franchise Director	Earnings Claim Statement: No
	Term of Contract (Years): 10/10
We provide consulting, education and guidance to people exploring self-employment as an additional career option. Using a unique profiling system, ENTREPRENEUR'S SOURCE consultants help people discover the best options for them.	Avg. # Of Employees: 1 FT
	Passive Ownership: Not Allowed
	Encourage Conversions: Yes
	Area Develop. Agreements: No
	Sub-Franchising Contracts: Yes
	Expand In Territory: Yes
BACKGROUND: IFA MEMBER	Space Needs: NR SF; N/A
Established: 1984; 1st Franchised: 1998	
Franchised Units: 195	**SUPPORT & TRAINING PROVIDED:**
Company-Owned Units 0	Financial Assistance Provided: Yes(I)
Total Units: 195	Site Selection Assistance: N/A
Dist.: US-43; CAN-1; O'seas-0	Lease Negotiation Assistance: N/A
North America: 27 States	Co-Operative Advertising: Yes
Density: 5 in GA, 5 in FL, 3 in SC,	Franchisee Assoc./Member: No
Projected New Units (12 Months): 40	Size Of Corporate Staff: 6
Qualifications: 4, 4, 1, 1, 2, 5	On-Going Support: D,H,I
Registered: CA,FL,MD,MI,MN,NY,VA, WA,WI	Training: 8 Days in CT.
FINANCIAL/TERMS:	**SPECIFIC EXPANSION PLANS:**
Cash Investment: $50K	US: All United States
Total Investment: $45-50K	Canada: All Canada
Minimum Net Worth: $100K	Overseas: Most Countries
Fees: Franchise — $35K	

The Entrepreneur's Source specializes in alternative career options, providing individuals and businesses with assessments and coaching to ease clients' transitions into new business opportunities. The Entrepreneur's Source's Franchise-Development Services division focuses on helping companies expand their businesses via franchising and other distribution methods.

No prior experience, inventory or large overhead investments in equipment, materials or employee labor is necessary. A laptop computer, telephone and initiative are all an Entrepreneur's Source franchisee requires. The company offers four franchise program options. The individual office program licenses franchisees for one office with the option for later expansion; the master developer program allows franchisees to develop a team of consultants and to work with an associate; and the regional director program is for franchisees who have the desire and ability to manage and support a team of consultants to develop many individual offices within a large geographic area. Franchisees can also take advantage of The Entrepreneur's Source international licensing programs, which are available in select locations.

Operating Units	12/31/2000	12/31/2001	12/31/2002
Franchised	40	83	175
% Change	--	107.5%	110.8%
Company-Owned	0	0	0
% Change	--	N/A	N/A
Total	40	83	175
% Change	--	107.5%	110.8%
Franchised as % of Total	100.0%	100.0%	100.0%

Investment Required
The fee for a The Entrepreneur's Source franchise is $45,000. Additional units are available at a reduced fee.

The Entrepreneur's Source provides the following range of investments required to open your initial franchise. The range assumes that all items are paid for in cash. To the extent that you choose to finance any of these expense items, your front-end investment could be substantially reduced.

Item	Established Low Range	Established High Range
Franchise Fee	$45,000	$45,000
Equipment	$3,000	$4,000
Intranet and Extranet Setup	$2,500	$2,500
Lead Generation and Support Fees	$6,000	$6,000
Marketing	$1,300	$2,300
Other Costs and Additional Funds	$9,700	$14,200
Training Expenses	$3,000	$4,500
Total Investment	$70,500	$78,500

On-Going Expenses
The Entrepreneur's Source franchisees pay monthly lead generation and support fees equaling $750.

What You Get—Training and Support
The Entrepreneur's Source training is thorough and enduring, making sure that each franchisee gets off to a comfortable, successful start. The first phase of training is pre-training with a personal Entrepreneur's Source coach. Upon completion, Entrepreneur's Source franchisees attend the E-Source Academy where they learn how to be a consultant by being led through every step of the experience, from first contacts to client placement. Finally, training concludes over the course of the next several months with the franchisee's participation in the "Jump Start" coaching program. Further training and support comes from the system's national and regional support offices and includes one-on-one coaching, tele-coaching, live training sessions and national conferences.

The Entrepreneur's Source's marketing and education tools focus on increasing exposure through international, national and regional channels. Advertising has appeared in the *International Herald Tribune*, the *Wall Street Journal*, *USA Today*, *The New York Times* and *The Los Angeles Times*. The Entrepreneur's Source also maintains a strong Internet presence with a company website, features on AOL and Yahoo and a company intranet system that provides 24-hour access to documents, manuals, e-mail, a library of franchise and business data, industry news, forums and a company support center.

Territory
The Entrepreneur's Source does not grant exclusive territories.

Expetec
Technology Services

	Aberdeen, SD 57402-0487
	Tel: (888) 297-2292 (605) 225-4122
	Fax: (605) 225-5176
	E-Mail: lisah@expetec.biz
12 2nd Ave. SW	Web Site: www.expetec.biz

Ms. Lisa Hinz, Franchise Sales

EXPETEC locations provide mobile, on-site or in-shop computer and printer repair, sales, service and upgrades. A multiple profit center in one franchise, with unlimited market potential, including communications, phone systems and retail point-of-sale systems.

BACKGROUND: IFA MEMBER
Established: 1992; 1st Franchised: 1996
Franchised Units: 150
Company-Owned Units: 0
Total Units: 150
Dist.: US-150; CAN-0; O'seas-0
North America: 28 States
Density: 19 in FL, 8 in TX, 5 in SD
Projected New Units (12 Months): 50
Qualifications: , , , , ,
Registered: NR

FINANCIAL/TERMS:
Cash Investment: $30K
Total Investment: $53.8-80K
Minimum Net Worth: $100K
Fees: Franchise — $27K

Royalty — 5%; Ad. — 2%
Earnings Claim Statement: No
Term of Contract (Years): 10
Avg. # Of Employees: 2 FT
Passive Ownership: Discouraged
Encourage Conversions: NR
Area Develop. Agreements: Yes/10
Sub-Franchising Contracts: Yes
Expand In Territory: Yes
Space Needs: 300-700 SF; FS,HB, IP, OB

SUPPORT & TRAINING PROVIDED:
Financial Assistance Provided: NR
Site Selection Assistance: Yes
Lease Negotiation Assistance: Yes
Co-Operative Advertising: No
Franchisee Assoc./Member: Yes/Yes
Size Of Corporate Staff: 13
On-Going Support: B,C,D,E,F,G,H,I
Training: 3 Weeks in Aberdeen, SD.

SPECIFIC EXPANSION PLANS:
US: All United States
Canada: All Canada
Overseas: No

Expetec provides businesses and consumers with mobile, on-site technology services. Expetec describes itself as a "franchise in a box;" the franchise fee includes all equipment and a new "Technical Assault Vehicle," armed with brand new graphics, a customization package, navigation system and on-site repair facilities.

All Expetec franchisees provide computer repair, the original Expetec service. For franchisees looking to expand, the Expetec Business Builder system drafts a strategic growth plan to help them expand into additional service options, including business phone system sales, installations and upgrades, point-of-sales modules, web modules and value added reseller modules. All modules are described in-depth during training and may require extra investment and training to execute.

243

Operating Units	2000	2001	2002
Franchised	31	52	53
% Change	--	67.7%	1.9%
Company-Owned	0	0	0
% Change	--	N/A	N/A
Total	31	52	53
% Change	--	67.7%	1.9%
Franchised as % of Total	100.0%	100.0%	100.0%

Investment Required
The fee for an Expetec franchise is $20,000.

Expetec provides the following range of investments required to open your initial franchise. The range assumes that all items are paid for in cash. To the extent that you choose to finance any of these expense items, your front-end investment could be substantially reduced.

Item	Established Low Range	Established High Range
Franchise Fee	$20,000	$28,000
Business Management System	$7,000	$7,000
Facility Improvements/ Office Equipment/Signs/ Supplies	$1,500	$4,500
Insurance	$600	$1,000
Inventory	$500	$1,000
Marketing Fee	$12,000	$20,000
Training Expenses	$4,000	$6,000
Vehicle	$3,600	$7,200
Other Costs and Additional Funds	$8,000	$13,500
Total Investment	$57,200	$88,200

On-Going Expenses

For the first eight weeks of operation, Expetec franchisees pay royalties equaling $50 per week and advertising marketing fund contributions equaling $50. Thereafter, royalties equal $150 to $300 per week and advertising fund contributions equal $100 to $275 per week, depending on each individual franchisee's gross volume.

What You Get—Training and Support

Expetec training primes any franchisee, regardless of background, to run a successful Expetec. Integrating the business management program with hands-on technical training modules, training instructs franchisees on financial management, customer relations, call center procedures, communications, local marketing, operations analysis, technical procedures and scheduling.

Expetec franchisees receive support from: an online support system, local marketing and promotional materials, a national customer service call center, management staff, annual conventions, monthly newsletters, operations analysis, yellow pages advertising, a media library, a preferred vendor program, certification training and an extended warranty program to ensure that customers are always happy.

Territory

Expetec grants exclusive territories encompassing up to 2000 businesses.

Express Oil Change

190 W. Valley Ave.
Birmingham, AL 35209-3621
Tel: (888) 945-1771 (205) 945-1771
Fax: (205) 940-6026
E-Mail: kfeazell@expressoil.com
Web Site: www.expressoil.com

Mr. R. Kent Feazell, VP Franchise Develop.

We are among the top ten fast oil change chains in the world. Per unit, sales out-pace our competitors by over 40%. Attractive, state-of-the-art facilities offer expanded, highly profitable services in addition to our ten minute oil change. We also provide transmission service, air conditioning service, brake repair, tire rotation and balancing and miscellaneous light repairs... Most extensive training and franchise support in the industry.

BACKGROUND:	IFA MEMBER	Encourage Conversions:	Yes
Established: 1979; 1st Franchised: 1986		Area Develop. Agreements:	Yes
Franchised Units:	130	Sub-Franchising Contracts:	No
Company-Owned Units	13	Expand In Territory:	Yes
Total Units:	143	Space Needs:	22,000 SF; FS
Dist.:	US-143; CAN-0; O'seas-0		
North America:	5 States	**SUPPORT & TRAINING PROVIDED:**	
Density:	62 in AL, 35 in GA, 6 in TN	Financial Assistance Provided:	Yes(I)
Projected New Units (12 Months):	15	Site Selection Assistance:	Yes
Qualifications:	5, 5, 1, 3, 3, 5	Lease Negotiation Assistance:	Yes
Registered:	NR	Co-Operative Advertising:	Yes
		Franchisee Assoc./Member:	No
FINANCIAL/TERMS:		Size Of Corporate Staff:	37
Cash Investment:	$115-249K	On-Going Support:	A,B,C,D,E,F,G,H,I
Total Investment:	$130K-1.1MM	Training: 8 Weeks Closest Training Center; 1 Yr.	
Minimum Net Worth:	$450K	On-Site, Post-OpeningTraining; Continuous	
Fees:	Franchise — $17.5K		Training.
	Royalty — 5%; Ad. — 3%		
Earnings Claim Statement:	Yes	**SPECIFIC EXPANSION PLANS:**	
Term of Contract (Years):	10/10	US:	Southeast
Avg. # Of Employees:	7 FT	Canada:	No
Passive Ownership:	Allowed	Overseas:	No

Quick oil change franchisees behind the Express brand frequently trounce the competition in the number of cars their stores service per day, the average amount of each customer's receipt and average store sales chainwide. No doubt this opportunity for success is fueled by current industry conditions. The average life of a car has increased—and good maintenance is needed to support this increase, the population continues to grow—putting more cars on the road and, because of environmental concerns and lifestyle changes, many of those who usually changed their automotive oil themselves, now pay for the service.

Express Oil Change has expanded services and divides each unit into an oil change department, which performs speedy oil changes and transmission checks, and a mechanical department, which covers maintenance such as tire rotation, brakes and air conditioning. Together, both departments provide customers with one-stop shopping for their car maintenance needs.

Seeing a new market arising in quick oil changes, Jim Lunceford opened the first Express Oil Change in 1979. The first franchise opened in 1984 and in less than 20 years, there were more than 50 locations in Alabama.

In March of 1996, two established Express franchisees, who owned a total of

14 units, purchased the chain. They began expanding into Florida, Mississippi, Tennessee and Georgia and, in 1998, incorporated 25 Tune-Up Clinics into their fleet. There were 137 units in southeast America by the end of 2001. The company is looking to expand only in the Southeast.

Operating Units	12/31/1999	12/31/2000	12/31/2001
Franchised	95	112	125
% Change	--	17.9%	11.6%
Company-Owned	12	12	12
% Change	--	0.0%	0.0%
Total	107	124	137
% Change	--	15.9%	10.5%
Franchised as % of Total	88.8%	90.3%	91.2%

Investment Required
The fee for an Express Oil Change franchise is $17,500.

Express Oil Change provides the following range of investments required to open your initial franchise. The range assumes that all items are paid for in cash. To the extent that you choose to finance any of these expense items, your front-end investment could be substantially reduced.

Item	Established Low Range	Established High Range
Franchise Fee	$17,500	$17,500
Advertising	$5,000	$5,000
Inventory	$18,000	$22,000
Training Expenses	$2,000	$5,000
Other Costs and Additional Funds (for 3 months)	$63,000	$87,000
Total Investment (does not include real estate and assumes leasing equipment and signage)	$105,500	$136,500

On-Going Expenses

Express Oil Change franchisees pay royalties equaling 5% (with a volume discount available), with a required advertising expenditure of 3% of gross revenue per month.

What You Get—Training and Support

Express Oil Change franchisees undergo eight weeks of training in the classroom and the field. A certified trainer will also work with them at their locations throughout the first year and as needed thereafter.

Further perks and support include mass purchasing power and marketing programs, effective advertising that focuses on specific demographics and superior staffing and compensation systems to bring the best personnel to all Express Oil locations.

Territory

Express Oil Change grants protected territories of a one-mile radius around each unit.

Express
Personnel Services

8516 Northwest Expy.
Oklahoma City, OK 73162-5145
Tel: (877) 652-6400 (405) 840-5000
Fax: (405) 717-5665
E-Mail: tom.gunderson@expresspersonnel.com
Web Site: www.expressfranchising.com
Mr. Tom Gunderson, VP Franchising
Three sales divisions - permanent placement, temporary placement and executive search - offering full and complete coverage of the employment field.

BACKGROUND: IFA MEMBER
Established: 1983; 1st Franchised: 1985
Franchised Units: 407

Company-Owned Units	0
Total Units:	407
Dist.:	US-392; CAN-9; O'seas-6
North America:	45 States
Density:	48 in TX, 32 in OK, 24 in WA
Projected New Units (12 Months):	40
Qualifications:	4, 4, 3, 4, 4, 4
Registered:	All States

FINANCIAL/TERMS:

Cash Investment:	$120-160K
Total Investment:	$120-160K
Minimum Net Worth:	$100K
Fees:	Franchise — $17.5-20.5K
	Royalty — 8-9%; Ad. — 0.6%
Earnings Claim Statement:	No
Term of Contract (Years):	5/5
Avg. # Of Employees:	2 FT, 1 PT
Passive Ownership:	Not Allowed

Encourage Conversions:	Yes	Franchisee Assoc./Member:	No
Area Develop. Agreements:	Yes	Size Of Corporate Staff:	169
Sub-Franchising Contracts:	No	On-Going Support:	A,C,D,E,G,H,I
Expand In Territory:	Yes	Training:	2 Weeks Oklahoma City, OK; Plus 1
Space Needs:	1,200 SF; SC, RM, SF		Week On-Site.
SUPPORT & TRAINING PROVIDED:		**SPECIFIC EXPANSION PLANS:**	
Financial Assistance Provided:	Yes(D)	US:	All United States
Site Selection Assistance:	Yes	Canada:	All Except AB
Lease Negotiation Assistance:	Yes	Overseas:	UK, Australia.
Co-Operative Advertising:	Yes		

Express Personnel Services provides temporary help, flexible staffing, evaluation, direct hire employees, contract and professional placement, labor relations and management consulting to individuals and businesses in over 400 locations in the United States, Canada and South Africa. Focusing on product lines in light industrial, office services and professional staffing, Express is a sales-focused personal business opportunity with annual sales over $800 million in 2001. Their mission statement: "to professionally market and provide quality human resource solutions through an international franchising network that profits our associates, customers, franchisees, corporate staff, stockholders and communities." The company has an employee base exceeding 250,000 and a client roster of more than 75,000.

Operating Units	2000	2001	2002
Franchised	82	90	76
% Change	--	9.7%	-15.5%
Company-Owned	0	1	1
% Change	--	100.0%	0.0%
Total	82	91	77
% Change	--	11.0%	-15.4%
Franchised as % of Total	100.0%	98.9%	98.7%

Investment Required

The fee for an Express Personnel franchise ranges from $17,500 to $20,500, depending on territory population.

Express Personnel provides the following range of investments required to open your initial franchise. The range assumes that all items are paid for in cash. To the extent that you choose to finance any of these expense items, your front-end investment could be substantially reduced.

Item	Established Low Range	Established High Range
Franchise Fee	$17,500	$20,500
Equipment/Furniture/Signs	$27,300	$35,300
Insurance	$1,000	$3,500
Inventory/Supplies	$750	$1,000
Real Estate	$4,200	$16,000
Other Costs and Additional Funds	$69,150	$76,000
Total Investment	$119,900	$152,300

On-Going Expenses

In exchange for a 60/40% split of the monthly gross margin, Express Personnel Services provides franchisees with payroll processing, client invoicing, collection and risk management and worker compensation administration.

What You Get—Training and Support

When you purchase an Express Personnel franchise, Express provides you with: 100% financing of payroll for temporary associates, rights to four services in one franchise agreement, workers' compensation, liability and unemployment insurance for temporary and contract associates, advertising and marketing campaigns at volume prices, comprehensive operations and management manuals, three weeks of start-up training, continuing on-site visits by field support representatives, territory research and expertise, annual and regional meetings, year-round courses via Express University and regional training centers, franchisee assistance and technical support centers, sales tools, crisis support and credit and collections monitoring.

New franchisees undergo five days of operations training, five days of sales training and two days of business management instruction at the Express Personnel Service International headquarters in Oklahoma City, Oklahoma. An additional five days is spent in a regional field office.

Territory

Express Personnel Services grants exclusive territories.

FasTracKids International Ltd.

"Enrichment Education for Tomorrow's Leaders"

6900 E. Belleview Ave., 1st Fl.
Greenwood Village, CO 80111-1619
Tel: (888) 576-6888 (303) 224-0200
Fax: (303) 224-0222
E-Mail: kevin.krause@fastrackids.com
Web Site: www.fastrackids.com
Mr. Kevin Krause, Dir. Franchise Development

FASTRACKIDS® is an exciting advancement in the education of young children, powered by innovative technology, a strong curriculum, and the leadership of franchise owners throughout the world. Based on the premise that, given proper instruction and reinforcement, most children can perform at the level we now call gifted, FasTracKids fosters the early development of creativity, leadership and communication skills.

BACKGROUND:	IFA MEMBER
Established: 1998; 1st Franchised: 1998	
Franchised Units:	170
Company-Owned Units	0
Total Units:	170
Dist.:	US-32; CAN-8; O'seas-130
North America:	11 States
Density:	NR

Projected New Units (12 Months):	55
Qualifications:	4, 4, 4, 4, 5, 5
Registered:	All States

FINANCIAL/TERMS:	
Cash Investment:	$20.9-39.7K
Total Investment:	$20.9-39.7K
Minimum Net Worth:	$NR
Fees:	Franchise — $15K
	Royalty — 1.5%; Ad. — 5%
Earnings Claim Statement:	Yes
Term of Contract (Years):	5/5
Avg. # Of Employees:	1-5 FT
Passive Ownership:	Discouraged
Encourage Conversions:	N/A
Area Develop. Agreements:	Yes/5
Sub-Franchising Contracts:	No
Expand In Territory:	Yes
Space Needs:	700 SF; N/A

SUPPORT & TRAINING PROVIDED:	
Financial Assistance Provided:	No
Site Selection Assistance:	Yes
Lease Negotiation Assistance:	No
Co-Operative Advertising:	Yes
Franchisee Assoc./Member:	No
Size Of Corporate Staff:	12
On-Going Support:	C,G,h,I
	Training: 5 Days in Denver, CO.

SPECIFIC EXPANSION PLANS:	
US:	All United States
Canada:	All Canada
Overseas:	All Countries

The advent of the knowledge economy, combined with mounting dissatisfaction with the dismal state of many public schools, is creating vast openings for for-profit companies.
—Business Week Magazine

Based on a tested academic curriculum, innovative technology and a thriving classroom enterprise, FasTracKids® delivers enrichment education services to children ages three to six. Children enrolled for FasTracKids® instruction typically attend four 2-hour sessions each month and receive instruction in 12 subject areas over the course of two years. FasTracKids® Academy instruction also integrates innovative technology that is used by some of the most prestigious universities in the world.

A unique aspect of the FasTracKids® franchise opportunity is the screening/evaluation process for new licensees. Before prospects are asked to make a financial investment in FasTracKids®, the company is willing to make an investment in qualified applicants by putting them through an intensive Initial Training course. This allows prospects to determine whether the FasTracKids® opportunity is right for them.

FasTracKids® began operations in 1998 and has already appointed 170 FasTracKids® Academy licensees in 31 countries. The FasTracKids® management team has nearly 40 years of experience in franchising and also founded and operates Crestcom International, Ltd., one of the world's leading management training companies.

Operating Units	12/31/2000	12/31/2001	12/31/2002
Franchised	12	13	15
% Change	--	8.3%	15.4%
Company-Owned	0	0	0
% Change	--	--	--
Total	12	13	15
% Change	--	8.3%	15.4%
Franchised as % of Total	100.0%	100.0%	100.0%

Investment Required

The primary license sold by FasTracKids is for an Academy, which runs classes of 16 students. The fee for the Academy is $15,000. The fee for a Home-Study Program add-on license if $10,000. There are also master area developer licenses available in some locations.

FasTracKids provides the following range of investments required to open your initial franchise. The range assumes that all items are paid for in cash. To the extent that you choose to finance any of these expense items, your front-end investment could be substantially reduced.

Item	Established Low Range	Established High Range
Franchise Fee	$15,000	$25,000
Classroom/Other Real Estate Costs	$0	$2,000
Educational Package Access Fee	$1,975	$1,975
Equipment/Furniture/ Signs/Supplies	$880	$2,100
Insurance	$0	$1,800
Marketing and Promotion	$250	$2,500
Training	$0	$2,550
Other Costs and Additional Funds (for 3 months)	$2,750	$11,775
Total Investment	$20,855	$49,700

On-Going Expenses
FasTracKids franchisees have several royalty options based on the type and location of the franchise.

What You Get—Training and Support
In the FasTracKids training program franchisees learn the FasTracKids' educational philosophy as well as how to identify and market to prospective parents, create a localized business strategy, enroll students, operate learning stations, conduct classes and evaluate student progress.

For additional support, FasTracKids franchisees have regional seminars, an annual international conference, newsletters, a company website, and a procedures manual at their disposal.

Territory
FasTracKids territories are based on the population of a given area.

FASTSIGNS

FASTSIGNS.

2550 Midway Rd., # 150
Carrollton, TX 75006-2357
Tel: (800) 827-7446 + 283 (214) 346-5616
Fax: (972) 248-8201
E-Mail: bill.mcpherson@fastsigns.com
Web Site: www.fastsigns.com
Mr. Bill McPherson, VP Franchise Sales

FASTSIGNS, the sign and graphic solutions provider for businesses worldwide, continues to receive accolades as the premier business-to-business franchise concept. FASTSIGNS was recently named the #1 sign franchise in Success Magazine's Franchisee Satisfaction Survey and has been featured in Entrepreneur for 11 years. Average per store gross sales has increased 10 of the last 11 years to $475,000 in 2002. We're proud of our franchise owners and their remarkable success stories. Come join the team!

BACKGROUND:	IFA MEMBER
Established: 1985; 1st Franchised: 1986	
Franchised Units:	451
Company-Owned Units	0
Total Units:	451
Dist.:	US-383; CAN-9; O'seas-59
North America:	43 States, 2 Provinces
Density:	53 in TX, 36 in CA, 20 in IL
Projected New Units (12 Months):	20
Qualifications:	5, 4, 1, 1, 3, 5
Registered:	All States and AB

FINANCIAL/TERMS:

Cash Investment:	$50-75K
Total Investment:	$152-225K
Minimum Net Worth:	$240K
Fees:	Franchise — $20K
	Royalty — 6%; Ad. — 2%
Earnings Claim Statement:	Yes
Term of Contract (Years):	20/10
Avg. # Of Employees:	3 FT
Passive Ownership:	Not Allowed
Encourage Conversions:	Yes
Area Develop. Agreements:	Yes
Sub-Franchising Contracts:	Int
Expand In Territory:	Yes
Space Needs:	1,750 SF; SC

SUPPORT & TRAINING PROVIDED:

Financial Assistance Provided:	Yes(I)
Site Selection Assistance:	Yes
Lease Negotiation Assistance:	Yes
Co-Operative Advertising:	Yes
Franchisee Assoc./Member:	Yes
Size Of Corporate Staff:	83
On-Going Support:	C,D,E,G,H,I
Training:	4 Weeks in Dallas, TX.

SPECIFIC EXPANSION PLANS:

US:	All United States
Canada:	All Canada
Overseas:	France, Germany, Italy, Spain, UK, New Zealand, Australia, Colombia, Mexico, Brazil

FASTSIGNS franchisees deliver high-quality, on-time service, expert consultation and a range of sign and graphics solutions. A FASTSIGNS franchise is a high-energy environment where quality is not only expected, but showcased; glass-walled showrooms allow customers to observe all steps of the signmaking process, from layout to completion. FASTSIGNS franchisees also have the opportunity to provide clients with large-scale creative needs (such as vehicle lettering and trade show exhibits) and complete signage systems and to subcontract, offering products such as electrical signage and sign development and consultation on a national and international level.

The first FASTSIGNS opened in the summer of 1985. The company holds one goal above all others: to help franchisees attain high sales volumes and profit potential. FASTSIGNS prides itself on its network growth, profitability, sales performance, customer loyalty and franchisee satisfaction.

Operating Units	12/31/2000	12/31/2001	12/31/2002
Franchised	371	374	382
% Change	--	0.8%	2.1%
Company-Owned	0	0	0
% Change	--	N/A	N/A
Total	371	374	382
% Change	--	0.8%	2.1%
Franchised as % of Total	100.0%	100.0%	100.0%

Investment Required
The fee for a FASTSIGNS franchise is $20,000.

FASTSIGNS provides the following range of investments required to open your initial franchise. The range assumes that all items are paid for in cash. To the extent that you choose to finance any of these expense items, your front-end investment could be substantially reduced.

Item	Established Low Range	Established High Range
Franchise Fee	$20,000	$20,000
Advertising	$9,300	$11,500
Equipment/Signs/Supplies	$58,102	$72,180
Fixtures/Signs	$12,779	$21,911
Insurance	$2,000	$3,500
Inventory	$8,553	$11,379
Real Estate	$25,761	$534,500
Store Graphics	$4,375	5,030
Training Expenses	$9,490	$19,720
Other Costs and Additional Funds	$34,000	$55,000
Total Investment	$184,360	$754,720

On-Going Expenses

FASTSIGNS franchisees pay service fees equaling 6%, national advertising council fees equaling 2% and advertising co-op fees equaling a maximum of 2% of gross revenue. Franchisees may also be responsible for varying advertising and promotional material costs.

What You Get—Training and Support

The first step on the road to becoming a successful FASTSIGNS franchisee is the completion of the system's four-week training program. Courses include technical signmaking design and production, as well as operating, managing, sales, subcontracting and marketing techniques. Other forms of training include written materials, annual conventions and video and audio training tapes.

The key figure of support for every FASTSIGNS franchisee is the field support representative, a personal business consultant and the primary liaison between franchisees and the corporate office. Franchisees also receive assistance from the system's management and clerical staffs, including experts in finance, personnel, training, subcontracting, direct marketing, telemarketing and public relations, and the tech support specialists, all of whom are available via a FASTSIGNS telephone hotline. Additional support consists of on-site visits, financial analysis, sales and sales management, production techniques, personnel management, vendor referrals, research and development, a logo bank and monthly updates from the FASTSIGNS operations department.

FASTSIGNS maintains a national co-op advertising council. The elected board of the council oversees the use of funds for advertising and marketing programs and materials to increase national visibility and ensure that all franchisees benefit from each campaign. Typical advertising expenditures finance yellow page placement, radio and television commercials, telemarketing, direct mail, trade shows, national promotions, continuing education and marketing research.

Furthermore, a national accounts team works for the benefit of each franchisee to establish relationships with clients operating worldwide and to bring their business into individual FASTSIGNS stores.

Territory
FASTSIGNS grants exclusive territories.

Fiducial

10480 Little Patuxent Pkwy., 3rd Fl.
Columbia, MD 21044
Tel: (800) 323-9000 (410) 910-5860
Fax: (410) 910-5903
E-Mail: howard.margolis@fiducial.com
Web Site: www.fiducial.com
Mr. Howard J. Margolis, Manager Field Operations/ Dev.

A FIDUCIAL franchise is a business which provides small businesses and individuals with back office support and accounting and financial management services, tax services, financial services, business counseling services and payroll services. Franchise offices operate out of commercial spaces furnished in such a manner that clients walking in immediately realize that their business, financial and tax needs will be taken care of by qualified individuals who will be there for them year after year.

BACKGROUND: IFA MEMBER
Established: 1999; 1st Franchised: 1999
Franchised Units: 677

257

Company-Owned Units	20	Area Develop. Agreements:	No
Total Units:	697	Sub-Franchising Contracts:	No
Dist.:	US-697; CAN-0; O'seas-0	Expand In Territory:	No
North America:	48 States	Space Needs:	800-3,200 SF; OB
Density:	N/A		
Projected New Units (12 Months):	59	**SUPPORT & TRAINING PROVIDED:**	
Qualifications:	5, 4, 5, 2, 3, 4	Financial Assistance Provided:	Yes(I)
Registered:	All States	Site Selection Assistance:	Yes
		Lease Negotiation Assistance:	No
FINANCIAL/TERMS:		Co-Operative Advertising:	Yes
Cash Investment:	$60-75K	Franchisee Assoc./Member:	No
Total Investment:	$44.4-115.5K	Size Of Corporate Staff:	82
Minimum Net Worth:	$150K	On-Going Support:	a,b,C,D,g,h,I
Fees: Franchise —	$12.5-25K	Training: 10-15 Days in Columbia, MD; 86 Hours
Royalty — 1.5-6%;	Ad. — 2%		Home Study.
Earnings Claim Statement:	No		
Term of Contract (Years):	10/5	**SPECIFIC EXPANSION PLANS:**	
Avg. # Of Employees:	1-8 FT, 1-2 PT	US:	All United States
Passive Ownership:	Discouraged	Canada:	No
Encourage Conversions:	Yes	Overseas:	No

Fiducial is the world's 13th largest accounting firm. Fiducial franchisees provide small businesses and individuals with accounting and financial management, tax, payroll, business counseling and financial services. The franchise's market includes all small- and medium-sized businesses as well as individual tax filers. Fiducial provides franchisees with a non-seasonal and recession-proof suite of services to meet needs of their customers.

Fiducial was founded in 1970 by Christian Latouche. The company acquired Income Tax Services in 1999 and Century Small Business Solutions in 2000, ultimately combining five franchise systems that date back as far as 1935. Fiducial is now the largest U.S. network of professional service advisors.

Operating Units	9/30/1999	9/30/2000	9/30/2001
Franchised	815	729	693
% Change	--	-10.5%	-4.9%
Company-Owned	8	20	20
% Change	--	150.0%	0.0%
Total	823	749	713
% Change	--	-9.0%	-4.8%
Franchised as % of Total	99.0%	97.3%	97.2%

Investment Required

The fee for a Fiducial franchise ranges from $12,000 to $25,000. Additional franchises cost $7,500. Conversions are allowed. Initial training costs also apply.

Fiducial provides the following range of investments required to open your initial franchise. The range assumes that all items are paid for in cash. To the extent that you choose to finance any of these expense items, your front-end investment could be substantially reduced.

Item	Established Low Range	Established High Range
Franchise Fee	$12,500	$25,000
Equipment/Supplies	$500	$10,000
Fixtures/Real Estate/Signs	$75	$4,500
Insurance	$100	$150
Inventory	$5,000	$20,000
Telephone Listing/Other Advertising	$2,000	$8,000
Training (per person)	$2,700	$6,500
Other Costs and Additional Funds	$21,500	$41,400
Total Investment	$44,375	$115,550

On-Going Expenses

Fiducial franchisees pay royalties equaling 1.5 to 6% (depending upon gross) and national awareness fund contributions equaling 2% of gross revenue.

What You Get—Training and Support

Fiducial provides franchisees with two weeks of initial training at their Technical and Administrative Support Center which is located in Columbia, Maryland. An optional third week of field training is also provided by Fiducial staff. Fiducial provides a comprehensive continuous education program, including support manuals, annual professional services seminars, profitability meetings and conventions and online education programs.

Franchisees also benefit from national branding programs and Fiducial's Local Marketing System™ that includes everything needed to build their business and retain clients as well as client acquisition assistance, toll-free tax research and advice hotlines, processing centers, purchasing power, a company intranet site, franchise committees, field operations support, on-site support and visits, product managers, product development teams, and proprietary software and support.

Territory
Fiducial does not grant protected territories.

Fish Window Cleaning Services

FISH WINDOW CLEANING SERVICES
148 Chesterfield Industrial Blvd., # G
Chesterfield, MO 63005
Tel: (877) 707-3474 (636) 530-7334
Fax: (636) 530-7856
E-Mail: matt@fishwindowcleaning.com
Web Site: www.fishwindowcleaning.com
Mr. Matt Merrick, Dir. Franchise Development

There is no glass ceiling when it comes to the potential you will have to grow your own unique service business in a large protected territory, specializing in year-round commercial and residential low-rise window cleaning. You can have the satisfaction of owning a business that requires no night or weekend work, backed by a franchisor with 25 years of experience.

BACKGROUND: IFA MEMBER
Established: 1978; 1st Franchised: 1998
Franchised Units: 76
Company-Owned Units: 1
Total Units: 77
Dist.: US-77; CAN-0; O'seas-0
  North America: 26 States

Density:	6 in MO, 6 in IN, 6 in FL
Projected New Units (12 Months):	40
Qualifications:	4, 4, 1, 2, 3, 5
Registered:	All States

FINANCIAL/TERMS:
Cash Investment:	$60-120K
Total Investment:	$60-120K
Minimum Net Worth:	$80-500K
Fees:	Franchise — $24.5-49.5
	Royalty — 6-8%; Ad. — 0.5%
Earnings Claim Statement:	No
Term of Contract (Years):	10/5
Avg. # Of Employees:	3-12 FT
Passive Ownership:	Discouraged
Encourage Conversions:	Yes
Area Develop. Agreements:	No
Sub-Franchising Contracts:	No
Expand In Territory:	Yes
Space Needs:	N/A SF; NA

SUPPORT & TRAINING PROVIDED:
Financial Assistance Provided:	Yes(I)
Site Selection Assistance:	NA
Lease Negotiation Assistance:	NA
Co-Operative Advertising:	Yes
Franchisee Assoc./Member:	Yes
Size Of Corporate Staff:	11
On-Going Support:	A,B,C,D,E,G,H,I
Training:	10 Days Chesterfield, MO.

SPECIFIC EXPANSION PLANS:		Canada:	No
US:	All United States	Overseas:	No

Initially, the window cleaning market may seem small, but, in reality, the niche market is actually large and diverse. Small businesses, major companies and national chains all benefit from Fish's three-story window cleaning. Moreover, many home cleaning services don't clean windows, but by joining with Fish Window Cleaning, homeowners receive full-service cleaning. Also, Fish Window Cleaning can come in handy even before the homeowner moves in! Many contractors, builders and painters hire services like Fish to clean up commercial and residential windows after construction and before move-in. Accordingly, the simple business of window cleaning profits from high demand and repeat business. Start-up costs are low, but profit margins are high. Fish franchisees keep Monday-to-Friday, daytime business hours.

Fish has been cleaning windows since 1978.

Operating Units	12/31/2000	12/31/2001	12/31/2002
Franchised	26	36	66
% Change	--	38.5%	83.3%
Company-Owned	1	1	1
% Change	--	0.0%	0.0%
Total	27	37	67
% Change	--	37.0%	81.1%
Franchised as % of Total	96.3%	97.3%	98.5%

Investment Required

The fee for a Fish Window Cleaning franchise varies by territory size. The fee for a small territory is $24,500, the fee for a standard territory is $29,500 and the fee for an executive territory is $49,500.

Fish Window Cleaning provides the following range of investments required to open your initial franchise. The range assumes that all items are paid for in cash. To the extent that you choose to finance any of these expense items, your front-end investment could be substantially reduced.

261

Item	Established Low Range	Established High Range
Franchise Fee	$24,500	$49,500
Advertising/Literature	$13,500	$27,000
Equipment and Office Packages	$9,500	$11,500
Real Estate	$600	$1,200
Training Expenses	$1,000	$3,000
Other Costs and Additional Funds	$6,600	$23,600
Total Investment	$55,700	$115,800

On-Going Expenses

Fish Window Cleaning franchisees pay royalties equaling 6 to 8% and advertising fees equaling 0.5% of gross revenue. Franchisees also pay local marketing fees equaling a minimum of $500 per month and a weekly marketing program fee of $250 to $750, depending on territory size. Additional training is also available for $100 per day.

What You Get—Training and Support

Fish franchisees begin their business at the Fish Window Cleaning Franchise Management School. Training covers business fundamentals, sales, marketing and bidding, cleaning techniques, ladder safety, scheduling and routing, employee recruiting, retention and management, office procedures, financial planning and management and software use.

Following two weeks of training at the St. Louis, Missouri institution, the Fish Window Cleaning staff visits all new franchisees for the sole purpose of establishing commercial window cleaning accounts, simultaneously supplying additional hands-on training and building franchisees' confidence in their personal abilities and those of the Fish Window Cleaning system.

Forms of Fish's extensive, on-going franchisee support include: a toll free support hotline, a company website, a personal webpage for each franchisee, newsletters, weekly fax updates and annual regional meetings, discounted purchasing power, training "Refresher Courses," field visits and product development.

Territory
Fish Window Cleaning grants exclusive territories.

Foliage Design Systems

Foliage Design Systems

4496 35th St.
Orlando, FL 32811-6504
Tel: (800) 933-7351 (407) 245-7776
Fax: (407) 245-7533
E-Mail: john@foliagedesign.com
Web Site: www.foliagedesign.com
Mr. John S. Hagood, Chairman

FOLIAGE DESIGN SYSTEMS is one of the largest interior plant maintenance companies in the U.S., according to Interiorscape Magazine. FOLIAGE DESIGN franchisees learn the business from the ground up in an intensive training program followed by training sessions in the field. Franchisees are taught design, sales and maintenance of interior foliage plants.

BACKGROUND:	IFA MEMBER
Established: 1971; 1st Franchised: 1980	
Franchised Units:	37
Company-Owned Units	3
Total Units:	40
Dist.:	US-40; CAN-0; O'seas-0
North America:	16 States
Density:	13 in FL, 4 in SC, 3 in MS
Projected New Units (12 Months):	3
Qualifications:	4, 5, 3, 3, 1, 5
Registered:	FL

FINANCIAL/TERMS:

Cash Investment:	$14.4-44.4K
Total Investment:	$49.4-144.4K
Minimum Net Worth:	$NR
Fees:	Franchise — $25-100K
	Royalty — 6%; Ad. — 0%
Earnings Claim Statement:	No
Term of Contract (Years):	10
Avg. # Of Employees:	4 FT, 2 PT
Passive Ownership:	Discouraged
Encourage Conversions:	No
Area Develop. Agreements:	Yes
Sub-Franchising Contracts:	No
Expand In Territory:	Yes
Space Needs:	200 SF; Greenhouse, Warehouse

SUPPORT & TRAINING PROVIDED:

Financial Assistance Provided:	No
Site Selection Assistance:	Yes
Lease Negotiation Assistance:	No
Co-Operative Advertising:	No
Franchisee Assoc./Member:	NR
Size Of Corporate Staff:	8
On-Going Support:	A,B,C,D,F,G,H,I
Training:	8-10 Days Headquarters; 3-5 Days in Field.

SPECIFIC EXPANSION PLANS:

US:	All United States
Canada:	All Canada
Overseas:	Europe, Asia, Mexico, South America

Foliage Design Systems combines two fields that aren't typically associated with franchising—plants and design. Franchisees of Foliage Design Systems provide design, installation and maintenance services of live plants and related products to commercial businesses and properties like office buildings, hotels, restaurants, atriums and malls. Some franchisees also work with landscape architects and interior designers. With many national accounts and references to supplement personal client lists, Foliage Design Systems franchisees have the potential to attract steady, repeat revenue from initial design and installation services, in addition to guaranteed monthly plant maintenance and seasonal and holiday decoration and displays. Other services include plant health management and integrated pest management.

Foliage Design Systems opened for business in 1971 and is now one of the top two interiorscape firms in North America. The system began franchising in 1980.

Operating Units	10/31/1999	10/31/2000	10/31/2001
Franchised	36	36	36
% Change	--	0.0%	0.0%
Company-Owned	3	3	3
% Change	--	0.0%	0.0%
Total	39	39	39
% Change	--	0.0%	0.0%
Franchised as % of Total	92.3%	92.3%	92.3%

Investment Required
The fee for a Foliage Design Systems franchise ranges from $25,000 to $100,000, depending on the size, location and demographics of the assigned territory.

Foliage Design Systems provides the following range of investments required to open your initial franchise. The range assumes that all items are paid for in cash. To the extent that you choose to finance any of these expense items, your front-end investment could be substantially reduced.

Item	Established Low Range	Established High Range
Franchise Fee	$25,000	$100,000
Cargo Van or Truck	$1,500	$1,500

Equipment/Fixtures/Signs	$3,000	$6,500
Insurance	$1,500	$2,500
Inventory/Supplies	$2,500	$3,600
Real Estate	$5,800	$11,100
Training Expenses	$1,500	$2,000
Other Costs and Additional Funds	$8,600	$17,200
Total Investment	$49,400	$144,400

On-Going Expenses

Foliage Design Systems franchisees pay royalties equaling 6% and local advertising fees equaling 1% of gross revenue.

What You Get—Training and Support

The corporate staff of Foliage Design Systems is the franchisees' key source for training and additional award-winning design, installation and maintenance expertise, all available via a toll-free phone line, e-mail and fax. Company-owned units keep the corporate staff in touch with the realities and needs of operating a Foliage Design System location and allow the company to test and develop new ideas and techniques. Individual owners are trained to provide plant care and to train and hire qualified plant service technicians.

Foliage Design Systems is the preferred interior foliage designer and caretaker for many large corporations with locations the world over, supplying franchisees with easy connections and pre-made leads. Franchisees also receive product and supply discounts, volume purchasing prices and the best plants from approved growers located in Florida, California and Hawaii.

Support also comes in operations manuals, national and regional franchisee meetings and informative sessions, newsletters and professional marketing materials—national advertising appears at trade shows and in magazines, newspapers and trade journals. The system's franchise executive council, composed of both elected and appointed Foliage Design Systems franchisees, meets with the corporate staff to bring the concerns and input of the franchisees to the attention of central management.

Territory

Foliage Design Systems grants exclusive territories.

Furniture Medic

FURNITURE MEDIC®
"the prescription for damaged furniture"

860 Ridge Lake Blvd.
Memphis, TN 38120-9421
Tel: (800) 255-9687 (901) 820-8600
Fax: (901) 820-8660
E-Mail: dmessenger@smclean.com
Web Site: www.furnituremedicfranchise.com
Mr. David Messenger. VP Market Expansion

FURNITURE MEDIC is a division of ServiceMaster Consumer Services. It has grown into an international franchise operation providing complete on-site precision repair as well as furniture stripping and refinishing. Targeting the residential, commercial and insurance markets, their patented Restoration-Refinishing process yields efficiency plus cost saving to customers. A solid training program and strong business support has effectively positioned FURNITURE MEDIC as the premier furniture repair company.

BACKGROUND:	IFA MEMBER
Established: 1992; 1st Franchised: 1992	
Franchised Units:	635
Company-Owned Units	0
Total Units:	635
Dist.:	US-460; CAN-71; O'seas-104
North America:	47 States,10 Provinces
Density:	36 in FL, 28 in CA, 24 in VA
Projected New Units (12 Months):	50

Qualifications:	4, 4, 2, 3, 3, 5
Registered:	All States

FINANCIAL/TERMS:

Cash Investment:	$15-25K
Total Investment:	$35.5-78.9K
Minimum Net Worth:	$100K
Fees:	Franchise — $25K
Royalty — 7%/$250 Min.;	Ad. — 1%/$50 Min.
Earnings Claim Statement:	No
Term of Contract (Years):	5/5
Avg. # Of Employees:	1 FT, 1 PT
Passive Ownership:	Not Allowed
Encourage Conversions:	N/A
Area Develop. Agreements:	No
Sub-Franchising Contracts:	No
Expand In Territory:	Yes
	Space Needs: NR SF; N/A

SUPPORT & TRAINING PROVIDED:

Financial Assistance Provided:	Yes(D)
Site Selection Assistance:	N/A
Lease Negotiation Assistance:	No
Co-Operative Advertising:	No
Franchisee Assoc./Member:	Yes/Yes
Size Of Corporate Staff:	21
On-Going Support:	A,B,G,h,I
	Training: 2 Weeks Memphis, TN.

SPECIFIC EXPANSION PLANS:

US:	All United States
Canada:	All Canada
Overseas:	All Countries

Furniture Medic, a furniture cleaning and restoration service, is a business with wide and varied market appeal—residential, moving and transportation companies, furniture retailers, insurance claims, fire and disaster restoration, city, county, state, and federal buildings, hotels, restaurants, bed and breakfast inns, country clubs, office complexes and commercial buildings. The company requires no prior technical experience.

Furniture Medic is part of the ServiceMaster corporation, which was founded in 1952 and now has more than 5,000 franchise partners on 4 continents. As a Furniture Medic franchisee, you reap the rewards of the ServiceMaster family, with the resources of each franchise used to develop and enhance the training and marketing of all.

Operating Units	12/31/2000	12/31/2001	12/31/2002
Franchised	444	447	460
% Change	--	0.7%	2.9%
Company-Owned	0	0	0
% Change	--	--	--
Total	444	447	460
% Change	--	0.7%	2.9%
Franchised as % of Total	100.0%	100.0%	100.0%

Investment Required
The fee for a Furniture Medic franchise is $35,500. All franchisees receive a $1,000 reimbursement for attending the international convention that follows the acquisition of their franchise.

Furniture Medic provides the following range of investments required to open your initial franchise. The range assumes that all items are paid for in cash. To the extent that you choose to finance any of these expense items, your front-end investment could be substantially reduced.

Item	Established Low Range	Established High Range
Franchise Fee	$4,400	$22,000
Advertising Fund Contribution/Marketing/ Royalty Fee (for 3 months)	$1,500	$3,900
Equipment	$2,700	$13,500
Insurance	$1,400	$2,200
Vehicle/Van Detail Package	$2,260	$25,644

Training Expenses	$1,000	$3,750
Other Costs and Additional Funds (for 3 months)	$2,445	$7,850
Total Investment	$15,705	$78,844

On-Going Expenses
Furniture Medic franchisees pay royalty fees equaling 7%, or $250 per month, and advertising fees equaling 1%, or $50 per month, of gross revenue.

What You Get—Training and Support
The first part of your Furniture Medic training begins with 21 days of pre-Academy coursework that prepares you for both the coming Academy training and business ownership. Part two consists of two weeks of intensive hands-on training at Furniture Medic's National Service Academy in Memphis, Tennessee. The program includes daily lunches and all materials and workbooks. Third and last, you must attend a week-long post-Academy seminar 90 to 120 days after graduation to review and hone your technical skills, business plans, marketing and record keeping. Furniture Medic pays for all associated airfare, hotel, transfers and meals.

In addition to training, the purchase of a Furniture Medic franchise gives the buyer the franchise license itself; all tools, supplies, equipment, products and cases required for most services; a notebook computer, with recommended business software, including financial and customer database management programs and other Furniture Medic proprietary management software.

Furniture Medic franchisees are entitled to on-going regional visits, continued training, national account usage, new product development, and on-call experts ready to answer any technical and marketing questions. Furniture Medic's association with the ServiceMaster franchises also allow for cross-selling and joint marketing ventures.

Territory
Furniture Medic does not grant exclusive territories.

Gymboree
Play & Music

GYMBOREE PLAY & MUSIC

700 Airport Blvd., # 200
Burlingame, CA 94010-1912
Tel: (800) 520-7529 (650) 696-7440
Fax: (650) 696-7452
E-Mail: eva_crosland@gymboree.com
Web Site: www.playandmusic.com
Ms. Eva Crosland, Manager Franchise Development

GYMBOREE, the world's largest development play and music program, offers weekly classes to parents and their children, ages newborn through 4 years, with custom-designed equipment. The program is based on sensory integration theory, positive parenting, child development principles and the importance of play. GYMBOREE has recently rolled out a new Arts Program designed to support your child's development through an array of enriching experiences and Fun!

BACKGROUND: IFA MEMBER
Established: 1976; 1st Franchised: 1978

Franchised Units:	512
Company-Owned Units:	23
Total Units:	537
Dist.:	US-354; CAN-22; O'seas-161
North America	43 States, 3 Provinces
Density:	49 in CA, 31 in NY, 29 in NJ
Projected New Units (12 Months):	15
Qualifications:	4, 4, 3, 3, 2, 4
Registered: CA,FL,HI,IL,IN,MD,MI,MN,NY,OR,	

RI,SD,VA,WA,WI,DC,AB

FINANCIAL/TERMS:

Cash Investment:	$35-60K
Total Investment:	$80-150K
Minimum Net Worth:	$150K
Fees:	Franchise — $35K
	Royalty — 6%; Ad. — 2.25%
Earnings Claim Statement:	No
Term of Contract (Years):	10/10
Avg. # Of Employees:	1 FT, 3 PT
Passive Ownership:	Not Allowed
Encourage Conversions:	No
Area Develop. Agreements:	No
Sub-Franchising Contracts:	No
Expand In Territory:	Yes
Space Needs:	2,200 SF; SF, SC, RM

SUPPORT & TRAINING PROVIDED:

Financial Assistance Provided:	No
Site Selection Assistance:	Yes
Lease Negotiation Assistance:	Yes
Co-Operative Advertising:	Yes
Franchisee Assoc./Member:	Yes
Size Of Corporate Staff:	19
On-Going Support:	B,D,G,h,I
Training:	7 Days Headquarters.

SPECIFIC EXPANSION PLANS:

US:	All United States
Canada:	All Canada
Overseas:	Asia, Europe

Gymboree is the originator of movement and play programs, which foster the natural activity and children's health, growth and learning. The format is based upon childhood education, educational psychology, physical therapy, recreation and fitness. Gymborees offer 45-minute weekly classes, in which parental participation is essential to children four years of age and younger. The play is organized around 40 pieces of proprietary equipment. In addition, there are also music and art programs offered in Gymboree style.

In 1976, Joan Barnes, wishing that their were classes for parents and infants

269

to take together, began to test her own classes. Two years later, she franchised her first Gymboree. There are now more than 510 Gymboree play centers and 570 Gymboree retail stores that promote the play centers and sell activewear for children aged zero to eight years.

Operating Units	2/3/2001	2/2/2002	2/1/2003
Franchised	410	459	512
% Change	--	11.9%	11.5%
Company-Owned	26	25	23
% Change	--	-3.8%	-8.0%
Total	436	484	537
% Change	--	11.0%	10.9%
Franchised as % of Total	94.0%	94.8%	95.3%

Investment Required

The fee for a Gymboree franchise is $35,000. A second unit costs $27,000 and a third $23,000. All others cost $20,000. Third party financing is available.

Gymboree provides the following range of investments required to open your initial franchise. The range assumes that all items are paid for in cash. To the extent that you choose to finance any of these expense items, your front-end investment could be substantially reduced.

Item	Established Low Range	Established High Range
Franchise Fee	$35,000	$35,000
Décor/Equipment/ Furniture/Signs/Supplies	$29,350	$52,850
Insurance	$900	$1,500
Inventory	$6,400	$11,000
Real Estate	$600	$90,250
Training Expenses	$0	$4,000
Other Costs and Additional Funds (for 3 months)	$4,442	$19,555
Total Investment	$76,692	$214,155

On-Going Expenses

Gymboree franchisees pay royalties equaling 6% and marketing and public relations fees equaling up to 5% of gross revenue. Franchisees must also pay regional advertising fees, which vary by region.

What You Get—Training and Support

The Gymboree initial investment covers equipment, marketing material, office and location setup, insurance, training, resale product, computer and software.

Gymboree's initial training is mandatory and covers program development, sales, operations, teacher development, marketing and public relations. Additional business and program training is held regionally about twice a year and at the annual convention.

Aside from general support in programs, operations, marketing, resale, teacher training and personnel, franchisees can also receive professionally developed marketing and advertising materials and research and development of products, programs and markets.

Territory

Gymboree determines the number of sites located in one territory based upon the number of children who reside in the territory and are aged zero up to five years.

House Doctors
Handyman Service

6355 E. Kemper Rd., # 250

Cincinnati, OH 45241-2300
Tel: (800) 319-3359 (513) 469-2443
Fax: (513) 469-2226
E-Mail: scohen@housedoctors.com
Web Site: www.housedoctors.com
Mr. Steve M. Cohen, President

There's big money in house calls. Millions of dollars are being spent every day on those odd jobs around

the house that people don't have the time or skill to do. You don't need a screwdriver or hammer to own this franchise. Financing and training provided.	Term of Contract (Years):	10/10/10
	Avg. # Of Employees:	3 FT, 2 PT
	Passive Ownership:	Discouraged
	Encourage Conversions:	Yes
BACKGROUND:	Area Develop. Agreements:	Yes/10
Established: 1994; 1st Franchised: 1995	Sub-Franchising Contracts:	No
Franchised Units: 225	Expand In Territory:	No
Company-Owned Units 0	Space Needs: N/A SF; N/A	
Total Units: 225		
Dist.: US-224; CAN-0; O'seas-1	**SUPPORT & TRAINING PROVIDED:**	
North America: 42 States	Financial Assistance Provided:	Yes(D)
Density: 10 in OH, 9 in IN, 9 in IL	Site Selection Assistance:	N/A
Projected New Units (12 Months): 30	Lease Negotiation Assistance:	N/A
Qualifications: 2, 3, 2, 2, 4, 5	Co-Operative Advertising:	N/A
Registered: CA,FL,IL,IN,MD,MI,MN,NY,	Franchisee Assoc./Member:	No
ND,OR,RI,VA,WA,WI	Size Of Corporate Staff:	12
	On-Going Support:	A,B,C,D,E,G,H,I
FINANCIAL/TERMS:	Training:	1 Week Cincinnati, OH.
Cash Investment: $12-23K		
Total Investment: $19-46K	**SPECIFIC EXPANSION PLANS:**	
Minimum Net Worth: $10K	US:	All United States
Fees: Franchise — $12-30K	Canada:	All Canada
Royalty — 6%; Ad. — 3%	Overseas:	All Countries
Earnings Claim Statement: No		

House Doctor has reinvented the medical house call. While doctors may no longer stop by to fix health ailments, house doctors are more than happy to perform domestic odd jobs and repairs. However, no construction experience is necessary; House Doctor franchisees don't do the work themselves. Rather, they manage a team of craftsmen who do it all, eliminating the need for multiple craftsmen to perform diverse tasks and lowering costs for both franchisees and their clients. One of House Doctor's main objectives is to help its franchisees control costs without sacrificing their business's quality.

House Doctor is the ideal franchise for those who those who relish simplicity. There is no inventory, equipment expenditures, account receivables or seasonal slumps. Start-up fees for the cash business are low and franchisees can run their business from their home or a small office.

Operating Units	12/31/2000	12/31/2001	12/31/2002
Franchised	115	132	145
% Change	--	14.8%	9.8%
Company-Owned	0	0	0
% Change	--	N/A	N/A
Total	115	132	145
% Change	--	14.8%	9.8%
Franchised as % of Total	100.0%	100.0%	100.0%

Investment Required

The fee for a House Doctor franchise varies depending on the size of the franchisee's territory. The fee for a small territory is $13,900, the fee for a medium-sized territory is $21,900 and the fee for a large territory is $27,900. Financing is available.

House Doctor provides the following range of investments required to open your initial franchise. The range assumes that all items are paid for in cash. To the extent that you choose to finance any of these expense items, your front-end investment could be substantially reduced.

Item	Established Low Range	Established High Range
Franchise Fee	$13,900	$32,900
Equipment/Furniture	$1,500	$3,500
Insurance	$1,000	$3,000
Pre-opening Promotion	$1,000	$3,000
Rent/Deposits	$550	$1,150
Additional Funds (for 3 months)	$6,000	$8,000
Total Investment	23,950	51,550

On-going Expenses

House Doctor franchisees pay royalties equaling 6% and advertising fees equaling 3%, or $12.50 per week, of gross revenue.

273

What You Get—Training and Support

House Doctor training covers all the basics, including how to hire quality crafts-men, bid work, computers, accounting software, budgeting, time management and marketing. The opening of every House Doctor franchise is also buttressed by pre-opening promotional assistance and grand opening support.

Initial training is backed by extensive on-going support—field visits, telephone support, corporate newsletters, technical assistance, regional meetings, the home remedies newsletter, advertising/marketing, a public relations package and client incentive programs—and an array of management tools—computer software, employment agreements, quality controls and administrative help.

Word-of-mouth has proven to be tne most effective form of House Doctor adver-tising. However, to supplement this network of home owners, real estate agents, friends and neighbors, House Doctor supplies franchisees with artwork for direct mail, newspaper and magazine ads, color brochures, rebate certificates, coupons, site signs, realtor presentations, trade show exhibits and publicity releases.

Territory

House Doctor grants exclusive territories of three sizes: small—with a popula-tion of up to 100,000, medium—with a population up to 300,000 and large—with a population of up to 500,000.

InterContinental Hotels Group

INTERCONTINENTAL.
H O T E L S   G R O U P

3 Ravinia Dr., # 100
Atlanta, GA 30346-2118
Tel: (770) 604-2000
Fax: (770) 604-2107
E-Mail: brown.kessler@ichotelsgroup.com
Web Site: www.ichotelsgroup.com
Mr. Brown Kessler, VP Franchise Sales/Dev.

INTERCONTINENTAL HOTELS GROUP is the world's global hotel company. Operates or fran-chises more than 3,300 hotels and 515,000 guest rooms in more than 100 countries. Franchisor of INTER-CONTINENTAL HOTELS, CROWNE PLAZA HOTELS, HOLIDAY INN, HOLIDAY INN EXPRESS AND STAYBRIDGE SUITES HOTELS.

BACKGROUND:	IFA MEMBER
Established: 1952; 1st Franchised: 1952	
Franchised Units:	2,751
Company-Owned Units	510
Total Units:	3,261
Dist.:	US-; CAN-; O'seas-
North America:	50 States

Density:	NR	Space Needs:	NR SF; FS
Projected New Units (12 Months):	100+		
Qualifications:	5, 4, 4, , ,	**SUPPORT & TRAINING PROVIDED:**	
Registered:	All States and AB	Financial Assistance Provided:	Yes(I)
		Site Selection Assistance:	Yes
FINANCIAL/TERMS:		Lease Negotiation Assistance:	No
Cash Investment:	$1-20MM	Co-Operative Advertising:	Yes
Total Investment:	$Varies	Franchisee Assoc./Member:	Yes
Minimum Net Worth:	$Varies	Size Of Corporate Staff:	1,000
Fees: Franchise — $500/Rm,40Kmin		On-Going Support:	C,D,E,H,I
Royalty — 5%; Ad. — 2.5-3%		Training: 4 - 5 Days Atlanta, GA. 4 - 5 Days	
Earnings Claim Statement:	Yes		Regional.
Term of Contract (Years):	10/10		
Avg. # Of Employees:	Varies	**SPECIFIC EXPANSION PLANS:**	
Passive Ownership:	Allowed	US:	All United States
Encourage Conversions:	Yes	Canada:	All Canada
Area Develop. Agreements:	No	Overseas:	All Countries
Sub-Franchising Contracts:	No		
Expand In Territory:	Yes		

IHG franchises some of the most recognized hotel brands in the world—Holiday Inn Hotels and Resorts and HI Express Hotels, Staybridge Suites, and Crowne Plaza Hotels and Resorts. Guest needs are too diverse to be met by one single hotel, so IHG has a brand for every patron. However, despite the magnitude of the IHG system, management doesn't treat their hotels like a mere licensees. The company is an invested real estate owner. IHG continually works on developing and improving their hotels, all the while maintaining the standards they've spent years establishing.

You can be anywhere in the world, but the same familiar IHG signs will greet you wherever you are, and along with that familiar sign, comes consistent quality, comfort and service. Over 90% of American travelers frequent IHG lodgings.

Operating Units	9/30/2000	9/30/2001	9/30/2002
Franchised	2062	2148	2841
% Change	--	4.2%	32.3%
Company-Owned	91	94	189
% Change	--	3.3%	101%
Total	2153	2242	3030
% Change	--	4.1%	35.1%
Franchised as % of Total	95.8%	95.8%	93.8%

Investment Required

IHG license applicants must pay an application fee of $500 per guest room.

IHG provides the following range of investments required to open your initial franchise. The range assumes that all items are paid for in cash. To the extent that you choose to finance any of these expense items, your front-end investment could be substantially reduced. The following figures refer to the opening of a 100-room, two-story Holiday Inn/Holiday Inn Hotel & Suites.

Item	Established Low Range	Established High Range
Application Fee	$500 per guest room, $40,000 minimum	$500 per guest room, $40,000 minimum
Building	$3,503,500	$5,018,000
Computer and Reservations Equipment and Systems	$51,500	$58,600
Equipment/Fixtures/Signs	$824,000	$1,095,000
Insurance	$75,000	$200,000
Inventory	$100,000	$200,000
Training	$3,000	$3,000
Other Costs and Additional Funds (for 3 months)	$200,000	$425,000
Total Investment (does not include land)	$4,807,000	$7,049,600

On-Going Expenses

IHG franchisees pay royalties equaling 5%, service contributions equaling 2.5 to 3% and marketing fees equaling 5% of gross room revenue. There is also a technology fee of $8.74 per room, per month.

What You Get—Training and Support

The marketing provided to you as an IHG franchisee varies according to which hotel brand you run. Each different brand has different marketing not only for itself, but also for business, leisure and conference guests. Alliances with American Express, Delta, Visa and AT&T strengthen the visibility, ability and reputation of all IHG brands. Sales and marketing are integrated on a local, regional and global level, so every marketing effort benefits every franchisee. There are approximately 300 members of the Six Continents sales team throughout the world.

IHG fosters the development of customer relationships, leading to word of mouth recommendations and repeat business, to reduce marketing costs and still increase customer yield. Efforts toward building these relationships include Priority Club rewards, a hotel loyalty program with more than 15 million members. Members earn points toward hotel stays, airline miles and more. These members account for 30% of Six Continents occupancy in the Americas.

Personal support comes in the form of a hotel-assigned field services representative, an on-site consultant that dispenses guest service, product quality and revenue management advice. These representatives also host occasional regional workshops. Each hotel also has a dedicated service manager who is accessible through a toll-free number specified for just this purpose. The service managers can provide quick answers to questions regarding policy, procedures, systems and new initiatives. Between the service manager and the field representative, franchisees can get an around-the-clock response to any concern or question.

Quality consultants conduct routine inspections of the IHG hotels and train staff in product quality and the human resources department ensures employee quality and commitment through training and education.

IHG is on the cutting edge of technology with their property-based and centralized reservation management systems. These ease the burden of reservations on human resources and increase efficiency, productivity and costs. These instantly respond to demand shifts, make predictions about your business and monitor occupancy, all the while also determining the best strategies to help your business. In addition, IHG was the first to allow guests to make real-time reservations online; the site is one of the top ten most visited travel industry websites. The voice reservation system accounts for the booking of more than 13 million nights per year, more than $1.2 billion in revenue. IHG technology also assists travel agents with convenient access to vacancies and locations, providing an easy-to-use, real time intermediary between them and the IHG system and bringing more travelers to IHG rooms.

IHG also offers leveraged purchasing of software and other supplies and design and plan review services from architects, engineers and quantity surveyors in the initial stages of your business development.

Territory
IHG does not grant exclusive territories.

Interiors by Decorating Den

I N T E R I O R S
by Decorating Den

19100 Montgomery Village Ave., # 200
Montgomery Village, MD 20886-3701
Tel: (800) 332-3367 (301) 272-1500
Fax: (301) 272-1520
E-Mail: victoriaj@decoratingden.com
Web Site: www.decoratingden.com
Ms. Victoria Jenkins, VP Franchise Marketing

Established in 1969, INTERIORS BY DECORATING DEN is the oldest international, shop-at-home interior decorating franchise in the world. Our company-trained interior decorators bring thousands of samples including window coverings, wallcoverings, floor coverings, furniture and accessories to their customers' homes in our uniquely equipped COLORVAN ©. Special business features include: home-based, marketing systems, business systems, training, support and complete sampling.

BACKGROUND: IFA MEMBER
Established: 1969; 1st Franchised: 1970

Franchised Units:	465
Company-Owned Units	1
Total Units:	466
Dist.:	US-401; CAN-50; O'seas-15
North America:	NR
Density:	33 in FL, 28 in NC, 27 in TX
Projected New Units (12 Months):	50
Qualifications:	5, 5, 3, 3, 5, 5
Registered:	All States

FINANCIAL/TERMS:

Cash Investment:	$15K
Total Investment:	$40-70K
Minimum Net Worth:	$40K
Fees:	Franchise — $24.9K
	Royalty — 7-9%; Ad. — 4%/$100 Min
Earnings Claim Statement:	Yes
Term of Contract (Years):	10/10
Avg. # Of Employees:	1 FT
Passive Ownership:	Not Allowed
Encourage Conversions:	Yes
Area Develop. Agreements:	Yes/10
Sub-Franchising Contracts:	Yes
Expand In Territory:	No
Space Needs:	N/A SF; HB

SUPPORT & TRAINING PROVIDED:		Training: 10.5 Days in Montgomery Village, MD; Continuous.
Financial Assistance Provided:	Yes(D)	
Site Selection Assistance:	N/A	**SPECIFIC EXPANSION PLANS:**
Lease Negotiation Assistance:	N/A	US: All United States
Co-Operative Advertising:	Yes	Canada: All Canada
Franchisee Assoc./Member:	Yes/Yes	Overseas: No
Size Of Corporate Staff:	40	
On-Going Support:	C,D,E,G,H,I	

If you're attracted to the security and proven success of franchising, but also yearn to utilize personal creativity, an Interiors by Decorating Den franchise may be the perfect fit. Interiors franchisees offer home design services, from conception to delivery and installation, tailored to reflect each clients' preferences, style and budget. In addition, since each Interiors's gig varies by client, no inventory is necessary.

Operating Units	12/31/1999	12/31/2000	12/31/2001
Franchised	415	403	369
% Change	--	-2.9%	-8.4%
Company-Owned	0	0	0
% Change	--	N/A	N/A
Total	415	403	369
% Change	--	-2.9%	-8.4%
Franchised as % of Total	100.0%	100.0%	100.0%

Investment Required

The fee for an Interiors by Decorating Den franchise is $23,900.

Interiors by Decorating Den provides the following range of investments required to open your initial franchise. The range assumes that all items are paid for in cash. To the extent that you choose to finance any of these expense items, your front-end investment could be substantially reduced.

Item	Established Low Range	Established High Range
Franchise Fee	$23,900	$23,900
Advertising/Grand Opening	$1,700	$2,500
Business Materials	$500	$750
Equipment/Fixtures	$2,525	$3,445
Insurance	$742	$1,369
Additional Funds	$5,000	$8,500
Total Investment	$34,367	$40,464

On-Going Expenses

Interiors franchisees pay service fees equaling 7 to 9% and national marketing fund contributions equaling 4%, or $100 a month, of gross revenue.

What You Get—Training and Support

Interiors' training is thorough. Thirty to 45 days of home study prepares each franchisee for the two-week training course held at Decorating Den headquarters. Courses cover everything from design, products, sales, marketing, business management and personal development. Grand opening planning and support follows training and each franchisee is required to participate in 12 "Directions" follow-up training modules within the first three to six months of operation. As business continues, franchisees may take advantage of further training through the regional coordinator mentor program, monthly regional training meetings, "Lifestyle University" on-going training and supplier and vendor training.

Interiors' full-time merchandising department supplies its franchisees and their clients with manufacturer direct buying power and 75 brand name companies selling warrantied products. They also maintain personal purchase discounts and coupons, a "frequent buyer" points program and an annual market conference with suppliers.

The Interiors's national public relations department does its best to build Interiors by Decorating Den's brand image and awareness. Tools include exposure on cable and network television, the Dream Room Contest and articles in magazines, books and newspapers.

Interiors's marketing support is also extensive, including the services of a national advertising department, co-op advertising, a turnkey direct mail subscription program, workshop invitations, ad slicks, newspaper inserts and client newsletters.

Other Interiors by Decorating Den perks: corporate and regional support teams, the DecoNet intranet, system-wide and individual franchisee websites, a franchise advisory board and annual conferences.

Territory
Interiors by Decorating Den grants exclusive territories.

Jackson Hewitt

TAX SERVICE

7 Sylvan Way, 2nd Fl.
Parsippany, NJ 07054-0657
Tel: (800) 475-2904 (973) 496-1040
Fax: (973) 496-2760
E-Mail: william.scavone@jtax.com
Web Site: www.jacksonhewitt.com
Mr. William Scavone, SVP Franchise Sales/Devel.

JACKSON HEWITT prepares tax returns for customers throughout over 4,000 franchised offices in more than 48 states, including locations within Wall-Nart, Kmart, Staples, etc. Since its founding in 1986, JACKSON HEWITT is the fastest-growing national tax service. Offices are independently owned and operated, offering full-service individual tax preparation, electronic filing, refund anticipation loans (subj. to qualification), and audit representation. A subsid-

iary of Cendant Corp. since 1998.

BACKGROUND:	IFA MEMBER
Established: 1960; 1st Franchised: 1986	
Franchised Units:	3,792
Company-Owned Units	524
Total Units:	4,316
Dist.:	US-4,316; CAN-0; O'seas-0
North America:	48 States, DC
Density:	480 in TX, 381 in FL, 350 IL
Projected New Units (12 Months):	350
Qualifications:	5, 5, 3, 4, 4, 5
Registered:	All States

FINANCIAL/TERMS:	
Cash Investment:	$25-50K
Total Investment:	$47.4-75.2K
Minimum Net Worth:	$100K
Fees:	Franchise — $25K
	Royalty — 15%; Ad. — 6%
Earnings Claim Statement:	Yes
Term of Contract (Years):	10/10
Avg. # Of Employees:	1 FT, 6 PT
Passive Ownership:	Allowed
Encourage Conversions:	Yes
Area Develop. Agreements:	No

281

Sub-Franchising Contracts:	No	Size Of Corporate Staff:	235
Expand In Territory:	Yes	On-Going Support:	A,B,C,D,G,H,I
Space Needs: 400-1,000 SF; SF, SC, RM		Training:	5 Days in Parsippany, NJ.
SUPPORT & TRAINING PROVIDED:		**SPECIFIC EXPANSION PLANS:**	
Financial Assistance Provided:	Yes(I)	US:	All United States
Site Selection Assistance:	Yes	Canada:	No
Lease Negotiation Assistance:	No	Overseas:	No
Co-Operative Advertising:	Yes		
Franchisee Assoc./Member:	Yes/Yes		

With the canon of tax laws ever-changing, tax knowledge and services are valuable commodities. Accordingly, the number of Jackson Hewitt Tax Services franchises has doubled over the last three years. In addition to tax preparation expertise, Jackson Hewitt franchises retain customer devotion through specialized programs and promotions like pre-approved RALs and preferred customer sweepstakes mailings and the new Holiday Express Loan Program, which grants interest-free December loans.

Jackson Hewitt is a member of Cendant, the largest hotel and residential real estate brokerage franchiser, which interacts with millions of consumers every year. Such an association provides invaluable opportunities for cross-marketing, broadening Jackson Hewitt's customer base and increasing revenue.

Operating Units	1/1/2000	1/1/2001	2/5/2002
Franchised	2720	3344	3816
% Change	--	22.9%	14.1%
Company-Owned	37	7	440
% Change	--	-81.1%	6185.7%
Total	2757	3351	4256
% Change	--	21.5%	27.0%
Franchised as % of Total	98.7%	99.8%	89.7%

Investment Required

The fee for a Jackson Hewitt franchise in a standard-sized territory is $25,000. The fee in small markets is $16,500.

Jackson Hewitt Tax Services provides the following range of investments required to open your initial franchise. The range assumes that all items are paid for in cash. To the extent that you choose to finance any of these expense items, your front-end investment could be substantially reduced.

Item	Established Low Range	Established High Range
Franchise Fee	$16,500	$25,000
Application Fee	$500	$500
Deposits/Telephone/ Utilities	$1,615	$2,580
Equipment/Signs	$9,460	$12,960
Insurance	$260	$310
Real Estate	$5,075	$13,775
Supplemental Advertising	$5,000	$5,000
Training Expenses	$1,600	$3,500
Other Costs and Additional Funds	$7,420	$11,580
Total Investment (does not include royalties, advertising, electronic filing fee or debt service)	$47,430	$75,205

On-Going Expenses
Jackson Hewitt franchisees pay royalties equaling 15% and advertising fees equaling 6% of gross revenue.

What You Get—Training and Support
Jackson Hewitt training is executed by a team of experts who train franchisees in the usage of company systems and programs and teach them everything from how to build customer bases to how to recruit and train employees. Instructional sessions are held in many locations, but primarily at Jackson Hewitt's hands-on training facility in Parsippany, New Jersey.

Included with the franchise license is the ProFiler software, an easy-to-use and easy-to-learn Windows-based application that prompts tax preparers with step-by-step questions personalized for each tax customer and situation. With the ProFiler to lead them through the tax filing process, preparers are less likely to commit calculation and formatting errors that often occur when maximizing deductions by hand.

All Jackson Hewitt software is updated every year by certified public accountants and other knowledgeable tax professionals.

Regional directors service specific geographical markets and provide franchisees with site selection, local advertising and public relations, workshops, training, signage and staffing guidance. Franchise service management provides quick responses to franchisee questions as well as communication system updates and ways to strengthen franchise relations. Also, all franchisees have operator access to Jackson Hewitt's senior management and other corporate personnel to address any concerns. In addition, during the tax season, technical support for the ProFiler support is available through the company help desk.

JHnet on the internet provides up-to-date franchise services information, marketing tips, technological developments, training topics and headquarter messages, keeping franchisees informed of news within Jackson Hewitt and the greater tax world.
All franchisees receive an annual ad kit based upon a national advertising campaign designed to increase brand awareness and regional marketing programs to entice more local customers. The kit includes newspaper, direct mail, yellow pages and billboard artwork. Regional marketing focuses on specific market needs and supports the national campaign. The ad campaign is brought into the office through materials such as posters, banners, brochures, sales aides, window signage and educational resources.

Territory
Jackson Hewitt grants exclusive territories.

Kinderdance International

Education Through Dance

INTERNATIONAL

268 N. Babcock St.
Melbourne, FL 32935-6766
Tel: (800) 554-2334 (321) 242-0590
Fax: (321) 254-3388
E-Mail: kindercorp@kinderdance.com
Web Site: www.kinderdance.net
Mr. Jerry M. Perch, VP Sales/Marketing

KINDERDANCE franchisees are trained to teach 4 developmentally-unique dance and motor development programs: KINDERDANCE, KINDERGYM, KINDERTOTS and KINDERCOMBO, which are designed for boys and girls ages 2-8. They learn the basics of ballet, tap, gymnastics and creative dance, as well as learning numbers, colors, shapes and words. No studio or dance experience required. Franchisee teaches at child care center sites. Area development agreements available.

BACKGROUND:	IFA MEMBER
Established: 1979; 1st Franchised: 1985	
Franchised Units:	83
Company-Owned Units	1
Total Units:	84
Dist.:	US-81; CAN-1; O'seas-2
North America:	28 States, 3 Provinces
Density:	10 in TX, 8 in FL, 7 in CA
Projected New Units (12 Months):	20

Qualifications:	2, 2, 1, 2, 2, 5
Registered:	CA,FL,HI,IL,MD,MI,MN,NY ,OR,VA,WA,DC,AB

FINANCIAL/TERMS:

Cash Investment:	$6.4-25.6K
Total Investment:	$9-25.6K
Minimum Net Worth:	$N/A
Fees:	Franchise — $6.5-20K
	Royalty — 6-15%; Ad. — 3%
Earnings Claim Statement:	No
Term of Contract (Years):	10/10
Avg. # Of Employees:	1 PT
Passive Ownership:	Discouraged
Encourage Conversions:	Yes
Area Develop. Agreements:	Yes/10
Sub-Franchising Contracts:	No
Expand In Territory:	Yes
Space Needs:	NR SF; NR

SUPPORT & TRAINING PROVIDED:

Financial Assistance Provided:	Yes(D)
Site Selection Assistance:	N/A
Lease Negotiation Assistance:	N/A
Co-Operative Advertising:	Yes
Franchisee Assoc./Member:	Yes/Yes
Size Of Corporate Staff:	7
On-Going Support:	A,B,C,D,E,F,G,H,I
Training:	6 Days in Melbourne, FL and On-Site.

SPECIFIC EXPANSION PLANS:

US:	All United States
Canada:	All Canada
Overseas:	All Countries

Kinderdance is an "on-site location," educational dance program that takes educational dance classes to daycare centers and pre-schools and eliminates the parental hassle of coordinating multiple extracurricular activities. Focusing on the idea that children learn with their bodies and their minds, the original Kinderdance program caters to children ages two to eight and blends creative movement, gymnastics, fitness, acrobatics and dance with colors, numbers, shapes, words and songs to build physical and language skills, imagination, socialization, self-confidence and self-esteem. New programs include Kindertots, a program specially designed for

285

two-year-olds; Kindergym, which uses basic floor gymnastic skills to foster perceptual motor development; and Kindercombo, a ballet, tap and modern dance program for older children aged six to eight. Franchisees are qualified to teach all four programs and manage a team of additional program instructors.

Today, busy schedules make daycare a necessity and daycare centers want programs that will attract parents to their centers. Kinderdance's year-round, high-quality, moderately-price programs are just the thing. Suitable for churches, YMCAs, public and private schools, military bases and community centers, the market for the Kinderdance program is wide and varied. Franchisees pay nearly no overhead, make their own hours (which never need to include nights or weekends) and can even manage the business from their home. Moreover, a line of customized Kinderdance dancewear can provide extra income for inclined franchisees. No dance experience is required—the procedures are simple and demand high.

In 1980, Carol Kay Harsell was trying to increase enrollment in the pre-school dance program, a.k.a. Kinderdance, at the American Academy of Dance in Phoenix, Arizona. The problem was, it seemed, that the children the program targeted were in daycare and pre-schools and couldn't make it to the dance academy. Along with businessman Bernard Friedman, Harsell decided to take the dance classes to the children. Six months later, classes were being held in more than 30 childcare centers around Phoenix. Kinderdance incorporated in 1981 and its first franchise, in Houston, Texas, opened in 1985.

Operating Units	12/31/2000	12/31/2001	12/31/2002
Franchised	65	71	85
% Change	--	9.2%	19.7%
Company-Owned	1	1	1
% Change	--	0.0%	0.0%
Total	66	72	86
% Change	--	9.1%	19.4%
Franchised as % of Total	98.5%	98.6%	98.8%

Investment Required

Kinderdance offers three different franchise agreements—Gold for $21,000,

Silver for $14,000 and Bronze for $7,000. Gold is ideal for franchisees with previous management experience; the agreement grants franchisees the right to hire additional teachers and teach at an unlimited number of locations in an exclusive market with a population not exceeding 400,000 people. Franchises outside the United States and Canada are only available at the gold level with fees starting at $25,000. Silver grants franchisees a full-time license to teach at no more than 12 locations with the option of hiring new teachers as necessary. Bronze is for franchisees who want to work part-time and teach all the classes themselves at no more than six locations. Although a license may allow franchisees to work at a limited number of locations, they may conduct multiple classes of various Kinderdance programs at each location. Financing is available.

Kinderdance provides the following range of investments required to open your initial franchise. The range assumes that all items are paid for in cash. To the extent that you choose to finance any of these expense items, your front-end investment could be substantially reduced.

Item	Established Low Range	Established High Range
Franchise Fee	$7,000	$21,000
Insurance	$400	$600
Inventory	$100	$500
Training Expenses	$450	$1,000
Additional Funds	$2,000	$4,000
Total Investment	$9,950	$27,100

On-Going Expenses

Gold franchisees pay royalties equaling 6 to 7%, or $250, silver franchisees pay royalties equaling 7 to 10%, or $200 a month, Bronze franchisees pay royalties equaling 15%, or $100 a month, and all franchisees pay advertising fees equaling 3% of gross revenue. Training costs $500 per employee.

What You Get—Training and Support

Each Kinderdance franchisee must attend the Kinderdance Franchisee Training class, taught by Harsell and Friedman. The six-day course takes place at corporate headquarters in Melbourne, Florida and consists of classroom lessons, video instruction, individual meetings and on-site work with children. Each teacher, whether franchisee or not, is trained in the Kinderdance curriculum and must be certified for every program they instruct. Annual continuing education conferences, quarterly updates and a toll-free hotline provide additional training opportunities at no additional cost.

The simplicity of the Kinderdance system puts franchisees in business within weeks of completing their training and Kinderdance support and services kick in right away. Franchisees receive supplies including leotards, business cards, music, business forms and operations manuals; marketing help including brochures and posters; advertising help including sample ad copy, press releases and promotional letters; and ideas and management help including sales agreements, order forms, bookkeeping and an accounting and billing system

Territory
Kinderdance grants exclusive territories only to Gold level franchisees.

Kumon North America

MATH & READING CENTERS
Learning How To Learn™

300 Frank W. Burr Blvd., 5th Fl.
Teaneck, NJ 07666-6703
Tel: (866) 633-0740 (201) 928-0444 + 303
Fax: (201) 928-0044
E-Mail: mmele@kumon.com
Web Site: www.kumon.com
Mr. Mark Mele, Asst. VP Fran. Recruitment

Kumon is the world's largest provider of supplemental math and reading programs. Our neighborhood learning centers serve students of all ages and abilities, from pre-school through high school.

BACKGROUND:		IFA MEMBER
Established: 1958; 1st Franchised: 1980		
Franchised Units:		1,338
Company-Owned Units		22
Total Units:		1,360
Dist.:	US-1,015; CAN-345; O'seas-20,705	
North America:		50 States, 9 Provinces
Density:	232 in CA, 93 in NY, 92 NJ	
Projected New Units (12 Months):		150
Qualifications:		4, 3, 3, 4, 4, 4
Registered:		All States
FINANCIAL/TERMS:		
Cash Investment:		$NR
Total Investment:		$5.9-30.6K
Minimum Net Worth:		$NR
Fees:		Franchise — $1K
	Royalty — $30-33.8K; Ad. — N/A	
Earnings Claim Statement:		No
Term of Contract (Years):		2/5
Avg. # Of Employees:		1 FT, 1-3 PT

Passive Ownership:	Not Allowed	Franchisee Assoc./Member:	Yes
Encourage Conversions:	N/A	Size Of Corporate Staff:	NR
Area Develop. Agreements:	No	On-Going Support:	B,C,D,E,G,H,I
Sub-Franchising Contracts:	No	Training:	9-12 Weeks Local Branch Office; 9-12
Expand In Territory:	Yes		Weeks Local Kumon Center.
Space Needs:	Varies SF; FS, SF, SC, RM		

SPECIFIC EXPANSION PLANS:

SUPPORT & TRAINING PROVIDED:		US:	All United States
Financial Assistance Provided:	N/A	Canada:	All Canada
Site Selection Assistance:	Yes	Overseas:	All Countries
Lease Negotiation Assistance:	Yes		
Co-Operative Advertising:	N/A		

Kumon gives franchisees the opportunity to help others and make money. As the largest franchisor in the supplemental education industry, with more than 12 million success stories, Kumon has proven that discipline, practice and concentration work for all, whether franchisee, teacher or student. Kumon Learning Centers offer individualized, self-paced learning programs designed to help children reach and exceed their grade levels. A Kumon franchise is affordable and community-oriented, and its franchisees must enjoy working with children. Each week, all centers must initially open for at least two consecutive weekdays for a minimum of three consecutive after-school hours. Franchisees may choose, and will eventually be expected, to open their center more than two times a week.

High school teacher Toru Kumon created the Kumon idea and basic materials in 1954 to help his young son learn math. Four years later, he founded the Kumon Institute of Education, where children were spared the expectation of having to keep up with their peers and were able to progress at their own pace, free of embarrassment or worry. Their progress, and Kumon's success, were dramatic. In February of 2003, enrollment in Kumon programs worldwide was 3,275,469.

Operating Units	12/31/2000	12/31/2001	12/31/2002
Franchised	1,002	1,021	1,053
% Change	--	1.9%	3.1%
Company-Owned	20	20	23
% Change	--	0.0	15.0%

Total	1,022	1,041	1,076
% Change	--	1.8%	3.4
Franchised as % of Total	98.0%	98.1%	97.9%

Investment Required

The fee for a Kumon math and reading franchise is $1,000.

Kumon provides the following range of investments required to open your initial franchise. The range assumes that all items are paid for in cash. To the extent that you choose to finance any of these expense items, your front-end investment could be substantially reduced.

Item	Established Low Range	Established High Range
Franchise Fee	$1,000	$1,000
Advertising	$100	$1,500
Computer/Equipment/ Furniture/Signs/Supplies	$3,500	$14,470
Rent	$550	$3,500
Training Expenses	$1,900	$3,000
Other Costs and Additional Funds	$825	$6,575
Total Investment	$7,875	$30,045

On-Going Expenses

The amount of royalties due to Kumon depends upon the number of students enrolled at each individual center. Franchisees pay monthly royalties equaling $15 for each new student and $33.75 for each full-paying (i.e. non-exempt and non-pro-rated students) during their temporary license period. Once the temporary license period has passed, franchisees pay $30 for each full-paying student. Franchisees must also purchase insurance costing $3.50 per student per year.

What You Get—Training and Support

Kumon franchisees obtain start-up training at the National Training Department in Oakbrook Terrace, Illinois. Over a two-month period, franchisees undergo seven days of training in Kumon management and instruction policies and procedures.

Kumon also provides site selection assistance and most teaching and management supplies at no extra cost. Generally, marketing is solely the responsibility of the franchisee. However, all marketing materials and campaigns must be pre-approved the corporate office. The company also maintains a marketing professional to assist with graphics.

Territory

Kumon grants exclusive territories.

Meineke Car Care Centers, Inc.

128 S. Tryon St., # 900
Charlotte, NC 28202-5001
Tel: (800) 275-5200 (704) 377-8855
Fax: (704) 372-4826
E-Mail: paul_baratta@meineke.com
Web Site: www.ownameineke.com
Mr. Paul Baratta, Interim Dir. Fran. Devel.

MEINEKE CAR CARE CENTERS is the nation's largest discount muffler and brake repair specialist with more than 860 shops across the nation. They have been offering great service at discount prices for more than 25 years. Their franchisees come from all walks of life and represent many nationalities.

BACKGROUND:	IFA MEMBER
Established: 1972; 1st Franchised: 1973	
Franchised Units:	844
Company-Owned Units	25

Total Units:	869
Dist.:	US-830; CAN-30; O'seas-9
North America:	49 States, 5 Provinces
Density:	73 in NY, 73 in PA, 55 in TX
Projected New Units (12 Months):	65
Qualifications:	4, 3, 3, 2, 2, 5
Registered:	All States
FINANCIAL/TERMS:	
Cash Investment:	$50K
Total Investment:	$180-365K
Minimum Net Worth:	$150K
Fees:	Franchise — $30K
	Royalty — 3-7%; Ad. — 8%
Earnings Claim Statement:	Yes
Term of Contract (Years):	15/15
Avg. # Of Employees:	4 FT
Passive Ownership:	Not Allowed
Encourage Conversions:	Yes
Area Develop. Agreements:	Yes/Varies
Sub-Franchising Contracts:	No
Expand In Territory:	Yes
Space Needs:	2,880-3,880 SF; FS

SUPPORT & TRAINING PROVIDED:		On-Going Support:	A,B,C,D,G,h,I
Financial Assistance Provided:	Yes(I)	Training:	4 Weeks Charlotte, NC.
Site Selection Assistance:	Yes		
Lease Negotiation Assistance:	No	**SPECIFIC EXPANSION PLANS:**	
Co-Operative Advertising:	Yes	US:	All United States
Franchisee Assoc./Member:	Yes/Yes	Canada:	All Canada
Size Of Corporate Staff:	88	Overseas: Caribbean, Central AmericaAll Countries	

Meineke Car Care Centers, Inc. strives to fix vehicles correctly the first time, and to provide quality products and workmanship at a fair price. With annual U.S. sales of $193 billion in the auto industry, an increasing average vehicle age and the disappearance of repair-providing service stations, Meineke franchisees get more than enough opportunities to meet the company's aforementioned objectives.

Sam Meineke opened the first Meineke auto store in Houston, Texas in 1972. In 1983, Meineke became a subsidiary of Parts Industries Corporation, a British-owned group that is a leading supplier of automotive and agricultural products. Now part of the Brambles Group, Meineke stores have serviced more than 50 million cars since their beginning in 1972.

Operating Units	1999	2000	2001
Franchised	852	862	861
% Change	--	1.2%	-0.1%
Company-Owned	12	20	25
% Change	--	66.7%	25.0%
Total	864	882	886
% Change	--	2.1%	0.4%
Franchised as % of Total	98.6%	97.7%	97.2%

Investment Required
The fee for a Meineke franchise is $30,000. Funding can be arranged.

Meineke provides the following range of investments required to open your initial franchise. The range assumes that all items are paid for in cash. To the extent that you choose to finance any of these expense items, your front-end investment could be substantially reduced. The following figures apply to the opening of a 4-bay location.

Item	Established Low Range	Established High Range
Franchise Fee	$30,000	$30,000
Equipment/Freight/ Installation/Shop Supplies/ Signs	$84,790.25	$86,690.25
Insurance	$672	$3,664
Inventory	$25,330.87	$25,330.87
Real Estate	$2,250	$8,400
Training Expenses	$1,500	$2,400
Other Costs and Additional Funds (for 3 months)	$40,900	$176,900
Total Investment	$185,443.12	$333,385.12

On-Going Expenses

Meineke franchisees pay royalties equaling 3 to 7%, depending on the product or service sold, and advertising fees equaling 8% of gross revenue. Four and one-half percent of advertising fees fund yellow pages and local media efforts, while 3.5% fund national media, marketing programs and other creative endeavors.

What You Get—Training and Support

When you purchase a Meineke franchise, you get: the Meineke brand name, marketing and advertising featuring a nationally recognized spokesperson (most recently George Foreman), national television coverage, internet advertisements and in-depth local programs, a protected territory, site selection assistance, the *Pipe Bender* and *Pro Tech* weekly newsletters and company training.

Meineke University conducts a four-week training program in Charlotte, North Carolina that teaches new franchisees management and technical skills. Meineke covers the hotel and travel expenses of up to two franchisees. Continued field training is available through Meineke's one-of-a-kind electronic, interactive training program and the operations and training departments, which have administered more than 24,000 hours of training in one year.

Further support is provided by the operations department. An operations manager will work individually with you to improve performance. Meineke also offers its franchisees the purchasing power of over 850 shops, more than 30 years of experience, a growing and diverse product line, a nationwide warranty program and a private label credit card.

Territory
Meineke grants protected territories of a two-mile radius and considers customer impact upon territories through the encroachment insurance policy.

Merry Maids

merry maids.

860 Ridge Lake Blvd.
Memphis, TN 38120-9421
Tel: (800) 798-8000 (901) 537-8100
Fax: (901) 537-8140
E-Mail: franchisesales@mmhomeoffice.com
Web Site: www.merrymaids.com
Mr. Rob Sanders, Director Market Expansion

MERRY MAIDS is the largest and most recognized company in the home cleaning industry. The company's commitment to training and on-going support is unmatched. MERRY MAIDS is highly-ranked as an established and fast growing franchise opportunity according to leading national publications. We offer low investment, cross-selling promotions with our partner companies, research and development and excellent marketing support.

BACKGROUND: IFA MEMBER
Established: 1979; 1st Franchised: 1980
Franchised Units: 1,245
Company-Owned Units   128
Total Units: 1,373
Dist.:   US-880; CAN-67; O'seas-426
  North America: 49 States, 7 Provinces
  Density: 123 in CA, 51 in TX, 42 IL
Projected New Units (12 Months):   32

Qualifications:	5, 3, 1, 3, 4, 5
Registered:	All States
FINANCIAL/TERMS:	
Cash Investment:	$21-23K
Total Investment:	$42-50K
Minimum Net Worth:	$Varies
Fees:	Franchise — $17-25K
	Royalty — 5-7%; Ad. — 0.25-1%
Earnings Claim Statement:	No
Term of Contract (Years):	5/5
Avg. # Of Employees:	2 FT, 12 PT
Passive Ownership:	Discouraged
Encourage Conversions:	Yes
Area Develop. Agreements:	No
Sub-Franchising Contracts:	No
Expand In Territory:	Yes
Space Needs:	800 Minimum SF; FS
SUPPORT & TRAINING PROVIDED:	
Financial Assistance Provided:	Yes(D)
Site Selection Assistance:	No
Lease Negotiation Assistance:	No
Co-Operative Advertising:	N/A
Franchisee Assoc./Member:	No
Size Of Corporate Staff:	60
On-Going Support:	C,D,G,H,I
Training:	8 Days Headquarters, Memphis, TN.
SPECIFIC EXPANSION PLANS:	
US:	All United States
Canada:	All Canada
Overseas:	All Countries

Merry Maids offers its clients more than a clean home—it offers time. Merry Maids is the largest home-cleaning franchise in the United States; it has more franchises than the next three competitors combined. With more than 70% of women working outside the home and increased demands for leisure, home cleaning franchises are growing two to three times faster than other franchises. In addition to these market factors, Merry Maids attributes its personal growth to its two-person cleaning teams, systematic approach to training, cleaning, office management and exclusive territory agreements.

In 1988, Merry Maids joined the ServiceMaster corporation, which was founded in 1952 and now has more than 5,000 franchise partners on 4 continents. As a Merry Maid franchisee, you reap the rewards of the ServiceMaster family, with the resources of each franchise used to develop and enhance the training and marketing of all.

Operating Units	12/31/1999	12/31/2000	12/31/2001
Franchised	775	755	755
% Change	--	-2.6%	0.0%
Company-Owned	77	104	110
% Change	--	35.1%	5.8%
Total	852	859	865
% Change	--	0.8%	0.7%
Franchised as % of Total	91.0%	87.9%	87.3%

Investment Required

Merry Maids offers three different franchise agreements, which vary by market size. The fee for a Merry Maids franchise is $24,000 in a full-sized market, $20,000 in a mid-sized market and $16,000 in a small market. Financing is available.

Merry Maids provides the following range of investments required to open your initial franchise. The range assumes that all items are paid for in cash. To the extent that you choose to finance any of these expense items, your front-end investment could be substantially reduced. The following figures apply to the opening of a franchise in a mid-sized market.

Item	Established Low Range	Established High Range
Franchise Fee	$4,000	$20,000
Advertising (for 3 months)	$4,000	$5,000
Equipment	$4,000	$5,000
Real Estate	$2,000	$4,000
Training Expenses	$500	$1,000
Other Costs and Additional Funds (for 3 months)	$7,000	$10,500
Total Investment	$21,500	$45,500

On-Going Expenses

Merry Maids franchisees pay service fees equaling 7% of gross revenue. Franchisees must also pay $14.40 a week for software.

What You Get—Training and Support

The Merry Maids franchise fee covers training for two and the opening inventory package, which includes equipment, supplies and cleaning products to equip two cleaning teams.

Merry Maids want to make sure that its franchisees are well-rounded and understand all aspects of the business. Training begins with eight days at the Merry Maids home office and concludes with support from the franchise development team and a mentor relationship with an established franchisee. Trainees learn operations, management, hiring, training, marketing, selling, scheduling and cleaning. Further training, if desired, is available from manuals, videos, CD-ROMs, on-the-job experience, a company Intranet site, newsletters, regional meetings, invitational conferences, seminars, field instruction and an annual national convention.

Support after a franchisee's initial training is complete can be obtained from the home office, regional coordinators, field visits and the franchisee "buddy" program, which remains uncompromised thanks to the protected territories awarded to each Merry Maids franchisee. Without the threat of competition, each franchisee is free to give and receive advice and insight from other franchisees.

Merry Maids's exclusive software is also supplied by the franchise fee. The software streamlines operations and assists with management, covering scheduling, payroll, bookkeeping and accounting, taxes and data transfer. Ideally, the Merry Maids Customer Information System takes care of the daily grind of the franchise, allowing franchisees to focus on the business as a whole.

Merry Maids's resource center houses more than 300 cleaning-related products that franchisees can order via telephone, modem or Intranet at prices discounted from retail. All products are researched, developed and manufactured by ServiceMaster Technical Services.

Franchisees also receive a package of tools and materials tailored to assist in selecting, training and compensating employees. Package contents include hiring and safety videos, recognition and reward programs and the quarterly Team Member newsletter.

Merry Maids marketing focuses first on neighborhood promotion and grows along with each franchisee's customer base to build market awareness and sales. Advertising includes television commercials, company-wide Internet sites with franchise locators and customizable Internet sites for each owner. Merry Maids's association with the other ServiceMaster franchises also allows for cross-selling and joint marketing ventures.

Territory
Merry Maids grants exclusive territories. Franchise territories in a full-sized market have a minimum of 10,000 qualified households, in a mid-sized market a minimum of 5,000 qualified households and in a small market a maximum of 5,000 qualified households.

Midas Auto Services

1300 Arlington Heights Rd.
Itasca, IL 60143-3174
Tel: (800) 365-0007 (630) 438-3000
Fax: (630) 438-3700
E-Mail: bkorus@midas.com
Web Site: www.midasfran.com
Ms. Barbara Korus, Franchise Recruitment Coord.

MIDAS is one of the world's largest providers of auto-motive service, offering exhaust, brake, steering and suspension services, as well as batteries, climate control and maintenance services at 2,700 franchised, company-owned and licensed MIDAS shops in 19 countries, including nearly 2,000 in the United States and Canada.

BACKGROUND: IFA MEMBER
Established: 1956; 1st Franchised: 1956
Franchised Units: 2,603
Company-Owned Units: 111
Total Units: 2,714
Dist.: US-1,726; CAN-233; O'seas-755
  North America: NR
  Density: NR
Projected New Units (12 Months): 40
Qualifications: 4, 4, 2, 2, 3, 5
Registered: All States

FINANCIAL/TERMS:
Cash Investment: $100-150K
Total Investment: $360-487K
Minimum Net Worth: $300K
Fees: Franchise — $20K
  Royalty — 10%; Ad. — Incl. Roy.
Earnings Claim Statement: No
Term of Contract (Years): 20/20
Avg. # Of Employees: 6 FT, 4 PT
Passive Ownership: Discouraged
Encourage Conversions: Yes
Area Develop. Agreements: Varies
Sub-Franchising Contracts: No
Expand In Territory: Yes
Space Needs: 4,000-5,000 SF; FS

SUPPORT & TRAINING PROVIDED:
Financial Assistance Provided: Yes(I)
Site Selection Assistance: Yes
Lease Negotiation Assistance: Yes
Co-Operative Advertising: Yes
Franchisee Assoc./Member: Yes/Yes
Size Of Corporate Staff: NR
On-Going Support: B,C,D,e,f,G,H,I
Training: 1-2 Weeks of Self Study; 1-2 Weeks In-Shop Assignment; 3 Weeks in Palatine, IL.

SPECIFIC EXPANSION PLANS:
US: All United States
Canada: All Canada
Overseas: Select Countries

The standard Midas location has eight bays and offers exhaust, suspension, brakes, alignment, starting and charging, heating and cooling, scheduled and general maintenance and cv joint and driveshaft services. Since the company expanded their core services, their market share has increased from $19.3 billion to $34.3 billion.

Operating Units	12/31/1999	12/31/2000	12/31/2001
Franchised	1,831	1,769	1,622
% Change	--	-3.4%	-8.3%
Company-Owned	10	10	108
% Change	--	0.0%	980%
Total	1,841	1,779	1,730
% Change	--	-3.4%	-2.7%
Franchised as % of Total	99.4%	99.4%	93.7%

Investment Required

The fee for a Midas franchise is $20,000. If requested, Midas will provide you with a list of preferred lenders.

Midas provides the following range of investments required to open your initial franchise. The range assumes that all items are paid for in cash. To the extent that you choose to finance any of these expense items, your front-end investment could be substantially reduced.

Item	Established Low Range	Established High Range
Franchise Fee	$20,000	$20,000
Advertising	$4,350	$7,500
Construction Management/ Site Selection Fees	$6,000	$7,500
Equipment/Fixtures/ Machinery/Signs	$230,000	$294,000
Insurance	$9,000	$14,000
Inventory/Supplies	$50,000	$75,000
Real Estate (for 3 months)	$14,000	$36,000
Training Expenses	$3,000	$4,000
Other Costs and Additional Funds (for 3 months)	$43,000	$70,000
Total Investment	$379,350	$528,000

On-Going Expenses
Midas franchisees pay royalties equaling 10% of gross revenue.

What You Get—Training and Support
Midas franchisees have the option to buy their own facilities or to lease them from the company itself. The equipment to furnish these facilities are approved and tested by Midas and are available to their franchisees at discounted national account prices.

Midas training is long and thorough. Initial training lasts for five to seven weeks and consists of: self-study, in which the franchisee is guided by a company representative through competitive analysis, including market research, shop experience and business plan evaluation; the Midas Institute of Technology in Palatine, Illinois, where they instruct new franchisees on business problems, day to day operations and policies. The tuition for these two segments of training are included in the franchise fee, but franchisees are responsible for travel, room and board expenses. Corporate discounts may be available. Training continues with follow-up courses and instructional videotapes.
Fifty percent of Midas royalties fund advertising. Not only is Midas the third-largest yellow pages advertiser, making any location always easy to find, but the company spends more than $50 million on annual national and local advertising, reaching 97% of American households through television advertisements on NBC, CBS, ABC, FOX and the major cable networks.

Because of this exposure, despite the youth of any new Midas location, the name is already known. However, local marketing, such as television and radio spots, newspaper advertisements, outdoor billboards and direct mail help draw customers to any budding franchise. The Midas public relations department also provides guidance with all media, including that for grand openings, helps get Midas franchisees involved in the community they seek to serve and raises awareness of the Midas brand as well as individual locations.

Territory
Midas does not grant exclusive territories.

Miracle Auto Painting and Body Repair

3157 Corporate Pl.
Hayward, CA 94545
Tel: (877) 647-2253 (510) 887-2211
Fax: (510) 887-3092
E-Mail: jim@miracleautopainting.com
Web Site: www.miracleautopainting.com
Mr. Jim Jordan, Vice President

Cash Investment:	$75-100K
Total Investment:	$215-275K
Minimum Net Worth:	$400K
Fees: Franchise —	$35K
Royalty — 5%;	Ad. — 5%
Earnings Claim Statement:	No
Term of Contract (Years):	10/10
Avg. # Of Employees:	10 FT, 2 PT
Passive Ownership:	Discouraged
Encourage Conversions:	Yes
Area Develop. Agreements:	Yes/5
Sub-Franchising Contracts:	Yes
Expand In Territory:	Yes
Space Needs:	9,000-11,000 SF; FS, SF

MIRACLE is a production collision repair and refinishing company that specializes in complete paint jobs. MIRACLE caters to individual vehicle owners, insurance carriers, other body shop facilities and new and used automobile dealers.

BACKGROUND: IFA MEMBER
Established: 1953; 1st Franchised: 1964

Franchised Units:	28
Company-Owned Units	3
Total Units:	31
Dist.:	US-31; CAN-0; O'seas-0
North America:	4 States
Density:	23 in CA, 6 in TX, 1 in AZ
Projected New Units (12 Months):	1
Qualifications:	3, 3, 3, 1, 2, 5
Registered:	CA,OR,WA

FINANCIAL/TERMS:

SUPPORT & TRAINING PROVIDED:

Financial Assistance Provided:	Yes(I)
Site Selection Assistance:	Yes
Lease Negotiation Assistance:	Yes
Co-Operative Advertising:	No
Franchisee Assoc./Member:	Yes/Yes
Size Of Corporate Staff:	20
On-Going Support:	B,C,D,E,G,H
Training:	10 Days Headquarters; 10 Days On-Site.

SPECIFIC EXPANSION PLANS:

US:	West, Southwest
Canada:	No
Overseas:	No

Miracle Auto Painting and Body Repair has provided body collision repair and auto painting under the same ownership since 1953, with the same management team for the last 20 years. Miracle franchises require little inventory, keeping costs low and profits high. However, this franchise opportunity isn't for everyone—the company seeks franchisees in the west and southwest of the United States and, in California, in San Jose, Oakland and San Francisco.

Operating Units	9/30/1999	9/30/2000	9/30/2001
Franchised	32	31	30
% Change	--	-3.1%	-3.2%
Company-Owned	4	3	3
% Change	--	-25.0%	0.0%
Total	36	34	33
% Change	--	-5.5%	-2.9%
Franchised as % of Total	88.9%	91.2%	90.9%

Investment Required
The fee for a Miracle Auto franchise is $35,000 for an entire territory. If you wish to be one of a number of franchisees within one territory, a slightly lower fee applies. No direct financing is available.

Miracle Auto provides the following range of investments required to open your initial franchise. The range assumes that all items are paid for in cash. To the extent that you choose to finance any of these expense items, your front-end investment could be substantially reduced.

Item	Established Low Range	Established High Range
Franchise Fee	$35,000	$35,000
Advertising Fees (for 5 months)	$15,000	$15,000
Equipment/Signs	$112,000	$112,000
Inventory	$7,500	$7,500
Real Estate	$10,000	$40,000
Training Expenses	$2,000	$3,500
Other Costs and Additional Funds (for 6 months)	$35,000	$60,000
Total Investment	$216,500	$273,000

On-Going Expenses
Miracle Auto franchisees pay royalties equaling 5%, perhaps less under the parts rebate program, and advertising fees equaling 5% of gross rev-

enue. Two percent of your advertising contribution funds local advertising of your choice. The remaining 3% funds system-wide umbrella advertising.

What You Get—Training and Support

The purchase of a Miracle Auto franchise includes: intensive four-week training (two weeks of classroom lessons at company headquarters and two weeks on the job in a Miracle Auto shop), a comprehensive operation manual, proven systems and procedures, an experienced management team and marketing and advertising programs.

Start-up support also includes site evaluation assistance, lease negotiation, facility design and layout and operating, advertising and marketing manuals.

Furthermore, all franchisees benefit from Miracle Auto's association with one of the largest and most cost-effective suppliers, MAS Warehousing, with which all inventory orders are placed.

Territory

Miracle Auto grants protected territories with a minimum population of 50,000 people.

Money Mailer

"Like Getting Money In Your Mailbox".

14271 Corporate Dr.
Garden Grove, CA 92843-4937
Tel: (800) 508-6663 (714) 265-8494
Fax: (714) 265-8311
E-Mail: djenkins@moneymailer.com
Web Site: www.moneymailer.com
Mr. Dennis Jenkins, VP Franchise Licensing

MONEY MAILER is one of America's leading direct mail advertising companies with over 300 franchises in the U.S. and Canada. Over its 20 year history, MONEY MAILER has been at the forefront of introducing innovative direct mail advertising products and programs to the marketplace - helping businesses get and keep more customers and helping consumers save money everyday.

BACKGROUND: IFA MEMBER
Established: 1978; 1st Franchised: 1980
Franchised Units: 244
Company-Owned Units   8
Total Units: 252
Dist.:   US-312; CAN-6; O'seas-1

North America:	NR	Sub-Franchising Contracts:	Yes
Density:	31 in CA, 23 in NJ, 20 in NC	Expand In Territory:	Yes
Projected New Units (12 Months):	40	Space Needs:	NR SF; HB
Qualifications:	4, 3, 4, 3, 4, 5		
Registered:	CA,FL,IL,IN,NY,VA,WA,WI	**SUPPORT & TRAINING PROVIDED:**	
		Financial Assistance Provided:	No
		Site Selection Assistance:	N/A
FINANCIAL/TERMS:		Lease Negotiation Assistance:	N/A
Cash Investment:	$37-71.5K	Co-Operative Advertising:	No
Total Investment:	$37-71.5K	Franchisee Assoc./Member:	Yes/Yes
Minimum Net Worth:	$Varies	Size Of Corporate Staff:	300
Fees:	Franchise — $25-35K	On-Going Support:	C,D,H,I
	Royalty — Varies; Ad. — N/A	Training: 1 Week Regional Office; 2 Weeks Corpo-	
Earnings Claim Statement:	No	rate Headquarters; 1 Week Regional Office.	
Term of Contract (Years):	10/10		
Avg. # Of Employees:	1 FT, 1 PT	**SPECIFIC EXPANSION PLANS:**	
Passive Ownership:	Not Allowed	US:	All United States
Encourage Conversions:	N/A	Canada:	No
Area Develop. Agreements:	No	Overseas:	No

A leader in the $47 billion direct mail industry, Money Mailer serves as a local business consultant specializing in direct response and Internet advertising. The company delivers both profits and savings by remaining committed to its mission: "To help businesses get and keep more customers and to help customers save money every day."™ Its franchisees mail more than 105 million over-sized "Like Getting Money in Your Mailbox" envelopes and services more than 30,000 advertisers each year.

Money Mailer offers its franchisees just as much as it offers its customers. With a variety of direct marketing services to offer clients, Money Mailer is a program whose new and repeat client list and growth knows no limits. The franchise requires no employees, no inventory and no storefront. In other words, overhead is low. Also, franchisees can work from their own homes, allowing them to set their own hours.

Money Mailer was first established in Garden Grove, California in 1979.

Operating Units	11/30/2000	11/30/2001	11/30/2002
Franchised	201	211	245
% Change	--	5.0%	16.1%

Company-Owned	0	0	0
% Change	--	N/A	N/A
Total	201	211	245
% Change	--	5.0%	16.1%
Franchised as % of Total	100.0%	100.0%	100.0%

Investment Required

The minimum fee for a Money Mailer franchise is $30,500. The ultimate fee varies according to the number of mail targets located in the franchisee's territory. The fee includes the $3,000 training and materials fee.

Money Mailer provides the following range of investments required to open your initial franchise. The range assumes that all items are paid for in cash. To the extent that you choose to finance any of these expense items, your front-end investment could be substantially reduced.

Item	Established Low Range	Established High Range
Franchise Fee	$30,500	$41,500
Equipment/Supplies	$2,750	$4,750
Initial Map and List Creation	$175	$245
Insurance	$500	$1,500
Rent/Security Deposit/ Telephone	$100	$1,000
Training Expenses	$1,500	$3,500
Additional Funds	$12,500	$17,000
Total Investment	$48,025	$69,495

On-Going Expenses

Money Mailer franchisees pay annual regional royalties equaling $440 to $544 per 10,000 home area per mailing (the more mailings sent by a franchisee, the lower the fee), national royalties equaling $217 for areas scheduled to be mailed but not mailed, annual advertising fund contributions equaling $300 and on-going advertising fund contributions equaling $21 per 10,000 home area mailing.

What You Get—Training and Support

A Money Mailer business begins with interactive classroom and field training to familiarize all franchisees with the Money Mailer operating system.

Money Mailer wants its franchisees to hit the ground running, thus, upon start-up, the company provides each franchisee with its free mailing program, which provides mailing production for two 10,000 home areas at no cost to the franchisee. The company also strives to supply its franchisees with low-cost, turnkey client lead generation. To this end, Money Mailer makes available a series of postcards to send to target businesses with the aim of signing them to the Money Mailer advertising system. The series is further strengthened by a corresponding turnkey telemarketing program that is available for a small additional fee.

In addition, both new and mature franchisees benefit from SmartZones®, Money Mailer's proprietary mapping and report generating software. Franchisees use SmartZones as a valuable tool to help them better educate their small business clients about the demographic make-up of the consumers in their market.

As on-going support, franchise development and regional support teams back up Money Mailer franchisees with assistance and advice. In addition, the Money Mailer intranet website, which is updated daily, provides information on selling techniques, marketing programs and other industry news. Money Mailer also conducts regular "Quarterly Sales Meetings" to brief franchisees on topics of current importance.

Money Mailer also maintains the Chain Partners Program, which establishes Money Mailer as the preferred vendor for national businesses by partnering the companies' local branches with Money Mailer franchisees. Franchisees take over from there by simply contacting the local branch and providing them with advertising services utilizing the pre-approved ads, artwork and logos established for each partner. The Chain Partners Program even makes it possible for brand new franchisees to handle accounts for big name chain restaurants and automotive stores as soon as they open for business.

Territory
Money Mailer grants exclusive territories.

Mr. Electric Corp.

P.O. Box 3146
Waco, TX 76707
Tel: (800) 805-0575 (254) 745-2439
Fax: (800) 209-7621
E-Mail: mhawkins@dwyergroup.com
Web Site: www.mrelectric.com
Mr. Mike Hawkins, VP Franchising

Serving the electrical repair needs of residential and light commercial establishments, in addition to offering other electrical products to the 'same user,' including such items as surcharge protectors, communication and data cabling, ceiling fans, decorative light fixtures, security and landscape lighting, etc.

BACKGROUND:	IFA MEMBER
Established: 1994; 1st Franchised: 1994	
Franchised Units:	117
Company-Owned Units	0
Total Units:	117
Dist.:	US-109; CAN-4; O'seas-4
North America:	37 States, 2 Province
Density:	11 in CA, 5 in IL, 4 in TX
Projected New Units (12 Months):	18
Qualifications:	3, 2, 5, 3, 2, 4
Registered:	All States

FINANCIAL/TERMS:	
Cash Investment:	$30.2-68K
Total Investment:	$64-157K
Minimum Net Worth:	$75K
Fees:	Franchise — $19.5K
	Royalty — 3-6%; Ad. — 2%
Earnings Claim Statement:	No
Term of Contract (Years):	10/5
Avg. # Of Employees:	3 FT, 1 PT
Passive Ownership:	Discouraged
Encourage Conversions:	Yes
Area Develop. Agreements:	No
Sub-Franchising Contracts:	Yes
Expand In Territory:	Yes
Space Needs:	500-1,000 SF; FS, HB

SUPPORT & TRAINING PROVIDED:	
Financial Assistance Provided:	Yes(B)
Site Selection Assistance:	N/A
Lease Negotiation Assistance:	N/A
Co-Operative Advertising:	No
Franchisee Assoc./Member:	No
Size Of Corporate Staff:	8
On-Going Support:	C,D,E,G,h,I
Training:	5 Business Days at Corporate Offices; 3 Business Days On-Site in Business.

SPECIFIC EXPANSION PLANS:	
US:	All United States
Canada:	Not This Year
Overseas:	Most Latin American and Asian Countries

Mr. Electric provides electrical repair and service to customers ranging from homeowners and commercial construction companies to utility companies, retail stores, national accounts and plumbing contractors. Mr. Electric is able to retain such a diverse customer base through its menu pricing, fast response time, professional image, prompt and attentive service, trained and courteous professionals, round-the-clock availability and satisfaction guaranteed policy. Not surprisingly, the business also thrives on repeat business and referrals. Mr. Electric also offers franchisees and customers with national alliances with quality electrical manufacturers and indoor and outdoor lighting design and maintenance. What's more, Mr. Electric has no comparable competitor in the franchise industry. The market is virtually untapped.

Mr. Electric is an ideal franchise for electrical contractors and technicians interested in the security and freedom a franchise offers. Mr. Electric offers these electricians more control over their business lives, as well as owner and employee benefits and a more professional, national image behind which to sell their services. Mr. Electric offers franchisees the strength to weather the industry changes threatened by deregulation and big corporations and greater long-term business value with a recognized name.

Mr. Electric is part of The Dwyer Group, a national corporation of service-based franchises. The Dwyer Group mission: "To teach our franchisees the principles of personal and business success so they, and all people they touch, will live happier and more successful lives." Accordingly, Mr. Electric fosters open correspondence between itself and its franchisees to help both parties reach their full potential.

Operating Units	12/31/2000	12/31/2001	12/31/2002
Franchised	91	103	106
% Change	--	13.2%	2.9%
Company-Owned	0	0	0
% Change	--	N/A	N/A
Total	91	103	106
% Change	--	13.2%	2.9%
Franchised as % of Total	100.0%	100.0%	100.0%

Investment Required
The fee for a Mr. Electric franchise is $19,500.

Mr. Electric provides the following range of investments required to open your initial franchise. The range assumes that all items are paid for in cash. To the extent that you choose to finance any of these expense items, your front-end investment could be substantially reduced.

Item	Established Low Range	Established High Range
Franchise Fee	$19,500	$19,500
Advertising and Promotion	$5,000	$35,000
Equipment/Inventory/ Supplies	$9,500	$9,500
Insurance	$1,200	$2,500
Training Expenses	$2,000	$6,000
Vehicle	$850	$26,000
Other Costs and Additional Funds (for 3 months)	$26,000	$52,500
Total Investment (does not include real estate)	$64,050	$151,000

On-Going Expenses

Mr. Electric franchisees pay royalties equaling 3 to 6% and national advertising fees equaling 1 to 2% of gross revenue. Franchisees are also responsible for an advertising co-op fee. The franchise fee covers training for three people; additional training is available for $1,000 a person. The annual convention registration fee ranges from $137.50 to $220, depending on the timelines of payment.

What You Get—Training and Support

Initial training covers business, marketing and management. Training continues through national training conferences and franchisee information exchanges. Support includes field support, a toll-free phone line to Mr. Electric's head-quarters, a regional director, the Sure Start Program, regional and national conferences and regular on-site visits.

All franchisees use Mr. Electric's streamlined, time-saving systems and forms to document and manage procedures, safety, marketing and other aspects of operation.

In addition to national name recognition, Mr. Electric franchisees receive professional marketing, including custom-decaled service vans, professionally prepared advertising, and promotional programs and materials—all designed to build the company's national image while reaching franchisee's local markets.

Mr. Electric franchisees can also choose to take advantage of many optional benefit packages, such as health plans, 401Ks, life insurance and stock purchases.

In addition, Mr. Electric's association with The Dwyer Group provides it and its franchisees with gross marketing opportunities, national buying power and an extensive peer network through which to expand and prosper.

Territory
Mr. Electric grants exclusive territories with a minimum population of approximately 100,000 and a maximum population of approximately 1,500,000 people.

Mr. Rooter Corp.

PLUMBING

1020 N. University Parks Dr.
Waco, TX 76707
Tel: (800) 298-6855 (254) 745-2439
Fax: (800) 209-7621
E-Mail: mhawkins@dwyergroup.com
Web Site: www.mrrooter.com
Mr. Mike Hawkins, VP Franchising

Full-service plumbing and sewer/drain cleaning. Franchise specializing in conversion of existing trades people to our method of doing business.

BACKGROUND: IFA MEMBER
Established: 1968; 1st Franchised: 1972
Franchised Units: 192
Company-Owned Units   0
Total Units: 192

Dist.:	US-170; CAN-16; O'seas-6
North America:	41 States, 4 Provinces
Density:	35 in CA, 18 in ON, 17 in TX
Projected New Units (12 Months):	40
Qualifications:	3, 3, 5, 2, 3, 4
Registered:	All States

FINANCIAL/TERMS:
Cash Investment:	$NR
Total Investment:	$NR
Minimum Net Worth:	$Varies
Fees:	Franchise — $22.5K
	Royalty — 3-6%; Ad. — 2%
Earnings Claim Statement:	No
Term of Contract (Years):	10/5
Avg. # Of Employees:	Depends on Sales
Passive Ownership:	Not Allowed
Encourage Conversions:	Yes
Area Develop. Agreements:	Yes/10
Sub-Franchising Contracts:	Yes
Expand In Territory:	Yes
Space Needs:	NR SF; N/A

SUPPORT & TRAINING PROVIDED:		On-Going Support:	C,D,E,F,G,H,I
Financial Assistance Provided:	Yes(I)	Training:	I Week Waco, TX.
Site Selection Assistance:	N/A		
Lease Negotiation Assistance:	N/A	**SPECIFIC EXPANSION PLANS:**	
Co-Operative Advertising:	No	US:	Uncovered Areas
Franchisee Assoc./Member:	No	Canada:	All Canada
Size Of Corporate Staff:	13	Overseas:	All Countries

If you're a plumbing contractor or technician seeking a franchise opportunity, Mr. Rooter is for you. Mr. Rooter is designed for those who are comfortable with the technical aspects of a plumbing business, but not the business matters, and gives the franchisee control with proven, streamlined operations system.

Since 1974, Mr. Rooter has provided franchisees with relief from the anxiety of service industry consolidation while maintaining their autonomy, as Mr. Rooter franchisees retain their freedom but benefit from the security of membership in a greater organization. Mr. Rooter also offers franchisees greater long-term business value, granting their business a nationally-recognized name and a proven system.

Mr. Rooter is part of The Dwyer Group, a national corporation of service-based franchises. The Dwyer Group mission: "To teach our franchisees the principles of personal and business success so they, and all people they touch, will live happier and more successful lives."

Operating Units	12/31/1999	12/31/2000	12/31/2001
Franchised	173	186	188
% Change	--	7.5%	1.1%
Company-Owned	0	0	0
% Change	--	N/A	N/A
Total	173	186	188
% Change	--	7.5%	1.1%
Franchised as % of Total	100.0%	100.0%	100.0%

Investment Required

The fee for a Mr. Rooter franchise is $22,500.

Mr. Rooter provides the following range of investments required to open your initial franchise. The range assumes that all items are paid for in cash. To the extent that you choose to finance any of these expense items, your front-end investment could be substantially reduced.

Item	Established Low Range	Established High Range
Franchise Fee	$22,500	$22,500
Advertising and Promotion	$2,000	$4,000
Equipment/Inventory/ Supplies	$9,500	$30,000
Insurance	$1,000	$2,000
Training Expenses	$1,200	$4,000
Vehicle	$550	$27,000
Other Costs and Additional Funds (for 3 months)	$10,000	$31,000
Total Investment (does not include real estate)	$46,750	$120,500

On-Going Expenses

Mr. Rooter franchisees pay royalties equaling 4 to 7% and national advertising fees equaling 2% of gross revenue. Franchisees are also responsible for an undetermined advertising co-op fee. The franchise fee includes training for three people; additional training comes at a cost of $1,000 per person. There is also an annual convention attendance fee of $125 to $200, depending on the timeliness of payment.

What You Get—Training and Support

Mr. Rooter wants its franchisees to manage their business better and have more free time. Training focuses on operations, marketing and advertising, human resources, customer service, salesmanship, management, finance, business and more, with an emphasis on: identifying and attracting new customers; keeping customers; controlling overhead; recruiting and retaining plumbing technicians; setting and updating goals to ensure consistent growth; financial, accounting and marketing systems and arrangements for long-term rewards.

On-going support includes national conferences; regional seminars and advanced classes; mentoring; one-on-one visits; forms and marketing materials; national advertising and promotion programs; customer retention tools; national accounts initiative; vendor discounts; research development into new products, services, business systems and equipment; and buying power negotiations. Mr. Rooter's objective is to ease the burden of franchisees' tasks so that they can concentrate on their customers.

In addition, Mr. Rooter's association with The Dwyer Group provides it and its franchisees with gross marketing opportunities, national buying power and an extensive peer network through which to expand and prosper.

Territory
Mr. Rooter does grant exclusive territories with populations of 100,000 to 1,500,000 people.

New Horizons Computer Learning Center

New Horizons®
Computer Learning Centers

1900 S. State College Blvd., # 200
Anaheim, CA 92806
Tel: (714) 940-8230
Fax: (714) 938-6008
E-Mail: ralph.loberger@newhorizons.com
Web Site: www.newhorizons.com
Mr. Ralph Loberger, VP Franchise Development

NEW HORIZONS COMPUTER LEARNING CENTERS, Inc. is the world's largest independent IT training company, meeting the needs of more than 2.4 million students each year. NEW HORIZONS offers a variety of flexible training choices: instructor-led classes, Web-based training, computer-based training, computer labs, certification exam preparation tools and 24-hour, 7-day-a-week help-desk support.

BACKGROUND: IFA MEMBER
Established: 1982; 1st Franchised: 1992

Franchised Units:	246
Company-Owned Units:	26
Total Units:	272
Dist.:	US-159; CAN-1; O'seas-113
North America:	42 States, 1 Province
Density:	19 in CA, 11 in FL, 8 in NY
Projected New Units (12 Months):	20
Qualifications:	5, 5, 2, 3, 3, 5
Registered:	All States

FINANCIAL/TERMS:

Cash Investment:	$150-200K
Total Investment:	$400-500K
Minimum Net Worth:	$500K
Fees:	Franchise — $25-75K
	Royalty — 6%; Ad. — 1%
Earnings Claim Statement:	No
Term of Contract (Years):	10/5
Avg. # Of Employees:	15 FT

Passive Ownership:	Discouraged	Co-Operative Advertising:	Yes
Encourage Conversions:	Yes	Franchisee Assoc./Member:	Yes/Yes
Area Develop. Agreements:	Yes/10	Size Of Corporate Staff:	200+
Sub-Franchising Contracts:	Yes	On-Going Support:	B,C,D,E,G,H
Expand In Territory:	Yes	Training: 2 Weeks Headquarters; 1 Week Franchise
Space Needs: 4,000-5,000 SF; FS, OB, IP, Business Park		Location; 2 Days Regional.

SPECIFIC EXPANSION PLANS:

SUPPORT & TRAINING PROVIDED:

Financial Assistance Provided:	Yes(D)	US:	All United States
Site Selection Assistance:	Yes	Canada:	All Canada
Lease Negotiation Assistance:	Yes	Overseas:	All Countries

With the advent of computers and the internet, business will never be the same. The ever-changing pace and format of the technological world requires that companies employing such methods must continue to update, integrate and learn these evolving developments. For these same reasons, New Horizons' cutting-edgeness is eternally renewed. New Horizons offers computer and technology instruction with flexible course options that can be tailored to any student's specific needs. They offer classes in linux, cisco and A+ certification, the internet, Microsoft training and certification, technical training, skills assessment and exam preparation for all experience levels. More recently, the company began to offer online learning in addition to their traditional classroom learning.

New Horizons asks that a prospective franchisee have the strong management skills necessary to operate a business, an entrepreneurial spirit and the discipline to learn and follow the New Horizons system.

Founder Mike Brinda opened the first New Horizons in southern California nearly twenty years ago. Ten years of testing and refining later, he offered his first New Horizons franchise.

Operating Units	12/31/1999	12/31/2000	12/31/2001
Franchised	145	186	186
% Change	--	28.3%	0.0%
Company-Owned	14	16	18
% Change	--	14.3%	12.5%

Total	159	202	204
% Change	--	27.0%	1.0%
Franchised as % of Total	91.2%	92.1%	91.2%

Investment Required

The fee for a New Horizons franchise ranges from $10,000 to $75,000, depending upon territory size.

New Horizons provides the following range of investments required to open your initial franchise. The range assumes that all items are paid for in cash. To the extent that you choose to finance any of these expense items, your front-end investment could be substantially reduced.

Item	Established Low Range	Established High Range
Franchise Fee	$25,000	$75,000
CMS Site Survey/Training/ Usage and Monthly Support Fees	$5,436	$10,925
Computer	$95,000	$155,000
Furnishings/Signs	$30,200	$57,000
Insurance	$1,000	$4,000
Inventory/Supplies	$1,500	$3,000
Real Estate	$8,000	$53,000
Training Expenses	$2,000	$5,000
Additional Funds (for 4 to 6 months)	$200,000	$200,000
Total Investment	$368,136	$562,925

On-Going Expenses

New Horizons' franchisees must pay royalties equaling 6% and a marketing and advertising fee equaling 1% of gross monthly revenue. Delivery fees for online class delivery apply whenever the classes are requested.

What You Get—Training and Support

Payment of the New Horizons franchise fee gives you: use of the New Horizons sales model, on-going comprehensive training, support from regional managers and field specialists, an extensive courseware library of over 1,000 titles (many of which are authorized by companies like Microsoft and Corel) in a host of languages, videos and other reference materials, web-based training solutions, a computer-based training library for use by instructors or students, assistance with industry vendor authorizations (such as those with Microsoft, Novell, Lotus and Prometric), the strength of an international system and a globally recognized brand.

Before each center's opening, franchisees take part in a two-week training course that teaches daily operations, management and marketing.

Regional offices, an online resource library, discussion forums and international conferences keep franchisees informed and business management honed.

Territory

New Horizons grants exclusive territories, usually with a minimum radius of 25 miles.

Perma-Glaze

1638 S. Research Loop Rd., # 160
Tucson, AZ 85710
Tel: (800) 332-7397 (520) 722-9718
Fax: (520) 296-4393
E-Mail: daleyoung@permaglaze.com
Web Site: www.permaglaze.com
Mr. Dale R. Young, President/CEO

PERMA GLAZE specializes in multi-surface restoration of bathtubs, sinks, countertops, appliances, porcelain, metal, acrylics, cultured marble and more. PERMA GLAZE licensed representatives provide valued services to hotels/motels, private residences, apartments, schools, hospitals, contractors, property managers and many others.

BACKGROUND:	IFA MEMBER
Established: 1978; 1st Franchised: 1981	
Franchised Units:	178
Company-Owned Units	2
Total Units:	180
Dist.:	US-104; CAN-3; O'seas-40
North America:	36 States, 3 Provinces
Density:	15 in CA, 7 in AZ, 6 in PA
Projected New Units (12 Months):	20
Qualifications:	4, 2, 1, 3, 4, 3
Registered:	CA,IL,IN,MD,MI,MN,NY, ND,OR,SD,VA,WA,WI

FINANCIAL/TERMS:

Cash Investment:	$2.5-3K
Total Investment:	$NR
Minimum Net Worth:	$21.5K
Fees:	Franchise — $21.5K+
	Royalty — 6/5/4%/$200 Min.; Ad. — NR
Earnings Claim Statement:	Yes
Term of Contract (Years):	10/10
Avg. # Of Employees:	1 FT
Passive Ownership:	Allowed
Encourage Conversions:	N/A
Area Develop. Agreements:	Yes/10
Sub-Franchising Contracts:	No
Expand In Territory:	Yes
Space Needs:	N/A SF; HB

SUPPORT & TRAINING PROVIDED:

Financial Assistance Provided:	Yes
Site Selection Assistance:	Yes
Lease Negotiation Assistance:	N/A
Co-Operative Advertising:	N/A
Franchisee Assoc./Member:	Yes
Size Of Corporate Staff:	6
On-Going Support:	C,D,G,H,I
Training:	5 Days Tucson, AZ.

SPECIFIC EXPANSION PLANS:

US:	All United States
Canada:	All Canada
Overseas:	All Countries

Perma-Glaze specializes in multi-surface restoration services, such as the renewal of worn and damaged fixtures and surfaces, whether bathtubs, tile, porcelain, metal, acrylic, fiberglass, appliances, formica, cultured marble, countertops or floors. Their wide range of services have a wide range of potential applications, including hotels, motels, private homes, schools, hospitals, contractors and property managers. To be a Perma-Glaze franchisee no experience is necessary.

The refinishing industry is young, but its merits are great. Refinishing is faster and cheaper than replacement and ensures the same quality as the original product—because it is the original product. Perma-Glaze's special formula is safer for kitchen and bathroom use than most and doesn't chip or discolor.

The start-up cost for a Perma-Glaze franchise is low. Franchisees can work from home, most equipment fits in the trunk of a car and all supplies are included in the franchise fee. In addition, surface restoration is a cash business. When the job is done, the paycheck is due. The company is also devoted to environmental safety and awareness.

Operating Units	7/31/1997	7/31/1998	7/31/1999
Franchised	128	118	112
% Change	--	-7.8%	-5.1%
Company-Owned	1	1	1

% Change	--	0.0%	0.0%
Total	129	119	113
% Change	--	-7.8%	-5.0%
Franchised as % of Total	99.2%	99.1%	99.1%

Investment Required

The fee for a Perma-Glaze franchise, available in three different licenses—platinum, silver or gold—ranges from $21,500 to $42,500 depending on population.

Perma-Glaze provides the following range of investments required to open your initial franchise. The range assumes that all items are paid for in cash. To the extent that you choose to finance any of these expense items, your front-end investment could be substantially reduced. The following figures apply to the opening of a Perma-Glaze franchise. Floortastic franchises and combined franchises carry different costs.

Item	Established Low Range	Established High Range
Franchise Fee	$21,500	$42,500
Additional Funds (for 3 months)	$5,000	$5,000
Total Investment	$26,500	$47,500

On-going Expenses

Perma-Glaze franchisees pay royalties equaling 4 to 6%, depending on income, of gross revenue.

What You Get—Training and Support

Perma-Glaze franchisees undergo a fully paid-for training course in Tucson, Arizona. Here, they learn tool and material use and business administration and development, such as job pricing estimations.

New franchisees are also provided with: start-up printing needs; professional marketing in the form of television commercials, radio spots, direct mail art, ad slicks, full color photos, press releases and vehicle signage; an international advertising program and website; the franchise operations manual; consulting services; research and development; regional meetings; newsletters and a toll-free 24-hour support phone line.

Territory

Depending on the population of the territory and franchisee compliance, Perma-Glaze does grant exclusive territories.

Pop-A-Lock

1018 Harding St., # 205
Lafayette, LA 70503
Tel: (337) 233-6211
Fax: (337) 233-6655
E-Mail: dmarks@thelsrgroup.com
Web Site: www.pop-a-lock.com
Mr. Don Marks, Chief Executive Officer

POP-A-LOCK is America's largest car door unlocking, roadside assistance, and locksmith service. We provide fast, professional, guaranteed service using our proprietary tools and opening techniques. We also offer an outstanding community service through our emergency car door unlocking program. You will provide lockout and roadside assistance to the public, businesses and various motor clubs. Franchisees are presently authorized but not required to offer full locksmith services.

BACKGROUND:	IFA MEMBER
Established: 1991; 1st Franchised: 1994	
Franchised Units:	105
Company-Owned Units:	0
Total Units:	105
Dist.:	US-105; CAN-0; O'seas-0
North America:	29 States
Density:	22 in TX, 15 in LA, 14 in FL

Projected New Units (12 Months):	10-20
Qualifications:	3, 3, 2, 3, 3, 4
Registered:	CA,FL,IL,IN,MD,MI,NY,OR,VA,WA
FINANCIAL/TERMS:	
Cash Investment:	$
Total Investment:	$8-65K
Minimum Net Worth:	$Varies
Fees:	Franchise — $26.1-48.9K
	Royalty — 6%; Ad. — 1%
Earnings Claim Statement:	No
Term of Contract (Years):	10/10
Avg. # Of Employees:	8 FT
Passive Ownership:	Allowed
Encourage Conversions:	No
Area Develop. Agreements:	No
Sub-Franchising Contracts:	No
Expand In Territory:	No
Space Needs:	N/A SF; N/A
SUPPORT & TRAINING PROVIDED:	
Financial Assistance Provided:	No
Site Selection Assistance:	N/A
Lease Negotiation Assistance:	
Co-Operative Advertising:	No
Franchisee Assoc./Member:	Yes/No
Size Of Corporate Staff:	6
On-Going Support:	C,D,G,H,I
Training:	2-3 Days in Houston, TX; 5 Days in Lafayette, LA.

SPECIFIC EXPANSION PLANS:	
US:	All United States
Canada:	No
Overseas:	No

319

Pop-A-Lock is the locksmith of the twenty-first century, providing trained and courteous service, using state-of-the-art equipment, dispatched live from a national dispatch center, 24 hours a day. The business prides itself on three trademarks—timeliness, efficiency and reliability—and is fully insured, endorsed and used by the country's top automotive clubs and insurance companies. Their services include automotive, residential, commercial and safe locksmithing, flat tire assistance, battery jumping and gas delivery.

Pop-A-Lock was founded in Lafayette, Louisiana in 1991. Widely appreciated by its clients, Pop-A-Lock grew to become the largest franchise of its kind. Employee uniform and grooming standards, along with marked, well-maintained vehicles keep the Pop-A-Lock image consistent and professional. The company also maintains an emergency car door unlocking service, which was developed to help emergency medical personnel, police and fire departments enter locked cars. The program provides free locksmithing in any situation when a child is trapped in a vehicle or a life is in danger.

Operating Units	1/1/1999	1/1/2000	1/1/2001
Franchised	105	103	107
% Change	--	-1.9%	3.9%
Company-Owned	0	0	0
% Change	--	N/A	N/A
Total	105	103	107
% Change	--	-1.9%	3.9%
Franchised as % of Total	100.0%	100.0%	100.0%

Investment Required
The fee for a Pop-A-Lock franchise varies, but consists of a fixed base of $5,000 plus an additional $30 for every 1,000 people living in the territory.

Pop-a-Lock provides the following range of investments required to open your initial franchise. The range assumes that all items are paid for in cash. To the extent that you choose to finance any of these expense items, your front-end investment could be substantially reduced.

Item	Established Low Range	Established High Range
Franchise Fee	$6,500	$50,000
Advertising	$2,000	$69,000
Equipment	$9,000	$85,000
Printed Materials	$300	$5,000
Tool Kits	$750	$7,500
Training	$1,750	$17,500
Other Costs and Additional Funds	$5,800	$255,000
Total Investment	$26,100	$489,000

On-Going Expenses

Pop-A-Lock franchisees pay royalties equaling 6% and advertising and marketing fees equaling 1% of gross revenue. Franchisees also pay local advertising fees equaling the greater of $3 per every 100 persons in the territory or $250 and are responsible for telephone directory advertising costs.

What You Get—Training and Support

Pop-A-Lock's proprietary tools and techniques, which are frequently updated as new car makes and models appear, open most doors in less than a minute and are mastered by technicians in the company's national technical training and certification program.

Pop-A-Lock also sponsors an on-going research and development program to find the best technology to serve its customers and franchisees.

Territory

Pop-A-Lock grants exclusive territories.

PostNet Postal & Business Services

181 N. Arroyo Grande Blvd., # 100 A
Henderson, NV 89014-1630
Tel: (800) 841-7171 (702) 792-7100
Fax: (702) 792-7115
E-Mail: spin@postnet.com
Web Site: www.postnet.net
Mr. Brian Spindel, Executive Vice President

Become a POSTNET Pro! POSTNET's franchise opportunity offers a proven method of marketing products and services, which consumers need on a daily basis. The opportunity to get in on the ground floor of a rapidly expanding business is a rarity -- POSTNET's domestic and international franchisees have the opportunity to tap into the world market, offering personal and business services including UPS and FedEx Shipping, B/W and color copy services, private mail boxes, fax, printing and much more.

BACKGROUND: IFA MEMBER
Established: 1992; 1st Franchised: 1993
Franchised Units: 750
Company-Owned Units   1
Total Units: 751
Dist.:   US-400; CAN-0; O'seas-350
  North America: 39 States, 2 Provinces
  Density: 17 in CA, 14 in IL, 11 in FL
Projected New Units (12 Months):   75
Qualifications: 5, 3, 1, 3, 4, 5

Registered: All States

FINANCIAL/TERMS:
Cash Investment: $35-50K
Total Investment: $120-150K
Minimum Net Worth: $200K
Fees: Franchise — $27.9
                       Royalty — 4%; Ad. — 2%
Earnings Claim Statement: No
Term of Contract (Years):   15/15
Avg. # Of Employees: 2 FT, 1 PT
Passive Ownership: Not Allowed
Encourage Conversions: Yes
Area Develop. Agreements: Yes/Varies
Sub-Franchising Contracts: No
Expand In Territory: Yes
Space Needs: 1,200 SF; SC

SUPPORT & TRAINING PROVIDED:
Financial Assistance Provided: Yes(I)
Site Selection Assistance: Yes
Lease Negotiation Assistance: Yes
Co-Operative Advertising: No
Franchisee Assoc./Member: No
Size Of Corporate Staff: 30
On-Going Support: C,D,E,F,G,H,I
Training: 1 Week Henderson, NV; 1 Week at Store
                Opening; 2-3 Days Follow-Up.
SPECIFIC EXPANSION PLANS:
US: All United States
Canada: All Canada
Overseas: All Countries Not Currently Represented

PostNet is the fastest growing, privately held company in the postal and business services industry. With locations the world over, PostNet does its best to unite people the world over with UPS and FedEx services; private mailbox rentals; packaging and office supplies; greeting cards; copy, fax, computer and printing services, document binding and bulk mail.

PostNet seeks detail-oriented "people" people, those who enjoy working with others—both peers and the public—to provide outstanding customer service and to contribute to the PostNet community online, at local and regional functions and at annual franchise conventions.

Operating Units	1999	2000	2001
Franchised	649	671	732
% Change	--	3.4%	9.1%
Company-Owned	0	0	0
% Change	--	N/A	N/A
Total	649	671	732
% Change	--	3.4%	9.1%
Franchised as % of Total	100.0%	100.0%	100.0%

Investment Required
The fee for a PostNet franchise is $27,900.

PostNet provides the following range of investments required to open your initial franchise. The range assumes that all items are paid for in cash. To the extent that you choose to finance any of these expense items, your front-end investment could be substantially reduced.

Item	Established Low Range	Established High Range
Franchise Fee	$27,900	$27,900
Equipment/Supplies	$28,890	$35,080
Fixtures/Turnkey Build Out	$0	$65,900
Insurance	$900	$1,500
Inventory Package (optional)	$0	$5,000
Promotional Activities	$2,500	$4,000
Real Estate	$19,950	$30,967
Training Expenses	$875	$1,550
Additional Funds (for 8 to 12 months)	$30,000	$30,000
Total Investment	$111,015	$201,897

On-Going Expenses

PostNet franchisees pay royalties equaling 4% and a national ad fund contribution equaling 2% of gross sales. Royalties fund regional meetings, national conventions, franchise support systems, franchisee updates, operation manuals, new service and product research and proprietary services development. The national ad fund prepares and produces marketing and advertising materials.

What You Get—Training and Support

The PostNet franchise fee, PostNet claims, is the most inclusive and the most competitive in the postal and business services industry. It includes site selection, layout and design services; training and grand opening support, initial customized printed materials and the use of proprietary marks. The store development assistance provided by PostNet includes construction management, store fixtures, painting, carpeting, signage, start-up inventory and supplies and an equipment package including the Store Management System.

PostNet training takes a three-step approach—classroom management training, on-site opening training and follow-up visits and online learning. Franchisees also continue their PostNet education through a full-time knowledge base, regional meetings and national convention workshop programs.

PostNet's marketing program seeks to identify competition, target opportunities and build commercial accounts to maximize the profit assets of your territory. Franchisees have access to a library of professionally-produced advertising materials and programs and benefit from national advertising fund inventions, such as the CNN commercial "Cookies for Grandma" and the "Sizzlin' Summer Specials" full-page color newspaper inserts.

Other franchisee resources include the franchisee web, store management system, digital copy center and computer services.

Territory

PostNet grants exclusive territories.

Puroclean

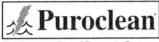

The Paramedics of Property Damage

5350 NW 35th Ave.
Ft. Lauderdale, FL 33309-6314
Tel: (800) 247-9047 (954) 777-2431
Fax: (954) 731-1915
E-Mail: msmith@puroclean.com
Web Site: www.puroclean.com
Mr. C. Monty Smith, VP Sales & Marketing

PUROCLEAN. is a true property disaster mitigation service. We are the "Paramedics of Property Damage," serving the customer when a mishap results in damage caused by water, fire and smoke. Property owners and insurance companies rely on mitigation services as a first step to solving an insurance claim. Insurance restoration is an $80 billion, recession-proof industry. Claims are due to damage caused by everyday occurrences, such as washing machine hose breaks, kitchen fires, chimney fires, etc.

BACKGROUND:

Established: 1985; 1st Franchised: 1991	
Franchised Units:	88
Company-Owned Units	0
Total Units:	88
Dist.:	US-88; CAN-0; O'seas-0
North America	25 States
Density:	14 in CA, 11 in PA, 7 in NJ
Projected New Units (12 Months):	30

Qualifications:	3, 1, 1, 3, 1, 3
Registered:	CA,FL,IL,IN,MI,NY,OR,WA,WI

FINANCIAL/TERMS:

Cash Investment:	$15K
Total Investment:	$76.3-119.2K
Minimum Net Worth:	$NR
Fees:	Franchise — $25K
	Royalty — 10-8%; Ad. — 0%
Earnings Claim Statement:	No
Term of Contract (Years):	20/10
Avg. # Of Employees:	2 FT, 2 PT
Passive Ownership:	Discouraged
Encourage Conversions:	No
Area Develop. Agreements:	No
Sub-Franchising Contracts:	No
Expand In Territory:	Yes
Space Needs:	Varies SF; FS, SF, HB

SUPPORT & TRAINING PROVIDED:

Financial Assistance Provided:	Yes(I)
Site Selection Assistance:	No
Lease Negotiation Assistance:	No
Co-Operative Advertising:	No
Franchisee Assoc./Member:	Yes/Yes
Size Of Corporate Staff:	16
On-Going Support:	C,G,H,I
Training: 10 Days Ft. Lauderdale, FL; 5 Days Franchise Location.	

SPECIFIC EXPANSION PLANS:

US:	Southeast, Midwest, West
Canada:	No
Overseas:	No

The first step in the settlement of disaster claims, Puroclean franchisees are mitigation and restoration specialists, serving both property owners and insurance companies in the event of a water, smoke or fire-related disaster. Everyday accidents like kitchen fires ensure the consistent need for Puroclean's clean-up services, and the system's nature—recession-proof with unlimited growth potential in a high volume niche—and experience—30 years of tested success and recognition in the insurance industry—along with its low cash investment requirement, make it an ideal prospect for those interested in owning a service-based franchise.

Operating Units	12/31/2000	12/31/2001	12/31/2002
Franchised	85	73	79
% Change	--	-14.1%	8.2%
Company-Owned	0	0	0
% Change	--	N/A	N/A
Total	85	73	79
% Change	--	-14.1%	8.2%
Franchised as % of Total	100.0%	100.0%	100.0%

Investment Required

The fee for a Puroclean franchise ranges from $15,000 to $30,000 depending on the type of system purchased and the territory's population. Financing is available.

Puroclean provides the following range of investments required to open your initial franchise. The range assumes that all items are paid for in cash. To the extent that you choose to finance any of these expense items, your front-end investment could be substantially reduced.

Item	Established Low Range	Established High Range
Franchise Fee	$15,000	$30,000
Advertising/Marketing	$100	$250
Equipment and Supplies Package	$30,000	$30,000
Insurance	$1,100	$1,100
Office Supplies	$250	$400
Real Estate	$350	$2,000
Van	$0	$25,000
Other Costs and Additional Funds	$20,250	$35,750
Total Investment	$67,050	$124,500

On-Going Expenses

Puroclean franchisees pay royalties equaling 8 to 10% of gross revenue.

What You Get—Training and Support

Franchisees are trained at the Puroclean national support and training center located at the company's headquarters in Fort Lauderdale, Florida. The programs, which take place in the classroom and in hands-on training simulators, are run by certified restorers and trainers from the Institute of Inspection and Restoration and cover topics like water mitigation, smoke and odor removal and marketing techniques. For later reference, franchise operations and marketing manuals document everything learned in the classroom and the field.

Additional regional marketing support, such as professional marketing materials catered to the insurance world, builds business and enables franchisees to participate in insurance vendor programs. Puroclean franchisees use state-of-the-art equipment and products; the company's customized software tracks customers, schedules jobs, provides estimates and manages employees and bookkeeping.

Other on-going franchisee support includes toll-free, 24-hour access to certified restorers, a franchise advisory council, field consultation and monthly technical bulletins outlining technology developments and industry trends.

Territory

Puroclean grants protected territories.

Ramada Franchise Systems

RAMADA®

A very good place to be.℠

One Sylvan Way
Parsippany, NJ 07054
800#: (800) 758-8999
Tel: (973) 428-9700
Fax: (800) 643-2107
E-Mail: tom.bernardo@cendant.com

Web Site: www.ramada.com	Total Investment: $380K-6.2MM
Contact: Mr. Thomas P. Bernardo, EVP Franchise Sales	Minimum Net Worth: $N/A
	Fees: Franchise — $35K, $350/rm
	Royalty — 4.%; Ad. — 4.5%
RAMADA is proud to be one of the fastest-growing hotel chains in the world, with nearly 1,000 properties in the US and Canada. The mid- to upper-mid market chain has classified its hotels into 3 distinct tiers for the discerning business traveler and vacationer - Limiteds, Inns and Plaza Hotels. The RAMADA brand was created in Flagstaff, AZ in 1954. In 1990, the brand was acquired by Cendant Corp, formerly HFS Inc. RAMADA FRANCHISE SYSTEMS is a subsidiary of Cendant Corp. (NYSE: CD).	Earnings Claim Statement: Yes
	Term of Contract (Years): 15 or 20
	Avg. # Of Employees: 2-4 FT, 4-10 PT
	Passive Ownership: Discouraged
	Encourage Conversions: Yes
	Area Develop. Agreements: No
	Sub-Franchising Contracts: No
	Expand In Territory: No
	Space Needs: Varies SF; FS
	SUPPORT & TRAINING PROVIDED:
	Financial Assistance Provided: Yes(D)
BACKGROUND: IFA MEMBER	Site Selection Assistance: No
Established: 1954; 1st Franchised: 1954	Lease Negotiation Assistance: No
Franchised Units: 945	Co-Operative Advertising: Yes
Company-Owned Units 0	Franchisee Assoc./Member: Yes/Yes
Total Units: 945	Size Of Corporate Staff: 600
Dist.: US-875; CAN-70; O'seas-0	On-Going Support: b,C,D,E,G,H,I
North America: 39 States	Training: 5-10 Days, New Jersey; 3-6 Days On
Density: CA,BC,TX	Site; 1 Day Various Locations
Projected New Units (12 Months): N/A	**SPECIFIC EXPANSION PLANS:**
Qualifications: , , , ,	US: All United States
Registered: All States	Canada: All Canada
	Overseas: No
FINANCIAL/TERMS:	
Cash Investment: $N/A	

Ramada Inns brings comfort and economy together, a traveler's dream. Catering to mid-market travelers and seeking to meet both every guest and every franchisee's need, Ramada offers three brands of hotel franchises. The Ramada Limited features a hospitality area in addition to its guest rooms and serves a complimentary signature breakfast to its visitors. The Ramada Inn features an on-site restaurant and lounge, plus facilities like meeting rooms and swimming pools and services like voicemail. The Ramada Plaza Hotel is a mid- or high-rise inn that houses a full-service restaurant, a lounge, banquet facilities and other business and leisure capacities.

The first Ramada opened in Flagstaff, Arizona in 1954. Since 1990, Ramada has been part of Cendant Corporation, the largest of hotel franchisors and an international source of travel, real estate, vehicle and financial services.

Operating Units	2000	2001	2002
Franchised	988	978	899
% Change	--	-1.0%	-8.1%
Company-Owned	0	0	0
% Change	--	N/A	N/A
Total	988	978	899
% Change	--	-1.0%	-8.1%
Franchised as % of Total	100.0%	100.0%	100.0%

Investment Required

The fee for a Ramada Inns franchise is the greater of $35,000 or $350 per each guest room located in the franchised unit.

Ramada provides the following range of investments required to open your initial franchise. The range assumes that all items are paid for in cash. To the extent that you choose to finance any of these expense items, your front-end investment could be substantially reduced. The following figures apply to the opening of a 100-room, newly constructed facility.

Item	Established Low Range	Established High Range
Application Fee/Initial Fee	$18,500	$36,000
Advertising	$15,000	$30,000
Construction	$2,132,500	$4,287,500
Equipment/Fixtures/Signs	$548,000	$1,582,000
Insurance	$10,500	$18,100
Inventory/Supplies	$27,000	$35,000
Training Expenses	$2,500	$6,600
Other Costs and Additional Funds (for 3 months)	$158,500	$183,500
Total Investment (does not include land acquisition)	$2,912,500	$6,178,700

On-Going Expenses

Ramada franchisees pay royalties equaling 4% and service assessment fees equaling 4.5% of gross room revenue. Soon, franchisees will also be responsible for a special assessment fee equaling 5% of revenue acquired from guests who belong to Ramada's loyalty program.

What You Get—Training and Support

As a Cendant franchise, Ramada offers its franchisees cross-marketing opportunities through other travel-related businesses, national advertising campaigns, on-line room reservation capabilities, on-call experts and thorough hotel management training.

Ramada wants to be sure that no franchisee is alone throughout the development and management process. Support begins with on-site experts whose mission is to walk you through renovation, construction, landscape design, market analysis, signage design and installation, supplier selection, insurance procurement, sales and reservations systems installation, advertising and press release composition. "Personal Best Hospitality" training, covering both administration and housekeeping, takes place on-site at each hotel to recruit and train employees.

For on-going support, each franchisee's primary contact for answers, advice, even supplies, is the franchise support manager. In addition, franchisees receive monthly management reports from corporate headquarters to help assess and build their businesses. Franchisees also have access to the company intranet site, from which they can order training manuals and hotel supplies, at reduced prices, at any time of day. For additional fees, Ramada sharpens and expands franchisee skills and knowledge through the orientation program and professional seminars offered at Cendant's state-of-the-art Hospitality Training Center in Parsippany, New Jersey. The company also hosts regional workshops throughout the United States and Canada. Exceptional franchisees are honored with the Gold Key award in recognition of great guest service.

Ramada marketing is of national, regional and local scope. Services include a reservations system that is supported by 1-800 call centers 24 hours a day;

ramada.com, where visitors can locate Ramada units and book rooms; an international sales team that promotes Ramada's interests in the group traveling industry and the TripRewards guest rewards program, which encourages frequent travelers to return to Cendant hotels.

Awareness of and publicity for the Ramada brand is built through national ad campaigns; the Ramada Management Association, a regional franchisee board that pools franchisee funds and combines them with matched amounts from Ramada to support regional marketing, co-op promotions; discounted rates on local ads and on-site meetings with regional managers who help personalize and develop each individual Ramada's operating and marketing strategy.

Territory
Ramada grants protected territories or uses the "impact policy" to determine whether a new franchise might negatively impact an existing Ramada unit.

Red Roof Inns

14651 Dallas Pkwy., # 500
Dallas, TX 75254
Tel: (972) 702-6951
Fax: (972) 702-3610
E-Mail: dsavas@accor-na.com
Web Site: www.redroof.com
Mr. Dean Savas, SVP of Franchising

With 3,700 hotels worldwide, Accor is the industry leader. Of Accor's 1,200+ N. American properties, today 230 are franchised. An integral part of our strategy will include franchise relationships with a diverse mix of entrepreneurs that share the Accor spirit of quality, fairness and respect. We received the AAFD Fair Franchising Seal of Approval. RED ROOF INNS, a well-established brand, has a quality product, proven operational results and is easy to operate. Many open markets are available.

BACKGROUND:	IFA MEMBER
Established: 1972; 1st Franchised: 1996	
Franchised Units:	101
Company-Owned Units:	259
Total Units:	360
Dist.:	US-360; CAN-0; O'seas-0
North America:	39 States
Density:	37 in OH, 25 in TX, 22 in GA
Projected New Units (12 Months):	17
Qualifications:	4, 4, 1, 1, 1, 3
Registered:	All States
FINANCIAL/TERMS:	
Cash Investment:	$100-500K
Total Investment:	$2.6-3.4MM
Minimum Net Worth:	$1.5MM
Fees:	Franchise — $30K
	Royalty — 4.5-5%; Ad. — 4%
Earnings Claim Statement:	Yes

331

Term of Contract (Years):	20/10	Site Selection Assistance:	N/A
Avg. # Of Employees:	2-4 FT, 4-10 PT	Lease Negotiation Assistance:	No
Passive Ownership:	Allowed	Co-Operative Advertising:	Yes
Encourage Conversions:	Yes	Franchisee Assoc./Member:	Yes/Yes
Area Develop. Agreements:	No	Size Of Corporate Staff:	537
Sub-Franchising Contracts:	No	On-Going Support:	A,B,C,D,E,G,h,I
Expand In Territory:	No	Training:	2.5 Weeks Columbus, OH.
Space Needs:	15,000+ SF; FS		

SPECIFIC EXPANSION PLANS:

		US:	All United States
SUPPORT & TRAINING PROVIDED:		Canada:	All Canada
Financial Assistance Provided:	Yes(I)	Overseas:	No

James R. Trueman incorporated Red Roof Inns, a company built on value, consistency and excellence, in 1972 and opened his first location in Columbus, Ohio a year later. A single room went for $8.50. The company franchised in 1996 and now serves millions of patrons every year.

In 1990, Accor Lodging North America added Red Roof Inns to its economy lodging division. Accor Economy Lodging is the largest owner and operator of economy lodgings in the United States. Its inns, including Motel 6 and Studio 6, represent nearly 1,200 properties housing 128,000 rooms, and command a 10% share of the entire U.S. economy lodging market. Accor is also a worldwide hotel management company, with 145,000 associates offering travel, tourism and corporate services in 140 countries. Despite Red Roof Inn's association with other economy lodgings, in order to maintain independent integrity and optimize growth potential, each Accor Economy Lodging brand is managed by its own distinct operating group.

Operating Units	12/31/1999	12/31/2000	12/31/2001
Franchised	73	87	100
% Change	--	19.2%	14.9%
Company-Owned	258	263	261
% Change	--	1.9%	-0.8%
Total	331	350	361
% Change	--	5.7%	3.1%
Franchised as % of Total	22.0%	24.8%	27.7%

Investment Required

The fee for a Red Roof Inns franchise is $30,000.

Red Roof Inns provides the following range of investments required to open your initial franchise. The range assumes that all items are paid for in cash. To the extent that you choose to finance any of these expense items, your front-end investment could be substantially reduced.

Item	Established Low Range	Established High Range
Franchise Fee	$30,000	$30,000
Construction	$2,075,750	$2,311,850
Equipment/Fixtures/Signs	$375,740	$425,000
Insurance	$13,800	$17,250
Inventory/Opening/Supplies	$32,500	$40,700
Training Expenses	$7,800	$11,300
Other Costs and Additional Funds	$95,000	$132,000
Total Investment (does not include land acquisition)	$2,630,590	$2,968,100

On-Going Expenses

Red Roof Inns franchisees pay first year royalties equaling 4.5% (later 5%), marketing and reservation contributions equaling 4% and cooperative contributions equaling no more than 1% of gross room revenue. Franchisees also pay variable booking fees and commissions and 3% of the gross room revenue of members of the Redicard preferred member program.

What You Get—Training and Support

The most powerful aspect of the Red Roof Inns franchise system is its brand power, built upon 30 years of consistent service. Contributing to that strength is initial and on-going training, written and video materials, refresher courses, newsletters and reports, marketing support and advertising focused on high guest approval ratings, the Redicard preferred member program, directory distribution (over three million distributed per year) and the Red Roof Inns website and reservations line (which accounts for the booking of more than 28% of Red Roof's room nights).

Furthermore, as part of the Accor family, Red Roof Inn franchisees can take advantage of the purchasing power of 1,200 lodging properties and the Accor Economy Lodging Quality Team, which protects the image and reputation of the entire Accor and Red Roof Inn system by ensuring that each individual lodging unit maintains appropriate system standards.

Territory
Red Roof Inns grants protected territories.

Schooley Mitchell Telecom Consultants

187 Ontario St.
Stratford, ON N5A 3H3 CANADA
Tel: (800) 465-4145 (519) 275-3339
Fax: (519) 273-7979
E-Mail: james.young@schooleymitchell.com
Web Site: www.schooleymitchell.com
Mr. James Young, VP Franchise Development

SCHOOLEY MITCHELL is the nation's largest independent consulting franchise. We offer a strong value proposition for both small- and medium-sized businesses centering on cost reduction in telecommunication. Commitment to independence and objectivity. Roughly 80% of our initial consultative agreements are cost reduction, contingency billing-based engagements which include a two-year commitment and on-going reviews. No telecom experience needed. Sales/management/consulting experience preferred.

BACKGROUND: IFA MEMBER
Established: 1996; 1st Franchised: 1997
Franchised Units: 160
Company-Owned Units: 0

Total Units:	160
Dist.:	US-110; CAN-50; O'seas-0
North America:	35 States, 7 Provinces
Density:	30 in ON, 13 in CA, 7 in FL
Projected New Units (12 Months):	120
Qualifications:	3, 5, 3, 4, 4, 4
Registered:	All States and AB

FINANCIAL/TERMS:

Cash Investment:	$NR
Total Investment:	$75-100K
Minimum Net Worth:	$125K
Fees:	Franchise — $37.5K
	Royalty — 8%; Ad. — 2%
Earnings Claim Statement:	No
Term of Contract (Years):	10/5
Avg. # Of Employees:	4 FT, 2 PT
Passive Ownership:	Discouraged
Encourage Conversions:	NA
Area Develop. Agreements:	No
Sub-Franchising Contracts:	No
Expand In Territory:	Yes
Space Needs:	NA SF; NA

SUPPORT & TRAINING PROVIDED:

Financial Assistance Provided:	No
Site Selection Assistance:	NA
Lease Negotiation Assistance:	NA
Co-Operative Advertising:	No

Franchisee Assoc./Member:	Yes/No	US:	All United States
Size Of Corporate Staff:	40	Canada:	All Canada
On-Going Support:	A,D,G,h,I	Overseas:	No

Training: 2 Weeks Stratford, ON; 1 Week On-Site
- Business Membership.

SPECIFIC EXPANSION PLANS:

Schooley Mitchell is a network of consultants who help business professionals and corporations navigate their way through the ever-quickly-changing world of telecommunications. *USA Today* listed telecommunications expenses as one of the top five largest items in business budgets. However, most of these businesses are spending much more on this item than necessary. Many are unaware of the existence of consultants like Schooley Mitchell, consultants whose cost is easily justified by the savings they deliver to their clients' telecommunications accounts.

Since people want to save money in boom times and bust times, the telecommunications industry is expected to grow 12% annually. To meet this need, Schooley Mitchell began franchising in 1997 and is currently the largest independent telecommunications consulting company in North America. It is a franchise that is well-suited to business-oriented, networking people. Schooley Mitchell's product relies upon business skills and practices, which many franchisees develop throughout their other career manifestations, to build strong relationships with other business professionals. There is little overhead and capital expenditure and franchisees often work out of their homes. Clients range from local businesses to large corporations with multiple locations, allowing independent franchisees to team up to serve the same company from their respective locations.

Operating Units	2000	2001	2002
Franchised	0*	17	77
% Change	--	N/A	352.9%
Company-Owned	0	0	0
% Change	--	0.0%	0.0%
Total	0	17	77
% Change	--	N/A	352.9%
Franchised as % of Total	N/A	100.0%	100.0%

* Schooley Mitchell did not offer U.S. franchises until 2001.

Investment Required

The fee for a Schooley Mitchell franchise is $37, 500.

Schooley Mitchell provides the following range of investments required to open your initial franchise. The range assumes that all items are paid for in cash. To the extent that you choose to finance any of these expense items, your front-end investment could be substantially reduced.

Item	Established Low Range	Established High Range
Franchise Fee	$30,000	$30,000
Business Development Fee	$7,500	$7,500
Equipment/Fixtures/ Supplies	$600	$6,600
Insurance/Inventory/ Licenses/Professional Fees/ Security Deposits/Utilities	$0	$3,000
Real Estate	$0	$750
Training Expenses	$1,000	$3,000
Additional Funds (for 3 months)	$1,000	$2,000
Total Investment	$40,100	$52,850

On-Going Expenses

Schooley Mitchell franchisees pay royalties equaling 8% and advertising fund fees equaling 2% of gross revenue. The company also charges a monthly fee of $100 for software licensing.

What You Get—Training and Support

Training with Schooley Mitchell last three weeks and takes the form of live client cases and sales, marketing, telecommunications, computer and technical training. One week of the training program is devoted to business development mentoring and takes place at each franchisee's personal office with the aim of versing franchisees in the sales process and helping franchisees acquire and retain clients, which has been reported as the biggest challenge in the development of a Schooley Mitchell franchise. Following the opening of your franchise, the head office (via a toll-free phone number) will continue to provide support and training as needed and the field consulting staff will provide marketing and sales assistance. The company also maintains a company intranet site and holds a franchisee training conference annually.

Schooley Mitchell does its best to provide its consultants with as many connections and as much information as possible. To that end, many telecommunications providers have formed liaisons with Schooley Mitchell, granting its consultants access to support and information from the providers themselves, those who are responsible for the telecommunications services clients receive.

Other perks that come with the franchise fee include computer software, the latest research and industry developments (a minimum of one update per week); publicity and public relations campaigns in the form of newspaper articles, magazine coverage, newsletters and a national charity campaign; frequently updated operations manuals; a vast franchisee network and a franchisee advisory council.

Territory
Schooley Mitchell does not grant exclusive territories.

ServiceMaster Clean

860 Ridge Lake Blvd.
Memphis, TN 38120-9421
Tel: (800) 230-2360 (901) 684-7500
Fax: (901) 684-7580
E-Mail: dmessenger@smclean.com
Web Site: www.ownafranchise.com
Mr. David Messenger, Vice President

SERVICEMASTER CLEAN provides heavy-duty cleaning services to both residential and commercial customers. Services include carpet, upholstery, window, drapery, disaster restoration and janitorial cleaning that is recognized around the world. With over 50 years experience, SERVICEMASTER CLEAN offers state-of-the-art equipment, research and development, continuous training, cross-selling promotions with our partner companies and a strong franchise relations base.

BACKGROUND:	IFA MEMBER
Established: 1947; 1st Franchised: 1952	
Franchised Units:	4,488
Company-Owned Units	0
Total Units:	4,488
Dist.:	US-2,951; CAN-176; O'seas-1,398
North America:	50 States, 9 Provinces

Density:	203 in IL, 157 in CA, 134 OH	Space Needs:	N/A SF; N/A
Projected New Units (12 Months):	130		
Qualifications:	5, 3, 2, 2, 3, 5	**SUPPORT & TRAINING PROVIDED:**	
Registered:	All States and AB	Financial Assistance Provided:	Yes(D)
		Site Selection Assistance:	No
FINANCIAL/TERMS:		Lease Negotiation Assistance:	No
Cash Investment:	$5.1-9.7K	Co-Operative Advertising:	Yes
Total Investment:	$18.5-90.5K	Franchisee Assoc./Member:	Yes/Yes
Minimum Net Worth:	$100K	Size Of Corporate Staff:	200
Fees: Franchise —	$16.9-31.5K	On-Going Support:	A,B,C,D,F,G,H,I
Royalty — 4-10%;	Ad. — 0.5-1%		
Earnings Claim Statement:	No	Training: 2 Weeks Memphis, TN; 1 Week on Loca-	
Term of Contract (Years):	5/5		tion.
Avg. # Of Employees:	3 FT, 2 PT		
Passive Ownership:	Discouraged	**SPECIFIC EXPANSION PLANS:**	
Encourage Conversions:	Yes	US:	All United States
Area Develop. Agreements:	No	Canada:	All Canada
Sub-Franchising Contracts:	Yes	Overseas:	All Countries
Expand In Territory:	Yes		

ServiceMaster Clean is a commercial cleaning service that covers six separate markets—residential services, commercial services, small business services, disaster restoration services, janitorial services, and small market services.

ServiceMaster Clean is part of the ServiceMaster corporation, which was founded in 1952 and now has more than 5,000 franchise partners on 4 continents. As a ServiceMaster Clean franchisee, you reap the rewards of the ServiceMaster family, with the resources of each franchise used to develop and enhance the training and marketing of all.

Operating Units	12/31/2000	12/31/2001	12/31/2002
Franchised	2732	2637	2645
% Change	--	-3.5%	0.3%
Company-Owned	0	0	0
% Change	--	0.0%	0.0%
Total	2732	2637	2645
% Change	--	-3.5%	0.3%
Franchised as % of Total	100.0%	100.0%	100.0%

Investment Required

ServiceMaster Clean offers six different franchise licenses. A residential services license costs $16,900; commercial services, $18,900; small business services, $18,500; disaster restoration services, $31,500; janitorial services, $28,500 and small market services, $25,000. Financial assistance is offered.

ServiceMaster Clean provides the following range of investments required to open your initial franchise. The range assumes that all items are paid for in cash. To the extent that you choose to finance any of these expense items, your front-end investment could be substantially reduced. The following figures apply to the opening of a residential cleaning services franchise.

Item	Established Low Range	Established High Range
Franchise Fee	$3,380	$16,900
Advertising (for 3 months)	$600	$6,400
Computer Equipment/Internet Connection	$2,560	$3,650
Opening Package	$3,947	$19,735
Vehicle Costs	$4,000	$5,000
Other Costs and Additional Funds (for 3 months)	$12,850	$21,700
Total Investment (does not include real estate)	$27,337	$73,385

On-Going Expenses

ServiceMaster Clean franchisees must pay royalty fees equaling 10%, or $250 per month, national advertising fund royalties equaling 1%, or $20.

What You Get—Training and Support

The franchise fee includes an extensive two-week training program that includes both classroom and hands-on instruction, a franchise orientation guide, start-up materials, a notebook computer and software.

ServiceMaster Clean's association with the other ServiceMaster brands, such as Terminix, TruGreen Chemlawn, Merry Maids, Furniture Medic and AmeriSpec, also allows for cross-selling and joint marketing ventures.

Territory

ServiceMaster Clean does not grant exclusive territories.

Sign-A-Rama

 SIGN★A★RAMA®

1801 Australian Ave., S.
West Palm Beach, FL 33409-6465
Tel: (800) 776-8105 (561) 640-5570
Fax: (561) 640-5580
E-Mail: csimnick@signarama.com
Web Site: www.signarama.com
Mr. Christopher Simnick, Franchise Director

World's largest full-service sign franchise. Over 550 locations in 20 countries. Ranked #1 in industry. No experience needed. Full training, local back-up and support. Financing available.

BACKGROUND: IFA MEMBER
Established: 1986; 1st Franchised: 1987
Franchised Units: 625
Company-Owned Units: 0
Total Units: 625
Dist.: US-612; CAN-0; O'seas-485
 North America: 44 States
 Density: 54 in CA, 41 in FL, 25 in NJ
Projected New Units (12 Months): 100
Qualifications: 5, 4, 1, 1, 4, 5
Registered: All States and AB

FINANCIAL/TERMS:

Cash Investment:	$40-50K
Total Investment:	$112-117K
Minimum Net Worth:	$60K
Fees:	Franchise — $37.5K
	Royalty — 6%; Ad. — 0%
Earnings Claim Statement:	No
Term of Contract (Years):	35/35
Avg. # Of Employees:	3 FT
Passive Ownership:	Discouraged
Encourage Conversions:	Yes
Area Develop. Agreements:	No Domestic
Sub-Franchising Contracts:	Yes
Expand In Territory:	Yes
Space Needs:	1,200 SF; SC

SUPPORT & TRAINING PROVIDED:

Financial Assistance Provided:	Yes(I)
Site Selection Assistance:	Yes
Lease Negotiation Assistance:	Yes
Co-Operative Advertising:	Yes
Franchisee Assoc./Member:	Yes/Yes
Size Of Corporate Staff:	85
On-Going Support:	A,B,C,D,E,F,G,H,I
Training:	2 Weeks West Palm Beach, FL; 2 Weeks On-Site; 1 Week Mentor.

SPECIFIC EXPANSION PLANS:

US:	All United States
Canada:	All Canada
Overseas:	All Countries

When they began to franchise in 1987, Sign-A-Rama introduced automated graphic design to an industry traditionally dominated by individual craftspeople. The introduction paid off. Now, Sign-A-Rama has more than 600 stores worldwide and is the largest full-service sign company in the world.

Seventy percent of the sign business is repeat business. Sign-A-Rama's full-service sign centers service the eight billion dollar market by providing a product for any and every kind of business. No technical experience is necessary and inventory needs are low. With twenty regional offices, help is never far away. Furthermore, Sign-A-Rama's corporate office does it all—site selection, marketing and training—for budding Sign-A-Rama franchisees.

The first Sign-A-Rama was located in Farmingdale, New York and was opened in 1986 by father and son Roy and Ray Titus. A second store in Palm Beach County, Florida proved that automated graphic design could effectively service business sign needs, and Sign-A-Rama offered its first franchise in 1987.

Operating Units	12/31/1999	12/31/2000	12/31/2001
Franchised	483	521	570
% Change	--	7.9%	9.4%
Company-Owned	0	0	0
% Change	--	N/A	N/A
Total	483	521	570
% Change	--	7.9%	9.4%
Franchised as % of Total	100.0%	100.0%	100.0%

Investment Required

The fee for a Sign-A-Rama franchise is $37,500. All additional units are $19,500. Financial assistance is available.

Sign-A-Rama provides the following range of investments required to open your initial franchise. The range assumes that all items are paid for in cash. To the extent that you choose to finance any of these expense items, your front-end investment could be substantially reduced.

Item	Established Low Range	Established High Range
Franchise Fee	$17,500	$37,500
Equipment Package	$78,983	$78,983

Equipment Package Security Deposit (if leased)	$3,705	$7,898
Insurance	$750	$2,000
Real Estate Expenses	$0	$3,000
Training Expenses	$210	$490
Yellow Page Advertisement (for 6 months)	$300	$1,200
Additional Funds (for 6 months)	$2,500	$55,000
Total Investment (leasing equipment, does not include real estate)	$47,465	$107,088
Total Investment (purchasing equipment, does not include real estate)	$151,413	$293,159

On-Going Expenses
Sign-A-Rama franchisees pay royalties equaling 6% of gross revenue.

What You Get—Training and Support
With the purchase of a Sign-A-Rama franchise, comes all of the following at no extra cost: research and development; annual world expos; leasing assistance; local regional seminars; direct mail, mentoring, royalty incentive and store evaluation programs; local support; software updates; certified training; point-of-sale systems; the Sign-A-Rama website; the quarterly newsletter; the franchise advisory council; a toll-free support number; a private bulletin board service; training manuals; mass purchasing power; industry association memberships; in-store assistance; lease negotiations; corporate advertising; online vendor access and trade show support.

The Sign-A-Rama franchise fee includes a two-week introductory program, including airfare, lodging, lunch and daily transportation, in West Palm Beach, Florida. The program covers both the technical—sign production and computer graphics—and the business—bookkeeping, sales and marketing techniques and management—aspects of running a Sign-A-Rama franchise. A third week of training takes place with a mentor at the franchisee's own store. A local field representative follows to help set up each Sign-A-Rama franchise.

Territory
Sign-A-Rama does not grant exclusive territories.

The Sports Section

2150 Boggs Rd., # 200
Duluth, GA 30096
Tel: (800) 321-9127 (678) 740-0800
Fax: (678) 740-0808
E-Mail: jan@sports-section.com
Web Site: www.sports-section.com
Mr. Jan Rhodes, Dir. Franchise Development

'The Best in Youth & Sports Memories.' THE SPORTS SECTION franchisees earn income from 3 profit centers: youth and sports photo keepsakes, uniforms and trophies/awards. Complete training is provided. No experience in photography required. Exclusive, protected territories. No royalties. Operate from home or office, full or part-time. Finance plan available.

BACKGROUND:

Established: 1983; 1st Franchised: 1984	
Franchised Units:	165
Company-Owned Units	0
Total Units:	165
Dist.:	US-165; CAN-0; O'seas-0
North America:	43 States
Density:	12 in GA, 10 in FL, 9 in CA
Projected New Units (12 Months):	30
Qualifications:	5, 4, 1, 3, 3, 4

Registered:	All States

FINANCIAL/TERMS:

Cash Investment:	$10.9-30.9K
Total Investment:	$15-45K
Minimum Net Worth:	$N/A
Fees:	Franchise — $10.9-30.9K
	Royalty — 0%; Ad. — 0%
Earnings Claim Statement:	Yes
Term of Contract (Years):	10/10
Avg. # Of Employees:	2 FT, 2 PT
Passive Ownership:	Discouraged
Encourage Conversions:	Yes
Area Develop. Agreements:	Yes (Int'l.)
Sub-Franchising Contracts:	Yes
Expand In Territory:	Yes
Space Needs:	N/A SF; HB, OB

SUPPORT & TRAINING PROVIDED:

Financial Assistance Provided:	No
Site Selection Assistance:	N/A
Lease Negotiation Assistance:	N/A
Co-Operative Advertising:	N/A
Franchisee Assoc./Member:	Yes/Yes
Size Of Corporate Staff:	35
On-Going Support:	A,b,C,D,G,H,h,I
Training:	5 Days in Franchisee's Territory; On-Going Training.

SPECIFIC EXPANSION PLANS:

US:	All United States
Canada:	All Canada
Overseas:	Master Franchises Only

As photographers of youth sports and peddlers of photo keepsakes, trophies and awards, Sports Section franchisees sell memories. Moreover, The Sports Section system is determined to do whatever it takes to make their franchisees and those memories the best they can be. No photography experience is necessary.

The Sports Section has been photographing leagues and organizations throughout North America since 1983.

Operating Units	5/31/1999	5/31/2000	5/31/2001
Franchised	126	125	130
% Change	--	-0.8%	4.0%
Company-Owned	0	0	0
% Change	--	N/A	N/A
Total	126	125	130
% Change	--	-0.8%	4.0%
Franchised as % of Total	100.0%	100.0%	100.0%

Investment Required
The Sports Section offers franchisees four fee options, which differ depending on territory size. The fee for a population of up to 100,000 people is $10,900; for a population of up to 200,000, $15,900; for a population of up to 350,000, $23,900; and for a population of up to 500,000 people, $30,900.

The Sports Section provides the following range of investments required to open your initial franchise. The range assumes that all items are paid for in cash. To the extent that you choose to finance any of these expense items, your front-end investment could be substantially reduced.

Item	Established Low Range	Established High Range
Franchise Fee	$10,900	$30,900
Advertising	$0	$4,700
Equipment/Furniture/Supplies	$3,700	$8,465

Film Processing and Developing Fees	$500	$1,250
Real Estate	$50	$100
Training Expenses	$1,000	$1,100
Other Costs and Additional Funds	$1,550	$9,200
Total Investment	$17,700	$55,715

On-Going Expenses

On-going expenses vary, but additional fees include those for film processing and developing, e-commerce sales and fulfillment and express print charges. Additional training is available for $300 per person.

What You Get—Training and Support

The Sports Section believes that franchisees succeed through dedication and willingness to learn. To that end, The Sports Section provides comprehensive training in both sales and photography for the beginning and the advanced franchisee. Each franchisee is visited by an expert trainer for three days of sales training. All training takes place in the franchisee's territory, where they will establish, build and operate their business. Together, the trainer and the franchisee will identify sales opportunities, make sales calls, set up office, survey competitors and draft a development plan. Photography training is conducted by professional photographers as well as fellow franchisees and ensures that all franchisees are well-versed in the use of lenses, film, lighting shading, poses, equipment, shoot day procedures and troubleshooting.

The Sports Section's collection of marketing materials is just as extensive as its training program. Materials are specifically designed to overcome client objections and answer typical sales and picture day situations to ease franchisees' burdens, allowing them to focus on the big picture. Products and services include: presentation and proposal folders, order envelopes, sales brochures, product catalogs, a custom website, flyers, posters, display materials, sample products and special promotions.

In addition, The Sports Section provides franchisees with a product line encompassing more than 250 products and partnerships with national organizations that exist in nearly every existing and proposed Sports Section territory. These organizations include Girl Scouts of America, the YMCA, the Police Athletic League and the National Recreation and Park Association.

Territory
The Sports Section grants exclusive territories.

Studio 6

14651 Dallas Pkwy., # 500
Dallas, TX 75254
Tel: (972) 702-6951
Fax: (972) 702-3610
E-Mail: dsavas@accor-na.com
Web Site: www.motel6.com
Mr. Dean Savas, SVP of Franchising

With 3,700 hotels worldwide, Accor is the industry leader. Of Accor's 1,200+ N. American properties, today 230 are franchised. An integral part of our strategy will include franchise relationships with a diverse mix of entrepreneurs that share the Accor spirit of quality, fairness and respect. We received the AAFD Fair Franchising Seal of Approval. STUDIO 6 has a quality product, proven operational results and is easy to operate. Many open markets are available. STUDIO 6 is a well-established brand.

BACKGROUND:	IFA MEMBER
Established: 1962; 1st Franchised: 1999	
Franchised Units:	2
Company-Owned Units	35
Total Units:	37
Dist.:	US-33; CAN-4; O'seas-0
North America:	11 States
Density:	17 in TX, 4 in GA

Projected New Units (12 Months):	2
Qualifications:	4, 4, 1, 1, 1, 3
Registered:	All States

FINANCIAL/TERMS:	
Cash Investment:	$100-500K
Total Investment:	$2.7-3.4MM
Minimum Net Worth:	$1.5MM
Fees:	Franchise — $25K
	Royalty — 5%; Ad. — 2%
Earnings Claim Statement:	No
Term of Contract (Years):	10-15/10
Avg. # Of Employees:	2-4 FT, 4-10 PT
Passive Ownership:	Allowed
Encourage Conversions:	Yes
Area Develop. Agreements:	No
Sub-Franchising Contracts:	No
Expand In Territory:	No
Space Needs:	15,000 SF; FS

SUPPORT & TRAINING PROVIDED:	
Financial Assistance Provided:	Yes(I)
Site Selection Assistance:	N/A
Lease Negotiation Assistance:	No
Co-Operative Advertising:	No
Franchisee Assoc./Member:	No/No
Size Of Corporate Staff:	537
On-Going Support:	A,B,C,D,E,G,h,I
Training:	2 Weeks in Dallas, TX for Owners and Managers.

SPECIFIC EXPANSION PLANS:	
US:	All United States
Canada:	All Canada
Overseas:	No

Since 1986, Motel 6 has devoted more than $200 million to make itself a household name. Launching itself from the high awareness level and name recognition of its sister brand, Studio 6, offering extended-stay lodging, taps into the power and success of Motel 6's $200 million investment. Hence, while a relatively young concept, Studio 6's corporate affiliation, name and image ensures instant consumer recognition, trust and traffic.

Studio 6 first appeared in the summer of 1999. In October of the following year, the concept went international in Mississauga, Canada. The first franchised unit opened in Port Arthur, Texas in 2001.

Studio 6 is part of Accor Economy Lodging, the largest owner and operator of economy lodgings in the United States. Its inns, including Motel 6 and Red Roof Inns, represent nearly 1,200 properties housing 128,000 rooms, and command a 10% share of the entire U.S. economy lodging market. Accor is also a worldwide hotel management company, with 145,000 associates offering travel, tourism and corporate services in 140 countries. Despite Studio 6's association with other economy lodgings, in order to maintain independent integrity and optimize growth potential, each Accor Economy Lodging brand is managed by its own distinct operating group.

Operating Units	12/31/1999	12/31/2000	12/31/2001
Franchised	0	0	2
% Change	--	N/A	N/A
Company-Owned	8	11	34
% Change	--	37.5%	209.1%
Total	8	11	36
% Change	--	37.5%	209.1%
Franchised as % of Total	0.0%	0.0%	5.6%

Investment Required
The fee for a Studio 6 franchise is $25,000.

Studio 6 provides the following range of investments required to open your initial franchise. The range assumes that all items are paid for in cash. To the extent that you choose to finance any of these expense items, your front-end investment could be substantially reduced.

Item	Established Low Range	Established High Range
Franchise Fee	$25,000	$25,000
Construction	$2,126,200	$2,359,000
Equipment/Fixtures/Signs	$435,000	$550,000
Insurance	$16,600	$20,000
Inventory/Opening/Supplies	$35,500	$43,000
Training Expenses	$1,000	$5,000
Other Costs and Additional Funds (for 3 months)	$65,000	$102,000
Total Investment (does not include land acquisition)	$2,704,300	$3,104,000

On-Going Expenses

Studio 6 franchisees pay royalties equaling 5% and marketing and reservation contributions equaling 2% of gross room revenue. Franchisees will also be charged for use of the Studio 6 Welcome Card program—$100 for program installation and 2 to 5% of all subsequent Welcome Card charges.

What You Get—Training and Support

As part of the Studio 6 family, franchisees receive franchisor support through: initial and on-going training, written and video materials, refresher courses, newsletters and reports, award-winning advertising campaigns, marketing, the Studio 6 Welcome Card program, directory distribution (over five million distributed per year) and the Studio 6 and Motel 6 websites and reservations line.

Furthermore, as part of the greater Accor family, Studio 6 franchisees can take advantage of the purchasing power of 1,200 lodging properties and the Accor Economy Lodging Quality Team, which protects the image and reputation of the entire Accor and Studio 6 system by ensuring that each individual lodging unit maintains appropriate system standards.

Territory
Studio 6 grants protected territories.

Sylvan Learning Centers

SYLVAN LEARNING CENTERS®

1001 Fleet St.
Baltimore, MD 21202-4382
Tel: (800) 284-8214 (410) 843-8000
Fax: (410) 843-6265
E-Mail: greg.helwig@educate.com
Web Site: www.sylvanfranchise.com
Mr. Greg Helwig, VP Franchise Sales/Dev.

SYLVAN is the leading provider of educational services to families, schools and industry. SYLVAN services kindergarten through adult-levels from more than 900 SYLVAN LEARNING CENTERS worldwide.

BACKGROUND: IFA MEMBER
Established: 1979; 1st Franchised: 1980

Franchised Units:	849
Company-Owned Units	129
Total Units:	978
Dist.:	US-903; CAN-75; O'seas-4
North America:	50 States
Density:	CA, TX, NY
Projected New Units (12 Months):	50
Qualifications:	4, 4, 2, 3, 2, 5
Registered:	All States

FINANCIAL/TERMS:

Cash Investment:	$101.1-171.3K
Total Investment:	$121.1-219.3K
Minimum Net Worth:	$N/A
Fees:	Franchise — $38-46K
	Royalty — 5-13%; Ad. — 1.5%
Earnings Claim Statement:	Yes
Term of Contract (Years):	10/10
Avg. # Of Employees:	2 FT, 5 PT
Passive Ownership:	Not Allowed
Encourage Conversions:	No
Area Develop. Agreements:	Yes/Varies
Sub-Franchising Contracts:	No
Expand In Territory:	Yes
Space Needs:	1,600-2,500 SF; FS, SF, SC

SUPPORT & TRAINING PROVIDED:

Financial Assistance Provided:	Yes(B)
Site Selection Assistance:	Yes
Lease Negotiation Assistance:	No
Co-Operative Advertising:	Yes
Franchisee Assoc./Member:	Yes
Size Of Corporate Staff:	500
On-Going Support:	B,C,D,E,G,H,I
Training:	6 Days Baltimore, MD; 5 Days in Various Other Locations.

SPECIFIC EXPANSION PLANS:

US:	All United States
Canada:	All Canada
Overseas:	Asia, Europe, South America

Sylvan Learning Centers provides supplementary education to students of all ages and needs—remedial students, students wishing to maintain knowledge and students seeking to enrich knowledge. The demand for services like Sylvan's can only increase as public school enrollment increases and budgets shrink. Today, individualized lesson plans simply aren't feasible in traditional educational settings. Thus, Sylvan franchisees acquire not only financial success, but also the satisfaction of increasing life's opportunities.

Sylvan uses individualized, diagnostic and prescriptive methods to discover students' individual needs, to better their study, math, reading and writing skills or to prepare them for the SAT or ACT standardized college entrance exams.

Sylvan is accredited by the commission of international and trans-regional accreditation.

Operating Units	12/31/1999	12/31/2000	12/31/2001
Franchised	664	709	735
% Change	--	6.8%	3.7%
Company-Owned	71	82	90
% Change	--	15.5%	9.7%
Total	735	791	825
% Change	--	7.6%	4.3%
Franchised as % of Total	90.3%	89.6%	89.1%

Investment Required
The fee for a Sylvan franchise ranges from $60,0120 to $68,012, depending on territory.

Sylvan provides the following range of investments required to open your initial franchise. The range assumes that all items are paid for in cash. To the extent that you choose to finance any of these expense items, your front-end investment could be substantially reduced.

Item	Established Low Range	Established High Range
Franchise Fee	$46,000	$46,000
Furniture/Supplies	$30,900	$45,320
Inventory	$22,012	$22,012
Real Estate	$10,000	$55,000
Training Expenses	$2,815	$4,015
Additional Funds (for 6 months)	$48,000	$48,000
Total Investment	$159,727	$220,347

On-Going Expenses

Sylvan franchisees pay royalties equaling 8 to 9%, national advertising fees equaling 1.5 to 5% and local advertising fees equaling at least 8% of gross revenue.

What You Get—Training and Support

A group of regional consultants, consisting of both Sylvan and supplementary education veterans is at each franchisee's disposal as they open and operate their learning centers. They can assist with tasks like educational program administration, operations management and business growth.

In addition, Sylvan franchisees benefit from highly visible national advertising, professionally researched and created ad slicks, brochures, television and radio commercials and direct mail campaigns. Sylvan publicity also comes from magazines like *Success, Fortune* and *Money* and television appearances on "Nightline," "The Today Show" and CNN.

The Sylvan system also focuses on identifying key partners to build relationships with organizations whose expertise and strength can complement its own.

Territory

Sylvan grants exclusive territories.

Thrifty Car Rental

5310 E. 31st St.
Tulsa, OK 74135
Tel: (800) 532-3401 (918) 669-2219
Fax: (918) 669-2061
E-Mail: gary.valentine@thrifty.com
Web Site: www.thrifty.com
Mr. Gary Valentine, Executive Director

THRIFTY operates in over 60 countries and territories, with over 1,100 locations throughout North and South America, Europe, the Middle East, Caribbean, Asia and the Pacific, and is one of the fastest-growing car rental company in Canada and Australia. THRIFTY has a significant presence both in the airport and local car rental markets. Approximately 60% of its business is in the airport market, 40% in the local market.

BACKGROUND:
Established: 1958; 1st Franchised: 1962
Franchised Units: 1,068

351

Company-Owned Units	89	Area Develop. Agreements:	No
Total Units:	1,157	Sub-Franchising Contracts:	No
Dist.:	US-426; CAN-140; O'seas-592	Expand In Territory:	Yes
North America:	46 States,10 Provinces	Space Needs:	Varies SF; FS, SF, SC, RM
Density:	59 in ON, 37 in FL, 34 in CA		
Projected New Units (12 Months):	50-75	**SUPPORT & TRAINING PROVIDED:**	
Qualifications:	5, 5, 5, 3, 3, 5	Financial Assistance Provided:	Yes(I)
Registered:	All States	Site Selection Assistance:	No
		Lease Negotiation Assistance:	Yes
		Co-Operative Advertising:	Yes
FINANCIAL/TERMS:		Franchisee Assoc./Member:	No
Cash Investment:	$150K	Size Of Corporate Staff:	450
Total Investment:	$200-250K	On-Going Support:	A,B,C,D,E,F,G,H,I
Minimum Net Worth:	$500K	Training:	5 Days + Mentor Program at Headquar-
Fees:	Franchise — $Varies		ters in Tulsa, OK.
	Royalty — 3%; Ad. — 2.5-5%		
Earnings Claim Statement:	No	**SPECIFIC EXPANSION PLANS:**	
Term of Contract (Years):	10/5	US:	Selected Markets Remaining
Avg. # Of Employees:	4-6 FT	Canada:	All Canada
Passive Ownership:	Not Allowed	Overseas:	All Countries
Encourage Conversions:	Yes		

Thrifty Car Rental is the largest car rental company in the world. Whether a vehicle is needed for travel, business, leisure, government or temporary replacement, Thrifty's wide selection ensures that each customer will receive the perfect car. Balancing most of its rental business between airport and local markets, Thrifty franchisees may also offer vehicle leasing and parking services.

Thrifty's service initiative is its top priority and its secret to success, and the company demands that its franchisees be able to meet that challenge. Accordingly, Thrifty is also devoted to nurturing community relationships, taking time out to help grade schools, support the American Red Cross or Big Brothers and Sisters and cheer for local sports teams, charities and other health and religious organizations.

Thrifty Car Rental incorporated in 1950 and is a subsidiary of Dollar Thrifty Automotive Group, Inc.

Operating Units	12/31/1999	12/31/2000	12/31/2001
Franchised	560	530	473
% Change	--	-5.3%	-10.7%
Company-Owned	4	3	17
% Change	--	-25.0%	467.0%
Total	564	533	490
% Change	--	-5.5%	-8.1%
Franchised as % of Total	99.3%	99.4%	96.5%

Investment Required

The fee for a Thrifty Car Rental franchise is generally determined by the following formula: $175 for every 1,000 territory inhabitants. However, the fee can vary depending on the territory's number of airline passengers, total airport rental revenue, level of other rental activity and more.

Thrifty provides the following range of investments required to open your initial franchise. The range assumes that all items are paid for in cash. To the extent that you choose to finance any of these expense items, your front-end investment could be substantially reduced.

Item	Established Low Range	Established High Range
Franchise Fee	$17,500	$1,725,000
Courtesy Vehicles/ Fleet Inventory	$11,019	$6,720,000
Equipment/Fixtures/ Supplies	$24,161	$160,480
Insurance Deposits	$1,000	$50,000
Real Estate	$5,150	$13,000
Training Expenses	$1,000	$1,400
Other Costs and Additional Funds	$84,600	$808,600
Total Investment	$144,430	$9,478,480

On-Going Expenses

Thrifty's on-going fees and expenses depend upon the gross revenue and the number of vehicles rented by each individual Thrifty location. Costs include administrative fees, the truck rental program fee, advertising fees, local advertising expenditures, reservation fees, airline booking fees, airport fees, third party website suppliers' fees and yellow page advertising.

What You Get—Training and Support

The overall goal and effect of Thrifty's training and support is to place each franchisee in a strategic position to make the most of the Thrifty brand name.

The licensee operations department hosts all new Thrifty owners at an orientation held at corporate headquarters in Tulsa, Oklahoma. In addition, before and after completion of the new team owner orientation, all franchisees meet with a franchise mentor, at the mentor's location, where they undergo hands-on training in the operation and management of a Thrifty Car Rental.

The scope of Thrifty's support services is only appropriate for a company of its size and influence. For the benefit of its franchisees, the Thrifty system maintains a fleet leasing program, a fully computerized worldwide reservation system and telephone sales, insurance programs, computer hardware and software, marketing and customer loyalty programs, agent rewards and volume purchasing prices on supplies, signs, stationery, advertising, uniforms, tires and more.

Numerous consulting services guide franchisees through opening, business planning, reviews and policy implementation. Peer groups provide another channel of improvement and support in semi-annual meetings that strengthen communications and focus on the best Thrifty business practices.

Operating manuals help franchisees qualify customers, manage and rent vehicles, hire employees, build and maintain travel agent relations and coordinate advertising in a consistent manner to ensure the reputation and success of each individual location and the entire Thrifty system. Online courses train new employees and test management skills.

Territory
Thrifty grants exclusive territories.

The UPS Store

6060 Cornerstone Ct. W.
San Diego, CA 92121-3762
Tel: (877) 623-7253
Fax: (858) 546-7493
E-Mail: jdring@mbe.com
Web Site: www.theupsstore.com/franchise/
fraopp.html
Mr. John Dring, Sr. Dir. Domestic Fran Sales

In April 2001, Mail Boxes Etc. (MBE), the world's largest franchisor of retail shipping, postal and business services, became a subsidiary of UPS, the world's largest express carrier and package delivery company. In 2003, we introduced The UPS STORE franchise opportunity to offer franchisees and customers the best of both businesses. With over 4,500 The UPS Store and MBE locations in more than 40 countries and territories, our network is the global leader in its market.

BACKGROUND:	IFA MEMBER
Established: 1980; 1st Franchised: 1980	
Franchised Units:	4,525
Company-Owned Units	0
Total Units:	4,525
Dist.:	US-3,424; CAN-263; O'seas-838
North America:	50 States,10 Provinces
Density:	501 in CA, 293 in FL, 190 TX

Projected New Units (12 Months):	250
Qualifications:	5, 4, 3, 3, 3, 5
Registered:	All States
FINANCIAL/TERMS:	
Cash Investment:	$50K
Total Investment:	$141-240K
Minimum Net Worth:	$150K
Fees:	Franchise — $29.9K
	Royalty — 5%; Ad. — 3.5%
Earnings Claim Statement:	No
Term of Contract (Years):	10/10
Avg. # Of Employees:	2 FT, 2+ PT
Passive Ownership:	Allowed
Encourage Conversions:	Yes
Area Develop. Agreements:	Yes/10
Sub-Franchising Contracts:	No
Expand In Territory:	Yes
Space Needs:	NR SF; FS, SF, SC, RM, Non-Tradit.
SUPPORT & TRAINING PROVIDED:	
Financial Assistance Provided:	Yes
Site Selection Assistance:	Yes
Lease Negotiation Assistance:	Yes
Co-Operative Advertising:	Yes
Franchisee Assoc./Member:	Yes/Yes
Size Of Corporate Staff:	300
On-Going Support:	B,C,D,E,G,H,I
Training:	2 Weeks San Diego, CA; On-going.
SPECIFIC EXPANSION PLANS:	
US:	All United States
Canada:	All Canada
Overseas:	All Countries

If you want to own a prominent non-food franchise, The UPS Store may be the opportunity for you. The UPS Store franchises market packaging, shipping, document, printing, mailbox, fax and postal services and office, packaging and mailing supplies. The labor and start-up costs are low and 97% of locations opened in the last three years are still operating. The UPS Store franchise can be customized to any location, even special venues with limited space—and heavy traffic—like college campuses, hotels, military bases and convention centers. A unique rural-center development program provides even more opportunities for you to open your own The UPS Store location.

Mail Boxes Etc., Inc., the world's largest franchisor of its kind, franchises The UPS Store opportunity in the United States, and the Mail Boxes Etc. opportunity internationally. The two brands combined form a worldwide network of more than 4,500 locations. The UPS Store franchisees not only benefit from the support and stability of such a large and well-respected system, but also the global brand recognition of the world's largest express carrier and package delivery company—UPS.

Operating Units	4/29/2000	4/30/2001	12/31/2001
Franchised	3,186	3,278	3,354
% Change	--	2.9%	2.3%
Company-Owned	2	0	0
% Change	--	-100.0%	0.0%
Total	3,188	3,278	3,354
% Change	--	2.8%	2.3%
Franchised as % of Total	99.9%	100.0%	100.0%

Investment Required
The fee for The UPS Store franchise is $29,950. Financing assistance is available.

The UPS Store provides the following range of investments required to open your initial franchise. The range assumes that all items are paid for in cash. To the extent that you choose to finance any of these expense items, your front-end investment could be substantially reduced.

Item	Established Low Range	Established High Range
Franchise Fee	$14,950	$29,950
Décor/Furniture/Real Estate/Signs	$36,345	$97,900
Equipment/Supplies	$16,498	$25,396
Grand Opening, Design and Center Development Fees	$7,950	$13,200
Insurance	$1,000	$2,000
Option Fee	$10,000	$10,000
Training	$9,000	$8,105
Other Costs and Additional Funds (for 3 months)	$31,500	$41,500
Total Investment	$127,243	$228,051

On-Going Expenses

The UPS Store franchisees pay royalties equaling 5%, marketing fees equaling 1% and national media fees equaling 2.5% of gross revenue. Depending on the regional location of the store, monthly advertising co-op dues average from $100 to $400 and all franchisees pay an annual $595 software development and upgrade fee.

What You Get—Training and Support

The UPS Store franchise fee covers the rights to trade names, logos, trademarks, proprietary technology and business methods.

Initial training is conducted in three phases, including two weeks at The UPS Store University in San Diego, California.

In preparation for your opening, the company also offers site selection guidance and design and construction oversight.

As a The UPS Store franchisee, you have continued access to local support, on-going training, multi-level marketing and corporate account programs.

Territory
The UPS Store grants exclusive territories.

Window Genie

350 Gest St.
Cincinnati, OH 45203
Tel: (800) 700-0022 (513) 241-8443
Fax: (513) 412-7760
E-Mail: rik@windowgenie.com
Web Site: www.windowgenie.com
Mr. Richard Nonelle, President

Residential window cleaning, window tint and pressure washing business.

BACKGROUND:

Established: 1994; 1st Franchised: 1998	
Franchised Units:	37
Company-Owned Units	0
Total Units:	37
Dist.:	US-37; CAN-0; O'seas-0
North America:	12 States
Density:	6 in OH, 4 in CO, 3 in KY
Projected New Units (12 Months):	19
Qualifications:	4, 4, 1, 3, 3, 5
Registered:	CA,FL,IL,IN,MD,MI,NY,VA,WA

FINANCIAL/TERMS:

Cash Investment:	$40-50K
Total Investment:	$40-50K
Minimum Net Worth:	$Varies
Fees:	Franchise — $19.5K
	Royalty — 6%; Ad. — 1%
Earnings Claim Statement:	No
Term of Contract (Years):	10/5
Avg. # Of Employees:	2 FT, 2 PT
Passive Ownership:	Discouraged
Encourage Conversions:	Yes
Area Develop. Agreements:	No
Sub-Franchising Contracts:	No
Expand In Territory:	Yes
Space Needs:	N/A SF; N/A

SUPPORT & TRAINING PROVIDED:

Financial Assistance Provided:	No
Site Selection Assistance:	N/A
Lease Negotiation Assistance:	N/A
Co-Operative Advertising:	N/A
Franchisee Assoc./Member:	No
Size Of Corporate Staff:	3
On-Going Support:	B,C,D,E,F,G,H,I
Training:	5 Days Corporate, Cincinnati, OH; 5 Days On-Site.

SPECIFIC EXPANSION PLANS:

US:	All United States
Canada:	All Canada
Overseas:	No

While it may not sound like a glamorous industry, Window Genie has impressive grounds for growth. The U.S. Bureau of Labor Statistics claims that cleaning services were the largest source of new jobs from 1994 to 2005. With the rise in two-income households, not only can more people afford cleaning services, but also more people need cleaning services as they don't have the time to keep their home themselves. Maid services typically don't cover window cleaning and Window Genie businesses benefit from both this and the repeating cycle of cleaning needs.

Furthermore, Window Genie operates on a typical business schedule, nine to five, Monday through Friday, and is designed around managing workers, not doing the actual work yourself. Window Genie is home-based, with limited receivables and inventory but a broad market.

Window Genie began in Cincinnati, Ohio and offers window, vinyl siding and gutter cleaning and deck, concrete, brick, driveway and patio cleaning and sealing to residential and commercial customers.

Operating Units	12/31/1999	12/31/2000	12/31/2001
Franchised	6	18	21
% Change	--	200.0%	16.7%
Company-Owned	0	0	0
% Change	--	N/A	N/A
Total	6	18	21
% Change	--	200.0%	16.7%
Franchised as % of Total	100.0%	100.0%	100.0%

Investment Required
The fee for a Window Genie franchise $19,500. The fee increases by $10,000 for every additional 75,000 households above the customary territory size of 100,000 households.

Window Genie provides the following range of investments required to open your initial franchise. The range assumes that all items are paid for in cash. To the extent that you choose to finance any of these expense items, your front-end investment could be substantially reduced.

Item	Established Low Range	Established High Range
Franchise Fee	$19,500	$19,500
Advertising	$3,000	$5,000
Equipment/Furniture	$5,000	$7,500
Inventory	$1,200	$1,500
Real Estate	$0	$500

Training	$600	$1,300
Vehicle	$0	$2,000
Other Costs and Additional Funds	$5,050	$10,000
Total Investment	$34,350	$47,300

On-Going Expenses
Window Genie franchisees pay royalties equaling 6%, regional and national advertising fees equaling 1 to 3% and local advertising fees equaling 10% of gross revenue.

What You Get—Support and Training
When you open a Window Genie franchise, you will be trained in equipment operation and maintenance, cleaning procedures, customer service, sales and marketing techniques, customer service, software operation and bookkeeping. You will also receive: grand opening assistance (with five days of on-site field support), proprietary software, use of the Window Genie name, logo and servicemarks, marketing and advertising programs, field and phone support, national product and equipment affiliations, Window Genie glass cleaner for promotion and resale, purchase discounts on equipment and supplies, publicity and public relations assistance, national programs for business and health insurance, assistance with employee hiring, cost estimation and selling, newsletters and conventions.

In addition, Window Genie franchisees have access to: business cards, stationery, envelopes, brochures, flyers, postcards, door hangers, ad slicks, uniforms, office and vehicle signage, printed forms like invoices, work orders and proposals, proprietary software for billing, scheduling and record keeping and radio scripts.

Territory
Window Genie grants protected marketing areas.

World Gym International

3223 Washington Blvd.
Marina Del Rey, CA 90292
Tel: (800) 544-7441 (310) 827-7705
Fax: (310) 827-6355
E-Mail: info@worldgym.com
Web Site: www.worldgym.com
Mr. Mike Uretz, President/CEO

Service oriented fitness centers featuring circuit training, cardiovascular equipment, free weights and personal training.

BACKGROUND:
Established: 1977; 1st Franchised: 1985

Franchised Units:	278
Company-Owned Units	0
Total Units:	278
Dist.:	US-262; CAN-3; O'seas-13
North America:	34 States
Density:	30 in FL, 24 in CA, 21 in NY
Projected New Units (12 Months):	45
Qualifications:	4, 5, 3, 3, 3, 2
Registered:	CA,FL,HI,IL

FINANCIAL/TERMS:
Cash Investment:	$300K-1MM
Total Investment:	$300K-1MM
Minimum Net Worth:	$300K-1MM
Fees:	Franchise — $13K
	Royalty — $6.5K/Yr.; Ad. — 0%
Earnings Claim Statement:	No
Term of Contract (Years):	5/5
Avg. # Of Employees:	8-15 FT, 5 PT
Passive Ownership:	Allowed
Encourage Conversions:	Yes
Area Develop. Agreements:	Yes/10
Sub-Franchising Contracts:	Yes
Expand In Territory:	Yes
Space Needs:	6,500-40,000 SF; FS,SF,SC,RM

SUPPORT & TRAINING PROVIDED:
Financial Assistance Provided:	Yes(I)
Site Selection Assistance:	Yes
Lease Negotiation Assistance:	No
Co-Operative Advertising:	No
Franchisee Assoc./Member:	No
Size Of Corporate Staff:	8
On-Going Support:	c,d,G,H,I
Training:	2 Days Las Vegas, NV University; 2 Days Columbus, OH University.

SPECIFIC EXPANSION PLANS:
US:	All United States
Canada:	All Canada
Overseas:	All Countries

With over 20,000 square feet of facilities and locker rooms, World Gym's supergyms are a telling testament to the wealth of the World Gym franchise system. However, not all World Gyms are the size of supergyms; World Gym accommodates both the big guy and the little guy. Most fitness centers need be only 15,000 square feet and conversions of existing gyms, if over 9,500 square feet, are allowed.

No one forgets the gorilla and with notaries like founder Joe Gold and actor Arnold Schwarzenegger behind the name, recognition of the World Gym

361

brand is guaranteed the world over. Its prevalence in the international fitness and bodybuilding world makes it seem like an old friend wherever it may be encountered and visitors know they will find up-to-date and top-of-the-line gym facilities and staff. Furthermore, because of World Gym's guest travel privileges, World Gym members truly are welcome at any World Gym across the globe. World Gym's clothing and accessories line, sold at most locations, is one of the most popular lines of fitness merchandise sold today.

Although Joe Gold once graced a 1935 cover of *Muscle Power* magazine, he never expected his gym to receive the same acclaim. The first World Gym franchise opened in Mentor, Ohio in 1981 and soon after Joe approved the creation of two more. Swamped by interest, Gold joined forces with attorney Mike Uretz. They set the guidelines and developed the systems that would shape the World Gym company.

Operating Units	12/31/1999	12/31/2000	12/31/2001
Franchised	230	240	230
% Change	--	4.3%	-4.2%
Company-Owned	0	0	0
% Change	--	N/A	N/A
Total	230	240	230
% Change	--	4.3%	-4.2%
Franchised as % of Total	100.0%	100.0%	100.0%

Investment Required
The fee for an initial World Gym franchise is $13,000. Each additional gym costs $3,000.

World Gym provides the following range of investments required to open your initial franchise. The range assumes that all items are paid for in cash. To the extent that you choose to finance any of these expense items, your front-end investment could be substantially reduced.

Item	Established Low Range	Established High Range
Franchise Fee	$13,000	$13,000
Annual License Fees	$7,000	$7,000
Equipment	$175,000	$550,000
Insurance	$3,500	$7,000
Real Estate	$7,000	$20,000
Additional Funds	$30,000	$60,000
Total Investment	$235,500	$657,000

On-Going Expenses

World Gym franchisees pay annual license fees equaling $7,000.

What You Get—Training and Support

World Gym franchisees benefit from national account pricing arrangements, giving them discounts on equipment sold through preferred vendors and access to the latest and best equipment.

World Gym believes that "A Well Informed Gym Owner is a Successful Gym Owner," and their support services prove this conviction. In addition to the grand opening services and sales staff training that the company provides, World Gym requires attendance at the quarterly educational seminars and World Gym Convention/Expo Seminars. At free business seminars and equipment expos, experts and peers share their secrets and teach franchisees how to make their gyms the best. Other services comprising the most extensive owner education program in the fitness business include the World Gym University and the annual convention in Columbus, Ohio.

World Gym also provides publications and business and operations manuals to keep its owners well-informed and knowledgeable. The glossy, four-color World Gym magazine features expert advice written expressly for gym owners, including general system news and gossip as well as the latest on successful marketing, management and operations programs. Other provided publications include instruction on gym operations, public relations, presales, corporate fitness and wellness and interior design.

Territory

World Gym grants protected territories based on population rather than mileage, a calculation unique in the fitness industry. Each territory has a radius of at least 50,000 people and often as many as 100,000 people, providing each owner with a great supply of potential members.

World Inspection Network

6500 6th Ave., NW
Seattle, WA 98117-5099
Tel: (800) 967-8127 (206) 728-8100
Fax: (206) 441-3655
E-Mail: traymond@wini.com
Web Site: www.wini.com
Mr. Tom Raymond, VP Franchise Development

The home inspection business is the highest growth business in real estate services today and we have the highest professional standards of any home inspection company in the industry. Our strategic partnership philosophy with our franchisees makes us different. We work together to build a strong market presence for our brand, WORLD INSPECTION NETWORK. Ask to see our strategic market growth plan for your area.

BACKGROUND: IFA MEMBER
Established: 1993; 1st Franchised: 1994
Franchised Units: 120
Company-Owned Units 0
Total Units: 120
Dist.: US-120; CAN-0; O'seas-0
  North America: 25 States
  Density: 21 in WA, 20 in CA, 12 in NY
Projected New Units (12 Months): 25
Qualifications: 5, 5, 2, 2, 5, 5

Registered:	CA,FL,IL,IN,MI,MN,NY,OR, VA,WA,WI
FINANCIAL/TERMS:	
Cash Investment:	$10K
Total Investment:	$33.1-47.8K
Minimum Net Worth:	$N/A
Fees:	Franchise — $23.9K
	Royalty — 7%; Ad. — 3%
Earnings Claim Statement:	Yes
Term of Contract (Years):	5/5
Avg. # Of Employees:	1 FT
Passive Ownership:	Discouraged
Encourage Conversions:	Yes
Area Develop. Agreements:	No
Sub-Franchising Contracts:	No
Expand In Territory:	Yes
Space Needs:	N/A SF; HB
SUPPORT & TRAINING PROVIDED:	
Financial Assistance Provided:	Yes(D)
Site Selection Assistance:	N/A
Lease Negotiation Assistance:	N/A
Co-Operative Advertising:	Yes
Franchisee Assoc./Member:	Yes/Yes
Size Of Corporate Staff:	10
On-Going Support:	B,C,D,G,H,I
Training:	2 Weeks Training Facility, Seattle, WA.
SPECIFIC EXPANSION PLANS:	
US:	All United States
Canada:	No
Overseas:	No

The service real estate agents most widely recommend to buyers is home inspection. Now, most buyers even require that a contingency be placed in their contract and a home inspection be performed. Buying a home is a big investment, and World Inspection Network helps buyers decide if it's the right one for them.

In addition to providing a valuable and often requested service, World Inspection Network also allows franchisees to work from home and make their own schedule, allowing them to fit their business lives into and around their family and social responsibilities.

Operating Units	12/31/1999	12/31/2000	12/31/2001
Franchised	71	90	106
% Change	--	26.8%	17.8%
Company-Owned	0	0	0
% Change	--	N/A	N/A
Total	71	90	106
% Change	--	2.7%	17.8%
Franchised as % of Total	100.0%	100.0%	100.0%

Investment Required

The fee for a World Inspection Network franchise is $23,900.

World Inspection Network provides the following range of investments required to open your initial franchise. The range assumes that all items are paid for in cash. To the extent that you choose to finance any of these expense items, your front-end investment could be substantially reduced.

Item	Established Low Range	Established High Range
Franchise Fee	$23,900	$26,900
Equipment/Vehicles	$3,700	$10,400
Insurance	$900	$1,300
Marketing/Career Clothing	$2,300	$2,500
Training Expenses	$1,400	$2,600
Other Costs and Additional Funds	$1,100	$4,500
Total Investment	$33,300	$48,200

On-Going Expenses

World Inspection Network franchisees pay royalties equaling 7% and a marketing fund contribution equaling 3% of gross revenue.

What You Get—Training and Support

World Inspection Network's training starts at home. A support advisor visits new franchisees and helps them begin to learn inspection terminology, building systems and home construction methods. Following this independent study, franchisees attend a two-week interactive program at WIN's training facility. The program includes technical inspection, technology (software as well as screening for carbon monoxide and moisture), marketing, customer service, business operations and management. On-going weekly technical updates and monthly website newsletters continue training even as business begins.

The marketing fund provides franchisees with exclusive mailings and professional marketing and sales programs that bring national exposure and internet visibility.

Marketing and promotions also contribute to franchisee success with service-selling materials and programs, such as a signature van for brand recognition, the home sellers inspection program and the extended referral protection plan, which partners franchisees with real estate professionals.

Franchisees also use WIN's inspection report, a portable program that processes the information gathered in a home inspection and produces a final product for inspectors to share with clients immediately after the inspection.

Franchisees will also benefit from World Inspection Network's home office team, annual conferences and expos, advisory council and 24-hour internet support system of forums and library resources.

Territory

World Inspection Network grants exclusive territories.

Alphabetical Listing of Franchisors

367

Categorical Listing of Franchisors

Service-Based Franchises

DEFINITIVE FRANCHISOR DATABASE AVAILABLE FOR RENT

SAMPLE FRANCHISOR PROFILE

BLIMPIE SUBS AND SALADS

180 Interstate North Pkwy., SE, # 500
Atlanta, GA 30339

800/LocalTelephone #:	(800) 447-6256; (770) 984-2707
Fax #:	(404) 240-6540
E-Mail:	kietha@blimpie.com
Internet Address:	www.blimpie.com
# Franchised Units:	1,955
# Company-Owned Units:	1
# Total Units:	1,956
Company Contact/Title:	Mr. Keith Albright, VP Fran. Devel.
Contact Salutation:	Mr. Albright
President/Title:	Mr. Jeffrey Endervelt, President
President Salutation:	Mr. Endervelt
Industry Category (of 54):	16/Quick Service/Take-Out
IFA/CFA Member:	International Franchise Association

KEY FEATURES

- # of Active North American Franchisors   ~ 2,200
- Data Fields (See Above)   24
- Industry Categories   45
- Guaranteed Accuracy-$.50 Rebate/Returned Mailing
- Data Converted to Any Popular Database or Contact Management Program
- Initial Front-End Cost $1,000
- Quarterly Up-Dates (Optional) $75
- Mailing Labels Only - One-Time Use $400

For more information, please contact
Source Book Publications
P.O. Box 12488, Oakland, CA 94604
(800) 841-0873 or (510) 839-5471 or fax (510) 839-2104

Bond's Top 50 Food-Service Franchises
by Steve Schiller and Robert Bond

Key Features:

In response to the constantly asked question, *"What are the best franchises?"*, Bond's newest book focuses on the top 50 franchises in the food-service industry. Over 500 food-service systems were evaluated for consideration. Companies were analyzed on the basis of historical performance, brand identification, market dynamics, franchisee satisfaction, the level of training and on-going support, financial stability, etc. Detailed 3-4 page profiles on each company, as well as key statistics and industry overviews. All companies are proven performers and most have a national presence. Excellent starting point for someone focusing on the food-service industry.

Yes, I want to order ____ copy(ies) of *Bond's Top 50 Food-Service Franchises* at $19.95 each ($29.95 Canadian). Please add $7.00 per book for Shipping* & Handling ($5.75 Canada; International shipments at actual cost). California residents, please add appropriate sales tax.

Name_____ Title_____

Company _____ Telephone No. (_____) _____

Address _____

City _____ State/Prov._____ Zip _____

❑   Check Enclosed or

Charge my: ❑ MasterCard ❑   Visa

Card#:_____ Expiration Date:_____

Signature:_____

Please return to: **Source Book Publications**, P.O. Box 12488, Oakland, CA 94604

* Note: All books shipped by USPS Priority Mail.

Satisfaction Guaranteed. If not fully satisfied, return for a prompt, 100% refund.

Tips & Traps When Buying A Franchise
2nd Edition (Completely revised in 1999)

By Mary Tomzack, President of FranchiseHelp, Inc., an international information and research company servicing the franchising industry.

Key Features:

- Completely updated version of the 1994 reader-acclaimed classic on franchising, with the same practical advice, non-textbook approach. Provides an insightful crash course on selecting, negotiating and financing the right franchise, and turning it into a lucrative, satisfying business.
- How to select the best franchise for your personal finances and lifestyle; navigate the legal maze; and finance your investment.
- Reveals the hottest franchise opportunities for the 21st Century and discusses co-branding. Provides advice on building a business empire through franchising.
- "This book is the bible for anyone who is considering a franchise investment."

Yes, I want to order ____ copy(ies) of *Tips & Traps When Buying a Franchise* (2nd Edition) at US$19.95 each, plus US$7.00 for shipping & handling (international shipments at actual cost).

Name _____ Title _____

Company _____ Telephone No. (_____) _____

Address _____

City _____ State/Prov._____ Zip _____

❑   Check Enclosed or
Charge my: ❑   MasterCard ❑   Visa
Card #: _____ Expiration Date: _____
Signature: _____

Please return to: **Source Book Publications,** P.O. Box 12488, Oakland, CA 94604

* Note: All books shipped by USPS Priority Mail.
Satisfaction Guaranteed. If not fully satisfied, return for a prompt, 100% refund.

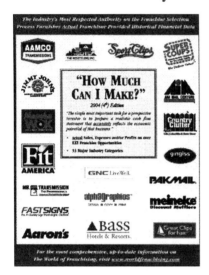